THE LITERARY
COMPANION TO SEX

Fiona Pitt-Kethley began writing professionally
in the late 1970s. Her first collection of poetry,
Sky Ray Lolly, caused a sensation when it was
first published in 1986; it was followed by *Private
Parts* (1987) and *The Perfect Man* (1989). *Journeys
to the Underworld* (1988) is a travel book and she
has written one novel, *The Misfortunes of Nigel*
(1991). She writes freelance journalism for
magazines and the quality newspapers. She lives
in Hastings.

THE LITERARY COMPANION TO SEX

An anthology of prose and poetry

collected by

Fiona Pitt-Kethley

Mandarin

A Mandarin Paperback
THE LITERARY COMPANION TO SEX

First published in Great Britain 1992
by Sinclair-Stevenson Limited
This edition published 1993
by Mandarin Paperbacks
an imprint of Reed Consumer Books Limited
Michelin House, 81 Fulham Road, London SW3 6RB
and Auckland, Melbourne, Singapore and Toronto

Reprinted 1993

Copyright Introduction, textual notes and editorial matter
© 1992 by Fiona Pitt-Kethley
The author has asserted her moral rights

A CIP catalogue record for this title
is available from the British Library
ISBN 0 7493 1383 8

Printed and bound in Great Britain
by Cox & Wyman Ltd, Reading, Berks

TEXTUAL NOTE

I have grouped the extracts into five wide periods. Within these sections the order is not strictly chronological, as I did not wish to get bogged down in academic arguments over precisely which year a particular poem or prose work was written. For the same reason, I have avoided giving authors' dates.

The texts I have used are, in most cases, simply those that were available to me and not necessarily definitive ones. I have retained the original spelling and punctuation. In a few cases – mainly seventeenth-century poems – I have taken the liberty of inserting the rude words omitted. I felt that dashes would slow down the reader. These words may well have been included in other editions, or in the manuscript versions, anyway. In most cases, the missing words were obvious, as an initial or rhyme was given – p for prick or pintle (the same thing), according to rhythm; c for cunt; swives (i.e. fucks) to rhyme with wives; tarse (prick) to rhyme with arse, etc. In 'The Delights of Venus' I had to use more guesswork as no initials were given. Any purist who wants the unadorned text will have to seek it out in the British Library.

In the case of translations I have used the most pleasing ones I could find, rather than necessarily opting for the most accurate. Again I would say that purists should read the originals for themselves. Where I have made my own translations I have indicated this by the initials F.P.

CONTENTS

THE MIDDLE AGES AND THE RENAISSANCE 57

THE RESTORATION AND THE EIGHTEENTH CENTURY 127

THE NINETEENTH CENTURY   281

ACKNOWLEDGEMENTS

I would like to acknowledge the help of all those who suggested works I should read, sent photographs or lent me books – in particular, my friends Professor J. P. Sullivan for introducing me to Eskimo Nell and Maximianus Etruscus, Bernard Stone for ideas and the loan of various books, Jeremy Reed for ideas and photocopies, Gary Pulsifer for books and Anthony Suter for ideas. I would also like to thank Richard Greville Clark for the loan of the text of *The Whore*.

I would like to thank the staff of the London Library for staggering down with countless heavy volumes from 'The Librarian's Room' and similarly those of the British Library, most especially the woman who bravely mounted an unsuccessful search by computer for *The Panegyrick upon Cundums* trying to nudge its memory banks in vain with umpteen different spellings of condom.

I would also like to express my gratitude to the following publishers, agents and writers for permission to print extracts:

To Polygon Books and Liz Lochhead for poems from *Dreaming of Frankenstein* and *Collected Poems* (Polygon 1984).

To André Deutsch Ltd; Alfred A. Knopf and John Updike for the extract from *A Month of Sundays* by John Updike. Copyright © 1974, 1975 by John Updike. Reprinted by permission of Alfred A. Knopf, Inc.

To Methuen, London, for the extracts from *The Orton Diaries* edited by John Lahr.

To Martin Secker and Warburg Ltd and Rogers Coleridge and White Ltd for an extract from Erica Jong's *Fear of Flying*.

To Methuen and Michèle Roberts for 'Magnificat' from *The Mirror of the Mother*.

To Peter Owen for extracts from Guillaume Apollinaire's *Les Onze Mille Verges* translated by Nina Rootes, from Anaïs Nin's *Little Birds* and from Violette Leduc's *La Bâtarde* translated by Derek Coltman.

To Grafton Books, a division of HarperCollins Publishers Ltd and Harcourt Brace and Jovanovich for items from the *Collected Poems* of e. e. cummings.

To HarperCollins, Sheil Land Associates and Wendy Perriam for the extract from *The Fifty Minute Hour*.

To Jonathan Meades for *Fur and Skin* from his collection, *Filthy English*, Jonathan Cape 1984, Paladin 1986.

To the Women's Press and Alfred A. Knopf for the excerpt from *Original Sins* by Lisa Alther. Copyright © 1981 by Lisa Alther, Inc. Reprinted by permission of Alfred A. Knopf, Inc.

To Dangaroo Press and David Dabydeen for use of his poem from *Slave Song*.

To Martin Secker and Warburg Ltd for lines from Colette's *La Vagabonde*, translated by Enid Bagnold.

To Random Century Ltd for an excerpt from J. R. Ackerley's *My Dog Tulip* published by the Bodley Head.

To Random Century Ltd and Jonathan Clowes Ltd for 'Nothing to Fear' from *Collected Poems* by Kingsley Amis published by Hutchinson.

To Random Century Ltd and Rogers Coleridge and White Ltd for an extract from Philip Roth's *Portnoy's Complaint* published by Jonathan Cape.

To Random Century Ltd and Peters Fraser and Dunlop Ltd for a poem from *Nineties* by Jeremy Reed.

To Carcanet Press Ltd for a poem from Sujata Bhatt's *Brunizem*, published in 1988.

To David Higham Associates for the excerpt from Robert Baldick's translation of Restif de la Bretonne's *Monsieur Nicholas*.

To New Beacon Books Ltd and to James Barry for his poem from *Fractured Circles*.

To Curtis Brown and John Farquharson for the extract from Henry Miller's *Tropic of Cancer* published by John Calder.

To the *New Statesman* and Roger Woddis for the use of his poem.

To Laurence Pollinger Ltd and the Estate of Frieda Lawrence Ravagli for the extract from *The First Lady Chatterley*.

To Sebastian Barker, Zygmunt Frankel, Molly Parkin, Jeremy Reed, Charles Thomson and John Whitworth for the use of their poems and John Adlard and my mother O. Pitt-Kethley for the use of their verse translations.

Lastly, I would like to acknowledge the intransigence of the Nabokov Estate via Nikki Smith of Smith/Kolnik in repeatedly denying me permission to use a piece from *Lolita* even though an extract from that book had appeared in an erotic anthology and even though I explained to them what good company Nabokov would be keeping – the Bible,

Richardson, etc. 'The Nabokov Estate' Nikki Smith wrote, 'has a firm policy of granting permission only for anthologies relating to the art of literature; requests for anthologies regarding sex per se are consistently denied'. Whilst I can certainly appreciate the problems caused to an author by typecasting, this smacks of a whitewash job. Whether his estate likes it or not, Nabokov was a remarkably good writer about sex.

In spite of all possible efforts I have been unable to trace G. R. Quaife, translators Bernard Guilbert Guerney and Clement Egerton or the owners of the Alexandre Kuprin rights. I would be grateful if either they or their estates (as appropriate) would get in touch with me.

Every effort has been made to trace the copyright holders of the quoted material. If, however, there are inadvertent omissions, these can be rectified in any future editions.

INTRODUCTION

FOR THE LAST eighteen months I have read nothing but sex literature in the cause of putting this book together. The last time I read piles of erotica by choice, I was fourteen. At that stage, having no experience with men beyond snogging, I took it all as gospel. Now, after I've lived a little, I read the same works again and think, 'Has this author ever really had sex?' All the classic myths occur – bedfuls of blood at the taking of a virginity, endlessly voracious women, and so on.

Lying authors were not the only problem. The manual type of book can be seriously boring. Even at fourteen, I can remember all those 'yonis' and 'lingams' of *The Kama Sutra* turning me off, not on, as I perused it under my desk during scripture lessons. It was hard for me to find a likeable passage in either that or *The Perfumed Garden*.

In the end I decided that my criteria in choosing would be these: realism, humour, or the unusual – preferably all three. It was important to find realistic writing, simply because there's so little of it.

If every passage or poem were directly about the sexual act in its many shapes and forms, there's a danger that even the most dedicated voyeur would not keep reading for 415 pages. For this reason, I have included a lot of peripheral matter – writing about various parts of the body, etc. How often are sex organs really well described? There are even some relatively clean pieces – just for the sake of variety.

I opted for arranging material according to period, not by sexual activity. If I had done that, there seemed to be a distinct possibility that the lazier reader would select his/her favourite kink and only read a certain section. I want to make you work harder than that. If you're only interested in knickers you are going to have to search for your pleasures.

Working by period had its rewards. As I stockpiled material in separate files, I found, slightly to my surprise, that a distinct character emerged in each pile – a theme almost – that transcended the bounds of creed or nationality. The writers of the ancient world, in the main, proved to be the most open and unashamed about sex, although a slightly prurient, shocked tone crept into their news reportage (the sensationalist historians, Suetonius and Procopius). But are the journalists of today any different?

The Middle Ages and the Renaissance, although bawdy, were over-shadowed by religion and doom. Conversely, their religious writing often had sexual overtones. The fate in hell of the adulteress in *Gesta Romanorum* provides a memorably kinky image of tortured womankind that must have provided good masturbation material for pious monks everywhere. The frankest writing of this period turns up in my favourite novel, the Chinese *Chin P'ing Mei*. Although the theme and tone of the book are similar to those in Western writing of the time, the inclusion of oral sex and sex aids is not. They had vanished from Western literature almost entirely after the Romans, whatever ordinary people were getting up to.

By the time we reach the seventeenth century, dildoes, and jokes about them, are big news, as are venereal diseases. The Restoration and the eighteenth century provide a period of frankness similar to that of the ancient world. It's probably the easiest period in which to find good sex writing. In prose, with the start of the novel and the fashion for writing autobiographies, writers were beginning to use sex to make interesting philosophical points. It was also a good period for women writers – they had considerable difficulties, yes, but many survived. It is from this period also that most of the best classical translations came. By the nineteenth century, classicists couldn't afford to be even half as frank as the originals. Victorian translation is responsible for giving us a deeply distorted view of Latin and Greek literature and the individuals who wrote it.

I knew from the start that the nineteenth century would give me the biggest problems. Apart from some good French literature and Byron, what was I to include? Literature became schizophrenic during Victoria's reign. Sex didn't happen in the official literature, but it happened non-stop – to an unrealistic extent – in *The Pearl* and other underground writing. Kinkiness was in. It was the great period for fetishism and sado-masochism. At the same time, censorship was paramount.

Censorship, incidentally, is something I've avoided totally in this collection. I have used three asterisks to indicate cuts in texts, but none of these cuts were made for reasons of censorship. Where ellipses (dots) are included, they are the original author's. De Sade may well have started this sort of punctuation with implications – fair enough when you're doing it all on prison notepaper in longhand – but there's little excuse for the proliferation of this corny device in the nineteenth century. The best use of the dot-dot-dot school of writing occurs in Lockhart's novel, *The Life of*

Mr Adam Blair. I couldn't resist including this example, even if the adultery implied is fairly quiet by today's standards.

Apart from mainstream writing and underground pornography, there's a third tradition in the nineteenth century – one that's often ignored. Isolated individuals had begun to collect folklore. Writing for 'the learned reader', these writers could be a little franker than those who wrote for the mass market, like Dickens. And mercifully, their style is usually of a far higher quality than that of the average nineteenth-century pornographer. These folk tales hark back to older traditions, keeping alive the bawdy spirit of the Middle Ages and the Renaissance.

By the twentieth century we are into mixed territory. I sensed curious affinities across the eras – Apollinaire's erotic novel with Rochester's *Sodom*; one of e. e. cummings's poems with an anonymous seventeenth-century one; Eskimo Nell and Procopius's Empress Theodora – another fucker of cosmic proportions. There is also, alas, a great deal of bad writing. Authors frequently make great claims for their own honesty, only to get bogged down in prurience and their own embarrassment. I avoided all passages that talked about waves beating on shores. (That sort of writing's only permissible if the couple are doing it on a beach.) Still, on the plus side, there is a tremendous range of ideas and experience in the writing of the twentieth century – everything from bestiality to vibrators.

As I selected pieces for the anthology, my own ideas went through a lot of changes. Preconceived notions were thrown away. Sadism horrifies me so much that I had half thought of excluding de Sade when I took on the project. When I took the trouble to read a few works by him, I realised that he was far from being the most sadistic of writers. Besides, as long as you're not involved in sadism, it can be desperately funny. You can get a good laugh out of Victorian flagellation – *Le Vice Anglais*.

It's easy enough to find pieces on every known act of sexuality. Finding enough variety in writers is harder. I would have liked to have found a good many more books by women writers. Sex does not seem to be an area they've written about frequently – or if they have, as in the case of some classical poets, the work has been lost.

Where I could, I included examples of homosexuals writing about homosexuality, lesbians on lesbianism, etc. Bestiality proved a problem, though. The nearest I could get to insider authenticity was Jonathan Meades's well-imagined story.

Friends and acquaintances were more than helpful once they knew of my quest. I got an Olympia Press volume pressed into my hand every time I went into Bernard Stone's bookshop in Lamb's Conduit Street. Sadly, some friends misunderstood what was wanted. Some offered me their favourite well-chewed piece of porn. Others suggested things that weren't really about sex at all – something they found faintly erotic, or something with a rude word or two. Erotic literature and literature about sex are not necessarily the same.

I have included many unusual poems, in the interest of resurrecting little-known but likeable items such as Butler's 'Dildoides' and the pseudonymous 'Delights of Venus'. I have also included some much-used specimens. For a coy lady, Marvell's mistress has a habit of turning up absolutely everywhere. I thought about leaving her out for this reason. On the other hand, it is such an extremely filthy poem (think about the implications of worms trying her long preserved virginity) that its rightful place is in my anthology and not in all those school ones. I was always more pleased, though, when I came across an interesting, little-known poem. Two by black writers struck me with their clever handling of awkward subjects. Sujata Bhatt's 'Shérdi' must be the world's only poem by a woman that waxes lyrical about fellation – an act that the majority of us find extremely boring. David Dabydeen's 'Nightmare' is about a rape fantasy. A man writing about rape fantasies is on dangerous ground. He pulls it off by a clever trick – his fantasist is a slave-owner dreaming about being raped by her black slaves. That makes the poem wholly acceptable.

I also enjoyed, in a mischievous sense, finding sexy passages in respectable authors. Milton is rather good on how angels do it. Crabbe provided me with lecherous Peter Pratt, the gardener, who takes a great deal of pleasure in telling people how to propagate cucumbers. In a funny sort of way, it's one of the most erotic passages in the book, as well as being a good, realistic piece of observation. I have also included the odd respectable poem found in other anthologies – but only if it has a decidedly Freudian undertone. George Peele's 'The Voice from the Well' seems to have another meaning, as does Lady Catherine Dyer's epitaph on her husband, with its orgasmically necrophiliac end.

Since most of the pieces in the book are about sex or the lead up to it, it seems necessary to define sex. In the cause of equality, I believe that this has to include homosexual as well as heterosexual acts. Homosexual men often make good talkers and writers about sex. How many straight men can equal the realism of Orton's *Diary*? Perhaps all the best writers about sex are outsiders – homosexuals, the promiscuous, deviants. Those who have married young without any experimentation have usually swallowed all the standard values. They are unlikely to have thought deeply about sex and therefore will not be able to write well about it. Like Queen Victoria, they will probably refuse even to believe that lesbians exist. Should a book on sex also include masturbation? I think so. In the end it is perhaps easiest to define sex as anything that can end in orgasm – if you're lucky, that is.

Any anthology is subjective. Everyone will be able to think of some favourite passage that I have neglected. Some good books were left out simply because they were too subtle – in a way, the whole of their text would have been needed to build up to the sexual incidents they contain. Laclos's *Les Liaisons Dangereuses* and Richardson's *Clarissa* fell into this category.

Those who favour pretentious writing will find nothing here for them. I have much more sympathy with a doggerel poet than with the elegant writer who can't say what he means. I don't claim greatness for all my writers, but I would claim that all I've included wrote interestingly about sex – if only, in some cases, in the passage I've chosen from their works. Some readers will quarrel with the fact that I've cut tiny extracts from long poems. In a book that mixes poetry with prose, and chapters from novels with lyrics, I felt this was justified. An anthology should be like a Thai banquet, with a long series of dishes. If I've whetted your appetite with an extract, you can go away and read the rest. Of course, in some cases, the rest may be a disappointment. . . . Every book and every poem has its orgasm or high point – some, like *The Works of Rabelais* have multiples. What I have tried to do is collect together all these orgasms to make one long orgiastic read.

THE
ANCIENT
WORLD

THE BIBLE

Two Angels Visit Lot in Sodom

AND THERE CAME two angels to Sodom at even; and Lot sat in the gate of Sodom: and Lot seeing them rose up to meet them; and he bowed himself with his face toward the ground; And he said, 'Behold now, my lords, turn in, I pray you, into your servant's house, and tarry all night, and wash your feet, and ye shall rise up early, and go on your ways.' And they said, 'Nay; but we will abide in the street all night.' And he pressed upon them greatly; and they turned in unto him, and entered into his house; and he made them a feast, and did bake unleavened bread, and they did eat.

But before they lay down, the men of the city, even the men of Sodom, compassed the house round, both old and young, all the people from every quarter: and they called unto Lot, and said unto him, 'Where are the men which came in to thee this night? bring them out unto us, that we may know them.' And Lot went out at the door unto them, and shut the door after him, and said, 'I pray you, brethren, do not so wickedly. Behold now, I have two daughters which have not known man; let me, I pray you, bring them out unto you, and do ye to them as is good in your eyes: only unto these men do nothing; for therefore came they under the shadow of my roof.'

Genesis 19: 1–8 (Authorised Version)

THE TALMUD

Joseph and Potiphar's Wife

JOSEPH FOUND GRACE in the eyes of Potiphar, and was placed over the house of the latter, and over all his possessions. And the Lord was with Joseph, and for his sake blessed Potiphar and all his household.

At this time Joseph was about eighteen years of age, and a lad of such beautiful appearance that his equal could not be found in the land of Egypt. Being obliged, in the pursuance of his duties, to enter freely all parts of his master's house, he attracted the attention of Zelicha, Potiphar's wife. She was fascinated by his manners and handsome form and face, and declared to him day by day her passion, praying for a return upon his part of the favour with which she regarded him. Joseph refused to listen to her, and endeavoured to rid himself of her attentions. When she praised his beauty, and said, 'Thou art fairer than all the rest of the world,' he replied, 'The same One who created me created also all mankind.' When she admired his fine eyes, he replied, 'What can they avail me; they will not move or sparkle in the grave.'

When Zelicha found that Joseph could not be induced by fair words to desecrate his master's house, she tried threats of death and loss of freedom in case of further obstinacy; but Joseph replied to them, 'The God who hath created man, looseneth the fetters of those who are bound, and He will deliver me from thy chastisement.'

Her female friends who called to see her also admired Joseph, and lauded his beauty. On one occasion when fruit was set before the visitors, one of them, paring the same, cut her fingers, and knew nothing of the accident till her attention was called to the blood upon her garments, for her eyes were fixed on Joseph, and her mind was filled with thoughts of his appearance.

Thus time passed on, and though Zelicha still entreated, Joseph remained cold to her allurements.

And it came to pass at the time of the overflowing of the Nile, that all the inhabitants of Egypt left their houses, the king, the princes, and all the people, to see the overflow and make a holiday in its honour. And with the rest of the people the family of Potiphar went also, all save Joseph, who remained to protect his master's goods, and Zelicha, who remained to be alone with Joseph.

She attired herself in her richest garments, and was more ardent than ever in her appeals to Joseph, so that to escape them he turned and fled abruptly from her presence. As he did so she caught his garment to stay him, but it sundered, and a portion remained in her hand. As she looked upon it, and became conscious of how she had been shamed, a deep feeling of hate entered her heart, and she was also terrified lest the affair might now become known to her husband. She quickly replaced her elegant clothing with her ordinary wear, and calling a lad she sent him to summon home the men of the house. When they arrived she met them with loud wailing, and related to them a story of Joseph's presumption, crediting him with the entreaties and protestations which she had herself made, and adding to them a charge of violence. 'I caught hold of his garment,' she said, 'and cried with a loud voice; he became frightened and fled, leaving this portion of his cloth in my hand.'

The men repeated these charges to Potiphar, who returned to his house in a great rage against Joseph, and commanded at once that the lad should be whipped severely. During the infliction of this punishment Joseph cried aloud, raising his hands to Heaven, 'Thou knowest, O God,' said he, 'that I am innocent of all these things; wherefore, shall I die through falsehood!'

Potiphar carried Joseph before the judges, and made an accusation against him, saying, 'Thus and thus has the slave done.' The judges then addressed Joseph, and he gave his version of the story, saying, 'Not so; but thus and thus did it occur.' The judges then ordered that the rent garment should be brought to them, and upon an examination of the same they pronounced Joseph 'not guilty.' But still they sent him to prison, that the character of the wife of one as high in the state as Potiphar might not suffer.

For twelve long years Joseph was confined in prison, and during this time Zelicha visited him, offering to restore him to honour and liberty if he would but do her will. Yet steadfastly he refused, till finally she abandoned the attempt. And while Joseph was thus in custody, deprived of his freedom, his father Jacob, in Canaan, mourned for him as a father mourns for a beloved child torn from him by death.

Transl. H. Polano

THE APOCRYPHA

The History of Susanna

THERE DWELT A man in Babylon, called Joacim: and he took a wife, whose name was Susanna, the daughter of Chelcias, a very fair woman, and one that feared the Lord. Her parents also were righteous, and taught their daughter according to the law of Moses. Now Joacim was a great rich man, and had a fair garden joining unto his house: and to him resorted the Jews; because he was more honourable than all others.

The same year were appointed two of the ancients of the people to be judges, such as the Lord spake of, that wickedness came from Babylon from ancient judges, who seemed to govern the people. These kept much at Joacim's house: and all that had any suits in law came unto them. Now when the people departed away at noon, Susanna went into her husband's garden to walk. And the two elders saw her going in every day, and walking; so that their lust was inflamed toward her. And they perverted their own mind, and turned away their eyes, that they might not look unto heaven, nor remember just judgments. And albeit they both were wounded with her love, yet durst not one shew another his grief. For they were ashamed to declare their lust, that they desired to have to do with her. Yet they watched diligently from day to day to see her. And the one said to the other, 'Let us now go home: for it is dinner time.' So when they were gone out, they parted the one from the other, and turning back again they came to the same place; and after that they had asked one another the cause, they acknowledged their lust: then appointed they a time both together, when they might find her alone.

And it fell out, as they watched a fit time, she went in as before with two maids only, and she was desirous to wash herself in the garden: for it was hot. And there was no body there save the two elders, that had hid themselves, and watched her. Then she said to her maids, 'Bring me oil and washing balls, and shut the garden doors, that I may wash me.' And they did as she bade them, and shut the garden doors, and went out themselves at privy doors to fetch the things that she had commanded them: but they saw not the elders, because they were hid.

Now when the maids were gone forth, the two elders rose up, and ran unto her, saying, 'Behold, the garden doors are shut, that no man can see us, and we are in love with thee; therefore consent unto us, and lie with us. If thou wilt not, we will bear witness against thee, that a young man was with thee: and therefore thou didst send away thy maids from thee.' Then Susanna sighed, and said, 'I am straitened on every side: for if I do this thing, it is death unto me: and if I do it not, I cannot escape your hands. It is better for me to fall into your hands, and not do it, than to sin in the sight of the Lord.' With that Susanna cried with a loud voice: and the two elders cried out against her. Then ran the one, and opened the garden door. So when the servants of the house heard the cry in the garden, they rushed in at a privy door, to see what was done unto her. But when the elders had declared their matter, the servants were greatly ashamed: for there was never such a report made of Susanna.

And it came to pass the next day, when the people were assembled to her husband Joacim, the two elders came also full of mischievous imagination against Susanna to put her to death; and said before the people, 'Send for Susanna, the daughter of Chelcias, Joacim's wife.' And so they sent. So she came with her father and mother, her children, and all her kindred. Now Susanna was a very delicate woman, and beauteous to behold. And these wicked men commanded to uncover her face, (for she was covered) that they might be filled with her beauty. Therefore her friends and all that saw her wept. Then the two elders stood up in the midst of the people, and laid their hands upon her head. And she weeping looked up toward heaven: for her heart trusted in the Lord. And the elders said, 'As we walked in the garden alone, this woman came in with two maids, and shut the garden doors, and sent the maids away. Then a young man, who there was hid, came unto her, and lay with her. Then we that stood in a corner of the garden, seeing this wickedness, ran unto them. And when we saw them together, the man we could not hold: for he was stronger than we, and opened the door, and leaped out. But having taken this woman, we asked who the young man was, but she would not tell us: these things do we testify.'

Then the assembly believed them, as those that were the elders and judges of the people: so they condemned her to death. Then Susanna cried out with a loud voice, and said, 'O everlasting God, that knowest the secrets, and knowest all things before they be: thou knowest that they have borne false witness against me, and, behold, I must die; whereas I never did such things as these men have maliciously invented against me.' And the Lord heard her voice.

Therefore when she was led to be put to death, the Lord raised up the holy spirit of a young youth, whose name was Daniel: who cried with a loud voice, 'I am clear from the blood of this woman.' Then all the people turned them toward him, and said, 'What mean these words that thou hast spoken?' So he standing in the midst of them, said, 'Are ye such fools, ye sons of Israel, that without examination or knowledge of the truth ye have condemned a daughter of Israel? Return again to the place of judgment: for they have borne false witness against her.' Wherefore all the people turned again in haste, and the elders said unto him, 'Come, sit down among us, and shew it us, seeing God hath given thee the honour of an elder.' Then said Daniel unto them, 'Put these two aside one far from another, and I will examine them.'

So when they were put asunder one from another, he called one of them, and said unto him, 'O thou that art waxen old in wickedness, now thy sins which thou hast committed aforetime are come to light: for thou hast pronounced false judgment, and hast condemned the innocent, and hast let the guilty go free; albeit the Lord saith, "The innocent and righteous shalt thou not slay." Now then, if thou hast seen her, tell me, Under what tree sawest thou them companying together?' Who answered, 'Under a mastick tree.' And Daniel said, 'Very well; thou hast lied against thine own head; for even now the angel of God hath received the sentence of God to cut thee in two.' So he put him aside, and commanded to bring the other, and said unto him, 'O thou seed of Chanaan, and not of Juda, beauty hath deceived thee, and lust hath perverted thine heart. Thus have ye dealt with the daughters of Israel, and they for fear companied with you: but the daughter of Juda would not abide your wickedness. Now therefore tell me, Under what tree didst thou take them companying together?' Who answered, 'Under a holm tree.' Then said Daniel unto him, 'Well; thou hast also lied against thine own head: for the angel of God waiteth with the sword to cut thee in two, that he may destroy you.'

With that all the assembly cried out with a loud voice, and praised God, who saveth them that trust in him. And they arose against the two elders, (for Daniel had convicted them of false witness by their own mouth;) and according to the law of Moses they did unto them in such sort as they maliciously intended to do to their neighbour: and they put them to death. Thus the innocent blood was saved the same day. Therefore Chelcias and his wife praised God for their daughter Susanna, with Joacim her husband, and all the kindred, because there was no dishonesty found in her.

The History of Susanna (Authorised Version)

HOMER

From the Homeric Hymn to Venus

Extract 1: Venus and Anchises

Venus has pretended to be an ordinary woman to set him at his ease.

> Resistless love invading thus his breast,
> The panting youth the smiling queen addrest.
> 'Since mortal you, of mortal mother came,
> And Otreus you report your father's name,

And since the immortal Hermes from above,
To execute the dread commands of Jove,
Your wondrous beauties hither has convey'd,
A nuptial life with me henceforth to lead;
This instant will I seize upon thy charms,
Mix with thy soul, and melt within thy arms:
Tho' Phoebus, arm'd with his unerring dart,
Stood ready to transfix my panting heart;
Tho' death, tho' hell, in consequence attend,
Thou shalt with me the genial bed ascend.'
He said, and sudden snatch'd her beauteous hand;
The goddess smil'd, nor did th'attempt withstand,
But fix'd her eyes upon the hero's bed,
Where soft and silken coverlets were spread,
And over all a counterpane was plac'd,
Thick sown with furs of many a savage beast,
Of bears and lions, heretofore his spoil,
And still remain'd the trophies of his toil.

   Now to ascend the bed they both prepare,
And he with eager haste disrobes the fair.

   Her sparkling necklace first he laid aside,
Her bracelets next, and braided hair unty'd;
And now his busy hand her zone unbrac'd,
Which girt her radiant robe about her waist;
Her radiant robe at last aside was thrown,
Whose rosy hue with dazzling lustre shone.

   The Queen of Love the youth thus disarray'd,
And on a chair of gold her vestments laid.
Anchises now (so Jove and Fate ordain'd)
The sweet extreme of ecstasy attain'd;
And mortal he was like th'immortals bless'd,
Not conscious of the goddess he possess'd.

Extract 2: Aurora and Tithonus

But when the golden thron'd Aurora made
Tithonus partner of her rosy bed
(Tithonus, too, was of the Trojan line,
Resembling gods in face and form divine),
For him she straight the Thunderer address'd,
That with perpetual life he might be bless'd;
But ah! how rash was she! how indiscreet!
The most material blessing to omit;
Neglecting, or not thinking, to provide
That length of days might be with strength supply'd,
And to her lover's endless life engage
An endless youth, incapable of age.
But hear what fate befel this heav'nly fair,
In gold enthron'd, the brightest child of Air;
Tithonus, while of pleasing youth possess'd,
Is by Aurora with delight caress'd;
Dear to her arms, he in her court resides,
Beyond the verge of earth, and oceans' utmost tides.

    But when she saw gray hairs begin to spread,
Deform his beard, and disadorn his head,
The goddess cold in her embraces grew,
His arms declin'd, and from his bed withdrew;
Yet still a kind of nursing care she show'd,
And food ambrosial and rich cloaths bestow'd;
But when of age he felt the sad extreme,
And ev'ry nerve was shrunk and limb was lame,
Lock'd in a room her useless spouse she left,
Of youth, of vigour, and of voice, bereft.

Attributed to HOMER, transl. William Congreve

SAPPHO

It is hard to make a fair judgement on the work of Sappho, because, musical though her style certainly is, most of what is extant is extremely fragmentary. The following poem is an improvisation of Swinburne's using the only line that survives of one of her poems.

I loved thee once, Atthis, long ago

I loved thee, – hark, one tenderer note than all –
Atthis, of old time, once – one low long fall,
Sighing – one long low lovely loveless call,
Dying – one pause in song so flamelike fast –
Atthis, long since in old time overpast –
One soft first pause and last.
One, – then the old rage of rapture's fieriest rain
Storms all the music-maddened night again.

ALGERNON SWINBURNE

The following poem, one of very few that have survived in a more or less complete form, has been much translated. Even Gladstone, Smollett and Sir Richard Burton had a bash. Unfortunately, Smollett was too free and the other two too pompous, so I've opted for a lesser-known translator.

Blest as the immortal gods is he,
The youth, who fondly sits by thee,
And hears and sees thee all the while
Softly speak and sweetly smile.

'Twas this deprived my soul of rest,
And raised such tumults in my breast;
For while I gazed, in transport tost,
My breath was gone, my voice was lost:

My bosom glowed; the subtle flame
Ran quick through all my vital frame;
O'er my dim eyes a darkness hung;
My ears with hollow murmurs rung.

In dewy damps my limbs were chilled;
My blood with gentle horror thrilled;
My feeble pulse forgot to play;
I fainted, sank, and died away.

Transl. Ambrose Philips

ARISTOPHANES

From Lysistrata

Lysistrata and the other women decide to formalise their now-famous oath by pledging it in wine.

LYSISTRATA: Put your hands on the wine-cup, all of you.
One of you speak, repeating after me.
The rest of you confirm it and swear too.

LYSISTRATA: I won't have my husband or my lover,

KALONIKE: I won't have my husband or my lover,

LYSISTRATA: Even if he comes in erect. Repeat!

KALONIKE: Even if he comes in erect. Oh God!
I'm trembling at the knees, Lysistrata.

LYSISTRATA: I'll lead the purest virgin's life at home,

KALONIKE: I'll lead the purest virgin's life at home,

LYSISTRATA: In saffron silks and beautifully made up,

KALONIKE: In saffron silks and beautifully made up,

LYSISTRATA: So that my husband has the hots for me.

KALONIKE: So that my husband has the hots for me.

LYSISTRATA: I'll never willingly give in to him;

KALONIKE: I'll never willingly give in to him;

LYSISTRATA:	And if I'm forced to it against my will,
KALONIKE:	And if I'm forced to it against my will,
LYSISTRATA:	I won't respond. I'll give with a bad grace.
KALONIKE:	I won't respond. I'll give with a bad grace.
LYSISTRATA:	I won't oblige, with legs up in the air
KALONIKE:	I won't oblige, with legs up in the air
LYSISTRATA:	Or do a lion couchant act for him.
KALONIKE:	Or do a lion couchant act for him.
LYSISTRATA:	May I drink wine while all these oaths are kept,
KALONIKE:	May I drink wine while all these oaths are kept.
LYSISTRATA:	But if I stray, may water fill my cup.
KALONIKE:	But if I stray, may water fill my cup.
LYSISTRATA:	Do you all swear these things?
MYRRHINE:	By Zeus, we do.

Transl. F.P.

MARCUS ACCIUS PLAUTUS

From The Braggard Captain

Two servants of the braggard captain talk together:

SCELEDRUS: Haply you do not know, what new mischance
Has just befall'n us.

PALAESTRIO: What mischance?

SCELEDRUS: A filthy.

PALAESTRIO: Then keep it to yourself, don't tell it me,
I would not know it.

SCELEDRUS: But you must . . . Today,
As I was looking for our monkey, here
Upon our neighbour's tiles . . .

PALAESTRIO: One worthless beast
Was looking for another.

SCELEDRUS: Plague confound you!

PALAESTRIO: You rather . . . But go on, as you've begun.

SCELEDRUS: I haply chanc'd to peep down through the sky-light
Into next house, and there did I espy
Our lady fondling with I know not whom.

From *Miles Gloriosus*, transl. as *The Braggard Captain* by Bonnell Thornton

PUBLIUS TERENTIUS AFER (TERENCE)

From Andria

Terence gives the conventional view of why a prostitute becomes
a prostitute. Sosia and Simo discuss a neighbour at the beginning
of the play:

> A certain woman from the isle of Andros
> Came o'er to settle in this neighbourhood,
> By poverty and cruel kindred driv'n:
> Handsome and young.
>
> SOSIA: Ah! I begin to fear
> Some mischief from this Andrian.
>
> SIMO: At first
> Modest and thriftily, tho' poor, she liv'd,
> With her own hands a homely livelihood
> Scarce earning from the distaff and the loom.
> But when a lover came with promis'd gold,
> Another, and another, as the mind
> Falls easily from labour to delight,
> She took their offers, and set up the trade.

Transl. as *The Andrian* by George Colman

FROM *THE GREEK ANTHOLOGY*

Charito's sixty now, her curly hair
Is still as black as it once was, her breasts,
Like marble cones, uplift without a bra.
Ambrosia distils from her firm flesh,
A thousand graces, everything that stirs . . .
You lovers who don't shrink from red-hot passion,
Roll up, and never mind the lady's years.

PHILODEMOS OF GADARA, transl. F.P.

On a Clyster

I, only, am allowed to fuck a wife,
Quite openly, at her own mate's request.
I mount young lads, those in the prime of life,
Old men, maids – at their grieving parents' behest.
I'm anti lust, loved by the healer's hand,
Performing Herculean[1] tasks each time.
I'll even take on Pluto and demand
The lives of those whom I've lain with. For I'm
The offspring of an elephant and goat –
A white-tusked child with a good leather[2] coat.

ANON., transl. F.P.

1 The Herculean task here referred to must be the cleansing of the Augean Stables. (H. diverted a river through them – he never did anything by halves.)
2 Not having the advantage of rubber, the Greeks made this instrument from goatskin with an ivory pipe attached. Judging by this poem, they used the same instrument for giving both enemas and douches.

If you should see a handsome man, strike while the iron is hot –
Speak your mind, grab him by the balls, and above all, do not
Tell him, 'I'd like to be your brother and I reverence you.' –
Or modesty will close the way for what you want to do.

ADAIOS OF MACEDON, transl. F.P.

On a Boat, Paid for by the Profits of a Brothel

I slip into the sea from which the goddess came,
I, a ship, paid for by Aphrodite's labours.
My master who built me, was in the white slave game.
He called me Courtesan – I'm friend to every man.
Board me in confidence, you can afford the fee;
I take on all who come – foreigners, neighbours.
I handle well, upon the ground, or out at sea.

PHILIP OF THESSALONIKA, transl. F.P.

Priapus said, seeing Kimon's cock erect,
'Alas, God's short of man in this respect.'

ANTIPATER OF THESSALONIKA, transl. F.P.

Now no one's round, wretch, hard and sinewy too!
But yesterday – no life at all in you.

STRATO, transl. F.P.

Konon's wife's six foot tall,
But he is only three;
While feet to feet in bed,
Think where his face will be.

Attributed to JULIAN THE APOSTATE, transl. F.P.

While I was hanging a garland at her door,
(After a party), Hermonassa threw
Some water from a pot, flattening the hair
I'd curled enough to last three days or more.
And yet, the water made me hot – I knew
The pot contained her sweet lips' hidden fire.

PAULOS THE SILENTIARY, transl. F.P.

VALERIUS CATULLUS

XLI

Well-shagged Ameana asked from me
A round ten thousand as her fee
(She of the ugly turned-up snout,
Whose Formian boyfriend's quite spent out).
You relatives, whose charge she's in,
Call doctors and her kith and kin.
The girl's not sane. She never inspects
What sort of thing her glass reflects.

Transl. F.P.

LVIII

O Celius! think, our Lesbia, once thy pride;
   Lesbia, that Lesbia whom Catullus prized
More than himself, and all the world beside,
   Now gives for hire to profligates despised
In the dark alley, or the common lane,
The charms he loved, the love he sigh'd to gain.

Transl. Lamb

PUBLIUS VERGILIUS MARO (VIRGIL)

The following poem, ascribed to Virgil, comes from a literary tradition of Priapic verses that never gets a mention in school anthologies. Images of the god, Priapus, were commonly placed in Roman gardens to deter scrumping. You might say that Priapus is the ancestor of Worzel Gummidge. The theory behind using him as a garden ornament was that the well-endowed god would come alive and bugger the burglars. I keep an open mind about superstitions, so I like to test their validity. One year I placed a small Priapic image made of baked dough on my mother's Worcester tree, and it bore the best crop of apples ever, even though the image wasn't large enough to bugger anything of greater size than a pigeon.

Priapeum

In the silence of the night, a fair boy
Lay there, withdrawn from my lukewarm embrace.
Love was at rest, nor could my dotard prick
Raise up its knob to a more manly state.

Does it please you, Priapus, who reside
Beneath the trees' shade, red, with blushing prick,
Your sacred head bound with a vine-leaf wreath?
For, threefold phallus, we have often twined
Fresh flowers, artlessly, about your hair,
Shouting when busy daws or ravens strike,
Their horny beak upon your sacred head.

Goodbye, I am forsaken, wretched cock.
Goodbye, Priapus, I owe you nothing.
You'll be thrown out between my unsown fields;
The savage yellow dog will frig himself
Against your muddy flanks, down to the wood.

But, wicked prick, my evil destiny,
You will atone the wrong by staying on
The rails. You can complain. No tender boy,
The sort that turns his mobile quivering bum
In artful play's at your disposal now.
No jolly girl will fondle with smooth hands
Or press her white, transparent thigh to you.
A two-toothed crone, who knew old Romulus
Is ready, in the midst of whose dark groin,
Lies hid a cavern, covered by her paunch
And pendulous skin that's icy all year through;
A cobwebbed must surrounds the vestibule.
This is prepared for you – there, three or four
Deep trenches may engulf your slippery head.
You'll lie (a sick chap may) clammier than
A snake. But, you'll be ground down there, until,
Ah wretch! you've filled that pit, three or four times.
This pride will get you nowhere when you plunge
Your errant head into her squelching muck.

What's up, limp one? Aren't you ashamed of sloth?
This once, withdrawal's permitted, unavenged:
But when the golden boy comes back again,
As soon as you perceive his pattering steps,
Stretch out your sinews, standing stiff with lust,
Restless tumescence animate my groin,
Don't cease to swell until the moment when
Glad Venus parts his yielding flanks for me.

Transl. F.P.

PUBLIUS OVIDIUS NASO (OVID)

From the Ars Amatoria *(The Art of Love)*

Sometimes your lover to incite the more,
Pretend your husband's spies beset the door:
Tho' free as Thais, still affect a fright;
For seeming danger heightens the delight.
Oft' let the youth in thro' your window steal,
Tho' he might enter at the door as well;
And sometimes let your maid surprise pretend,
And beg you in some hole to hide your friend.
Yet ever and anon dispel his fear,
And let him taste of happiness sincere;
Lest, quite dishearten'd with too much fatigue,
He should grow weary of the dull intrigue.

But I forgot to tell how you may try
Both to evade the husband and the spy.

That wives should of their husbands stand in awe,
Agrees with justice, modesty, and law;
But that a mistress may be lawful prize,
None but her keeper I am sure denies.
For such fair nymphs these precepts are design'd,
Which ne'er can fail, join'd with a willing mind.
Tho' stuck with Argus' eyes your keeper were,
Advis'd by me you shall elude his care.

When you to wash or bathe retire from sight,
Can he observe what letters then you write?
Or can his caution against such provide,
Which in her breast your confidant may hide?
Can he that note beneath her garter view,
Or that which, more conceal'd, is in her shoe?
Yet these perceiv'd, you may her back undress,
And writing on her skin your mind express.

New milk, or pointed spires of flax, when green,
Will ink supply, and letters mark unseen;
Fair will the paper show, nor can be read
Till all the writings' with warm ashes spread.

   Acrisus was with all his care betray'd,
And in his tow'r of brass a grandsire made.

   Can spies avail when you to plays resort,
Or in the Circus view the noble sport?
Or can you be to Isis' fane pursu'd,
Or Cybelle's, whose rites all men exclude?
Tho' watchful servants to the bagnio come,
They're ne'er admitted to the bathing-room.
Or when some sudden sickness you pretend,
May you not take to your sick-bed a friend?
False keys a private passage may procure,
If not, there are more ways beside the door.
Sometimes with wine your watchful foll'wer treat;
When drunk you may with ease his care defeat;
Or, to prevent too sudden a surprise,
Prepare a sleeping draught to seal his eyes:
Or let your maid, still longer time to gain,
An inclination for his person feign:
With faint resistance let him drill him on,
And after competent delays be won.

   But what need all these various doubtful wiles,
Since gold the greatest vigilance beguiles?
Believe me, men and gods with gifts are pleas'd,
Ev'n angry Jove with off'rings is appeas'd.
With presents fools and wise alike are caught;
Give but enough, the husband may be bought.
But let me warn you, when you bribe a spy,
That you for ever his connivance buy;
Pay him his price at once, for with such men
You'll know no end of giving now and then.

   Once I remember, I with cause complain'd

Of jealousy, occasion'd by a friend.
Believe me, apprehensions of that kind
Are not alone to our false sex confin'd.
Trust not too far your she-companions truth,
Lest she sometimes should intercept the youth:
The very confidant that lends the bed
May entertain your lover in your stead.

Transl. William Congreve

From the Amores

Oldham modestly calls the next two poems 'Imitations', but they
are close enough to the originals to rate as translations.

That he loves women of all sorts and sizes

Not I, I never vainly durst pretend
My Follies and my Frailties to defend:
I own my Faults, if it avail to own,
While like a graceless wretch I still go on:
I hate my self, but yet in spite of Fate
Am fain to be that loathed thing I hate:
In vain I would shake off this load of Love,
Too hard to bear, yet harder to remove:
I want the strength my fierce Desires to stem,
Hurried away by the impetuous stream.
'Tis not one Face alone subdues my Heart,
But each wears Charms, and every Eye a Dart:
And wheresoe're I cast my Looks abroad,
In every place I find Temptations strow'd.
The modest kills me with her down-cast Eyes,
And Love his ambush lays in that disguise.
The Brisk allures me with her gaity,

And shews how Active she in bed will be:
If Coy, like cloyster'd Virgins, she appears,
She but dissembles, what she most desires:
If she be vers'd in Arts, and deeply read,
I long to get a Learned Maidenhead:
Or if Untaught and Ignorant she be,
She takes me then with her simplicity:
One likes my Verses, and commends each Line,
And swears that [1]*Cowley's* are but dull to mine:
Her in mere Gratitude I must approve,
For who, but would his kind Applauder love?
Another damns my Poetry, and me,
And plays the Critick most judiciously:
And she too fires my Heart, and she too charms,
And I'm agog to have her in my arms.
One with her soft and wanton Trip does please,
And prints in every step, she sets, a Grace:
Another walks with stiff ungainly tread;
But she may learn more pliantness abed.
This sweetly sings; her Voice does Love inspire,
And every Breath kindles and blows the fire:
Who can forbear to kiss those Lips, whose sound
The ravish'd Ears does with such softness wound?
That sweetly plays: and while her Fingers move,
While o're the bounding Strings their touches rove,
My Heart leaps too, and every Pulse beats Love:
What Reason is so pow'rful to withstand
The magick force of that resistless Hand?
Another Dances to a Miracle,
And moves her numerous Limbs with graceful skill:
And she, or else the Devil's in't, must charm,
A touch of her would bed-rid Hermits warm.

[1] Abraham Cowley, the poet. Oldham has substituted his contemporary for Ovid's Callimachus.

If tall; I guess what plenteous Game she'l yield,
Where Pleasure ranges o're so wide a Field:
If low; she's pretty: both alike invite,
The Dwarf, and Giant both my wishes fit.
Undress'd; I think how killing she'd appear,
If arm'd with all Advantages she were:
Richly attir'd; she's the gay Bait of Love,
And knows with Art to set her Beauties off.
I like the Fair, I like the Red-hair'd one,
And I can find attractions in the Brown:
If curling Jet adorn her snowy Neck,
The beauteous Leda is reported Black:
If curling Gold; Aurora's painted so:
All sorts of Histories my Love does know.
I like the Young with all her blooming Charms,
And Age it self is welcom to my Arms:
There uncropt Beauty in its flow'r assails,
Experience here, and riper sense prevails.
In fine, whatever of the Sex are known
To stock this spacious and well-furnish'd Town;
Whatever any single man can find
Agreeable of all the num'rous kind:
At all alike my haggard Love does fly,
And each is Game, and each a Miss for me.

II, 4

To his mistriss that jilted him

Nay then the Devil take all Love! If I
So oft for its damn'd sake must wish to die:
What can I wish for but to die, when you,
Dear faithless Thing, I find, could prove untrue?
Why am I curs'd with Life? why am I fain
For thee, false Jilt, to bear eternal Pain?

'Tis not thy Letters, which thy Crimes reveal,
Nor secret Presents, which thy Falshood tell:
Would God! my just suspicions wanted cause,
That they might prove less fatal to my ease:
Would God! less colour for thy guilt there were,
But that (alas!) too much of proof does bear:
Bless'd he, who what he loves can justifie,
To whom his Mistriss can the Fact deny,
And boldly give his Jealousie the lye.
Cruel the Man, and uncompassionate,
And too indulgent to his own Regret,
Who seeks to have her guilt too manifest,
And with the murd'ring secret stabs his Rest.
I saw, when little you suspected me,
When sleep, you thought, gave opportunity,
Your Crimes I saw, and these unhappy eyes
Of all your hidden stealths were Witnesses:
I saw in signs your mutual Wishes read,
And Nods the message of your Hearts convey'd:
I saw the conscious Board, which writ all o're
With scrawls of Wine, Love's mystick Cypher bore:
Your Glances were not mute, but each bewray'd,
And with your Fingers Dialogues were made:
I understood the Language out of hand,
(For what's too hard for Love to understand?)
Full well I understood for what intent
All this dumb Talk, and silent Hints were meant:
And now the Ghests were from the Table fled,
And all the Company retir'd to bed.
I saw you then with wanton Kisses greet,
Your Tongues (I saw) did in your Kisses meet:
Not such as Sisters to their Brothers give,
But Lovers from their Mistrisses receive:
Such as the God of War, and [1]*Paphian* Queen

[1] Venus.

Did in the height of their Embraces joyn.
Patience, ye Gods! (cried I) *what is't I see?*
Unfaithful! why this Treachery to me?
How dare you let another in my sight
Invade my native Property and Right?
He must not, shall not do't: by Love I swear
I'll seize the bold usurping Ravisher:
You are my Free-hold, and the Fates design,
That you should be unalienably mine:
These Favours all to me impropriate are:
How comes another then to trespass here?
This, and much more I said, by Rage inspir'd,
While conscious shame her Cheeks with Blushes fir'd:
Such lovely stains the face of Heav'n adorn
When Light's first blushes paint the bashful Morn:
So on the Bush the flaming Rose does glow,
When mingled with the Lillies neighb'ring Snow:
This, or some other Colour much like these,
The semblance then of her Complexion was:
And while her Looks that sweet Disorder wore
Chance added Beauties undisclos'd before:
Upon the ground she cast her jetty Eyes,
Her Eyes shot fiercer Darts in that Disguise:
Her Face a sad and mournful Air express'd,
Her Face more lovely seem'd in sadness dress'd:
Urg'd by Revenge, I hardly could forbear,
Her braided Locks and tender Cheeks to tear:
Yet I no sooner had her Face survey'd,
But strait the tempest of my Rage was laid:
A look of her did my Resentments charm,
A look of her did all their Force disarm:
And I, that fierce outrageous thing e're-while,
Grow calm as Infants, when in sleep they smile:
And now a Kiss am humbly fain to crave,
And beg no worse than she my Rival gave:

She smil'd, and strait a throng of Kisses prest,
The worth of which, should *Jove* himself but taste,
The brandish'd Thunder from his Hand would wrest:
Well-pleas'd I was, and yet tormented too,
For fear my envied Rival felt them so:
Better they seem'd by far than I e're taught,
And she in them shew'd something new methought:
Fond jealous I my self the Pleasure grutch,
And they displeas'd, because they pleas'd too much:
When in my mouth I felt her darting Tongue,
My wounded Thoughts it with suspicion stung:
Nor is it this alone afflicts my mind,
More reason for complaint remains behind:
I grieve not only that she Kisses gave,
Tho that affords me cause enough to grieve:
Such never could be taught her but in Bed,
And Heav'n knows what Reward her Teacher had.

II, 5. Transl. John Oldham

TITUS PETRONIUS ARBITER (PETRONIUS)

A Fragment

I hate Fruition, now 'tis past,
'Tis all but nastiness at best;
The homeliest thing, that man can do,
Besides, 'tis short and fleeting too:
A squirt of slippery Delight,
That with a moment takes its flight:
A fulsom Bliss, that soon does cloy,
And makes us loath what we enjoy.
Then let us not too eager run,
By Passion blindly hurried on,

Like Beasts, who nothing better know,
Than what meer Lust incites them to:
For when in Floods of Love we're drench'd,
The Flames are by enjoyment quench'd:
But thus, let's thus together lie,
And kiss out long Eternity:
Here we dread no conscious spies,
No blushes stain our guiltless Joys:
Here no Faintness dulls Desires,
And Pleasure never flags, nor tires:
This has pleas'd, and pleases now,
And for Ages will do so:
   Enjoyment here is never done,
   But fresh, and always but begun.

Transl. John Oldham

From the Satyricon

GITON WAS STANDING there, helpless with laughter. Seeing this, Quartilla asked with great interest whose boy he was. When I told her that he was my 'brother', she said: 'Then why hasn't he kissed me?' She called him to her and put her lips to his. Then, she slipped her hand into his clothes and felt his little untried seed-pod. 'This,' she said, 'will serve as starters for our orgies tomorrow; for the moment, after that little stud, I'm not bothering with our daily rations.'

As she said this, Psyche came in, smiling, and whispered something in her ear. 'Yes, just so,' said Quartilla, 'I'm glad you reminded me. It's such a good opportunity, why shouldn't our Pannychis be deflowered?' She was produced at once – quite a pretty girl, who seemed to be no more than seven years old. It was she who had come into our chamber with Quartilla, earlier. Everyone applauded and demanded a wedding. I was aghast and objected that Giton was a very modest boy who wasn't up to this wantonness, nor was the girl of an age to be able to assume the role of a submissive woman. 'Oh yes?' said Quartilla. 'Is she younger than I was when I had my first man? May Juno strike me down, if I can remember when I was a virgin. When I was a kid I mucked around with other children, and after, in the succeeding years, I took up with older boys until I arrived at my present age. I think this must be the origin of the proverb 'Who can bear the calf is able to take on the bull.'

In case my boy should suffer greater injury in private, I got up to help with his wedding. Already, Psyche had put a flame-coloured bridal veil over the girl's head and the male prostitute was leading the way. The drunken women were clapping in a long line and had decked out the bridal chamber, draping it suggestively. Then Quartilla, aroused by the joke, got up, seized Giton and dragged him into the room.

Without doubt, the boy made no attempt to resist, and the girl showed no fear or sorrow at the word 'marriage'. And so, as soon as they were shut in and lying down, we sat outside the door of the bridal chamber and Quartilla was the first to put a watchful eye to a chink she'd widened and spy on the children's games with lustful eagerness. She drew me to the same sight with a clammy hand, and since our faces were pressed together while we watched, she would move her lips to mine in passing and torment me with furtive kisses.

XIV, 24. Transl. F.P.

GAIUS SUETONIUS TRANQUILLUS (SUETONIUS)

From The Lives of the Caesars

Tiberius in Capri

HAVING RETIRED TO Capri, he contrived a place for private orgies where bevies of girls and boys he'd procured, and those called *Spintriae*, who were known for kinky practices, would perform threesomes in succession in front of him to kindle his flagging lust. A number of small rooms were fitted out with tablet paintings of voluptuous scenes, erotic sculptures and manuals from Elephantis[1], from which the inmates couldn't fail to understand what the emperor wanted. In the woods and groves he also devised places for lovemaking and had both sexes dressed up as Pans and nymphs standing in front of caves and grottoes, so that the whole place became known as Goat Island.

---

[1] In Egypt.

Some of his infamies were too shameful to report, let alone to believe –
for instance, he trained tiny boys, calling them 'little fishes', to go between
his legs while he was swimming, licking and nibbling him. He also had
unweaned babies applied to his cock as to their mother's teats.

Transl. F.P.

DECIMUS JUNIUS JUVENALIS (JUVENAL)

From the Satires

Claudius and Messalina

The good old sluggard but began to snore,
When from his side up rose th'imperial whore:
She who preferr'd the pleasures of the night
To pomps, that are but impotent delight,
Strode from the palace, with an eager pace,
To cope with a more masculine embrace:
Muffl'd she march'd, like Juno in a cloud,
Of all her train but one poor wench allow'd,
One whom in secret service she cou'd trust;
The rival and companion of her lust.
To the known brothel-house she takes her way;
And for a nasty room gives double pay;
That room in which the rankest harlot lay.
Prepar'd for fight, expectingly she lies,
With heaving breasts, and with desiring eyes:
Still as one drops, another takes his place,
And baffled still succeeds to like disgrace.
At length when friendly darkness is expir'd,
And ev'ry strumpet from her cell retir'd,
She lags behind, and ling'ring at the gate,
With a repining sigh submits to Fate:

All filth without, and all a fire within,
Tir'd with the toil, unsated with the sin,
Old Casar's bed the modest matron seeks;
The stream of lamps still hanging on her cheeks
In ropy smut: thus foul, and thus bedight,
She brings him back the product of the night.

Philtres

The craving wife, the force of magic tries,
And philtres for th'unstable husband buys:
The potion works not on the part design'd;
But turns his brains, and stupefies his mind.
The sacred moon-calf gapes, and staring on,
Sees his own bus'ness by another done:
A long oblivion, a benumming frost,
Constrains his head; and yesterday is lost:
Some nimbler juice wou'd make him foam and rave
Like that Casonia[1] to her Caius gave:
Who, plucking from the forehead of the fole
His mother's love, infus'd it in the bowl:
The boiling blood ran hissing in his veins,
Till the mad vapour mounted to his brains.
The Thund'rer was not half so much on fire,
When Juno's girdle kindled his desire.
What woman will not use the pois'ning trade,
When Casar's wife the precedent has made?

Satire VI, transl. John Dryden

[1] These lines refer to Caesonia poisoning her husband, Caligula, by using the traditional aphrodisiac, Hippomanes, on him.

Entertainments

But you perhaps, expect a modish feast,
With am'rous songs and wanton dancers grac'd,
Where sprightly females to the middle bare,
Trip lightly o'er the ground, and frisk in air,
Whose pliant limbs in various postures move,
And twine and bound as in the rage of love:
Such sights the languid nerves to action stir,
And jaded lust springs forward with this spur:
Virtue would shrink to hear this lewdness told,
Which husbands now do with their wives behold;
A needful help to make 'em both approve
The dry embraces of long-wedded love:
In nuptial cinders this revives the fire,
And turns their mutual loathings to desire.

Satire XI, transl. William Congreve

MARCUS VALERIUS MARTIALIS (MARTIAL)

From the Epigrams

To Philaenis

Why don't I kiss you? You're bald as a coot . . .
Why don't I kiss you? You're bright red to boot . . .
Why don't I kiss you? You've only one eye . . .
Kissing you'd be just a blow job, that's why.

II, 33, transl. F.P.

Why, Thais, do you call me an old man?
Where blow jobs are concerned, even old men can.

IV, 1, transl. F.P.

No man among the people, or in all Rome can show
That he's fucked Thais – many'd like and many've asked, you know.
'Is Thais then so chaste?' I said.
'By no means. She sucks pricks instead.'

IV, 84, transl. F.P.

His tool was large and so was his nose,
Papylus could smell it whenever it rose.

VI, 36, transl. F.P.

Galla'll be fucked for two pieces of gold.
She'll do something more, for two more, I am told.
Aeschylus, why does she have ten from you?
Her blow jobs come cheaper. What then? Silence, too?

IX, 4, transl. F.P.

Lesbia swears she's never screwed for free.
That's true, for when she's fucked, she pays the fee.

IX, 62, transl. F.P.

When you fuck, Polycharmus, you end by shitting,
When poked, Polycharmus, what'll be fitting?

IX, 69, transl. F.P.

Abhorrent of all natural joys,
  Philaenis sodomises boys,
And like a spouse whose wife's away
  She drains of spend twelve cunts a day.
With dress tucked up above her knees
  She hurls the heavy ball with ease,
And, smeared all o'er with oil and sand,
  She wields a dumb bell in each hand,
And when she quits the dirty floor,
  Still rank with grease, the jaded whore
Submits to the schoolmaster's whip
  For each small fault, each trifling slip:
Nor will she sit her down to dine
  Till she has spewed two quarts of wine:
And when she's eaten pounds of steak
  A gallon more her thirst will slake.
After all this, when fired by lust,
  For pricks alone she feels disgust,
These cannot e'en her lips entice,
  Forsooth it is a woman's vice!
But girls she'll gamahuche for hours,
  Their juicy quims she quite devours.
Oh, you that think your sex to cloak
  By kissing what you cannot poke,
May God grant that you, Philaenis,
  Will yet learn to suck a penis.

                    VII, 67, transl. George Augustus Sala

Last night the soft charms of an exquisite whore
    Fulfilled every whim of my mind,
Till, with fucking grown weary, I begged something more,
    One bliss that still lingered behind.
My prayer was accepted; the rose in the rear
    Was opened to me in a minute;
One rose still remained, which I asked of my dear,
    'Twas her mouth and the tongue that lay in it.
She promised at once, what I asked her to do;
    Yet her lips were unsullied by me,
They'll not, my old friend, remain virgins for you,
    Whose penchant exceeds e'en her fee.

IX, 67, transl. George Augustus Sala

Lesbia, thou sinn'st still with an unpinn'd door,
And open, and ne'er cloak'st thy pleasure o'er,
Thy peepers more than active friends delight,
Nor are thy joys in kind if out of sight:
But yet the common wench with veil and key
Strives to expel the witness far away.
No chink doth in a brothel-house appear;
Of vulgar strumpets learn this modest care;
Stews hide this filthiness: but, Lesbia, see
If this my censure seem too hard to be?
    I don't forbid thee to employ thy prime,
    But to be taken, Lesbia, there's the crime.

I, 34, transl. Robert Fletcher

You grant your favours, Caelia, to all races –
Parthians, Germans, Dacians share your graces.
Cilicians, Cappadocians in your bed be,
And even a swarthy Indian from the Red Sea!
From Egypt's Memphis one sails to your door,
And Jews, though circumcised, you'll not ignore,
And that's not all! On his Sarmatian steed
No Scythian ever passed your door at speed.
You are a Roman girl, so tell me true,
Do Roman weapons have no charm for you?

VII, 30, transl. Olive Pitt-Kethley

Now no longer can you say
Paula, when you mean to stray,
'Caesar sent for me today.'
Circeian villa, Alban too,
Are no alibi for you.
Nerva rules now; you must be,
Though would-be whore, Penelope.
A problem, this. If you pretend
To visit family or sick friend,
Your dim old husband sticks like glue –
'You're going out dear? I'll come too.'
What on earth then can you say?
A lying whore would find a way,
In Sinuessa's springs redress
A bout of female nervousness.
But, Paula, you're no liar; you,
When off for an illicit screw,
Would first make sure your husband knew.

IX, 7, transl. Olive Pitt-Kethley

Lydia is as wide and slack
As a bronze horse's cul-de-sac,
Or sounding hoop with copper rings,
Or board from which an athlete springs,
Or swollen shoe from muddy puddle,
Or net of thrushes in a huddle,
Or awning that won't stay outspread,
In Pompey's theatre, overhead,
Or bracelet that, at every cough,
From a consumptive poof slips off,
French cushion, where the stuffing leaks,
Poor Breton's knackered, baggy breeks,
Foul pelican-crop, Ravenna-bred!
Now there's a rumour – he who said
I had her in the fish-pond joked;
It was the pond itself I poked.

IX, 21, transl. Olive Pitt-Kethley

LUCIUS APULEIUS

From The Golden Ass

Lucius sleeps with Fotis

I ROSE UP and went unto my chamber, where I found all things finely prepared, and the childrens bed (because they should not heare what we did in the night) was removed far off without the chamber doore. The table was all covered with those meats that were left at supper, the cups were filled halfe full with water, to temper and delay the wines, the flaggon stood ready prepared, and there lacked nothing that was necessary for the preparation of Venus. And when I was entring into the bed, behold my Fotis (who had brought her mistresse to bed) came in and gave me roses and floures which she had in her apron, and some she threw about the bed, and kissed mee sweetly, and tied a garland about my head, and bespred the chamber with the residue. Which when shee had done, shee tooke a cup of wine and delaied it with hot water, and profered it me to drinke; and before I had drunk off all she pulled it from my mouth, and then gave it me againe, and in this manner we emptied the pot twice or thrice together. Thus when I had well replenished my self with wine, and was now ready unto Venery not onely in minde but also in body, I removed my cloathes, and shewing to Fotis my great impatiencie I sayd, O my sweet heart take pitty upon me and helpe me, for as you see I am now prepared unto the battell, which you your selfe did appoint: for after that I felt the first Arrow of cruell Cupid within my breast, I bent my bow very strong, and now feare (because it is bended so hard) lest my string should breake: but that thou mayst the better please me, undresse thy haire and come and embrace mee lovingly: whereupon she made no long delay, but set aside all the meat and wine, and then she unapparelled her selfe, and unattyred her haire, presenting her amiable body unto me in manner of faire Venus, when shee goeth under the waves of the sea. Now (quoth shee) is come the houre of justing, now is come the time of warre, wherefore shew thy selfe like unto a man, for I will not retyre, I will not fly the field, see then thou bee valiant, see thou be couragious, since there is no time appointed when our skirmish shall cease. In saying these words she came to me to bed, and embraced me sweetly, and so wee passed all the night in pastime and pleasure, and never slept until it was day: but wee would eftsoones refresh our wearinesse, and provoke our pleasure, and renew our venery by drinking of wine. In which sort we pleasantly passed away many other nights following.

> Fotis's mistress is a witch. Lucius tries some of her ointment, wishing to become a bird, but instead is turned into an ass. In this guise he has many adventures.

WHEN HE HAD bought such things as was necessary, he would not returne home into his Countrey in Chariots, or waggon, neither would he ride upon Thessalian Horses, or Jenets of France, or Spanish Mules, which be most excellent as can be found, but caused me to be garnished and trimmed with trappers and barbs of Gold, with brave harnesse, with purple coverings, with a bridle of silver, with pictured cloths, and with shrilling bells, and in this manner he rode upon me lovingly, speaking and intreating me with gentle words, but above all things he did greatly rejoyce in that I was his Servant to beare him upon my backe, and his Companion to feed with him at the Table: After long time when we had travelled as well by Sea as Land, and fortuned to arive at Corinth, the people of the Towne came about us on every side, not so much to doe honour to Thiasus, as to see me: For my fame was so greatly spread there, that I gained my master much money, and when the people was desirous to see me play prankes, they caused the Gates to be shut, and such as entered in should pay money, by meanes whereof I was a profitable companion to them every day: There fortuned to be amongst the Assembly a noble and rich Matron that conceived much delight to behold me, and could find no remedy to her passions and disordinate appetite, but continually desired to have her pleasure with me, as Pasiphae had with a Bull. In the end she promised a great reward to my keeper for the custody of me one night, who for gaine of a little money accorded to her desire, and when I had supped in a Parler with my Master, we departed away and went into our Chamber, where we found the faire Matron, who had tarried a great space for our comming: I am not able to recite unto you how all things were prepared: there were foure Eunuches that lay on a bed of downe on the ground with Boulsters accordingly for us to lye on, the Coverlet was of cloth of Gold, and the pillowes soft and tender, whereon the delicate Matron had accustomed to lay her head. Then the Eunuches not minding to delay any longer the pleasure of their Mistresse closed the doores of the Chamber and departed away: within the Chamber were Lamps that gave a cleare light all the place over: Then she put off all her Garments to her naked skinne, and taking the Lampe that stood next to her, began to annoint all her body with balme, and mine likewise, but especially my nose, which done, she kissed me, not as they accustome to doe at the stewes, or in brothell houses, or in the Curtiant Schooles for gaine of money, but purely, sincerely, and with great affection, casting out these and like loving words: Thou art he whom I love, thou art he whom I onely desire, without thee I cannot live, and other like preamble of talke as women can use well enough, when as they mind to shew or declare their burning passions and great affection of love: Then she tooke me by the halter and cast me downe upon the bed, which was nothing strange unto me, considering that she was so beautifull a Matron and I so wel boldened out with wine, and perfumed with balme, whereby I was readily prepared for the purpose: But nothing grieved me so much as to think, how I should with my huge and great legs imbrace so faire a Matron, or how I should touch her fine, dainty, and silken skinne, with my hard hoofes, or how it was possible to kisse her soft, pretty and ruddy lips, with my monstrous mouth and stony teeth, or how she, who was young and tender, could be able to receive me.

And I verily thought, if I should hurt the woman by any kind of meane, I should be throwne to the wild Beasts: But in the meane season she kissed me, and looked in my mouth with burning eyes, saying: I hold thee my cunny, I hold thee my nops, my sparrow, and therewithall she eftsoones imbraced my body round about, and had her pleasure with me, whereby I thought the mother of Minotarus did not causelesse quench her inordinate desire with a Bull. When night was passed, with much joy and small sleepe, the Matron went before day to my keeper to bargaine with him another night, which he willingly granted, partly for gaine of money, and party to finde new pastime for my master. Who after he was informed of all the history of my luxury, was right glad, and rewarded my keeper well for his paine, minding to shew before the face of all the people, what I could doe: but because they would not suffer the Matron to abide such shame, by reason of her dignity, and because they could finde no other that would endeavour so great a reproach, at length they obtained for money a poore woman, which was condemned to be eaten of wilde beasts, with whom I should openly have to doe.

Transl. William Adlington

DECIUS MAGNUS AUSONIUS

The *Cento* (from the Greek for a needle, and later for patchwork) is a decadent Latin literary form, where the writer composes a poem on a subject, using a series of odd lines from the work of another poet (usually Virgil or Homer). One of the most famous of these was an epithalamium composed by Valentinian's tutor, Ausonius.

From the Cento

The Guests attending still; The beauteous Bride
Sits on the Bed, the Bridegroom by her Side.
But when alone, their ev'ry Glance imparts
The sweet Confusion of their meeting Hearts.

They talk, they toy, and as with weeping Eyes
She turns aside, and half repenting Sighs,
He seizes on her Lilly Hand, and cries,
With Kisses intermixt – My Love, my Life,
And ev'ry tender Name in One, my Wife,
Is it then giv'n me, in my longing Arms
To fold thee, guiltless thus, and taste thy Charms?
And canst thou now, my only Wish, my Spouse,
Refuse me the Reward of all my Vows?
Look up, and turn thy humid Eyes on mine,
They flame, and with their Fires will kindle thine
He said – And could no more his Heat command,
But she resists his Rage, and checks his Hand.
Downward she looks, and when the Bed she spies,
She shuts, so modest Maids affect, her Eyes,
And softly, sinking in his Arms, replies:
Oh lovely Youth! If ever to thy Ear,
A Father and a Mother's Names were dear;
By them let me conjure thee to forbear,
And but this Night a suppliant Virgin spare.
One Night again she begs, but begs in vain;
His Hand she can no more, nor he his Heat restrain.
Nor Words their Way, nor broken Accents find,
More Violent he grows, and she more Kind.
The rising Raptures break her swelling Sighs,
And breathless in the Bridegroom's Arms she lies.
Her Fears are flown, she clasps the furious Boy,
Gives all her Beauties up, and meets the Joy.

From an anonymous seventeenth-century translation in *Dryden's Miscellany*

LONGUS

From Daphnis and Chloe

Daphnis, a shepherd who's completely inept at sex, has to be
shown the ropes by a married woman.

HERE AND THERE, not without pleasure, the blating of the flocks was
heard, and the Lambs came skipping and inclined themselves
obliquely under the damms to riggle and nussle at their dugs. But those
which had not yet teemed, the Rams pursued; and when with some pains
they had made them stand, one rid another. There were seen too the
Chases of the he-goats, and their lascivious ardent leaps. Sometimes they
had battels for the she's, and every one had his own wives, and kept them
sollicitously, that no skulking adulterer should set upon them.

The old men seeing such incendiary fights as these, were prickt to
Venus: but the Young, and such as of themselves did itch, and for some
time had longed for the pleasure of Love, were wholly inflamed with what
they heard, and melted away with what they saw, and lookt for something
far more excellent then kisses and embraces were: and amongst them was
Daphnis chief. Therefore he, as being now grown up and lusty by keeping
at home, and following easie businesse all the Winter, was carried
furiously to kissing, and stung with the desire to embrace, and close; and,
in what he did, was now more curious, and more rampant then ever
before. And therefore he began to ask of Chloe that she would give him
free leave to do with her what he listed, and that she would lye naked with
him naked, and longer too then they were wont: For there was nothing but
that remaining of the Institutes of old Philetas, and that he would try, as
the onely Canon, the onely med'cine to ease the pain of Love.

But Chloe asking him, whether anything remain'd more than kissing,
embracing, and lying together upon the ground; or what he could do by
lying naked upon a naked Girle?

That (quoth he) which the Rams use to do with the Ewes, and the he-
Goats with the She's. Do you not see, how after that work, neither these
run away, not those weary themselves in pursuit of them; but afterwards
how enjoying a common pleasure, they feed together quietly. That . . . as
it seems is a sweet practice, and such as can master the bitternesse of
Love.

How Daphnis? And dost thou not see the she-Goats and the Ewes, the he-Goats and the Rams, how these do their work standing, and those suffer standing too; these leaping and those admitting them upon their backs? And yet thou askest me to lye down, and that naked. But how much rougher are they then I, although I have all my Clothes on?

Daphnis is persuaded, and laying her down, lay down with her, and lay long; but knowing how to do nothing of that he was mad to do, lifted her up, and endeavour'd to imitate the Goats. But at the first finding a mere frustration there, he sate up, and lamented to himself, that he was more unskilfull than a very Tup in the practice of the mystery and the Art of Love. But there was a certain neighbour of his, a landed man, Chromis his name, and was now by his age somewhat declining. He married out of the City a young, fair, and buxome girle, one that was too fine and delicate for the Country, and a Clown: Her name was Lycænium; and she observing Daphnis as every day early in the morning he drove out his Goats to the fields, and home again at the first twilight, had a great mind to purchase the youth by gifts to become her sweetheart. And therefore once when she had sculkt for her opportunity, and catcht him alone, she gave him a curious fine pipe, some pretious honey-combs, and a new Scrip of Stag-skin: but durst not break her mind to him, because she could easily conjecture at that dear love he bore to Chloe. For she saw him wholly addicted to the girle: which indeed she might well perceive before, by the winking, nodding, laughing and tittering that was between them: but one morning she made Chromis believe that she was to go to a womans labour, and followed softly behind them two at some distance, and then slipt away into a thicket and hid herself, and so could hear all that they said, and see too all that they did; and the lamenting untaught Daphnis was perfectly within her reach. Wherefore she began to condole the condition of the wretched Lovers, and finding that she had light upon a double opportunity; this, to the preservation of them; that, to satisfie her own wanton desire, she projected to accomplish both by this device. The next day making as if she were to go a Gossipping again, she came up openly to the Oak where Daphnis and Chloe were sitting together; and when she had skilfully counterfeited that she was feared, Help (Daphnis) help me, (quoth she), An Eagle has carried away from me the goodliest Goose of twenty in a flock, which yet, by reason of the great weight, she was not able to carry to the top of that her wonted high crag, but is fallen down with her into yonder Cops. For the Nymph's sake, and this Pan's, do thou Daphnis go in to the Wood, and rescue my Goose. For I dare not go in my self alone. Let me not thus lose the Tale of my Geese. And it may be thou mayest kill the Eagle too, and then she will scarce come hither any more to prey upon the Kids and Lambs. Chloe for so long will look to the flock; the Goats know her as thy perpetuall Companion in the fields. Now Daphnis suspecting nothing of that that was intended, gets up quickly, and taking his staff followed Lycænium, who lead him a great way off from Chloe. But when they were come to the thickest part of the wood, and she had bid him sit down by a Fountain: Daphnis (quoth she) Thou dost love Chloe, and that I learned last night of the Nymphs. Those tears which yesterday thou didst pour down, were shewn to me in a dream by them, and they commanded me, that I should save thee, and teach thee the secret practices of Love. But those are not Kisses, nor embracing, nor yet such things as thou seest the Rams, and the he-goats do. There are other leaps, there are other friskins than those, and far sweeter than them. For unto these there appertains a much longer duration of pleasure. If then thou wouldst be rid of thy misery, and make an Experiment of that pleasure, and sweetnesse which you have sought, and mist so long, come on, deliver thy self to me a sweet Schollar, and I, to gratifie the Nymphs, will be thy Mistris. At this Daphnis as being a rustick Goat-herd, a Sanguin Youth, and burning in desire, could not contain himself for meer pleasure, and that Lubency that he had to be taught; but throwes himself at the foot of Lycænium, and begs of her, that she would teach him quickly that Art, by which he should be able, as he would, to do Chloe; and he should not only accept it as a rare and brave thing sent from the gods, but for her kindnesse he would give her too a young Kid, some of the finest new-milk Cheeses; nay, besides, he promised her the dam her self. Wherefor Lycænium now she had found the Goat-herd so willing and forward beyond her expectation, began to instruct the Lad thus – She bid him sit down as near to her as possibly he could, and that he should kisse her as close and as often as he used to kisse Chloe; and while he kist her to clip her in his arms and hugg her to him, and lye down with her upon the ground. As now he was sitting, and kissing, and lay down with her; She, when she saw him itching to be at her, lifted him up from the reclination on his side, and slipping under, not without art, directed him to her Fancie, the place so long desired and sought. Of that which happened after this, there was nothing done that was strange, nothing that was insolent: the Lady Nature and Lycaenium shewed him how to do the rest. This wanton Information being over, Daphnis, who had still a Childish Pastorall mind, would presently be gone, and run up to Chloe, to have an experiment with her, how much he had profited by that magistery, as if indeed he had bin afraid lest staying but a little longer, he could forget to do his trick. But: Lycænium intercepted him thus: Thou art yet Daphnis, to learn this besides: I who am a woman, have suffered nothing in this close with thee, but what I am well acquainted withall. For heretofore another Youth taught me to play at this sport, and for his pains, he had my maidenhead. But if thou strive with Chloe in this list, she will squeak, and cry out, and bleed as if she were stickt. But be not thou afraid of her bleeding; but when thou hast persuaded her to thy pleasure, bring her hither into this place, that although she should cry and roar, no body can hear; and if she bleed, here's a clear Fountain, she may wash; and do thou, Daphnis, never forget it, that I before Chloe made thee a man. These advertisements given, Lycænium kist him, and went away through another glade of the Wood, as if still she would look for her Goose.

Gnatho

BUT GNATHO, a man that had learnt onely to guttle, and drink till he was drunk, and minded nothing but his belly, and his lasciviousnesse under that, he had taken a more curious view of Daphnis then others had, when he presented the gifts. And because from the beginning he was struck with Pœderastic (the Love of boys) by the Terrestriall gods, observing him to be such a beauty as all Mitylene could not shew, he resolved to tempt Daphnis to the purpose, and thought he had not much to do, because the Lad was but a Goat-herd. When he had now thus deliberated with himself, he went not with Astylus a hunting: but going down into the field where Daphnis kept, he said he came to see the Goats, but came indeed Spectator of the Youth. He began to palpe him with soft words, praised his Goats, call'd fondly on him for a Pastoral Tune, and said withall he would speedily impetrate his Liberty for him, as being able to do what he would with his Lord. And when he had found the harmlesse boy observant to him, when it was now grown somewhat dark, and Daphnis was to drive home, he watcht his time, and anon he ran at him, and lolled upon him; and when he had kist him o're and o're, he shuffled himself odly behind him, as if he meant to attempt something like the he-goats with the she's. But Daphnis at length perceiving it, and saying: That the he-goats rid the shees, That was very right indeed: but that a he-goat rid a he, that was never yet seen; nor the Rams, instead of the Ewes, to rid Rams; nor Cocks tread Cocks instead of Hens: Gnatho then laid hands on him, and offer'd to force him. But Daphnis flung off this drunken Sott, who scarce could stand upon his legs, and laid him on the ground, then whipt away, and left him to some sturdy Porter, as fitter to lead, or carry him.

Transl. George Thornley

MAXIMIANUS ETRUSCUS (MAXIMIAN)

From Elegies of Old Age

Elegy V

In the early parts of the poem, Maximianus talks of being sent to
the East as a legate. While there, he falls for a Greek girl, but when
he tries to have sex with her, impotence strikes.

I wish't, I ask't, and gain'd the Beautious She;
But, oh! what Witchcraft did Enervate me!
Lifeless I on that mass of Beauty lay,
Nor the due debts of Sacred Love could pay.
All vigorous warmth my languid Limbs forsook,
And left me cold, like an old sapless Oak.
My chief, yet basest Nerve, did then prove lank,
And, like a Coward, from the Battle shrank;
Shrivell'd, and dry, like a dead wither'd flow'r,
Depriv'd, and void of all vivisick pow'r.
No fertile Moisture, no prolifick Juice,
Could the enfeebled Instrument produce;
No unctious Substance, no kind Balm emit;
Balm, nourishing as Milk, as Honey sweet.
At last cry'd out the Disappointed Fair,
Thy dull unactive weight I cannot bear;
Thy heavy Limbs press me with joyless pain,
And all thy faint Endeavours are in vain.

Useless, I must confess, I then did lye,
O'er-come of Thuscan grave Simplicitie;
And in soft Græcian Dalliance unskill'd,
To Age's Impotence was forc'd to yield.
Those very Arts, those Stratagems of Love,
(Which did, of old, Troy's sad Destruction prove,

And, maugre Hector's Courage, could prevail,)
Us'd to one Old defective Man, did fail:
Nay, though a Beauty, ev'n as Hellen bright,
Did to the mighty Task of Love invite.
Yet in the vain performance did I tire,
Though giv'n up to th' Empire of Desire.
Nor need I blush to own, or be asham'd,
That I by such a Beauty was inflam'd;
For Jove himself, had he my Goddess seen,
Ev'n Jove himself her Captive must have been.
Yet ne'ertheless, such was my first sad Night,
That I could neither give nor take Delight.
But a base conscious shame possest each sence,
Nor left me pow'r to make the least defence,
Dash'd with the Guilt of my own Impotence.

But lo, the next ensuing Night came on,
And lo, my vig'rous heat again was gon;
Void of all warmth, and strength did I remain,
And as before was dull, and slow again.
But she much vex'd, that I would not fulfill
Her Expectation, but deceive her still:
Blam'd my neglectfull sloath, and angry too,
Claim'd the just Tribute which to Love was due;
And wond'ring why her Charms no more could move,
Said, Sluggard pay thy Debts to me, & Love.
But her just Anger, with me, nothing weigh'd,
Nothing her soothing Language could perswade.
In vain with either did she me assail,
'Gainst my unconquer'd Impotence both fail.
For what, alas, can those Defects supply,
Which weaken'd Nature do's to Age deny?
But then I blush't, and stupify'd became,
Much more debilitated by my Shame.

A conscious Terrour did possess my Mind,
And took away all pow'r of being kind.
Yet with her soft and active Hand she strove,
The frigid Member to adapt for Love:
But she the fainting thing did try in vain,
B'y inspiring touch to call to life again;
Nor answer'd it her Toil, nor my desire,
But cold remain'd i'th' midst of such a Fire:
So the starv'd Wretch in Northern Scythia sees,
Th' ungratefull Pot ev'n o'er the Fire to freeze.

    What cruel Woman, thou unkind, said she,
Has snatch'd thy Love, my Due alone from me?
Where hast thou been ungrateful? and with whom?
From whose Embraces do'st thou tir'd come?
I swore 'twas her mistake, and did protest,
No other Passion could invade my Breast;
She, only She was of my Heart possest.
And that it was excess of Love and Care,
Dash't me with such a trembling Awe, and Fear;
As render'd me uncapable to give,
Those Acts of Kindness, which she should receive.
Yet maugre this, the bright expecting Dame,
Believ'd 'twas all but a pretended Sham.
Thou ly'st, the much-offended Fair One cry'd,
For thou some other Nymph do'st love beside,
And art with me alone unsatisfy'd.
Variety affects thy Appetite,
And thou do'st in a frequent Change delight,
Why else would you my tendred Kindness slight?
Do's Sorrow damp you? then try to remove
Such heavy Griefs by the brisk Joys of Love.
Be not o'er-come by any sad Excess,
But intermit such Cares as over-press;
For Burthens oft laid down become the less.

Then I uncover'd in the Naked Bed,
To the inquiring Nymph thus weeping said,
Alas, Fair Greek, I am constrain'd to own,
What I endeavour'd to have kept unknown;
And lest you might suspect it want of Love,
Am forc'd by sad Defects my Age to prove.
Unhappy I, whose Vigour is quite dead;
Alas, my Will and Wishes are not fled:
Unfortunate, that I am judg'd to be
Unkind, because of my Debilitie.
Lo, I have brought you Arms, with Shame I own,
By a long lazy Rest defective grown,
Yet Arms devoted to thy Use alone.
Do what thou canst, all thy Endeavours try,
To move me, I submit most willingly:
Yet still I fail'd the more, the more I strove,
Desire's excess did Impotence improve.
Streight she began, with many a Græcian Art,
To give new Courage to the drooping Part:
But she, in vain, the cold dead thing, did strive,
With her gay Flames to quicken, and revive.
When she at last its Ruin did perceive,
And that the dear-lov'd Nerve no more could live;
But of its Resurrection all hopes lost,
On which she had bestow'd such pains, such cost.
Erected in the Bed, she mournfull sate,
Griev'd and tormented with her wretched state,
And thus deplor'd her miserable Fate.

Ah, fallen Member! who wert once to Me,
The best Improver of best Luxurie;
And at each sacred celebrated Feast,
My only Entertainment, only Guest;
My sweetest Darling, my Delight, my Health,
My dearest Honour, and my chiefest Wealth.

How thy dejected state shall I lament;
And in what Floods of Tears my sorrows vent?
Where shall I find equal, and worthy Verse,
Thy mighty Acts, and Prowess to reherse?
Oft, when inflam'd, with my too hot Desire,
Thou didst allay the raging of that Fire.
And oft didst thou (then when thou couldst be kind)
Charm the Diseases of my troubled Mind:
My dear Companion many tedious Nights,
Partaker of my Griefs, and my Delights;
To thee my choicest Secrets were disclos'd;
And with much Safety in thy trust repos'd.
Still wert thou watchfull, and wert still at hand,
To answer, and obey my least Command.
Whither! oh, whither is thy Fervour fled!
Why do'st thou hang thy cold, thy drooping Head?
What envious Power has depriv'd thee quite,
Of all that vigour, all that former spright,
Which made thee heretofore so bold in fight?
Frequent Engagements pleas'd thee heretofore,
But now thy Courage fails, and is no more;
For, lo, no more a lively chearfull Red,
Do's thee, as once it did, with warmth o'er-spread;
But pale and wan thou do'st dejected lye,
Nor dar'st look up to face thy Enemy;
The kindest, most endearing Words to thee,
Are lost, and altogether useless be.
The pow'rfull Charms of Verse, which can relieve,
Sorrowfull Minds, to thee no life can give.
Thee therefore justly I as dead bewail,
Since in all active Motion thou do'st fail.

Maximianus exhorts her to find a younger man . . .

> But she inrag'd, said, Fool, thou do'st not know
> The real Cause of all my real Woe;
> And why such floods of Tears my Eyes o'er-flow.
> Be not so fond and vain as to believe,
> That thy peculiar Fate I only grieve:
> No, this to my distracted Fancy, brings
> The sad Estate of all Created things:
> For if the gen'tive Pow'r were tane away,
> How soon, alas, would this vast World decay?
> And oh thou needfull Engine, without Thee,
> All things that breath would quickly cease to be!
> Mankind, Beast, Fish and Fowl, and all that live,
> From Thee their first Beginnings must receive.
> What Concord, or Agreement, could be made,
> In diff'rent Sexes, if without thy Aid;
> And if of thy most gratefull Favours void,
> The chiefest Good of Marriage is destroy'd.
> With such strong Leagues of Kindness thou canst bind,
> That of two diff'rent, thou mak'st up one Mind.
> So much thou do'st to Unitie incline,
> And separate Bodies can't so closely joyn,
> That Two grow into One by Am'rous Twine.
>
> Though to a Nymph Nature all Beauty grants,
> She wants her chief Reward, if Thee she wants:
> In Thee alone Valour and Vertue lyes,
> And thou of Beauty art the only Prize:
> Manhood by Thee alone is made compleat,
> Which, without Thee, were but a sordid Cheat.
> No sparkling Gems, nor yellow shining Gold,
> Can to thy solid real Worth be told;
> Not the most sordid Miser would, to be,
> Master of all the Wealth sunk in the Sea,

Or yet on shore, sell or dispose of Thee.
In vain, as Ornaments, such Toys are worn,
If thou as well do'st not the Man adorn:
Unlike those empty Trifles very much,
Thy kind increases by productive Touch;
But they by using, still the more decay,
And with a frequent rubbing wear away.
With Thee is Credit, and Fidelitie,
And Secrets told are safely lodg'd in Thee.
Oh! only true Reward of perfect Love,
To which thou do'st both kind and fruitfull prove:
To Thee both great things, and sublime give way,
And all thy mighty Mandates must obey.
All yield, and all submit without a Grief,
From the sweet Bondage wishing no Relief.
Thy angry Wounds are not so terrible,
But such as ev'n thy Friends desire to feel:
Ev'n that same Wisdom, which the World do's guide,
Declares her self of thy more equal side;
And to thy Rule and Governance thinks fit,
That all its Force and Power should submit.

   To Thee the trembling, conquer'd, yielding Maid,
Desiring that of which she seems afraid:
Prostrate falls down, just ready to receive
Those gratefull Wounds, which thou prepar'st to give
And when broke up, she still, and silent lyes,
Sheds her glad Blood, and with the Pleasure dyes.
Mangled, some Tears she drops, but more do's smile,
And stronger Joys her weaker Griefs begulle.
Pleas'd with the sweet Defeat, she clings more close,
And hugs the Conquerour that gives the murth'ring Blows.
Soft easie ways thou do'st not always chuse,
But sometimes acts of Force and Manhood use:
Thy toying Plays, and pretty gamesome Wiles,

Are sometimes mix't with more laborious Toils.
Oft Stratagems of Wit are your best course,
And sometimes you thrive best by down-right Force.
The cruel Hearts of Tyrants fierce, and wild,
Thou often canst convert to kind, and mild:
Ev'n thou the stubborn God of War canst move,
And melt, and soften into gentle Love.
Thou the enrag'd, and anger'd Jove canst charm,
And of his dreadfull Thunder quite disarm;
Nay, after the bold Gyant's overthrow,
Could'st clear his clouded, and incensed Brow.
The hungry Tyger, by thy strange Effects,
Grows tame, and the pursuit of Beasts neglects.
The humble Lover, courteous, meek, and mild,
By thee grows fierce, and, like a Lyon, wild.
Thy Vertue, and thy Patience wonders doe,
For all your Victims are belov'd by you;
And when you conquer, you are conquer'd too.
Triumphs you scorn, but love the active Fight,
And more in War than Conquest you delight.
O'ercome, you re-assume new Strength, new Life,
With double Courage to renew the Strife.
And then the Battle thus again renew'd,
You only fight to be again subdu'd.
Short is thy Rage, but Zeal do's longer live,
And Strength decay'd do's very oft revive.
And though thy Pow'r to doe and act is done,
Yet thy Good-will and Wishes are not gone.

   Thus she (as if she mourn'd the Obsequies
Of some dead Friend, as dear as her own Eyes)
Ended her long Complaint, and rose from me,
Abandon'd o'er to Grief, and Miserie.

Transl. H. Walker

PROCOPIUS OF CAESAREA

From Anecdota *or* The Secret History

The youth of the Empress Theodora

NOW, FOR THE time, Theodora was still too young to be able to sleep with a man, or have sex with them as a woman does, but she did have intercourse of the masculine kind with evil-minded slaves, who, following their masters to the theatre, took advantage of their leisure to commit this outrage; and she spent a lot of time in a brothel at this unnatural bodily activity. But, as soon as she came of age and reached maturity, she went on the stage and became a prostitute of the sort the men of the past used to call 'a streetwalker': for she was not a flute or harp player, and had not even learned to dance, but she sold her youth to anyone who came along, giving herself with total abandonment. Later, she went with the mime actors of the theatre and took part in their performances, getting laughs with bawdy comedy. For she was unusually witty and full of fun, and soon became known for that sort of act. For she had no modesty, and no one ever saw her embarrassed, but she'd take on shameless jobs without hesitation – she was the sort of person, for instance, who delights the audience by letting herself be knocked around and beaten over the head, and makes them laugh by stripping and showing bare to the spectators, those parts, back and front, which should be unseen and hidden from men.

As she toyed with her lovers, she kept trying new kinds of intercourse, succeeding in binding to her those of a licentious temperament. For she did not even wait for those she happened to meet to make the approach, but she swung into action, joking and waggling her hips in a comic way, tempting everyone, especially young boys. For there was never anyone who was such an addict to pleasure in all its forms. Often she'd go to dinner with ten young men or more, all at the peak of physical perfection, and sexual athletes as well, and have sex with all her banquet companions, all through the night; and when they were too worn out to go on, she would go on to their house-slaves, perhaps thirty in number, and pair off with each in turn – even so, she could not get her fill of this lewdness.

Once, visiting the house of someone well-known, during the after-dinner drinking, they say that, in full view of the drinkers, she climbed on to the projecting part of a couch, pulled up her clothes without decency and didn't refrain from showing her eagerness. And although she made use of three bore-holes, she ued to lament that Nature hadn't pierced a similar one between her tits, so that she could contrive another method of intercourse. She became pregnant frequently, but was practically always able to arrange to miscarry immediately.

Often, even in the theatre, before all the people, she undressed and stood naked in the midst; she had a G-string covering her private parts – not that she'd have minded showing them to the audience, as well as the rest – but because no one was allowed to enter there wholly naked, but must have a G-string over the groin. Dressed like this, she would spread her limbs, lying on her back on the stage; servants, whose work this was, scattered barley from above on to her genitals, and geese, provided for this purpose, ate it, picking it off with their beaks, grain by grain.

Transl. F.P.

VATSYAYANA

From The Kama Sutra

Of the auparishtaka or mouth congress

THERE ARE TWO kinds of eunuchs, those that are disguised as males, and those that are disguised as females. Eunuchs disguised as females imitate their dress, speech, gestures, tenderness, timidity, simplicity, softness and bashfulness. The acts that are done on the jaghana or middle parts of women, are done in the mouth of these eunuchs, and this is called Auparishtaka. These eunuchs derive their imaginable pleasure, and their livelihood from this kind of congress, and they lead the life of courtesans. So much concerning eunuchs disguised as females.

Eunuchs disguised as males keep their desires secret, and when they wish to do anything they lead the life of shampooers. Under the pretence of shampooing, a eunuch of this kind embraces and draws towards himself the thighs of the man whom he is shampooing, and after this he touches the joints of his thighs and his jaghana, or central portions of his body. Then, if he finds the lingam of the man erect, he presses it with his hands and chaffs him for getting into that state. If after this, and after knowing his intention, the man does not tell the eunuch to proceed, then the latter does it of his own accord and begins the congress. If however he is ordered by the man to do it, then he disputes with him, and only consents at last with difficulty.

The following eight things are then done by the eunuch one after the other:

> The nominal congress
> Biting the sides
> Pressing outside
> Pressing inside
> Kissing
> Rubbing
> Sucking a mango fruit
> Swallowing up

At the end of each of these, the eunuch expresses his wish to stop, but when one of them is finished, the man desires him to do another, and after that is done, then the one that follows it, and so on.

When, holding the man's lingam with his hand, and placing it between his lips, the eunuch moves about his mouth, it is called the 'nominal congress'.

When, covering the end of the lingam with his fingers collected together like the bud of a plant or flower, the eunuch presses the sides of it with his lips, using his teeth also, it is called 'biting the sides'.

When, being desired to proceed, the eunuch presses the end of the lingam with his lips closed together, and kisses it as if he were drawing it out, it is called the 'outside pressing'.

When, being asked to go on, he puts the lingam further into his mouth, and presses it with his lips and then takes it out, it is called the 'inside pressing'.

When, holding the lingam in his hand, the eunuch kisses it as if he were kissing the lower lip, it is called 'kissing'.

When, after kissing it, he touches it with his tongue everywhere, and passes the tongue over the end of it, it is called 'rubbing'.

When, in the same way, he puts the half of it into his mouth, and forcibly kisses and sucks it, this is called 'sucking a mango fruit'.

And lastly, when, with the consent of the man, the eunuch puts the whole lingam into his mouth, and presses it to the very end, as if he were going to swallow it up, it is called 'swallowing up'.

Transl. Sir Richard F. Burton

THE
MIDDLE AGES
AND THE
RENAISSANCE

FROM *THE ARABIAN NIGHTS*

At the opening of the story, Shah Zaman has discovered his wife in bed with the black cook and killed them both. He is ill with chagrin, but is comforted by finding out that his brother, Shahryar, has a wife as unfaithful. He shows him the Queen in action with a Moorish slave. They decide to leave their kingdoms and travel in search of another man similarly afflicted.

'DO NOT THWART me, O my brother, in what I propose,' and the other answered, 'I will not.' So he said, 'Let us up as we are and depart forthright hence, for we have no concern with Kingship, and let us overwander Allah's earth, worshipping the Almighty till we find some one to whom the like calamity hath happened; and if we find none then will death be more welcome to us than life.' So the two brothers issued from a second private postern of the palace; and they never stinted wayfaring by day and by night, until they reached a tree a-middle of a meadow hard by a spring of sweet water on the shore of the salt sea. Both drank of it and sat down to take their rest; and when an hour of the day had gone by, lo! they heard a mighty roar and uproar in the middle of the main as though the heavens were falling upon the earth; and the sea brake with waves before them, and from it towered a black pillar, which grew and grew till it rose skywards and began making for that meadow. Seeing it, they waxed fearful exceedingly and climbed to the top of the tree, which was a lofty; whence they gazed to see what might be the matter. And behold, it was a Jinni, huge of height and burly of breast and bulk, broad of brow and black of blee,[1] bearing on his head a coffer of crystal. He strode to land, wading through the deep, and coming to the tree whereupon were the two Kings, seated himself beneath it. He then set down the coffer on its bottom and out of it drew a casket, with seven padlocks of steel, which he unlocked with seven keys of steel he took from beside his thigh, and out of it a young lady to come was seen, white-skinned and of winsomest mien, of stature

[1] *Blee* – hue.

fine and thin, and bright as though a moon of the fourteenth night she had been, or the sun raining lively sheen. Even so the poet Utayyah hath excellently said:

She rose like the morn as she shone through the night and she
    gilded the grove with her gracious sight:
From her radiance the sun taketh increase when she unveileth and
    shameth the moonshine bright.
Bow down all beings between her hands as she showeth charms with
    her veil undight.
And she floodeth cities with torrent tears when she flasheth her look
    of leven-light.

The Jinni seated her under the tree by his side and looking at her said, 'O choicest love of this heart of mine! O dame of noblest line, whom I snatched away on thy bride night that none might prevent me taking thy maidenhead or tumble thee before I did, and whom none save myself hath loved or hath enjoyed: O my sweetheart! I would lief sleep a little while.' He then laid his head upon the lady's thighs; and, stretching out his legs which extended down to the sea, slept and snored and snarked like the roll of thunder. Presently she raised her head towards the tree-top and saw the two Kings perched near the summit; then she softly lifted off her lap the Jinni's pate which she was tired of supporting and placed it upon the ground; then standing upright under the tree signed to the Kings, 'Come ye down, ye two, and fear naught from this Ifrit.' They were in a terrible fright when they found that she had seen them and answered her in the same manner, 'Allah upon thee and by thy modesty, O lady, excuse us from coming down!' But she rejoined by saying, 'Allah upon you both that ye come down forthright, and if ye come not, I will rouse upon you my husband, this Ifrit, and he shall do you to die by the illest of deaths,' and she continued making signals to them. So, being afraid, they came down to her and she rose before them and said, 'Stroke me a strong stroke, without stay or delay, otherwise will I arouse and set upon you this Ifrit who shall slay you straightway.' They said to her, 'O our lady, we conjure thee by Allah, let us off this work, for we are fugitives from such and in extreme dread and terror of this thy husband. How then can we do it in such a way as thou desirest?' 'Leave this talk: it needs must be so,' quoth she, and she swore them by Him who raised the skies on high, without prop or pillar, that, if they worked not her will, she would cause them to be slain and cast into the sea. Whereupon out of fear King Shahryar said to

King Shah Zaman, 'O my brother, do thou what she biddeth thee do,' but he replied, 'I will not do it till thou do it before I do.' And they began disputing about futtering her. Then quoth she to the twain, 'How is it I see you disputing and demurring; if ye do not come forward like men and do the deed of kind ye two, I will arouse upon you the Ifrit.' At this, by reason of their sore dread of the Jinni, both did by her what she bade them do; and, when they had dismounted from her, she said, 'Well done!' She then took from her pocket a purse and drew out a knotted string, whereon were strung five hundred and seventy seal rings, and asked. 'Know ye what be these?' They answered her saying, 'We know not!' Then quoth she; 'These be the signets of five hundred and seventy men who have all futtered me upon the horns of this foul, this foolish, this filthy Ifrit; so give me also your two seal rings, ye pair of brothers. When they had drawn their two rings from their hands and given them to her, she said to them, 'Of a truth this Ifrit bore me off on my bride-night, and put me into a casket and set the casket in a coffer and to the coffer he affixed seven strong padlocks of steel and deposited me on the deep bottom of the sea that raves, dashing and clashing with waves; and guarded me so that I might remain chaste and honest, quotha! that none save himself might have connexion with me. But I have lain under as many of my kind as I please, and this wretched Jinni wotteth not that Destiny may not be averted nor hindered by aught, and that whatso woman willeth the same she fulfilleth however man nilleth. Even so saith one of them:

> Rely not on women; trust not to their hearts,
> Whose joys and whose sorrows are hung to their parts!
> Lying love they will swear thee whence guile ne'er departs:
> Take Yusuf[2] for sample, 'ware sleights and 'ware smarts!
> Iblis[3] ousted Adam (see ye not?) thro' their arts.

And another saith:

> Stint thy blame, man! 'Twill drive to a passion without bound;
> My fault is not so heavy as fault in it hast found.
> If true lover I become, then to me there cometh not
> Save what happened unto many in the by-gone stound.
> For wonderful is he and right worthy of our praise
> Who from wiles of female wits kept him safe and kept him sound.'

[2] The Joseph of the Koran.
[3] A revolting angel similar to our Satan as he caused Adam and Eve to lose Paradise.

Hearing these words they marvelled with exceeding marvel, and she went from them to the Ifrit and, taking up his head on her thigh as before, said to them softly, 'Now wend your ways and bear yourselves beyond the bounds of his malice.' So they fared forth saying either to other, 'Allah! Allah!' and, 'There be no Majesty and there be no Might save in Allah, the Glorious, the Great; and with Him we seek refuge from women's malice and sleight, for of a truth it hath no mate in might. Consider, O my brother, the ways of this marvellous lady with an Ifrit who is so much more powerful than we are. Now since there hath happened to him a greater mishap than that which befel us and which should bear us abundant consolation, so return we to our countries and capitals, and let us decide never to intermarry with womankind and presently we will show them what will be our action.' Thereupon they rode back to the tents of King Shahryar, which they reached on the morning of the third day; and, having mustered the Wazirs and Emirs, the Chamberlains and high officials, he gave a robe of honour to his Viceroy and issued orders for an immediate return to the city. There he sat him upon his throne and sending for the Chief Minister, the father of the two damsels who (Inshallah!) will presently be mentioned, he said, 'I command thee to take my wife and smite her to death; for she hath broken her plight and her faith.' So he carried her to the place of execution and did her die. Then King Shahryar took brand in hand and repairing to the Serraglio slew all the concubines and their Mamelukes. He also sware himself by a binding oath that whatever wife he married he would abate her maidenhead at night and slay her next morning to make sure of his honour; 'For,' said he, 'there never was nor is there one chaste woman upon the face of earth.' Then Shah Zaman prayed for permission to fare homewards; and he went forth equipped and escorted and travelled till he reached his own country. Meanwhile Shahryar commanded his Wazir to bring him the bride of the night that he might go in to her; so he produced a most beautiful girl, the daughter of one of the Emirs and the King went in unto her at eventide and when morning dawned he bade his Minister strike off her head; and the Wazir did accordingly for fear of the Sultan. On this wise he continued for the space of three years; marrying a maiden every night and killing her the next morning, till folk raised an outcry against him and cursed him, praying Allah utterly to destroy him and his rule; and women made an uproar and mothers wept and parents fled with their daughters till there remained not in the city a young person fit for carnal copulation.

From *The Arabian Nights' Entertainments, now entitled Book of the Thousand Nights and a Night*, transl. Sir Richard F. Burton

MARIE DE FRANCE

The Husband Who Saw his Wife with Another Man

A peasant lay in wait inside
His house to see what could be spied.
He saw another man instead
Of him, enjoying his wife in bed.
'Alas,' he said, 'what have I seen?'
His wife replied: 'What do you mean?
Fair lord, my love, what did you see?'
'Another man, I'm sure,' said he,
'Was on the bed in your embrace.'
His wife, with anger in her face,
Replied, 'A man? Oh, very well,
You're sick again, that I can tell.
You cling to lies, as if they're true.'
'I trust my eyes – that I must do.'
'You're mad,' she said 'to think you can
Insist you saw me with a man.
Now tell the truth, at once, be good.'
'I saw him leaving for the wood.'
'Oh no!' she said, 'that means that I
Today or next day'll surely die.
It happened to my Gran, you see,
My mother too, and now to me.
It happened just before they died –
A fact well-known both far and wide.
A young man led both off, you know –
They had no other cause to go.
My end is near, the die is cast –
Send for my cousins, I need them fast.
Let's split up all our property –
I mustn't waste my time, you see.

With all the stuff that is my share,
I'll to a nunnery repair.'
The peasant heard, and cried in fear:
'Let be, let be, my sweetheart, dear,
Don't leave me now, like this, I pray –
I made up all I saw today.'
'I dare not stay, it's far too late –
I'm thinking of my spiritual state,
Especially, after the shame
That you've attached to my good name.
I will be blamed, I know I will
For treating you so very ill,
Unless, perhaps, you'd rather swear,
With all my family standing there,
You never saw a man with me.
You must swear also, don't you see?
This subject will be dropped and you
Will never nag me for it, too.'
He answered 'Lady, I agree.'
They both went off to church, and he
Soon swore to all she'd asked him for
All that, ah yes, and much much more.
   Take warning from this tale, men, do,
That women know a thing or two –
For strange deceits and knavish tricks,
Their talent's greater than Old Nick's.

                              Marie de France, transl. F.P.

BERCHORIUS

Two tales from Gesta Romanorum

SOME TYME THERE was a man in Spayne, that hade be his wyfe a fayre doughter, ande no moo childryne; wherfore he louyde it mekille, ande cheryshede it. Afterward, when she was of sixtene or fiftene yere of age, the Deuylle, that is enemye to mankynde, that perceyuede, that he loude wele this childe, ande temptide hym to do fleshly synne with his doughter. Atte laste he brought hem bothe togedre to the dede of synne, ande fullefillede it in dede; ande than afterwarde she was with childe. Ande when the modre wiste it, she askide whose it was; but she wolde not telle here. The modire thratte hire, ande seide, she shulde abye, but she tolde hire, she nolde not. Then the modire pleaside here, ande gafe her goode drynke, ande made here merye; ande when she was wele merie, she askide who was the fadire? She seide, 'My fadire.' 'Thy fadire!' she sayde, 'oute on the, stronge strompette! were thou delyuerede, thou shuldyste neuer dwelle in my house lengere. Goddis curse haue thou, ande myne!' Ande with in few dayes after she was delyuerede of a fayre knave childe. Ande that tyme the fadir was oute. Ande alse sone as she was oute of here bedde, she toke the childe, ande wrothe in sondere the necke, ande wente, ande beriede it in the dunge-hille. Sone after that, the fadir come home, ande askede, whethere it were a man or a woman? He seide, 'Lette me se it.' She seide, 'It is dede.' He askyde, 'How?' She seide, 'I haue slayne it, ande beryede it in the donge-hille.' 'Alas!' he saide, 'that euer thou was borne, thoughe thou ande I be synfulle wrechis, the childe myght haue bene a seynte in Heuyne, ande now it is loste for euer! Alas the while!' The modire cursede ande wariede the doughtere ofte sithes, for here folye. The doughter sawe she myght not be in pease, ande on a nyght she slowe hire modire, for she thought the better to be in pease. Ande on the morowe, when the fadre wyste that she hade slayne her modre, he was a sorye man, ande seide, 'A! thou cursyde wreche, go oute of my house, for thou shalle neuer abyde with me more.' She sawe that she was forsakyne of here fadre, ande at euyne, when here fadre was in bedde on slepe, she toke an axe, ande kyllede here fadre. Ande whan she hade this done, she toke what she wolde, ande wente to a cite, into anothere contree; ande there she was a comyne woman, ande toke alle that wolde come. She

Abye – pay for it.
Nolde – would not.

reffusede none, monke ne frere, clerke ne lewde man; she was so comyne, that euery man that knewe here, lothede here company. She sawe that, ande wente to anothere cite, ande there she was as comyne as she was in the tothere cite. Atte laste, on a day as she wente in the strete, she sawe mych folke go into a chirche. Thought she, 'I will go wete what this folke do there.' Ande wente here into the chirche, ande sette here downe, as othere diddene. Sone after come a persone into the pullpite, ande prechide; ande his sermone was mych of the mercy of Gode, ande seide, though a man or a woman hade done as mych synne as alle men hade done, ande they hade sorowe in herte for theyre synnes, ande wolde amende hem, ande leue here synnes, God of his grete mercy wolde forgyve hem alle here synnes. This woman was right sorye, ande wepte faste, ande thought she wolde leue her synne, ande be shrevyn; ande longe she thought tille the sermone were done. Ande when it was done, she wente to the prechoure, ande prayde hym, for the loue of Gode, to here a synfulle wreche. He wente, ande herde here life; ande when he hade herde here, he was astonyede in hym selfe, what penaunce that he myghte gyve here, for here synnes were so grete. 'Sir,' she seide, 'why do ye so, that ye tary, ande gife me no penaunce? My herte is gretly tormentede for sorowe.' 'Doughter,' he seide, 'be not aferde, for thou shalte fare right wele. Go to yondere autere, ande knele downe before oure Ladie, ande pray here hertly ande deuoutely, that she wolde be goode meane to here sone; for she is alle weye modre of mercy, ande remedie for to helpe. Ande than shalle I telle the what thou shalle do.' She wente, ande dide as he bade here. He wente in the meane tyme to take counsaylle, what penaunce he myght gyve here. She in the meane tyme praide so hertly, ande with so mych sorowe, that hire herte braste; ande [she] deyede. Ande the confessoure come agayne, ande fownde here dede. Then he wente, ande sorowede, ande made grete mone; ande askide Gode mercy of his necligence, that he gafe here no penaunce. Then he herde a voice in the eyre, sayenge to hym thus, 'Be the grete mercy of Jhesu Criste, ande prayere of hys blessyde modre, ande the grete sorowe that she hade for here synnes, she is right wele, ande sittes fulle hye in Heuyne blisse, ande is as white as lille floure, ande as bryght as any golde in Goddis sight; therfore pray not for here, but pray here to pray for the, ande for alle that bene in dedly synne, that ye mow be alle in blisse that she is in.'

*   *   *

Wete – find out.

II

A woman there was some tyme, that hade a sone by here housbonde, that was sette to the scole; ande when he was of age, he was made a preste, ande studiede to lyve religeously. This wyfe hade conseyuede afterwarde two sonys in avoutery; ande when the childryne were waxen, she deyede. Then the fyrste sone, that she hade by here housbonde, that was a preste, was fulle besy for to pray the saluacione of his modyrs soule, ande songe many masses for here, prayenge to Gode deuoutely, that he myght wete how his modre farede. On a day as he prayde, there aperide to hym a fourme of a woman, fro whose hede he sawe a derke flawme rise vp; ande on here lippes ande on here tonge he sawe an horreble tode gnawe, ande sesid not; ande fro hire tetis he sawe hange two serpentes, sore soukynge hem; ande the skyn on here back was drawen downe to here hammes, ande traylede after here, alle on fyre. Then seide the preste, 'What arte thou, in the name of Gode?' She answeride, ande seide, 'I am thy modyre; beholde ande se to what paynes I ame putte euerlastyngly, for my synnes.' Then he askede here, for what synnes she suffrede thes paynes? She seide, 'I am tormentide with this blew fyre on my hede, for my lecherouse anourement of myne heere, ande other array ther on; in my lyppes ande my tonge, for wickede ande veyne speches, ande lecherouse kyssynges, I suffere thes todes to frete; on my tetis I haue thes two serpentes soukynge so sore, that me thinketh they souke oute my herte-blode, for I gafe souke, ande noryshede my two hore coppis; ande my brennynge skynne drawene of, ande folowynge me, is for my large trayne of clothe, that I was wonte to drawe aftire me, while I leuyde on erthe.' 'A! modre,' he seide, 'mowe ye not be sauyde?' 'No,' she seide; ande wente away frome his sighte.

From a Middle English translation of the Latin *Gesta Romanorum* (attributed to Berchorius)

Avoutery – adultery.
Waxen – grown up.
Anourement – anointing.
Hore coppis – children born from adulterous liaisons.

GIOVANNI BOCCACCIO

From The Decameron

The dumb gardener

THERE ARE MANY people so simple as to imagine, that, after a young lady puts on the veil, she is no longer subject to the passions of other women; as if by becoming a nun she were converted into stone: and if they hear any thing contrary to this opinion, are as much offended, as though some very heinous and unnatural crime were committed; never thinking of themselves, who cannot be satisfied, although they have the liberty of doing as they will; nor considering the prevalency of leisure and solitude. In like manner, there are others who think that the spade and pick-axe, with hard labour and gross feeding, quench all lustful appetites, depriving the people of all sense and understanding; but how much they are both mistaken, I shall, at the queen's command, now shew you, keeping close to the subject which she has given us.

There was formerly in our neighbourhood (and may be still) a monastery of nuns, famous for their sanctity (which shall be nameless, because I would not lessen their characters), in which were only eight young ladies with an abbess; there was also a gardener to look after the garden, who not being satisfied with his salary, made up his accounts with their steward, and returned to Lamporecchio, from whence he came. Amongst many others who were to welcome him home, was a young fellow called Masetto, who enquired of him where he had been all that time? The honest man (whose name was Nuto) told him. The other inquired again in what capacity he served the monastery? When he replied, 'I had the care of the garden, and used to go to the wood for faggots; I drew water for them also, with such-like services; but my wages were so small that they would scarcely find me shoes; and besides they are all so young and giddy, that I could do nothing to please them; for when I have been in the garden, one would cry do this, and another do that, and a third would take the spade out of my hand, and tell me that thing is in a wrong place, and they have given me so much trouble altogether, that I have left them; though the steward desired, at my departure, that if I met with a proper person, to send him; but let me be hanged if I do.' When Masetto heard this, he had a great desire to be amongst them, supposing, by what Nuto had said, that he might be able to gain his ends, and that it might be more difficult if he let the other into the secret. Therefore he said to him, 'You do very right to come away: what has a man to do among so many women? He might as well be with as many devils: for it is not once in ten times they know what they would be at.' After they had done talking together, Masetto began to contrive what method he should take to get introduced; and being assured that he could do all the work that Nuto had mentioned, he had no fears upon that account: all the danger seemed rather in his youth and person; whether for that reason he might not be rejected. After much reflection, he reasoned thus with himself: 'I live far enough off, and nobody knows me: suppose I feign myself dumb, they will certainly receive me then.' Resolved on this, without saying a word where he was going, he took an axe upon his shoulder, and went like a poor man to the monastery; and finding the steward in the monastery court, he made signs like a dumb person for a little bread, and that he would cleave wood if they had any occasion. The steward gave him something to eat, and afterwards shewed him divers pieces of wood, which Nuto was not able to rend, but which he, in a little time (being very strong), split all to pieces. The steward, having occasion to go to the wood, took him along with him; where, making him fell several trees, by signs he made him load the ass with them, and drive him home before him: this he did very well; and the steward wanting him for other things, he continued there for several days, till at length the abbess saw him, who asked the steward what the man did there? 'Madam,' he replied, 'this is a poor man, deaf and dumb, who came the other day to ask charity, which I gave him, and he has done many things for us since: I believe, if he knows any thing of a garden, and could be prevailed upon to stay, that he might be of good service, for we want such a person, and he is strong, and will do what work we please: besides, there will be no fear of his seducing any of the young ladies.' 'Why, truly,' quoth the abbess, 'you say right: do you see if he knows how to work, and try to keep him; and make much of him, giving him a pair of shoes, and an old coat, and let his belly be filled with victuals.' Which the steward promised to do. Masetto, who was at no great distance, but seemed busy in sweeping the court, heard all this, and said merrily to himself, 'Yes, if you let me stay here, I'll do your business, with a witness.' Now the steward perceiving that he knew how to work, inquired of him by signs whether he was willing to stay; and the other made him to understand that he was willing; therefore, taking him into the garden, he shewed him what he wished to have done, and went about other business relating to the monastery. Now the nuns used to come every day to tease and laugh at him, saying anything before him, imagining that he heard them not. Which the abbess took no notice of, not apprehending the least danger; and one day being laid down to rest himself, two nuns, who were walking in the garden, came to the place where he pretended to be asleep: and as they stood looking upon him, one, who was a little more forward than the other, said, 'Could I be assured of your secrecy, I would tell you of a thought I have often had in my head, which might be of service to yourself.' Said the other, 'You may speak safely, for I never will disclose it.' When the first nun began in this manner: 'We are kept here in strict confinement, and not a man suffered to come near us, but our steward, who is old, and this dumb man: wherefore I have often had a mind to gratify a certain curiosity with this fellow; for he is the fittest in the world for our purpose, being such an idiot, that he cannot expose us if he would: what is your opinion?' 'Alas!' quoth the other, 'what is that you say? Do not you know that we have promised our virginity to God?' 'Oh! but sister,' she replied, 'how many things do we promise every day, which we never perform? If we have promised, there will be others found that shall be more punctual.' 'But,' said the other lady, 'if we should be with child, what would become of us then?' She replied, 'You think of the worst before it happens: it will be time enough then to talk of that; there are a thousand ways of managing in such a case, that nobody will ever be the wiser, unless we ourselves make the discovery.' She was now prevailed upon, and said to her friend, 'How shall we contrive this matter?' The other replied, 'You see it is about nine o'clock, and I believe our sisters are all asleep; let us look round the garden, and if nobody be in it, what have we to do, but for one of us to lead him into yonder arbour, whilst the other keeps watch?' This was done accordingly, and they used to serve one another in the same manner, till at length they were discovered by the other nuns, who all took the same liberty: and last of all the lady abbess herself, excited by the same curiosity, had him conveyed into her chamber, and kept him there several days; till having satisfied his inclinations, he now resolved to depart. One night, therefore, he broke his long silence, and acquainted her with his intentions of going away. She was in the utmost astonishment to hear him speak, and said, 'What is the meaning of this? I thought you had been dumb.' 'Madam,' replied he, 'so I was, but not naturally; I had a long disorder, which deprived me of my speech, and which was restored to me but this night, for which I am very thankful.' The lady was too prudent to let him depart, for fear of his scandalizing the monastery; and in some little time, the steward happening to die, he was appointed to succeed him: and the people were made to believe that their prayers together with the merits of the saint to whom the monastery was dedicated, had effected this miracle. The affair was carried on so privately afterwards among them, that there was no suspicion of that sort till after the death of the abbess, when Masetto, being now in years, and wealthy, was desirous of going home: and their manner of living being no longer a secret, his desire was the more readily complied with. Thus, taking no care of his children, but bequeathing them to the place where they were bred and born, he returned to his native country, having taken such advantage of his youth, as amply to provide for the ease of his old age.

From a nineteenth-century translation

GEOFFREY CHAUCER

From The Canterbury Tales

The wedding night of Januarie and May, from The Marchantes Tale

Night with his mantel, that is dark and rude,
Gan oversprede the hemisperie aboute;
For which departed is this lusty route
Fro Januarie, with thank on every syde.
Hom to hir houses lustily they ryde,
Wher-as they doon hir thinges as hem leste,
And whan they sye hir tyme, goon to reste.
Sone after that, this hastif Januarie
Wolde go to bedde, he wolde no lenger tarie.
He drinketh ipocras, clarree, and vernage
Of spyces hote, t'encresen his corage;
And many a letuarie hadde he ful fyn,
Swiche as the cursed monk dan Constantyn
Hath writen in his book *de Coitu*;
To eten hem alle, he has no-thing eschu.
And to his privee freendes thus seyde he:
'For goddes love, as sone as it may be,
Lat voyden al this hous in curteys wyse.'

Ipocras – a cordial named after Hippocrates.
Clarree – wine clarified by mixing in honey and spices, then straining.
Vernage – an Italian wine.
Letuarie – electuary or remedy – here, an aphrodisiac.

And they han doon right as he wold devyse.
Men drinken, and the travers drawe anon;
The bryde was brought a-bedde as stille as stoon;
And whan the bed was with the preest y-blessed,
Out of the chambre hath every wight him dressed.
And Januarie hath faste in armes take
His fresshe May, his paradys, his make,
He lulleth hir, he kisseth hir ful ofte
With thikke bristles of his berd unsofte,
Lyk to the skin of houndfish, sharp as brere,
For he was shave al newe in his manere.
He rubbeth hir aboute hir tendre face,
And seyde thus, 'allas! I moot trespace
To yow, my spouse, and yow gretly offende,
Er tyme come that I wil doun descende,
But nathelees, considereth this,' quod he,
'Ther nis no werkman, what-so-ever he be,
That may bothe werke wel and hastily;
This wol be doon at leyser parfitly.
It is no fors how longe that we playe;
In trewe wedlok wedded be we tweye;
And blessed be the yok that we been inne,
For in our actes we mowe do no sinne.
A man may do no sinne with his wyf,
Ne hurte him-selven with his owene knyf;
For we han leve to pleye us by the lawe.'
Thus laboureth he til that the day gan dawe;
And than he taketh a sop in fyn clarree,
And upright in his bed than sitteth he,
And after that he sang ful loude and clere,
And kiste his wyf, and made wantoun chere.

Travers – a curtain. The term has survived in the theatre.
Make – mate.
Houndfish – dogfish, or rock salmon, a small member of the shark family. The skin is diabolically sharp and liable to scratch your hands, if handled without gloves, as I know to my own cost, having bought one for 50p from a wily fisherman who pretended he didn't have time to skin it.

He was al coltish, ful of ragerye,
And ful of jargon as a flekked pye.
The slakke skin aboute his nekke shaketh,
Whyl that he sang; so chaunteth he and craketh.
But god wot what that May thoughte in hir herte,
Whan she him saugh up sittinge in his sherte,
In his night-cappe, and with his nekke lene;
She preyseth nat his pleying worth a bene,
Than seide he thus, 'my reste wol I take;
Now day is come, I may no longer wake.'
And doun he leyde his heed, and sleep til pryme.
And afterward, when that he saugh his tyme,
Up ryseth Januarie; but fresshe May
Holdeth hir chambre un-to the fourthe day.

Ragerye – passion.
Pye – magpie.
Pryme – prime, 9 a.m.

REGINALD SCOT

From The Discovery of Witchcraft

Of bishop Sylvanus his lechery opened and covered again

YOU SHALL READ in the legend, how in the night-time Incubus came to a lady's bedside, and made hot love unto her: whereat she being offended, cried out so loud, that company came and found him under her bed in the likenesse of the holy bishop Sylvanus, which holy man was much defamed thereby, until at the length this infamy was purged by the confession of a devil made at St Jerome's tombe. Oh excellent peece of witchcraft wrought by Sylvanus!

How to procure the dissolving of bewitched love

THE PRIESTS SAY, that the best cure for a woman thus molested, next to confession, is excommunication. But to procure the dissolving of bewitched and constrained love, the party bewitched must make a jakes of the lover's shoe.

Of divers saints and holy persons, which were exceeding bawdy and lecherous, and by certain miraculous meanes became chaste

CASSIANUS WRITETH, THAT St Syren being of body very lecherous, and of mind wonderfull religious, fasted and prayed; to the end his body might be reduced miraculously to chastity. At length came an angel unto him by night, and cut out of his flesh certain kernels, which were the sparkes of concupiscence; so as afterwards he never had any more motions of the flesh. It is also reported, that the abbat Equicius, being naturally as unchaste as the other, fell to his beads so devoutly for recovery of honesty, that there came an angell unto him in an apparation, that seemed to geld him; and after that (forsooth) he was as chaste as though he had never had a stone in his breech; and before that time being a ruler over monkes, he became afterwards a governour over nunnes. Even as it is said Helias the holy monke gathered thirty virgins into a monastery, over whom he ruled and reigned by the space of two yeares, and grew so proud and hot in the cod-peece, that he was fain to forsake his holy house, and fly to a desert, where he fasted and prayed two daies, saying; Lord quench my hot, lecherous humors, or kill me. Wherupon in the night following, there came unto him three angels, and demanded of him why he forsook his charge: but the holy man was ashamed to tell them. Howbeit they asked him further, saying; Wilt thou returne to these damsels, if we free thee of all concupiscence? Yes (quoth he) with all my heart. And when they had sworne him solemnly so to do, they took him up, and gelded him; and one of them holding his hands, and another his feet, the third cut out his stones.

JOHN DONNE

The Apparition

When by thy scorne, O murdresse I am dead,
And that thou thinkst thee free
From all solicitation from mee,
Then shall my ghost come to thy bed,
And thee, fain'd vestall, in worse armes shall see;
Then thy sicke taper will begin to winke,
And he, whose thou art then, being tyr'd before,
Will, if thou stirre, or pinch to wake him, thinke
    Thou call'st for more,
And in false sleepe will from thee shrinke,
And then poore Aspen wretch, neglected thou
Bath'd in a cold quicksilver sweat wilt lye
    A veryer ghost than I;
What will I say, I will not tell thee now,
Lest that preserve thee; and since my love is spent,
I had rather thou shouldst painfully repent,
Than by my threatenings rest still innocent.

To his Mistris Going to Bed

Come, Madam, come, all rest my powers defie,
Until I labour, I in labour lie.
The foe oft-times having the foe in sight,
Is tir'd with standing though he never fight.
Off with that girdle, like heavens Zone glistering,
But a far fairer world incompassing.
Unpin that spangled breastplate which you wear,
That th'eyes of busie fooles may be stopt there.
Unlace your self, for that harmonious chyme,
Tell me from you, that now it is bed time.

Off with that happy busk, which I envie,
That still can be, and still can stand so nigh.
Your gown going off, such beautious state reveals,
As when from flowry meads th'hills shadow steales.
Off with that wyerie Coronet and shew
The haiery Diademe which on you doth grow:
Now off with those shooes, and then safely tread
In this loves hallow'd temple, this soft bed.
In such white robes, heaven's Angels us'd to be
Receavd by men; Thou Angel bringst with thee
A heaven like Mahomets Paradice; and though
Ill spirits walk in white, we easly know,
By this these Angels from an evil sprite,
Those set our hairs, but these our flesh upright.

    Licence my roaving hands, and let them go,
Before, behind, between, above, below.
O my America! my new-found-land,
My kingdome, safeliest when with one man man'd,
My Myne of precious stones, My Emperie,
How blest am I in this discovering thee!
To enter in these bonds, is to be free;
Then where my hand is set, my seal shall be.

    Full nakedness! All joyes are due to thee,
As souls unbodied, bodies uncloth'd must be,
To taste whole joyes. Gems which you women use
Are like Atlanta's balls, cast in mens views,
That when a fools eye lighteth on a Gem,
His earthly soul may covet theirs, not them.
Like pictures, or like books gay coverings made
For lay-men, are all women thus array'd;
Themselves are mystick books, which only wee
(Whom their imputed grace will dignifie)
Must see reveal'd. Then since that I may know;
As liberally, as to a Midwife, shew

Thy self: cast all, yea, this white lynnen hence,
There is no pennance due to innocence.
  To teach thee, I am naked first; why then
What needst thou have more covering than a man.

Sonnett

Madam that flea that Crept between your brests
I envied, that there he should make his rest:
The little Creatures fortune was soe good
That Angells feed not on so pretious foode.
How it did sucke how eager tickle you
(Madam shall fleas before me tickle you?)

Oh I can not holde; pardon if I kild it.
Sweet Blood, to you I aske this, that which fild it
Ran from my Ladies Brest. Come happie flea
That dide for suckinge of that milkie Sea.

Oh now againe I well could wishe thee there,
About hir Hart, about hir anywhere;
I would vowe (Dearest flea) thou shouldst not dye,
If thou couldst sucke from hir hir crueltye.

(Attributed to Donne)

The Baite

Come live with mee, and bee my love,
And wee will some new pleasures prove
Of golden sands, and christall brookes,
With silken lines, and silver hookes.

There will the river whispering runne
Warm'd by thy eyes, more than the Sunne.
And there th'inamor'd fish will stay,
Begging themselves they may betray.

When thou wilt swimme in that live bath,
Each fish, which every channell hath,
Will amorously to thee swimme,
Gladder to catch thee, than thou him.

If thou, to be so seene, beest loath,
By Sunne, or Moone, thou darknest both,
And if my selfe have leave to see,
I need not their light, having thee.

Let others freeze with angling reeds,
And cut their legges, with shells and weeds,
Or treacherously poore fish beset,
With strangling snare, or windowie net:

Let coarse bold hands, from slimy nest
The bedded fish in banks out-wrest,
Or curious traitors, sleavesilke flies
Bewitch poore fishes wandring eyes.

For thee, thou needst no such deceit,
For thou thy selfe art thine owne bait;
That fish, that is not catch'd thereby,
Alas, is wiser farre than I.

GEORGE PEELE

The Voice from the Well

Fair maiden, white and red,
Comb me smooth, and stroke my head;
And thou shalt have some cockle bread.
Gently dip, but not too deep,
For fear thou make the golden beard to weep.
Fair maid, white and red,
Comb me smooth, and stroke my head;
And every hair a sheave shall be,
And every sheave a golden tree.

SHAYKH NEFZAWI

From The Perfumed Garden

The sundry names given to the sexual parts of man

KNOW, O VIZIR (to whom God be good!), that man's member bears different names, as:

El de keur, the virile member.
El kamera, the penis.
El aïr, the member for generation.
El hamama, the pigeon.
El teunnana, the tinkler.
El heurmak, the indomitable.
El ahlil, the liberator.
El zeub, the verge.
El hammache, the exciter.
El nâasse, the sleeper.
El zodamme, the crowbar.

El khiake, the tailor.

Mochefi el relil, the extinguisher of passion.

El khorrate the turnabout.

El deukkak, the striker.

El âouame, the swimmer.

El dekhal, the housebreaker.

El âouar, the one-eyed.

El fortass, the bald.

Abou aïne, the one with an eye.

El âtsar, the pusher.

El dommar, the strong-headed.

Abou rokba, the one with a neck.

Abou quetaïa, the hairy one.

El besiss, the impudent one.

El mostahi, the shame-faced one.

El bekkai, the weeping one.

El hezzaz, the rummager.

El lezzaz, the unionist.

Abou lâaba, the expectorant.

El fattache the searcher.

El hakkak, the rubber.

El mourekhi, the flabby one.

El motelâ, the ransacker.

El mokcheuf, the discoverer.

As regard the names of *kamera*[1] and *dekeur*, their meaning is plain. *Dekeur* is a word which signifies the male of all creatures, and is also used in the sense of 'mention' and 'memory'. When a man has met with an accident to his member, when it has been amputated, or has become weak, and he can, in consequence, no longer fulfil his conjugal duties, they say of him: 'the member of such an one is dead;' which means: the remembrance of him will be lost, and his generation is cut off by the root. When he dies they will say, 'His member has been cut off,' meaning, 'His memory is departed from the world.'

*   *   *

[1] Kamera also means the glans of the penis.

The name of *el aïr* is derived from *el kir* (the smith's bellows). In fact if you turn in the latter word the k, *kef*, so that it faces the opposite way, you will find the word to read *el aïr*. The member is so called on account of its alternate swelling and subsiding again. If swollen up it stands erect, and if not it sinks down flaccid.

It is called *el hamama* (the pigeon), because after having been swelled out it resembles at the moment when it returns to repose a pigeon sitting on her eggs.[2]

El teunnana (the tinkler) – So called because every time it enters or comes out of the vulva in coition it makes a noise.

El heurmak (the indomitable) – It has received this name because when in a state of erection it begins to move its head, searching for the entrance to the vulva till it has found it, and it then walks in quite insolently, without asking leave.

El ahlil (the liberator) – Thus called because in penetrating into the vulva of a woman thrice repudiated it gives her the liberty to return to her first husband.[3]

El zeub (the verge) – From the word *deub*, which means creeping. This name was given to the member because when it gets between a woman's thighs and feels a plump vulva it begins to creep upon the thighs and the Mount of Venus, then approaches the entrance of the vulva, and keeps creeping in until it is in possession and is comfortably lodged, and having it all its own way penetrates into the middle of the vulva, there to ejaculate.

El hammache (the exciter) – It has received this name because it irritates the vulva by its frequent entries and exits.

El nâasse (the sleeper) – From its deceitful appearance. When it gets into erection, it lengthens out and stiffens itself to such an extent that one might think it would never get soft again. But when it has left the vulva, after having satisfied its passion, it goes to sleep.

There are members that fall asleep while inside the vulva, but the majority of them come out still firm; but at that moment they get drowsy, and little by little they go to sleep.

El zoddame (the crowbar) – It is called so because when it meets the vulva and the same will not let it pass in directly, it forces the entrance with its head, breaking and tearing everything, like a wild beast in the rutting season.

El khiate (the tailor) – It takes this name from the circumstance that it

[2] Arabic has the same word for eggs and testicles.
[3] In Mussulman law a wife that has been divorced by the thrice repeated formula cannot marry her first husband again until she has married another man and been divorced from him.

does not enter the vulva until it has manoeuvred about the entrance, like a needle in the hand of a tailor, creeping and rubbing against it until it is sufficiently roused, after which it enters.

Mochefi el relil (the extinguisher of passion) – This name is given to a member which is large, strong, and slow to ejaculate; such a member satisfies most completely the amorous wishes of a woman; for, after having wrought her up to the highest pitch, it allays her excitement better than any other. And, in the same way, it calms the ardour of the man. When it wants to get into the vulva, and arriving at the portal, finds it closed, it laments, begs and promises: 'Oh! my love! let me come in, I will not stay long.' And when it has been admitted, it breaks its word, and makes a long stay, and does not take its leave till it has satisfied its ardour by the ejaculation of the sperm, coming and going, tilting high and low, and rummaging right and left. The vulva protests, 'How about your word, you deceiver?' she says; 'you said you would only stop in for a moment.' And the member answers, 'Oh, certainly! I shall not retire till I have encountered your womb; but after having found it, I will engage to withdraw at once.' At these words, the vulva takes pity on him, and advances her matrix, which clasps and kisses its head, as if saluting it. The member then retires with its passion cooled down.

El khorrate (the turnabout) – This name was given to it because on arriving at the vulva it pretends to come on important business, knocks at the door, turns about everywhere, without shame or bashfulness, investigating every corner to the right and left, forward and backward, and then all at once darts right to the bottom of the vagina for the ejaculation.

El deukkak (the striker) – Thus called because on arriving at the entrance of the vulva it gives a slight knock. If the vulva opens the door, it enters; if there is no response, it begins to knock again, and does not cease until it is admitted. The parasite who wants to get into the house of a rich man to be present at a feast does the same: he knocks at the door; and if it is opened, he walks in; but if there is no response to his knock, he repeats it again and again until the door is opened. And similarly the *deukkak* with the door of the vulva.

By 'knocking at the door' is meant the friction of the member against the entrance of the vulva until the latter becomes moist. The appearance of this moisture is the phenomenon alluded to by the expression 'opening the door'.

El âouame (the swimmer) – Because when it enters the vulva it does not remain in one favourite place, but, on the contrary, turns to the right, to the left, goes forward, draws back, and then moves like swimming in the middle amongst its own sperm and the fluid furnished by the vulva, as if in fear of drowning and trying to save itself.

El dekhal (the housebreaker) – Merits that name because on coming to the door of the vulva this one asks, 'What do you want?' 'I want to come in!' 'Impossible! I cannot take you in on account of your size.' Then the member insists that the other one should only receive its head, promising not to come in entirely; it then approaches, rubs its head twice or thrice between the vulva's lips, till they get humid and thus lubricated, then introduces first its head, and after, with one push, plunges in up to the testicles.

El âouar (the one-eyed) – Because it has but one eye, which eye is not like other eyes, and does not see clearly.

El fortass (the bald one) – Because there is no hair on its head, which makes it look bald.

Abou aine (he with one eye) – It has received this name because its one eye presents the peculiarity of being without pupil and eyelashes.

El âtsar (the stumbler) – It is called so because if it wants to penetrate in the vulva, as it does not see the door, it beats about above and below, and thus continues to stumble as over stones in the road, until the lips of the vulva get humid, when it manages to get inside. The vulva then says, 'What has happened to you that made you stumble about so?' The member answers, 'O my love, it was a stone lying in the road.'

El dommar (the odd-headed) – Because its head is different from all other heads.

Abou rokba (the one with a neck) – That is the being with a short neck, a well developed throat, and thick at the end, a bald head, and who, moreover, has coarse and bristly hair from the navel to the pubis.

Abou quetaïa (the hairy one; who has a forest of hair) – This name is given to it when the hair is abundant about it.

El besiss (the impudent) – It has received this name because from the moment that it gets stiff and long it does not care for anybody, lifts impudently the clothing of its master by raising its head fiercely, and makes him ashamed while itself feels no shame. It acts in the same unabashed way with women, turning up their clothes and laying bare their thighs. Its master may blush at this conduct, but as to itself its stiffness and determination to plunge into a vulva only increase.

El mostahi (the shame-faced) – This sort of member which is met with sometimes, is capable of feeling ashamed and timid when facing a vulva which it does not know, and it is only after a little time that it gets bolder and stiffens. Sometimes it is even so much troubled that it remains incompetent for the coitus, which happens in particular when a stranger is present, in which case it becomes quite incapable of moving.

El bekkai (the weeper) – So called on account of the many tears it sheds; as soon as it gets in erection, it weeps; when it sees a pretty face, it weeps; handling a woman, it weeps. It goes even so far as to weep tears sacred to memory.

El hezzaz (the rummager) – It is named thus because as soon as it penetrates into the vulva it begins to rummage about vigorously, until it has appeased its passion.

El lezzaz (the unionist) – Received that name because as soon as it is in the vulva it pushes and works till fur meets fur, and even makes efforts to force the testicles into it.

Abou lâaba (the expectorant) – Has received this name because when coming near a vulva, or when it sees one, or even when merely thinking of it, or when its master touches a woman or plays with her or kisses her, its saliva begins to move and it has tears in its eye; this saliva is particularly abundant when it has been for some time out of work, and it will even wet then his master's dress. This member is very common, and there are but few people who are not furnished with it.

The liquid it sheds is cited by lawyers under the name of *medi*. Its production is the result of toyings and of lascivious thoughts. With some people it is so abundant as to fill the vulva, so that they may erroneously believe that it comes from the woman.

El fattache (the searcher) – From its habit, when in the vulva, of turning in every direction as if in search of something; and that something is the matrix. It will know no rest until it has found it.

El hakkak (the rubber) – It has got this name because it will not enter the vagina until it has rubbed its head against the entrance and the lower part of the belly. It is frequently mistaken for the next one.

El mourekhi (the flabby one) – The one who can never get in because it is too soft, and which is therefore content to rub its head against the entrance to the vulva until it ejaculates. It gives no pleasure to woman, but only inflames her passion without being able to satisfy it, and makes her cross and irritable.

El motelâ (the ransacker) – So named because it penetrates into unusual places, makes itself well acquainted with the state of vulvas, and can distinguish their qualities and faults.

El mokcheuf (the discoverer) – Has been thus denominated because in getting up and raising its head, it raises the vestments which hide it, and uncovers its master's nudities, and because it is also not afraid to lay bare the vulvas which it does not yet know, and to lift up the clothes which cover them without shame. It is not accessible to any sense of bashfulness, cares for nothing and respects nothing. Nothing which concerns the coitus is strange to it; it has a profound knowledge of the state of humidity, freshness, dryness, tightness or warmth of vulvas, which it explores assiduously. There are, in fact, certain vulvas of an exquisite exterior, plump and fine outside, while their inside leaves much to wish for, and they give no pleasure, owing to their being not warm, but very humid, and having other similar faults. It is for this reason that the *mokcheuf* tries to find out about things concerning the coitus, and has received this name.

These are the principal names that have been given to the virile member according to its qualities. Those who think that the number of these names is not exhaustive can look for more; but I think I have given a nomenclature long enough to satisfy my readers.

Transl. Sir Richard F. Burton

ROBERT BURTON

From The Anatomy of Melancholy

The dance of Bacchus and Ariadne

WHEN XENOPHON IN Symposio, or banquet, had discoursed of love, and used all the engins that might be devised to move Socrates; amongst the rest, to stir him the more, he shuts up all with a pleasant interlude or dance of Dionysius[1] and Ariadne. First, Ariadne dressed like a bride came in and took her place: by and by Dionysius entred, dancing to the musick. The spectators did all admire the yong mans carriage: and Ariadne herself was so much affected with the sight, that she could scarce sit. After a while Dionysius beholding Ariadne, and incensed with love, bowing to her knees, embraced her first, and kissed her with a grace; she embraced him again, and kissed him with like affection, &c. as the dance required; but they that stood by and saw this, did much applaud and commend them both for it. And when Dionysius rose up, he raised her up with him, and many pretty gestures, embraces, kisses, and love complements passed between them; which when they saw fair Bacchus and beautiful Ariadne, so sweetly and so unfainedly kissing each other, so

[1] More usually spelt 'Dionysus'.

really embracing, they swore they loved indeed, and were so enflamed with the object, that they began to rouse up themselves, as if they would have flown. At the last, when they saw them still, so willingly embracing, and now ready to go to the bride-chamber, they were so ravished with it, that they that were unmarried, swore they would forthwith marry; and those that were married, called instantly for their horses, and gallopped home to their wives.

The love of old men

HOW MANY DECREPIT, hoary, harsh, writhen, bursten-bellied, crooked, toothless, bald, blear-eyed, impotent, rotten old men shall you see flickering still, in every place? One gets him a young wife, another a curtisan; and when he can scarce lift his leg over a sill, and hath one foot already in Charons boat, when he hath the trembling in his joynts, the gout in his feet, a perpetual rhume in his head, a continuate cough, his sight fails him, thick of hearing, his breath stinks, all his moisture is dried up and gone, may not spit from him, a very child again, that cannot dress himself, or cut his own meat; yet he will be dreaming of, and honing after wenches; what can be more unseemly?

PETER HAUSTED

From Senilis Amor

II, i. Nicoläus, a petty official, is talking to Nicot (a tobacconist) about his wife, Mildreda, who is a chicken-breeder.

NICOLÄUS: When I discharge the duty of a loving husband, she grunts just like a sow giving birth to her first litter. Inarticulate cries of winged creatures assail my head as she mimics them all in bed. She coos, croaks, sings like a swan, croaks louder. Then she flaps her wings; then she caws like a crow, chirps and cackles.

NICOT: What! She cackles in bed, the indiscreet woman?

NICOLÄUS: She twitters like a swallow, pipes and chatters like a starling.

NICOT: What, does she chatter in bed, the indiscreet woman? I'll

write in my diary in capitals – MILDREDA CACKLES AND
CHATTERS IN BED.

NICOLÄUS: In truth, our sweethearts are made of better clay.

I, iv. Colossus, a braggart soldier, gives instruction to Vincentius,
before he meets two whores.

COLOSSUS: First you must salute them at the door.

VINCENTIUS: At the door. I'll remember that.

COLOSSUS: It must be done in the French fashion. Women of that
sort can't be kissed, they must be drooled over.

VINCENTIUS: I'm ready. I've got plenty of spit.

COLOSSUS: Then you press their hands; then you sigh.

VINCENTIUS: But why in the French fashion?

COLOSSUS: Because whores do everything in the French way. They
eat French food, drink French wine, and on top of that if they're ill
– it's the French sickness.

Translated from *Senilis Amor*, a Latin play attributed to Peter Hausted, by F.P.

II, i

FRANCIS BEAUMONT AND JOHN FLETCHER

From The Maid's Tragedy

Evadne prepares for her wedding night.

Ante-room to Evadne's bed-chamber.
Enter Evadne, Aspatia, Dula and other ladies.

DULA: Madam, shall we undress you for this fight?
The wars are nak'd that you must make to-night.

EVAD: You are very merry, Dula.

DULA: I should be
Far merrier, madam, if it were with me
As it is with you.

EVAD: How's that?

DULA: That I might go

To bed with him wi' th' credit that you do.

EVAD: Why, how now, wench?

DULA: Come, ladies, will you help?

EVAD: I am soon undone.

DULA: And as soon done:
Good store of clothes will trouble you at both.

EVAD: Art thou drunk, Dula?

DULA: Why, here's none but we.

EVAD: Thou think'st belike there is no modesty
When we're alone.

DULA: Ay, by my troth, you hit my thoughts aright.

EVAD: You prick me, lady.

FIRST LADY: 'Tis against my will.

DULA: Anon you must endure more and lie still;
You're best to practise.

EVAD: Sure, this wench is mad.

DULA: No, faith, this is a trick that I have had
Since I was fourteen.

EVAD: 'Tis high time to leave it.

DULA: Nay, now I'll keep it till the trick leave me.
A dozen wanton words, put in your head,
Will make you livelier in your husband's bed.

EVAD: Nay, faith, then take it.

DULA: Take it, madam! where?
We all, I hope, will take it that are here.

                                                                    II, i

Evadne has told Amintor on their wedding night that she is the
King's mistress and the marriage is only one of convenience. Out
of loyalty to the King, he goes along with this for a while, covering
up the situation in front of his friends.

Ante-room to Evadne's bed-chamber.
Enter Cleon, Strato, Diphilus.

CLEON: Your sister is not up yet.

DIPH: Oh, brides must take their morning's rest; the night is
troublesome.

STRA: But not tedious.

DIPH: What odds, he has not my sister's maidenhead to-night?

STRA: None; it's odds against any bridegroom living, he ne'er gets it while he lives.

DIPH: Y'are merry with my sister; you'll please to allow me the same freedom with your mother.

STRA: She's at your service.

DIPH: Then she's merry enough of herself; she needs no tickling. Knock at the door.

STRA: We shall interrupt them.

DIPH: No matter; they have the year before them. – Good morrow, sister! Spare yourself to-day; the night will come again.

Enter AMINTOR

AMIN: Who's there? my brother! I am no readier yet. Your sister is but now up.

DIPH: You look as you had lost your eyes to-night:
I think you ha' not slept.

AMIN: I'faith I have not.

DIPH: You have done better, then.

AMIN: We ventured for a boy: when he is twelve,
A'shall command against the foes of Rhodes.
Shall we be merry?

STRA: You cannot; you want sleep.

AMIN: 'Tis true; *[Aside]* but she,
As if she had drunk Lethe, or had made
Even with Heaven, did fetch so still a sleep,
So sweet and sound –

DIPH: What's that?

AMIN: Your sister frets
This morning, and does turn her eyes upon me,
As people on their headsman. She does chafe,
And kiss, and chafe again, and clap my cheeks!
She's in another world.

DIPH: Then I had lost: I was about to lay
You had not got her maidenhead to-night.

III, i

JOHN FORD

From 'Tis Pity She's a Whore

Giovanni has seduced his sister, Annabella.

GIO: Come, Annabella, no more Sister now,
    But Love, a name more gracious; do not blush,
    Beauty's sweet wonder, but be proud to know
    That yielding thou hast conquer'd, and inflamed
    A heart, whose tribute is thy brother's life.

ANN: And mine is his. Oh, how these stolen contents
    Would print a modest crimson on my cheeks,
    Had any but my heart's delight prevail'd!

GIO: I marvel why the chaster of your sex
    Should think this pretty toy call'd maidenhead,
    So strange a loss; when, being lost, 'tis nothing,
    And you are still the same.

ANN: 'Tis well for you;
    Now you can talk.

GIO: Music as well consists
    In th' ear, as in the playing.

ANN: Oh, you are wanton!
    Tell on 't, you were best; do.

GIO: Thou wilt chide me then.
    Kiss me – so! thus hung Jove on Leda's neck,
    And suck'd divine ambrosia from her lips.
    I envy not the mightiest man alive;
    But hold myself, in being king of thee,
    More great than were I king of all the world:
    But I shall lose you, sweetheart.

ANN: But you shall not.

GIO: You must be married, mistress.

ANN: Yes! to whom?

GIO: Some one must have you.

ANN: You must.

GIO: Nay, some other.

ANN: Now prithee do not speak so; without jesting
You'll make me weep in earnest.

GIO: What, you will not!
But tell me, sweet, canst thou be dared to swear
That thou wilt live to me, and to no other?

ANN: By both our loves I dare; for didst thou know,
My Giovanni, how all suitors seem
To my eyes hateful, thou wouldst trust me then.

GIO: Enough, I take thy word: sweet, we must part;
Remember what thou vow'st; keep well my heart.

ANN: Will you be gone?

GIO: I must.

ANN: When to return?

GIO: Soon.

ANN: Look you do.

GIO: Farewell.

ANN: Go where thou wilt, in mind I'll keep thee here,
And where thou art, I know I shall be there.
Guardian!

Enter PUTANA

PUT: Child, how is 't, child? well, thank heav'n, ha?

ANN: Oh, guardian, what a paradise of joy
Have I passed over!

PUT: Nay, what a paradise of joy have you passed under! why, now I
commend thee, charge. Fear nothing, sweetheart; what though he be
your brother? your brother's a man, I hope; and I say still, if a young
wench feel the fit upon her, let her take anybody, father or brother,
all is one.

II, i

JOHN WEBSTER

From The Duchess of Malfi

Enter Duchess, Antonio, and Cariola.

DUCH: Bring me the casket hither, and the glass.
  You get no lodging here tonight, my lord.

ANT: Indeed, I must persuade one.

DUCH: Very good:
  I hope in time 'twill grow into a custom,
  That noblemen shall come with cap and knee
  To purchase a night's lodging of their wives.

ANT: I must lie here.

DUCH: Must! you are a lord of misrule.

ANT: Indeed, my rule is only in the night.

DUCH: To what use will you put me?

ANT: We'll sleep together.

DUCH: Alas,
  What pleasure can two lovers find in sleep!

CARI: My lord, I lie with her often; and I know
  She'll much disquiet you.

ANT: See, you are complain'd of.

CARI: For she's the sprawling'st bedfellow.

ANT: I shall like her the better for that.

CARI: Sir, shall I ask you a question?

ANT: Ay, pray thee, Cariola.

CARI: Wherefore still, when you lie with my lady,
  Do you rise so early?

ANT: Labouring men
  Count the clock oftenest, Cariola,
  Are glad when their task's ended.

DUCH: I'll stop your mouth.   *[Kisses him*

ANT: Nay, that's but one; Venus had two soft doves
  To draw her chariot; I must have another.   *[She kisses him again*
  When wilt thou marry, Cariola?

CARI: Never, my lord.

ANT: Oh, fie upon this single life! forgo it.
We read how Daphne, for her peevish flight,
Became a fruitless bay-tree; Syrinx turn'd
To the pale empty reed; Anaxarete
Was frozen into marble; whereas those
Which married, or prov'd kind unto their friends,
Were by a gracious influence transhap'd
Into the olive, pomegranate, mulberry,
Became flowers, precious stones, or eminent stars.

III, ii

WILLIAM SHAKESPEARE

From Venus and Adonis

'Fair queen,' quoth he, 'if any love you owe me,
Measure my strangeness with my unripe years:
Before I know myself, seek not to know me;
No fisher but the ungrown fry forbears:
  The mellow plum doth fall, the green sticks fast,
  Or being early pluck'd is sour to taste.

'Look, the world's comforter, with weary gait,
His day's hot task hath ended in the west:
The owl, night's herald, shrieks, 't is very late;
The sheep are gone to fold, birds to their nest.
  And coal-black clouds, that shadow heaven's light,
  Do summon us to part, and bid good night.

'Now let me say good night; and so say you;
If you will say so, you shall have a kiss.'
'Good night,' quoth she; and, ere he says adieu,
The honey fee of parting tender'd is:
  Her arms do lend his neck a sweet embrace;
  Incorporate then they seem, face grows to face.

Till, breathless, he disjoin'd, and backward drew
The heavenly moisture, that sweet coral mouth,
Whose precious taste her thirsty lips well knew,
Whereon they surfeit, yet complain on drouth:
   He with her plenty press'd, she faint with dearth,
   (Their lips together glu'd,) fall to the earth.

Now quick desire hath caught the yielding prey,
And glutton-like she feeds, yet never filleth;
Her lips are conquerors, his lips obey,
Paying what ransom the insulter willeth:
   Whose vulture thought doth pitch the price so high,
   That she will draw his lips' rich treasure dry.

And having felt the sweetness of the spoil,
With blindfold fury she begins to forage;
Her face doth reek and smoke, her blood doth boil,
And careless lust stirs up a desperate courage;
   Planting oblivion, beating reason back,
   Forgetting shame's pure blush, and honour's wrack.

Hot, faint, and weary, with her hard embracing,
Like a wild bird being tam'd with too much handling,
Or as the fleet-foot roe that's tir'd with chasing,
Or like the froward infant still'd with dandling,
   He now obeys, and now no more resisteth,
   While she takes all she can, not all she listeth.

What wax so frozen but dissolves with tempering,
And yields at last to every light impression?
Things out of hope are compass'd oft with venturing,
Chiefly in love, whose leave exceeds commission:
   Affection faints not like a pale-fac'd coward,
   But then woos best, when most his choice is froward.

When he did frown, O! had she then gave over,
Such nectar from his lips she had not suck'd.
Foul words and frowns must not repel a lover;
What though the rose have prickles, yet 't is pluck'd:
  Were beauty under twenty locks kept fast,
    Yet love breaks through, and picks them all at last.

For pity now she can no more detain him;
The poor fool prays her that he may depart:
She is resolv'd no longer to restrain him,
Bids him farewell, and look well to her heart,
  The which, by Cupid's bow she doth protest.
    He carries thence incaged in his breast.

'Sweet boy,' she says, 'this night I'll waste in sorrow,
For my sick heart commands mine eyes to watch.
Tell me, Love's master, shall we meet to-morrow?
Say, shall we? shall we? wilt thou make the match?'
  He tells her, no; to-morrow he intends
    To hunt the boar with certain of his friends.

'The boar!' quoth she, whereat a sudden pale,
Like lawn being spread upon the blushing rose,
Usurps her cheek: she trembles at his tale,
And on his neck her yoking arms she throws;
  She sinketh down, still hanging by his neck,
    He on her belly falls, she on her back.

Now is she in the very lists of love,
Her champion mounted for the hot encounter:
All is imaginary she doth prove,
He will not manage her, although he mount her;
  That worse than Tantalus' is her annoy,
    To clip Elysium, and to lack her joy.

Even as poor birds, deceiv'd with painted grapes,
Do surfeit by the eye, and pine the maw,
Even so she languisheth in her mishaps,
As those poor birds that helpless berries saw.
    The warm effects which she in him finds missing,
    She seeks to kindle with continual kissing.

But all in vain; good queen, it will not be:
She hath assay'd as much as may be prov'd;
Her pleading hath deserv'd a greater fee;
She's Love, she loves, and yet she is not lov'd.
    'Fie, fie!' he says, 'you crush me; let me go:
    You have no reason to withhold me so.'

From Pericles, Prince of Tyre

Mitylene. A room in a brothel.
Enter Pander, Bawd and Boult.

PAND: Boult!

BOULT: Sir?

PAND: Search the market narrowly; Mitylene is full of gallants: we lost too much money this mart, by being too wenchless.

BAWD: We were never so much out of creatures. We have but poor three, and they can do no more than they can do; and they with continual action are even as good as rotten.

PAND: Therefore, let's have fresh ones, whate'er we pay for them. If there be not a conscience to be used in every trade, we shall never prosper.

BAWD: Thou say'st true: 't is not the bringing up of poor bastards – as I think, I have brought up some eleven –

BOULT: Ay, to eleven; and brought them down again. But shall I search the market?

BAWD: What else, man? The stuff we have, a strong wind will blow it to pieces, they are so pitifully sodden.

PAND: Thou say'st true; they're too unwholesome, o' conscience. The poor Transylvanian is dead, that lay with the little baggage.

BOULT: Ay, she quickly pooped him; she made him roast-meat for worms. But I'll go search the market.   *[Exit*

PAND: Three or four thousand chequins were as pretty a proportion to live quietly, and so give over.

BAWD: Why to give over, I pray you? is it a shame to get when we are old?

PAND: O! our credit comes not in like the commodity; nor the commodity wages not with the danger: therefore, if in our youths we could pick up some pretty estate, 't were not amiss to keep our door hatched. Besides, the sore terms we stand upon with the gods, will be strong with us for giving over.

BAWD: Come, other sorts offend as well as we.

PAND: As well as we? ay, and better too; we offend worse. Neither is our profession any trade; it's no calling. But here comes Boult.

Re-enter BOULT, *with the Pirates and* MARINA.

BOULT: [*To* MARINA.] Come your ways – My masters, you say she's a virgin?

PIR: O, sir! we doubt it not.

BOULT: Master, I have gone through for this piece, you see; if you like her, so; if not, I have lost my earnest.

BAWD: Boult, has she any qualities?

BOULT: She has a good face, speaks well, and has excellent good clothes: there's no further necessity of qualities can make her be refused.

BAWD: What's her price, Boult?

BOULT: I cannot be baited one doit of a thousand pieces.

PAND: Well, follow me, my masters, you shall have your money presently. Wife, take her in: instruct her what she has to do, that she may not be raw in her entertainment.   *[Exeunt Pander and Pirates*

BAWD: Boult, take you the marks of her, the colour of her hair, complexion, height, her age, with warrant of her virginity, and cry, 'He that will give most, shall have her first.' Such a maidenhead were no cheap thing, if men were as they have been. Get this done as I command you.

BOULT: Performance shall follow.   *[Exit*

MAR: Alack; that Leonine was so slack, so slow!
He should have struck, not spoke; or that these pirates
(Not enough barbarous) had not o'erboard thrown me
For to seek my mother!

BAWD: Why lament you, pretty one?

MAR: That I am pretty.

BAWD: Come, the gods have done their part in you.

MAR: I accuse them not.

BAWD: You are light into my hands, where you are like to live.

MAR: The more my fault.
To scape his hands where I was like to die.

BAWD: Ay, and you shall live in pleasure.

MAR: No.

BAWD: Yes, indeed, shall you, and taste gentlemen of all fashions.
You shall fare well: you shall have the difference of all complexions.
What! do you stop your ears?

MAR: Are you a woman?

BAWD: What would you have me be, an I be not a woman?

MAR: An honest woman, or not a woman.

BAWD: Marry, whip thee, gosling: I think I shall have something to do
with you. Come, you're a young foolish sapling, and must be bowed
as I would have you.

MAR: The gods defend me!

BAWD: If it please the gods to defend you by men, then men must
comfort you, men must feed you, men must stir you up – Boult's
returned.

Re-enter BOULT

Now, sir, hast thou cried her through the market?

BOULT: I have cried her almost to the number of her hairs: I have
drawn her picture with my voice.

BAWD: And, I pr'ythee, tell me, how dost thou find the inclination of
the people, especially of the younger sort?

BOULT: 'Faith, they listened to me, as they would have hearkened to
their father's testament. There was a Spaniard's mouth so watered,
that he went to bed to her very description.

BAWD: We shall have him here to-morrow with his best ruff on.

BOULT: To-night, to-night. But, mistress, do you know the French
knight that cowers i' the hams?

BAWD: Who? Monsieur Veroles?

BOULT: Ay: he offered to cut a caper at the proclamation; but he
made a groan at it, and swore he would see her to-morrow.

BAWD: Well, well; as for him, he brought his disease hither: here he does but repair it. I know, he will come in our shadow, to scatter his crowns in the sun.

BOULT: Well, if we had of every nation a traveller, we should lodge them with this sign.

BAWD: [*To* MARINA.] Pray you, come hither awhile. You have fortunes coming upon you. Mark me: you must seem to do that fearfully, which you commit willingly; to despise profit, where you have most gain. To weep that you live as ye do, makes pity in your lovers: seldom, but that pity begets you a good opinion, and that opinion a mere profit.

MAR: I understand you not.

BOULT: O! take her home, mistress, take her home: these blushes of hers must be quenched with some present practice.

BAWD: Thou say'st true, i' faith, so they must; for your bride goes to that with shame, which is her way to go with warrant.

BOULT: 'Faith, some do, and some do not. But, mistress, if I have bargained for the joint –

BAWD: Thou may'st cut a morsel off the spit.

BOULT: I may so?

BAWD: Who should deny it? Come, young one, I like the manner of your garments well.

BOULT: Ay, by my faith, they shall not be changed yet.

BAWD: Boult, spend thou that in the town: report what a sojourner we have; you'll lose nothing by custom. When nature framed this piece, she meant thee a good turn; therefore, say what a paragon she is, and thou hast the harvest out of thine own report.

BOULT: I warrant you, mistress, thunder shall not so awake the beds of eels, as my giving out her beauty stir up the lewdly-inclined. I'll bring home some to-night.

BAWD: Come your ways; follow me.

MAR: If fires be hot, knives sharp, or waters deep,
Untied I still my virgin knot will keep.
Diana, aid my purpose!

BAWD: What have we to do with Diana? Pray you, will you go with us?
[*Exeunt*

IV, iii

MARGARET, QUEEN OF NAVARRE

From The Heptameron

The muleteer's wife

IN THE TOWN of Amboise there was a muleteer in the service of the Queen of Navarre, sister to King Francis, first of that name. She being at Blois, where she had been brought to bed of a son, the aforesaid muleteer went thither to receive his quarterly payment, whilst his wife remained at Amboise in a lodging beyond the bridges.

Now it happened that one of her husband's servants had long loved her exceedingly, and one day he could not refrain from speaking of it to her. She, however, being a truly virtuous woman, rebuked him so severely, threatening to have him beaten and dismissed by her husband, that from that time forth he did not venture to speak to her in any such way again or to let his love be seen, but kept the fire hidden within his breast until the day when his master had gone from home and his mistress was at vespers at St Florentin, the castle church, a long way from the muleteer's house.

Whilst he was alone the fancy took him that he might obtain by force what neither prayer nor service had availed to procure him, and accordingly he broke through a wooden partition which was between the chamber where his mistress slept and his own. The curtains of his master's bed on the one side and of the servant's bed on the other so covered the walls as to hide the opening he had made; and thus his wickedness was not perceived until his mistress was in bed, together with a little girl eleven or twelve years old.

When the poor woman was in her first sleep, the servant, in his shirt and with his naked sword in his hand, came through the opening he had made in the wall into her bed; but as soon as she felt him beside her, she leaped out, addressing to him all such reproaches as a virtuous woman might utter. His love, however, was but bestial, and he would have better understood the language of his mules than her honourable reasonings; indeed, he showed himself even more bestial than the beasts with whom he had long consorted. Finding she ran so quickly round a table that he could not catch her, and that she was strong enough to break away from him twice, he despaired of ravishing her alive, and dealt her a terrible sword-thrust in the loins, thinking that, if fear and force had not brought her to yield, pain would assuredly do so.

The contrary, however, happened, for just as a good soldier, on seeing his own blood, is the more fired to take vengeance on his enemies and win renown, so her chaste heart gathered new strength as she ran fleeing from the hands of the miscreant, saying to him the while all she could think of to bring him to see his guilt. But so filled was he with rage that he paid no heed to her words. He dealt her several more thrusts, to avoid which she continued running as long as her legs could carry her.

When, after great loss of blood, she felt that death was near, she lifted her eyes to heaven, clasped her hands and gave thanks to God, calling Him her strength, her patience, and her virtue, and praying Him to accept her blood which had been shed for the keeping of His commandment and in reverence of His Son, through whom she firmly believed all her sins to be washed away and blotted out from the remembrance of His wrath.

As she was uttering the words, 'Lord, receive the soul that has been redeemed by Thy goodness,' she fell upon her face to the ground.

Then the miscreant dealt her several thrusts, and when she had lost both power of speech and strength of body, and was no longer able to make any defence, he ravished her. Having thus satisfied his wicked lust, he fled in haste, and in spite of all pursuit was never seen again.

The little girl, who was in bed with the muleteer's wife, had hidden herself under the bed in her fear; but on seeing that the man was gone, she came to her mistress. Finding her to be without speech or movement, she called to the neighbours from the window for aid; and as they loved and esteemed her mistress as much as any woman that belonged to the town, they came forthwith, bringing surgeons with them. The latter found that she had received twenty-five mortal wounds in her body, and although they did what they could to help her, it was all in vain.

Nevertheless she lingered for an hour longer without speaking, yet making signs with eye and hand to show that she had not lost her understanding. Being asked by a priest in what faith she died, she answered, by signs as plain as any speech, that she placed her hope of salvation in Jesus Christ alone; and so with glad countenance and eyes upraised to heaven her chaste body yielded up its soul to its Creator.

Just as the corpse, having been laid out and shrouded, was placed at the door to await the burial company, the poor husband arrived and beheld his wife's body in front of his house before he had even received tidings of her death. He inquired the cause of this, and found that he had double occasion to grieve; and his grief was indeed so great that it nearly killed him.

This martyr of chastity was buried in the Church of St Florentin, and, as was their duty, all the upright women of Amboise failed not to show her every possible honour, deeming themselves fortunate in belonging to a town where so virtuous a woman had been found. And seeing the honour that was shown to the deceased, such women as were wanton and unchaste resolved to amend their lives.

From a nineteenth-century translation

PIERRE DE BOURDEILLES, SEIGNEUR AND ABBÉ DE BRANTÔME

From Les Dames Gallantes

1

THE COURTESANS OF Rome and Italy, when they are old, hold by a certain maxim, 'Una gallina vecchia fa miglior brodo ch'un altra' (An old hen makes better broth than the other sort).

2

There once was a Spanish courtesan with two brave Spanish knights who picked a quarrel over her and went out of their pavilion, took up their swords and started to fight. She put her head out of the window and shouted down to them, 'My lovers, you can win me with gold and silver, not with iron.'

Transl. F.P.

WANG SHIH-CHEN

From Chin P'ing Mei

None of the critics or translators of *Chin P'ing Mei* seems prepared to give a translation of the title of this great Chinese novel, so I asked my Chinese obscene phone caller, Lee, to tell me what it means. His rendition, for what it's worth, was 'Pure as Snow'. If he was telling the truth, the title is an example of Chinese black comedy, because the book has been renowned throughout the ages for its pornographic passages.

For centuries, the book was attributed to Wang Shih-Chen, a

leading poet and essayist of the sixteenth century. Modern critics like to discredit this for the bizarre reason that they don't believe that such a dirty book could have been written by an intellectual. Personally, I like to accept the old attribution and also the legend that goes with it. Wang Shih-Chen, it is said, wrote the work to avenge the death of his father for which the Prime Minister, Yen Shih-fan, was responsible. He knew that Yen Shih-fan, a pornography addict, would not be able to put the book down, so he poisoned every page (there are about 1600 of them), knowing that the Prime Minister would lick and turn till he met his quietus.

To give an idea of the quality and feel of the book – it is the story of Hsi-Mên Ching, his wives and mistresses, and the fall of his house. It is a moral tale of corruption and its consequences. The murders and hauntings are probably even better than the sex passages. Parts of the book are Jacobean in their ferocity – a similarity to Webster's *White Devil* springs to mind. But it is *The White Devil* told by Richardson, with every subtlety of human character exposed – and for the fetishistic reader, every detail of dress noted. It is also a marvellous human record of the everyday life of that period. The lives of the rich and the poor are equally well depicted. As a feminist book, although not written by a woman, it's important. I have come across no other novel where the differences in the characters of a large cast of women are so well described. The majority of the women who people the book are wicked, but their wickedness is described with compassion and is largely explainable by the hard beginnings of loveless marriages, slavery or being forced into prostitution by their families at an early age.

The old procuress

Hsi-MEN CH'ING was desperately anxious to possess Golden Lotus. He gave the old woman no peace.

'Stepmother,' he said, 'if you bring this business to a happy end, I will give you ten taels of silver.'

'Sir,' said the old woman, 'you may have heard, perhaps, of "setting a love-snare". The expression implies much that is difficult and is, indeed, what is more commonly known as wife-stealing. Before a man can set about this wife-stealing business with any prospect of success, five things are essential. He must be as handsome as P'an An. His member must be at least as large as a donkey's. He must be as rich as Têng T'ung, and reasonably young. Finally, he must have plenty of time on his hands, and almost endless patience. If you are possessed of all these qualifications, you may think of going in for this sort of entertainment.'

'I think I may say I do possess them all,' Hsi-mên Ch'ing said. 'I would not venture to compare my handsome figure with that of P'an An, but it will serve. Ever since I was a boy, I have played in the lowest and most unsavoury haunts, and I must say I have succeeded in keeping a very fat turtle well content. I may not have as much money as Têng T'ung, but have a good deal put away, certainly sufficient to live upon. As for my patience, I should never think of retaliating though I received four hundred blows. Finally, if I had not plenty of time to waste, you would not be seeing me here so often. Stepmother, do this for me, and you shall not be disappointed with your reward.'

'There is one thing more, Sir,' the old woman said. 'You tell me that you possess the five essential qualifications, but I fear this too is indispensable.'

'What do you mean?' Hsi-mên Ch'ing cried.

'Forgive my speaking plainly,' the old woman said, 'but when a man would run off with somebody else's wife, there are very considerable difficulties in the way. A man may spend almost his last penny, and still fail. He must go to the absolute limit. I happen to know that you particularly dislike parting with your money, and that is the difficulty.'

'It shall be no difficulty in this case,' Hsi-mên said, 'for I will do anything you suggest.'

'Very well,' the old woman said, 'if you are really prepared to spend a few taels, I have a plan which should enable you to secure the lady.'

Hsi-mên would have liked to hear it, but the old woman said, with a laugh, 'It is too late today, and time you went home. Come back in six months, or perhaps three, and we will see what we can do.'

'Stepmother,' said Hsi-mên, 'don't joke about it. Only do this for me and you shall have a really handsome present.' But the old woman laughed all the more.

'You certainly seem to be very keen,' she said. 'Nobody ever comes to say his prayers to me at the temple of Wu Ch'êng Wang, but my plan is as good and better than any that fellow Sun Wu-tzǔ could have made. He was able to turn girls into soldiers, but I could have captured eight out of ten of them. Let me tell you all I know about this woman. She comes of a poor family, but she is as clever as can be. She knows how to play and sing, her embroidery is excellent, and she is expert at many games. In fact, there is nothing she doesn't know. Her surname is P'an, and her personal name, Golden Lotus. Her father was P'an Ts'ai, who used to live by the South

Gate. Originally, she was sold to Master Chang, and at his house she learned to sing and play. When Chang was very old, he made a present of her to Wu Ta. She does not go out very often and, when I am not busy, I go over to her place and get anything she happens to want. She always calls me "Stepmother".

'These last few days, Wu Ta has been going out early. If you wish to clinch the matter, you must buy some silk, one roll of blue, another of white, another of the finest white silk, and ten taels of good raw silk. Give them to me. I will go to her house to borrow a calendar, and ask her to tell me a day of good omen so that I can engage a dressmaker to come and make me some clothes. It may be that she will find a day for me, but not offer to come herself to make the clothes. In that case, there is nothing to be done. If she is very pleasant and says, "Don't get a dressmaker. I will come and make the clothes for you," that will be one to us. If I can persuade her to come here to sew, that will be another one to us. If she comes at noon, I will set out refreshments and invite her to have some. She may say, "I am very sorry but I can't," and go off home and, in that case, we shall have to give up. On the other hand, she may say nothing, but sit down and eat my lunch, and then we score again.

'You must not come tomorrow, but the day after. Put on your smartest clothes. Give a cough of warning, and then come to the door and call, "How do you do, Stepmother? May I come in and have a cup of tea?" I will come out and ask you in. It is possible that, as soon as she sees you, she may want to go home, and, if she does, I cannot stop her. That will be the end. But if she stays where she is, we shall be four points to the good.

'When you sit down, I shall say to her, "This is the gentleman who gave me the clothes. I can't tell you how grateful I am to him," and I shall say all sorts of pretty things about your generosity. Then you will compliment her on her sewing. If she does not answer, we are done. If she does answer, and enters into conversation with you, our fifth point is gained.

'Then I say, "Isn't this good lady kind to make my clothes for me?" and praise you both – you for giving me the money and her for making the clothes. I shall say, "This lady is indeed good-hearted. I was lucky to be able to persuade her to come. Perhaps you would like to offer her some refreshment." You will take some silver out of your pocket and ask me to go and buy something. If at that moment she decides to go, I can't hold her, and all is over. But, if she doesn't move, we shall have gained our sixth point.

'I shall take your silver and, as I go out, I shall say, "I wonder if you would mind keeping this gentleman company?" She may jump up at that and, if she does so, I can't very well put my arms round her and hold her, but, if she doesn't, we shall have gained another point.

'When I come back with the things, I shall put them on the table and say, "Lady, put the clothes aside for a while and let us drink a little wine. This gentleman has been good enough to spend his money on us." If she will not join us, but takes her leave, the matter is ended. But if she says, "Oh, really I can't stay," but does not make any effort to go, the eighth point is ours.

'If she drinks her wine contentedly and begins to talk to you, I shall say, "There is not enough wine," and you will ask me to buy some more, and some fruits too, and give me silver for the purpose. Then I shall shut the door upon you both. If she is shy and tries to run away, we can do no more. But if she lets me fasten the door and does not get angry, we are within an ace of our goal. The last stage is the critical one. You, Sir, will stay in the room with the woman and talk prettily to her, but you must not be too rough when you begin to take liberties. If you touch her, and spoil the whole game, it will not be my fault. But it is possible that you might knock down a pair of chop-sticks with your sleeve, and touch her foot when you pretend to pick them up. If this makes her angry, I shall come in and make peace between you, but all our chances will be gone and we can never hope to retrieve the position. If she says nothing, we gain our tenth point, and the game is ours. If I lead you to victory, what reward may I expect?'

Hsi-mên Ch'ing listened to all this, and was perfectly delighted. 'Your plan may not come from the Ling Yen temple,' he said, 'but it is absolutely flawless.'

'Don't forget those ten taels of silver,' old woman Wang said.

'If I get but a single piece of orange peel,' Hsi-mên said, 'I shall never forget the Tung-t'ing lake. But when do you propose to put this scheme into operation, Stepmother?'

'Come back this evening,' the old woman said, 'and you shall know. By this time Wu Ta has gone out, and I will go over about the calendar and say my part. You send somebody with the silk as quickly as possible. Don't waste any time.'

'I'll see to it at once,' Hsi-mên Ch'ing cried. 'You may count upon me absolutely.'

Golden Lotus plays the flute

Golden Lotus's speciality was *p'in hsiao* – playing the flute – the Chinese euphemism for fellatio.

GOLDEN LOTUS HAD taken particular pains to make herself look pretty and she had washed her body with perfumed water. She was expecting him and, when he came, she smiled sweetly. She took his clothes and told Plum Blossom to make tea. They went to bed, and, under the coverlets, embraced and pressed their tender bodies closely together. She used every one of her hundred charms to give him pleasure. They enjoyed each other for a while, then Hsi-mên Ch'ing found that he could not sleep. He told her how he had longed for her while he had been away. Then, as he was still unsatisfied, he asked her to play the flute for him. She was ready to do anything he asked, so that she might the more firmly establish her hold over him. They had been separated for a long time. She had been starved for love so long that passion set her afire. She would have made herself a part of him. *She played the flute all night, without letting it out of her mouth. He wanted to get up to pee, but she would not let him. 'My darling,' she said, 'let me take however much you've got stored up in my mouth* [1]. It is chilly tonight and you might take cold if you got out of bed. It would be more trouble.'

Hsi-mên Ch'ing was delighted. 'Dearest,' he said, 'I don't believe anyone else would love me as you do.' *Then he peed into her mouth and she drank it. Hsi-mên said, 'Do you like it?' 'It tastes acrid,' she said.* 'Give me some fragrant tea-leaves to take the taste away.'

'The tea-leaves are in my white silk coat,' Hsi-mên said, 'get them for yourself.' Golden Lotus pulled the coat to her, took the tea-leaves, and put them into her mouth.

[1] The sentences in italic are translated from Clement Egerton's Latin.

> Buddhist monks and nuns were as much profligates and conspirators as any Catholic ones in Western literature.

The temple novice

CHIN TSUNG-MING was not a good young man. He was about thirty years old, and spent much of his time in the bawdy-house. He was a great fellow for wine and women. He had some younger novices of his own, very smart, good-looking boys, and spent the night with them. When Ch'ên Ching-chi came, Tsung-ming saw how handsome he was, how white his teeth and how red his lips. He seemed so intelligent that he could make his eyes speak for him in place of his mouth. So he asked the young man to come and sleep in his room. In the evening they drank and, when Ching-chi was drunk, they went to bed together. At first, one had his head at one end of the bed and the other at the other end. But Chin Tsung-ming complained that Ching-chi's feet smelled, and asked him to come over the other way. Then he complained that Ching-chi's breath was bad, and asked him to turn his face around. Ching-chi pressed his back against the other monk's stomach and said nothing, feigning sleep. Then Chin Tsung-ming's penis became firm and erect like a spear. He smeared it with spittle and plunged in. When Ching-chi had been living among the beggars, two of his companions had misused his bottom and stretched it, so the monk's path was now easy. Ching-chi still said nothing. 'This fellow will fall into my hands', he thought. 'He doesn't know who I am and he can't do me much harm. I will let him have a taste and then I will get hold of his money.'

> Hsi-mên tries to boost his flagging powers with aphrodisiacs bought from an Indian monk, ignoring his advice about using them sparingly.

The Beginning of the end

WHEN THEY HAD drunk wine enough, and there was nobody in the room, Hsi-mên Ch'ing took the ribbon from his sleeve, put it round his penis and tied it round his waist. Then he drank some medicine mixed with wine. Porphyry stroked the prick, which quickly became proud and erect. The veins stood out; it looked like a piece of purple liver. The silk ribbon had far more effect than the clasp.[1] Hsi-mên Ch'ing lifted her onto his lap and pressed his prick into her queynt. They drank wine, each from the other's mouth, and their tongues played together.

In the evening, old woman Fêng made some pies with pork and radishes for them. Porphyry ate some with him and, when the maid had cleared away, they went to the bed. They pulled aside the silken curtains

---

[1] Throughout the book reference is made to various sex aids, that most often used being a clasp. This doesn't seem to be the *fibula* used by some Romans to clamp the foreskin together, and only to be taken off for a price. In this case it seems to be something clamped round the root of the penis, presumably to engorge it.

and took off their clothes. The woman knew that Hsi-mên Ch'ing liked to do things in the light and she set the lamp on a small table near the bed. Then she made fast the door and went to wash her queynt. When she came back she took off her trousers and went to bed. They lay down together and put their arms round one another. Hsi-mên Ch'ing was still thinking of Captain Ho's wife and his passion blazed like fire. His penis was very hard. He told her to get onto hands and knees like a horse, and he plunged to the flower in her bottom. He did this six hundred times, while her behind showed its noisy approbation. She felt down her body, played with the flower in her belly, and called him endearing names unceasingly.

Still Hsi-mên was not content. He sat up, put on a white short coat and set a pillow beneath him. Then he bade the woman turn over and tied her feet with two ribbons to the bed-posts. He began by playing the game of the golden dragon stretching its claws, and thrust this way and that, sometimes plunging deep, sometimes just a little way. He was afraid she might catch cold and wrapped a red silk coat about her body. He brought the light nearer and bent his head to watch the movements. Whenever he took out his penis, he put it in again right up to the hilt; he did this six hundred times. The woman, her voice trembling, called him every endearing word she could think of. Soon he withdrew completely and put some of the red powder on the tip of his penis; when it was set in motion again it so stimulated her queynt that she could hardly bear it. She climbed on top of him and begged him to go in deeper; but he deliberately played about the opening, touching the treasure inside only lightly and refusing to go in further. Love-juices flowed from her like slime from a snail. In the candlelight Hsi-mên beheld her white legs raised about his body on either side. He saw them quivering in response to his movements, which became still more violent.

'Do you love me, you strumpet?' he asked her.

'I have been thinking about you all the time,' she said. 'I can only hope that you will be like the pine tree and the cypress, evergreen. Do not weary of me and give me up. If you should do that, it would kill me. I dare not tell this to anyone else, and nobody knows it. And I shall not tell that turtle of mine. He is away and he has money. He has other women and need not bother about me.'

'My child,' Hsi-mên said, 'if you will give yourself entirely to me, I will find another wife for him when he comes back and then you can belong to me always.'

'Darling,' Porphyry said, 'do get him another wife. Whether you take me into your household or leave me outside does not matter. Do as you please. I give my worthless body to you utterly and entirely and I will do anything you wish.'

'I know you,' Hsi-mên Ch'ing said.

They went on for a very long time. Then Hsi-mên unloosed the ribbons which tied her feet, and they went to sleep together. About the third night-watch he got up, put on his clothes, and washed his hands. Porphyry opened the door and bade the maid bring them wine and food. They drank again. After more than ten cups of wine, Hsi-mên began to feel tipsy and asked for tea to rinse his mouth. He took a paper from his sleeve and gave it to Porphyry. 'Take this to clerk Kan, and ask him for a dress,' he said. 'You can choose your own pattern and design.' She thanked him, and he went away. Wang Ching carried a lantern and Tai An and Ch'in T'ung led his horse, one on either side.

It was the third night-watch. Dark clouds covered the sky, and the light of the moon could hardly pierce them. The street was deserted; only the barking of dogs could be heard in the distance. Hsi-mên Ch'ing went westwards. Suddenly, as he came near the stone bridge, a whirlwind swept before his horse. It was like a dark form advancing from the bridge to attack him. His horse was startled and reared. Hsi-mên shuddered. He whipped his horse. It shook its mane. Tai An and Ch'in T'ung clung to the bridle with all their strength, but they could not hold it, and the horse galloped wildly till it came to Hsi-mên's gateway. Then it stopped. Wang Ching, with the lantern, was left far behind. When Hsi-mên Ch'ing dismounted, his legs were almost useless, and servants came out to help him in. He went to Golden Lotus's room.

Golden Lotus had come back from the inner court, but she had not gone to bed. She was lying upon her bed, dressed, waiting for Hsi-mên Ch'ing. When he came, she got up at once. She took his clothes and saw that he was drunk, but she asked no questions. Hsi-mên put his hands on her shoulders and drew her towards him.

'You little strumpet!' he murmured, 'your darling is drunk. Get the bed ready: I want to go to sleep.'

She helped him to bed, and, as soon as he was on it, he began to snore like thunder. She could do nothing to wake him, so she took off her clothes and went to bed too. She played delicately with his weapon, but it was as limp as cotton-wool and had not the slightest spirit. She tossed about on the bed, consumed with passionate desire, almost beside herself. She pressed his prick, rubbed it up and down, bent her head to suck it; it was in vain. This made her wild beyond description. She shook him for a long time and at last he awoke. She asked him where his medicine was. Hsi-mên, still very drunk, cursed her.

'You little strumpet!' he cried, 'what do you want that for? You would like me to play with you, I suppose, but today your darling is far too tired for anything of that sort. The medicine is in the little gold box in my sleeve. Give it to me. You will be in luck if you make my prick stand up.'

Golden Lotus looked for the little gold box and, when she found it, opened it. There were only three or four pills left. She took a wine-pot and poured out two cups of wine. She took one pill herself, leaving three. Then she made the terrible mistake of giving him all three. She was afraid anything less would have no effect. Hsi-mên shut his eyes and swallowed them. Before he could have drunk a cup of tea, the medicine began to take effect. Golden Lotus tied the silken ribbon for him and his staff stood up. He was still asleep. She mounted upon his body, put some powder on the top of his penis, and put that in her queynt; immediately it penetrated right to the heart of her. Her body seemed to melt away with delight. Then, with her two hands grasping his legs, she moved up and down about two hundred times. First it was difficult, because she was dry, but soon the juices of love flowed and moistened her queynt. Hsi-mên Ch'ing let her do everything she wished, but himself was perfectly inert. She could bear it no longer. She put her tongue into his mouth. She held his neck and shook it. She writhed on his penis, which was entirely inside her queynt; only the two testicles remained outside. She caressed it with her hand, and it looked remarkably fine. The juices flowed; in no time she had used up five handkerchiefs. Still Hsi-mên persevered, although the head of his prick was swollen and hotter than burning coal. The ribbon felt so tight that he asked her to remove it, but the penis stayed erect, and he asked her to suck it. She bent down and, taking it in her lips, sucked it and moved up and down. Suddenly the white sperm squirted out like living silver; she took it in her mouth and could not swallow it fast enough. At first it was sperm and then it became an unceasing flow of blood. Hsi-mên Ch'ing had fainted and his limbs were stiff outstretched.

Golden Lotus was frightened. She hastily gave him some red dates. Blood followed sperm, cold air followed blood. Golden Lotus was terrified. She threw her arms round him and cried: 'Darling, how do you feel?'

From *Chin P'ing Mei*, attributed to Wang Shih-Chen, translated as *The Golden Lotus* by Clement Egerton

LORENZO DE' MEDICI

Dance Song

Deep in a valley, with a copse around,
A fountain of delight is to be found.

Out of this fountain such sweet waters flow
That none would choose to taste another spring:
To taste I was thought worthy and it so
Pleased me that now you see me hankering
For those sweet drops, sweeter than anything.
The elect alone drink on that wooded ground.

If I should give directions where it lay
Some savage animal might visit it,
But happy I shall be to show the way;
You must take two roads if you have the wit
(Unless, of course, you like the opposite
Journey to where another valley's found).

You travel first over a soft incline
That seems to be a field of dazzling snow
And, making for the fount in a straight line,
Between two gentle hillocks you must go;
And as you move across the smooth plateau
The way is shaded by each charming mound.

Feeling your way below them you may revel
In all the purity of a broad hill
Swelling so gently that it seems quite level;
Across its face you travel on until
Two valleys meet, and there you drink your fill
In that deep fountain with a copse around.

                                        Transl. John Adlard

FRANÇOIS RABELAIS

From The Works of Rabelais

How Panurge was in love with a lady of Paris

PANURGE BEGAN TO be in great reputation in the city of Paris, by means of this disputation, wherein he prevailed against the Englishman, and from thenceforth made his codpiece to be very useful to him; to which effect he had it pinked with pretty little embroideries, after the Romanese fashion: and the world did praise him publicly, in so far that there was a song made of him, which little children did use to sing when they went to fetch mustard. He was withal made welcome in all companies of ladies and gentlewomen; so that at last he became presumptuous, and went about to bring to his lure one of the greatest ladies in the city; and indeed, leaving a rabble of long prologues and protestations, which ordinarily these dolent contemplative lent-lovers make, who never meddle with the flesh; one day said he unto her, 'Madam, it would be a very great benefit to the common-wealth, delightful to you, honourable to your progeny, and necessary for me, that I cover you for the propagating of my race; and believe it, for experience will teach it you.' The lady at this word thrust him back above a hundred leagues, saying, 'You mischievous fool, is it for you to talk thus unto me? Whom do you think you have in hand? Begone! never come in my sight again; for, if it were not for one thing, I would have your legs and arms cut off.'

'Well,' said he, 'that were all one to me, to want both legs and arms, provided you and I had but one merry bout together at the brangle buttock-game: for here within is (in shewing her his long codpiece) master John Thursday, who will play you such an antique, that you shall feel the sweetness thereof even to the very marrow of your bones: he is a gallant, and doth so well know how to find out all the corners, creeks, and ingrained inmates in your carnal trap, that after him there needs no broom, he'll sweep so well before, and leave nothing to his followers to work upon.' Whereunto the lady answered, 'Go, villain! go! if you speak to me one such word more, I will cry out, and have you knocked down with blows.' 'Ha,' said he, 'you are not so bad as you say; no, or else I am deceived in your physiognomy: for sooner shall the earth mount up into the heavens, and the highest heavens descend into the abyss of hell, and all the course of nature be quite perverted, than that, in so great beauty and neatness as in you is, there should be one drop of gall or malice. They say, indeed, that hardly shall a man ever see a fair woman that is not also stubborn: yet that is spoke only of those vulgar beauties; but yours is so excellent, so singular, and so heavenly, that I believe nature hath given it you as a paragon and masterpiece of her art, to make us know what she can do, when she will employ all her skill, and all her power. There is nothing in you but honey, but sugar, but a sweet and celestial manna. To you it was to whom Paris ought to have adjudged the golden apple, not to Venus, no, nor to Juno, nor to Minerva: for never was there so much magnificence in Juno, so much wisdom in Minerva, nor so much comeliness in Venus, as there is in you.

'O heavenly Gods and Goddesses! how happy shall that man be to whom you will grant the favour to embrace her, to kiss her, and to rub his bacon with hers! By God that shall be I, I know it well; for she loves me already her belly-full, I am sure of it; and so was I predestinated to it by the fairies. And therefore, that we lose no time, put on, thrust out your gammons.' Then he would have embraced her; but she made as if she would put out her head at the window, to call her neighbours for help. Then Panurge on a sudden ran out, and in his running away said, 'Madam, stay here till I come again; I will go call them myself, do not you take so much pains.' Thus went he away, not much caring for the repulse he had got, nor made he any whit the worse cheer for it. The next day he came to the church, at the time that she went to mass: at the door he gave her some of the holy-water, bowing himself very low before her: afterwards he kneeled down by her very familiarly, and said unto her, 'Madam, know that I am so amorous of you, that I can neither piss nor dung for love: I do not know (lady) what you mean, but if I should take any hurt by it, how much would you be to blame?'

'Go,' said she, 'go, I do not care; let me alone to say my prayers.' 'Ay, but,' said he, 'equivocate upon a *Beaumont le viconte*.' 'I cannot,' said she. 'It is,' said he, 'a *beau con le vit monte*: and upon this pray to God to give you that which your noble heart desireth; and I pray you give me these patenotres.' 'Take them,' said she, 'and trouble me no longer.' This done, she would have taken off her patenotres, which were made of a kind of yellow stone, called cestrin, and adorned with great spots of gold: but Panurge nimbly drew out one of his knives, wherewith he cut them off very handsomely; and whilst he was going away to carry them to the brokers, he said to her, 'Will you have my knife?' 'No, no,' said she. 'But,' said he, 'to the point; I am at your commandment, body and goods, tripes and bowels.'

In the meantime the lady was not well content with the want of her patenotres; for they were one of her implements to keep her countenance by in the church: then thought with herself, 'This bold flouting royster is some giddy, fantastical, light-headed fool of a strange country; I shall never recover my patenotres again. What will my husband say? He will, no doubt, be angry with me; but I will tell him that a thief hath cut them off from my hands in the church; which he will easily believe, seeing the end of the ribbon left at my girdle.' After dinner Panurge went to see her, carrying in his sleeve a great purse full of palace-crowns, called counters, and began to say unto her, 'Which of us two loveth other best, you me, or I you?' Whereunto she answered, 'As for me, I do not hate you; for, as God commands, I love all the world.' 'But to the point,' said he, 'are not you in love with me?' 'I have,' said she, 'told you so many times already, that you should talk so no more to me; and, if you speak of it again, I will teach you that I am not one to be talked unto dishonestly: get you hence packing, and deliver me my patenotres, that my husband may not ask me for them.'

'How now, madam,' said he, 'your patenotres? Nay, by mine oath I will not do so, but I will give you others: had you rather have them of gold well enamelled in great round knobs, or after the manner of love-knots, or otherwise all massive, like great ingots? or if you had rather have them of ebony, of jacinth, or of grained gold, with the marks of fine turquoises, or of fair topazes, marked with fine sapphires, or of baleu rubies, with great marks of diamonds of eight and twenty squares. No, no, all this is too little. I know a fair bracelet of fine emeralds, marked with spotted ambergris, and at the buckle a Persian pearl as big as an orange; it will not cost above five and twenty thousand ducats: I will make you a present of it; for I have ready coin enough:' and withal he made a noise with his counters as if they had been French crowns.

'Will you have a piece of velvet, either of the violet colour, or of crimson died in grain; or a piece of broached or crimson satin? Will you have chains, gold, tablets, rings? You need no more but say yes; so far as fifty thousand ducats may reach, it is but as nothing to me.' By the virtue of which words he made the water come in her mouth. But she said unto him, 'No, I thank you; I will have nothing of you.' 'By God!' said he, 'but I will have somewhat of you; yet shall it be that which shall cost you nothing, neither shall you have a jot the less, when you have given it: hold,' (shewing his long codpiece) 'this is Master John Goodfellow, that asks for lodging,' and with that would have embraced her; but she began to cry out, yet not very loud. Then Panurge put off his counterfeit garb, changed his false visage, and said unto her, 'You will not then otherwise let me do a little? A turd for you; you do not deserve so much good, nor so much honour; but by God I will make the dogs ride you.' And with this he ran away as fast as he could, for fear of blows, whereof he was naturally fearful.

How Panurge served the Parisian lady a trick that pleased her not very well

NOW YOU MUST note that the next day was the great festival of Corpus Christi, called the sacre, wherein all women put on their best apparel; and on that day the said lady was cloathed in a rich gown of crimson satin, under which she wore a very costly white velvet petticoat.

Now on the vigil, Panurge searched so long of one side and another, that he found a hot or salt bitch, which, when he had tied her with his girdle, he led her to his chamber, and fed her very well all that day and night; in the morning thereafter he killed her, and took that part of her which the Greek geomancers know, and cut it into several pieces as small as he could: then carrying it away as close as might be, he went to the place where the lady was to come along to follow the procession, as the custom is upon the said holy-day. And when she came in, Panurge sprinkled some holy water on her, saluting her very courteously. Then, a little while after she had said her petty devotions, he sat down close by her upon the same bench, and gave her this roundelay in writing, in manner as followeth:

A ROUNDELAY

Lady for once, because my case
I told you, am I out of grace?
That you should so severely call
Me to be gone for good-and-all,
Who never had deserved your frown
By word, deed, letter, or lampoon.
You might deny me what I sought,
And not have call'd me all to nought,
Because I would have had a bout,
                Lady for once.

It hurts you not that I complain
Of my intolerable pain;
Of bloody wound, and deadly dart,
Wherewith your beauty thrills my heart:
And since from thence my torment came,
O grant some little of that same,
                                    Lady for once.

As she was opening this paper to see what it was, Panurge very promptly and lightly scattered the drug that he had upon her in divers places, but especially in the pleats of her sleeves, and of her gown: then said he unto her, 'Madam, the poor lovers are not always at ease. As for me, I hope that those heavy nights, those pains and troubles which I suffer for love of you, shall be a deduction to me of so much pain in purgatory: yet at the least pray to God to give me patience in my misery.' Panurge had no sooner spoke this, but all the dogs that were in the church came running to this lady with the smell of the drugs that he had strewed upon her, both small and great, big and little, all came, laying out their member; smelling to her, and pissing everywhere upon her: it was the greatest villany in the world.

Panurge made some offers of driving them away; then took his leave of her, and withdrew himself into a chapel or oratory of the said church, to see the sport; for these villanous dogs did compiss all her habiliments, and left none of her attire unbesprinkled with their staling; insomuch that a tall greyhound pissed upon her head; others in her sleeves; others on her crupper-piece; and the little ones pissed upon her pattins; so that all the women that were round about her, had much ado to save her. Whereat Panurge very hartily laughing, he said to one of the lords of the city, 'I believe that same lady is hot, or else that some greyhound hath covered her lately.' And when he saw that all the dogs were flocking about her, yarring at the retardment of their access to her, and every way keeping such a coil with her, as they are wont to do about a proud or salt bitch; he forthwith departed from thence, and went to call Pantagruel; not forgetting in his way along the streets through which he went, where he found any dogs, to give them a bang with his foot, saying, 'Will you not go with your fellows to the wedding? Away hence! avant! avant! with a devil avant!' And being come home, he said to Pantagruel, 'Master, I pray you come and see all the dogs of the country, how they are assembled about a lady, the fairest in the city, and would duffle and line her.' Whereunto

Pantagruel willingly condescended, and saw the mystery, which he found very pretty and strange. But the best was at the procession, in which were seen above six hundred thousand and fourteen dogs about her, which did very much trouble and molest her; and whithersoever she passed, those dogs that came afresh, tracing her footsteps, followed her at the heels, and pissed in the way where her gown had touched. All the world stood gazing at this spectacle, considering the action of those dogs, who leaping up, got about her neck, and spoiled all her gorgeous accoutrements; for the which she could find no remedy, but to retire unto her house, which was a palace. Thither she went, and the dogs after her: she ran to hide herself, but the chambermaids could not abstain from laughing. When she was entered into the house, and had shut the door upon herself, all the dogs came running, of half a league round, and did so well bepiss the gate of her house, that there they made a stream with their urine wherein a duck might very well have swum; and it is the same current that now runs at St Victor, in which Gobelin dyeth scarlet by the specifical virtue of these piss-dogs, as our master Doribus did heretofore preach publicly. So may God help you, a mill would have ground corn with it; yet not so much as those of Basacle at Toulouse.

How Gargantua was born in a strange manner

WHILST THEY WERE on this discourse, and pleasant tattle of drinking, Gargamelle began to be a little unwell in her lower parts; whereupon Grangousier arose from off the grass, and fell to comfort her very honestly and kindly, suspecting that she was in travail, and told her that it was best for her to sit down upon the grass, under the willows, because she was like very shortly to see young feet; and that, therefore, it was convenient she should pluck up her spirits, and take a good heart at the new coming of her baby; saying to her withal, that although the pain was somewhat grievous to her, it would be but of short continuance; and that the succeeding joy would quickly remove that sorrow, in such sort that she should not so much as remember it. 'On with a sheep's courage,' quoth he; 'despatch this boy, and we will speedily fall to work for the making of another.' 'Ha!' said she, 'so well as you speak at your own ease, you that are men: well, then, in the name of God, I'll do my best, seeing you will have it so; but would to God that it were cut off from you.' 'What?' said Grangousier. 'Ha!' said she, 'you are a good man indeed – you understand it well enough.' 'What, my member?' said he. 'Udzookers, if it please you, that shall be done instantly; bid 'em bring hither a knife.'

'Alas!' said she, 'the Lord forbid; I pray Jesus to forgive me; I did not say it from my heart: do it not any kind of harm, neither more nor less, for my speaking: but I am like to have work enough today, and all for your member; yet God bless both you and it.'

Transl. Robert Urquhart and P.A. Motteux

THOMAS DEKKER

From The Batchelars Banquet

The humour of a woman lying in childbed

THERE IS ANOTHER humor incident to a woman, when her husband sees her belly to grow big (though peraduenture by the help of some other friend) yet he perswades himselfe, it is a worke of his owne framing: and this breedes him new cares & troubles, for then must he trot up & down day & night, far, & neere, to get with great cost that his wife longs for: if she lets fall but a pin, he is diligent to take it up, least she by stouping should hurt her selfe. She on the other side is so hard to please, that it is a great hap when he fits her humor, in bringing home that which likes her, though he spare no paines nor cost to get it. And oft times through ease and plentie she growes so queasie stomackt, that she can brooke no common meates, but longs for strange and rare thinges, which whether they be to be had or no, yet she must have them, there is no remedie. She must have Cherries, though for a pound he pay ten Shillings, or greene Pescods at foure Nobles a peck: yea he must take a horse, and ride into the Countrey to get her greene Codlings[1], when they are scarcely so big as a Scotch button. In this trouble and vexation of mind and body, lives the silly man for six or seven months, all which time his wife doth nothing but complaine, and hee poore soule takes all the care, rising earely, going late to bed, and to be short, is faine to play both the husband and the huswife. But when the time drawes neere of her lying downe, then must he trudge to get Gossips, such as shee will appoint, or else all the fatte is in the fire. Consider then what cost and trouble it will bee to him to have all things fine against the Christning day, what store of Sugar, Biskets, Comphets and Carowayes, Marmilade, and marchpane, with all kind of sweete suckets,[2] and superfluous banquetting stuffe, with a hundred other odde

[1] *Codlings* – a type of apple.
[2] *Suckets* – sweetmeats.

and needlesse trifles which at that time must fill the pockets of daintie dames: Besides the charge of the midwife, she must have her nurse to attend and keepe her, who must make for her warme broaths, and costly caudels,[3] enough both for her selfe and her mistresse, being of the mind to fare no worse then she: If her mistresse be fed with partridge, plover, woodcocks, quailes, or any such like, the nurse must be partner with her in all these dainties: neither yet will that suffice, but during the whole month, she privily pilfers away the Sugar, the nutmegs and ginger, with all other spices that comes under her keeping, putting the poore man to such expense that in a whole yeare he can scarcely recover that one moneths charges.

[3] *Caudels*, or caudles – a mixture of barley and wine.

JOHN TAYLOR

From Taylor's Wit and Mirth

54

A MAN WAS riding through a village with his dog running by him, which dogs name was called Cuckold, leaping and frisking into every house hee past by where the doore was open. Whereupon the man, being afraid his dogge would bee lost, cals and whistles: here, here, Cuckold! to whom an old woman said: whom dost thou miscall? I would have thee know that no cuckold doth dwell in this house. Good woman, said the man, you mistake mee; I doe call nobody but my dog. Now out upon thee, thou misbeleeving knave, said shee, where learnest thou that manners to call a dog by a christian bodies name?

55

There was a lusty miller that in his younger daies had been much given to the flesh and the devill; so that not one pretty maid or female servant did or could bring grist to his mill to be grownd, but the knave miller would doe his best to undermine and blow up their chastity, and withal hee would bargaine with as many as his temptations overcame that, at his day of marriage, every one of them should give him a cake. In process of time the miller was married, and those aforesaid free-hearted wenches sent each one their cakes, to the number of 99. His wife the bride, who also went for a maid, did muse and aske what was the meaning of so many cakes. The miller told her the truth of all without any dissembling, to whom his wife answered: if I had beene so wise in bargaining as you have beene in your time, the young men of my acquaintance would have sent me 100 cheeses to eat with your cakes.

> This bawdy miller in a trap was catcht,
> Not onely married, but most fitly matcht:
> In this the proverb is approved plaine,
> What bread men breake, is broke to them againe.

115

A young fellow being newly married, having bin from home, came suddenly into his house, and found his wife at foule play with another man. The poor young cuckold ran presently, and told his wives father all the businesse, who replied thus: Sonne, I married her mother, and I tell thee plaine that thy wife seemes to bee her daughter in conditions as well as feature, for I have taken her mother many times in that manner, and no warning would serve her, till in the end age made her leave it, and so will thy wife doe, when she is old and past it.

PIETRO ARETINO

From I Ragionamenti *(The Dialogues)*

1 The lives of nuns

ANTONIA: Where did you go?

NANNA: To a crack through which could be seen a Sister who appeared to be the Mother of Discipline, the Aunt of the Bible, the Stepmother of the Old Testament, because of which I hardly dared watch her. She had twenty hairs on her head, like the bristles of a brush, all lousy, and perhaps a hundred wrinkles on her forehead; her eyebrows were grizzled and bushy; her eyes dripped something yellow.

ANTONIA: You've got good sight if you can spot nits from that distance.

NANNA: Listen to me. She had a slobbering mouth and a runny nose.
Her jaws were like a lousy man's bone comb with only two teeth left,
her lips were dried up and her chin pointed as a Genoese head,
graced with a few hairs, bristling like a lioness', and as hard, I
thought, as spines; her dugs looked like scrotums without testicles,
attached to the breast bone with cords; the stomach (mercy on me!)
was all shrivelled and shrunk with the navel turned inside out. It's
true, she had a garland of cabbage leaves round her pissing place
which looked as if they'd been on a scabby head for a month.

ANTONIA: Now St Nofrio wore a whole garland on his private parts.[1]

NANNA: So much the better. Her thighs were like twigs covered in
parchment, and her knees shook under her as if she was about to
fall, and while you imagine what her calves, her arms and feet were
like, I'll tell you that her finger nails were as long as the one
Roffiano wore on his little finger out of vanity, but hers were full of
muck. Now she was doubled up on the floor tracing stars, moons,
squares, circles, letters and a thousand other old charms with a piece
of charcoal. While she was doing this, she called on the demons by
various names which the devils themselves could not remember.
After going round the traced figures three times, she stood up
straight looking at the sky and muttering. Then she took up a little
mannikin of virgin wax into which needles were stuck (if you've ever
seen a mandrake, you've seen the figure) and she put it near enough
to the fire for it to feel it, turning it as one turns ortolans and
beccaficoes[2] to cook them without burning and she said:

> Fire, my own fire, devour
> The cruel man who flees my power.

And turning it with greater rage than that of those who give bread
to the hospital, she went on:

> May my great heart-break move
> Pity from the God of Love.

The image began to grow extremely hot. With her eyes fixed on
the ground, she said:

---

[1] On an inn sign.
[2] Fig-peckers – little birds that tasted very sweet because they lived on figs. They were eaten a great deal in the Middle Ages.

> Demon let my joy come nigh,
> Otherwise, spirit, let him die.

At the end of these verses, someone knocked at the door, panting like a man who's been caught stealing in the kitchen and who'd trusted his legs to save his shoulders a cudgelling. So she stopped her incantations at once and let him in.

ANTONIA: Naked, like that?

NANNA: Yes, naked. The poor man, compelled by black magic, as hunger is by famine, put his arms round her neck and kissing her as eagerly as if she'd been Rosa or Arcolana,[3] praised her beauty in the same words used by those who write sonnets to Lorenzina.[4] The awful vision bridled up and was transported. 'Was this flesh made to sleep alone?' she said.

ANTONIA: For shame!

NANNA: I shan't turn your stomach any more with the old witch. I don't know anything more, because I wouldn't look at any more. When the unlucky layman, barely old enough to shave, poked her on a stool, I did as Masino's cat who closes his eyes to avoid catching mice.

[3,4] Rosa, Arcolana and Lorenzina were three beautiful courtesans of the day.

2 The lives of married women

NANNA: Listen to this. One of the best women in the town had a husband who had more of a passion for gambling than a monkey has for cherries. His chief love was the game *primero*. A gang used to assemble in his house to play. Because he owned some land in the area, one of his labourer's wives, who was now a widow, used to come every fortnight to visit his wife, bringing some little things from her place, such as dried figs, nuts, olives, baked eggs and other goods. She'd stay a fair while, then return home. One time, on a half-holiday, she brought a collection of fine snails and twenty five plums or so, arranged on catmint in her little willow basket, and came to stop with the wife. The weather got worse. A wind came up, accompanied by rain so heavy that she was forced to stay the night. The lazy rake of a husband found out. (He was in the habit of saying anything that came into his mind in front of his wife.) Being a noted drinker, always full of jokes and wanting to be thought a good sort, he decided to fix up a *thirty-one*[1] for the widow. He talked about it to the gang that was in his house playing, which made them listen and roar with laughter; and it was fixed that they all return after dinner. He said to his wife: 'Put our labourer's widow to sleep in the room over the granary.' And she replied that she'd do that and sat down to dinner with him. The countrywoman sat at the foot of the table, blushing like a bunch of roses; and a little while after dinner, the troop returned. The husband retired with his wife, advising her to go to bed, and the widow likewise. The wife, who knew what the layabout was up to, said to herself: 'I've heard it said that whoever has a good time once, will never want. My husband, who has dishonour in place of honour, wants to ransack the shop and wardrobe of our labourer's widow, but I've decided to try out what a *thirty-one* is, what the nasty men really get up to and what sort of night-cap my lazy husband's gang are preparing for the good woman.' Saying this, she installed the widow in her own bed and herself in the one she'd made up for her. The husband came along the long corridors, puffing and blowing as he tried to hold his breath back. His friends, who were to have a share of the sweets after him, unable to hide their laughter, let rip, but so that they wouldn't be heard, they smothered the sound by putting hands over each others' mouths. (One of the *thirty-one* told me everything that happened. He used to come and give me a tumble from time to time.) The head of the gang of tilters came up breathing heavily to her (she'd never longed so much for anything in her life) and laid hold of her by the hair in a way that seemed to say, 'I know you won't escape me!' She made as if she had just woken up frightened and pretended she wanted to get up. He held her to him with all his strength, forced her legs wide apart with his knees and posted his letter. As he did it, he realised it was his own wife, about as much as one notices the leaves on the fig tree that gives one shade. Feeling him shaking her plum tree, not as a husband, but as a lover, she must have said to herself, 'The glutton devours other people's bread with appetite, but rejects that of his own home.' To sum up – he spent his load twice, and turning to his friends, wreathed in smiles, he said: 'What a bit of stuff! What a good lay! Her flesh is as firm as a lady's,' – in short, that her arse smelt like mint and pimpernels. As soon as he'd said that, he gave the signal to the next man, who, with the greed of a monk running for his broth, falls to feeding on the beef, as the Romanesco says. The nod was given to the third, who ran to the feast like fish to a worm. What made them laugh was his letting three thunder claps without lightning while his

[1] A gangbang.

pike was swimming in the reservoir. He brought the sweat to her temples and made her say: 'There's no discretion in this *thirty-one*!' Not to keep you till night with this and that – they did it to her in all fashions, all ways, all manners, by every method and in every wise (as Madrema-non-vuole'd[2] say). She began, with the twentieth one, to act like cats who screw and mew at the same time. In the meantime, one of them, who'd had both bag and pipes and found a good lodging in both for snails without shells, held back for a moment, then stuck it in behind, moving it this way and that: 'Madonna,' he said, 'wipe your noses and smell the capers! 'While he was talking, the queue stood listening to this speech, waiting to get at the girl in place of their friend, just as artisans, boys and peasants, on Maundy Thursday, Good Friday and Holy Saturday, watch the newly shriven penitent who's made his confession; and while they were waiting, more than one of them shook his dog from head to tail till it spat out its soul. In the end, four of those who'd waited till last, more stupid than wise, not having the guts to swim without a vessel in that mess of pottage, lit the stump of a torch, with which they used to give light to those who lost their money at cards and went home blaspheming, and, in spite of the leader of the *thirty-one*, went into the room where his wife was lying, in grease down to her knees. Seeing she was found out, assuming the look of a Ponte-Sisto girl, she said: 'It's a fantasy that came to me from hearing every day that such-and-such has had a *thirty-one*, and another one another. I wanted to see the *thirty-one*, face to face, whatever came of it.' The husband made a virtue out of necessity and answered: 'And what do you think of it, wife?' 'Nothing but good,' she said. And not being able to hold on any longer, after such a fill-up, she threw herself on the privy and let go like an overstuffed Abbot unloading all the stew from his belly, thus consigning to the earthly limbo twenty-seven unborn souls.

Transl. F.P.

[2] The nickname of a celebrated Roman courtesan.

WILLIAM CORKINE

Away, away! call back what you have said
When you did vow to live and die a maid:
Oh if you knew what chance to them befell
That dance about with bobtail apes in hell,[1]
Yourself your virgin girdle would divide
And put aside the maiden veil that hides
The chiefest gem of nature; and would lie
Prostrate to every peasant that goes by,
Rather than undergo such shame: no tongue can tell
What injury is done to maids in hell.

[1] There was a tradition that those who died virgins (of either sex) would lead apes in hell.

THE
RESTORATION
AND THE
EIGHTEENTH
CENTURY

Glossary for poems in this section

Pintle or *tarse* – prick
Swive – fuck
Cods – balls
Buboes – syphilitic swellings in the groin
Wame – womb

More unusual words are glossed separately on the texts themselves.

G. R. QUAIFE

From Wanton Wenches and Wayward Wives: Peasants and Illicit Sex in Early Seventeenth-Century England

Mary Combe

MAN AFTER MAN among the drinkers in her inn complained that she 'put her hand into his breeches to feel what he had' and then proclaimed that 'if it were ready to stand she was ready for him'. On the highway she was equally direct. She ridiculed one man because 'his prick would not stand' and claimed she had brought some starch and 'would draw it out and starch it, to make it stand'. She often 'layed her down in the highway between Axbridge and Crosse, and called to all persons passing, by spreading her legs abroad, saying: "Come play with my cunt and make my husband a cuckold."' Yet Mary Combe's activities are not that of the normal village slut. She provided more than her body. She deliberately encouraged and organised activities and sentiments opposed to traditional values. In 1653 she organised a drinking orgy to which only cuckolds and cuckold-makers, the outcasts of respectable society, were invited. When a respectable villager was ill, Mary visited him and tried to tempt him in front of his wife. She asked him 'whether he was able to do her a good turn. And more plainly whether he would .x.x. her or not, which is unseemly to write'. Before his wife could remove her she took up the man's underclothes and threw them in the fire. Whereas all the evidence points to sexual intercourse taking place almost exclusively by the male lying on top of the woman, Mary Combe was renowned for plucking up her coats and smock and sitting astride any man she found lying on his back. She wandered around the parish naked – another uncommon habit.

She delighted in shocking the godly. Several witnesses complained that she 'indecently would force an honest man to occupy her, spreading of her legs abroad and showing her commodity'. Another recalled that 'coming to her house she shut the door and would force him to be naught with her'. Yet again another found her molesting his apprentice, while a fourth subjected to her charms, 'being sickly and not subject to idleness got from her'. A respectable tradesman was confronted in his shop by the taunt: 'thou cuckold go into thy wife for she is fucking with William Fry'. The resultant disruption to the lives of two respectable families was indicated in his subsequent comment – that it 'caused a debate for a long time between me and my wife and likewise he and his wife'.

DANIEL DEFOE

From Roxana, or The Fortunate Mistress

AMY WAS DRESSING me one morning, for now I had two maids, and Amy was my chambermaid. 'Dear madam,' says Amy, 'what! ain't you with child yet?' 'No, Amy,' says I, 'nor any sign of it.' 'Law, madam,' says Amy, 'what have you been doing? Why, you have been married a year and a half; I warrant you master would have got me with child twice in that time.' 'It may be so, Amy,' says I, 'let him try, can't you?' 'No,' says Amy, 'you'll forbid it now; before, I told you he should with all my heart, but I won't now, now he's all your own.' 'Oh,' says I, 'Amy, I'll freely give you my consent, it will be nothing at all to me; nay, I'll put you to bed to him myself one night or other if you are willing.' 'No, madam, no,' says Amy, 'not now he's yours.'

'Why, you fool you,' says I, 'don't I tell you I'll put you to bed to him myself?'

'Nay, nay,' says Amy, 'if you put me to bed to him, that's another case; I believe I shall not rise again very soon.'

'I'll venture that, Amy,' says I.

After supper that night, and before we were risen from table, I said to him, Amy being by, 'Hark ye, Mr —, do you know that you are to lie with Amy tonight?' 'No, not I,' says he; but turns to Amy, 'Is it so, Amy?' says he. 'No, sir,' says she. 'Nay, don't say no, you fool; did not I promise to put you to bed to him?' But the girl said no still, and it passed off.

At night, when we came to go to bed, Amy came into the chamber to undress me, and her master slipped into bed first. Then I began and told him all that Amy had said about my not being with child, and of her being with child twice in that time. 'Ay, Mrs Amy,' says he, 'I believe so too; come hither and we'll try.' But Amy did not go. 'Go, you fool,' says I, 'can't you; I freely give you both leave.' But Amy would not go. 'Nay, you whore,' says I, 'you said if I would put you to bed you would with all your heart'; and with that I sat her down, pulled off her stockings and shoes, and all her clothes, piece by piece, and led her to the bed to him. 'Here,' says I, 'try what you can do with your maid Amy.' She pulled back a little, would not let me pull off her clothes at first, but it was hot weather and she had not many clothes on, and particularly no stays on; and at last, when she saw I was in earnest, she let me do what I would; so I fairly stripped her, and then I threw open the bed and thrust her in.

I need say no more; this is enough to convince anybody that I did not think him my husband, and that I had cast off all principle and all modesty and had effectually stifled conscience.

Amy, I dare say, began now to repent, and would fain have got out of bed again, but he said to her, 'Nay, Amy, you see your mistress has put you to bed, 'tis all her doing, you must blame her.' So he held her fast, and the wench being naked in bed with him, 'twas too late to look back, so she lay still and let him do what he would with her.

APHRA BEHN

From The Town Fop, or Sir Timothy Tawdrey

A bawdy house.
Enter Mrs Driver and Betty Flauntit.

FLAUNT: Driver, prithee call for a Glass, that I may set my self in order, before I go up; for really my Knight has not been at home all this Night, and I am so confus'd –

Enter one with a Glass, and two Wenches.

Lord Mrs Driver, I wonder you shou'd send for me, when other Women are in Company; you know, of all things in the World, I hate Whores, they are the pratingst leudest poor Creatures in Nature; and I wou'd not for any thing, Sir Timothy shou'd know that I keep Company, 'twere enough to lose him.

MRS DRIV: Truly Mrs Flauntit, this young Squire that you were sent to for, has two or three Persons more with him that must be accommodated too.

FLAUNT: Driver, tho I do recreate my self a little sometimes, yet you know I value my Reputation and Honour.

JENNY: Mrs Driver, why shou'd you send for us where Flauntit is? a stinking proud Flirt, who because she has a tawdry Petticoat, I warrant you, will think her self so much above us, when if she were set out in her own natural Colours, and her original Garments, wou'd be much below us in Beauty.

MRS DRIV: Look ye, Mrs Jenny, I know you, and I know Mrs Flauntit; but 'tis not Beauty or Wit that takes now-a-days; the Age is alter'd since I took upon me this genteel Occupation: but 'tis a fine Petticoat, right points, and clean Garments, that does me Credit, and takes the Gallant, tho on a stale Woman. And again, Mrs Jenny, she's kept, and Men love as much for Malice as for Lechery, as they call it. Oh 'tis a great Mover to Joy, as they say, to have a Woman that's kept.

JEN: Well! Be it so, we may arrive to that excellent Degree of Cracking, to be kept too one day.

MRS DRIV: Well, well, get yourselves in order to go up to the Gentlemen.

FLAUNT: Driver, what art thou talking to these poor Creatures? Lord, how they stink of Paint and Pox, faugh —

MRS DRIV: They were only complaining that you that were kept, shou'd intrude upon the Privileges of the Commoners.

FLAUNT: Lord, they think there are such Joys in Keeping, when I vow, Driver, after a while, a Miss has as painful a Life as a Wife; our Men drink, stay out late, and whore, like any Husbands.

DRIV: But I hope in the Lord, Mrs Flauntit, yours is no such Man; I never saw him, but I hear he's under decent Correction.

FLAUNT: Thou art mistaken, Driver, I can keep him within no moderate Bounds without Blows; but for his filthy Custom of Wenching, I have almost broke him of that — but prithee, Driver, who are these Gentlemen?

DRIV: Truly, I know not; but they are young, and fine as Princes: two of 'em were disguis'd in masking Habits last Night, but they have sent 'em away this Morning, and they are free as Emperors — One of 'em has lost a Thousand Pound at Play, and never repin'd at it; one's a Knight, and I believe his Courage is cool'd, for he has ferreted my Maids over and over to Night — But 'tis the fine, young, handsom Squire that I design you for.

FLAUNT: No matter for his Handsomness, let me have him that has most Money.

[*Exeunt*

From Familiar Letters

*A letter to the Earl of Kildare, dissuading him
from marrying Moll Howard*

My Lord,
We pity such as are by Tempest lost,
And those by Fortune's blind Disposal crost;
But when Men see, and may the Danger shun,
Yet headlong into certain Ruin run:
To pity such, must needs be Ridicule;
Do not (my Lord) be that unpity'd Fool.
There's a report, which round the Town is spread,
The fam'd *Moll Howard* you intend to Wed;

If it be true, my Lord, then guard your Head:
Horns, Horns, by wholesale, will adorn your Brows,
If e'r you make that rampant Whore your Spouse.
Think on the lewd Debauches of her Life;
Then tell me, if she's fit to be your Wife.
She that to quench her lustful, hot Desire,
Has Kiss'd with Dukes, Lords, Knights, and Country Squire;
Nay, Grooms and Footmen have been claw'd off by her.

Whoring has all her Life-time been her Trade,
And *Dorset* says, she is an exc'lent Baud:
But finding both will not defray Expence,
She lately is become an *Evidence*;
Swears against all that won't her Lust supply,
And says, they're false as Hell to Monarchy.

You had a Wife; but, rest her Soul, she's dead,
By whom your Lordship by the Nose was led:
And will you run into that Noose agen,
To be the greatest Monster among Men?
Think on the Horns that will adorn your Head,
And the Diseases that will fill your Bed:
Pox upon Pox, most horrid and most dire!
And Ulcers filled with Hell's Eternal Fire.

Forbear therefore, and call your Senses home;
Let Reason Love's blind Passion overcome:
For, if you make this base Report once true,
You'l wound your Honour, Purse, and Body too.

CHARLES SACKVILLE, LORD BUCKHURST AND SIXTH EARL OF DORSET

On Dolly Chamberlain, a Sempstress in the New Exchange

Dolly's beauty and art
Have so hemm'd in my heart
That I cannot resist the charm:
In revenge I will stitch
Up the hole next her breech
With a needle as long as my arm.

From A Faithful Catalogue of the Most Eminent Ninnies

On John Sheffield, 3rd earl of Mulgrave

How haughtily he cries: 'Page, fetch a whore;
Damn her, she's ugly; rascal, fetch me more;
Bring in that black-ey'd wench; woman, come near;
Rot you, you draggled bitch, what is't you fear?'
Trembling she comes, and with as little flame,
As he for the dear part from whence he came.
But by the help of an assisting thumb
Squeezes his chitterling into her bum;
And if it prove a straight, well-spincter'd arse,
Perhaps it rears a little his feeble tarse.

Duel of the Crabs

In Milford Lane[1] near to St Clement's steeple
There liv'd a nymph kind to all Christian people.
A nymph she was whose comely mien and stature,
Whose height of eloquence and every feature
Struck through the hearts of city and of Whitehall,
And when they pleas'd to court her, did 'em right all.
Under her beauteous bosom there did lie
A belly smooth as any ivory.
Yet nature to declare her various art
Had plac'd a tuft in one convenient part;
No park with smoothest lawn or highest wood
Could e'er compare with this admir'd abode.
Here all the youth of England did repair
To take their pleasure and to ease their care.

[1] Milford Lane was a mean street opposite St Clement Dane's – a sanctuary for debtors. It ran from the Strand to the Thames.

The next two poems were written as letters between Lord Buckhurst (Dorset) and his friend, Etherege.

A Letter from the Lord Buckhurst
to Mr George Etherege

Dreaming last night on Mrs Farley,[1]
My prick was up this morning early;
And I was fain without my gown
To rise in th' cold to get him down.
Hard shift, alas, but yet a sure,
Although it be no pleasing cure.

[1] *Mrs Farley* – Elizabeth Farley, alias Weaver, actress in the King's Company, 1660–1665.

Of old the fair Egyptian slattern,
For luxury that had no pattern,
To fortify her Roman swinger,
Instead of nutmeg, mace and ginger,
Did spice his bowels (as story tells)
With warts of rocks and spawn of shells.
It had been happy for her Grace,
Had I been in the rascal's place;
I, who do scorn that any stone
Shou'd raise my pintle but my own,
Had laid her down on every couch
And sav'd her pearl and diamond brooch
Until her hot-tail'd Majesty,
Being happily reclaim'd by me
From all her wild expensive ways,
Had worn her gems on holidays.
But since her cunt has long done itching,
Let us discourse of modern bitching.
    I must entreat you by this letter,
To inquire for whores, the more the better.
Hunger makes any man a glutton;
If Roberts, Thomas, Mrs Dutton,
Or any other bawds of note,
Inform of a fresh petticoat,
Inquire, I pray, with friendly care,
Where their respective lodgings are.
Some do compare a man t' a bark –
A pretty metaphor, pray mark –
And with a long and tedious story,
Will all the tackling lay before ye:
The sails are hope, the masts desire,
Till they the gentlest reader tire.
But howsoe'er they keep a pudder,
I'm sure the pintle is the rudder:

The pow'rful rudder, which of force
To town will shortly steer my course.
And if you do not there provide
A port where I may safely ride,
Landing in haste, in some foul creek,
'Tis ten to one I spring a leak.

Next, I must make it my request,
If you have any interest,
Or can be any means discover
Some lamentable rhyming lover,
Who shall in numbers harsh and vile,
His mistress 'Nymph' or 'Goddess' style,
Send all his labors down to me
By the first opportunity.

Or any Knights of your Round Table,
To other scribblers formidable,
Guilty themselves of the same crime,
Dress nonsense up in ragged rhyme,
As once a week they seldom fail,
Inspir'd by love and gridiron ale.

Or any paltry poetry,
Tho' from the university,
Who when the King and Queen were there,
Did both their wit and learning spare,
And have, I hope, endeavor'd since
To make the world some recompense.
Such damn'd fustian when you meet,
Be not too rash or indiscreet,
Tho' they can plead no just excuses,
To put 'em to their proper uses –
The fatal privy or the fire,
Their nobler foe – at my desire
Restrain your natural profuseness,
And spare 'em tho' you have a looseness.

GEORGE ETHEREGE

Mr Etherege's Answer

As crafty harlots use to shrink
From lechers dozed with sleep and drink,
When they intend to make up pack
By filching sheets or shirt from back,
So were you pleas'd to steal away
From me, whilst on your bed I lay;
But long you had not been departed
When pinch'd with cold from thence I started;
Where missing you I stamp'd and star'd,
Like Bacon when he wak'd and heard
His Brazen Head in vain had spoke,
And saw it lie in pieces broke.
Sighing, I to my chamber make,
Where ev'ry limb was stiff as stake,
Unless poor pintle, which did feel
Like slimy skin of new-stripped eel,
Or pudding that mischance had got,
And spent itself half in the pot.
With care I cleans'd the sneaking varlet
Which late had been in pool of harlot;
But neither shirt nor water cou'd
Remove the stench of lech'rous mud.
The Queen of Love from sea did spring,
Whence the best cunts still smell like ling.
But sure this damn'd notorious bitch
Was made o' th' foam of Jane Shore's[1] ditch;
Or else her cunt could never stink
Like pump that's foul, or nasty sink.

---

[1] *Jane Shore's ditch* – Shoreditch, 'a ditch of loathsome scent' according to a ballad in Percy's *Reliques*.

When this was done, to bed I went,
Where that whole day in sleep I spent;
But the next morning, fresh and gay
As citizen on holiday,
I wander'd in the spacious Town,
Amongst the bawds of best renown,
Making enquiry far and near
To find out fresh and wholesome gear.
To Temple I a visit made –
Temple, the beauty of her trade!
The only bawd that ever I
For want of whore could occupy.
She made me friends with Mrs Cuffley,
Whom we indeed had us'd too roughly,
For by a gentler way I found
The nymph would fuck under ten pound.
So resty jades that scorn to stir,
Tho' oft provok'd by whip and spur,
By milder usage may be got
To fall into their wonted trot.
  But what success I further had,
And what discoveries good and bad
I made by roving up and down,
I'll tell you when you come to town.
  Further, I have obey'd your motion,
Tho' much provok'd by pill and potion,
And sent you down some paltry rhymes,
The greatest grievance of our times,
When such as Nature never made
For poets daily do invade
Wit's empire, both the stage and press –
And what is worse, with good success.

A further poem from the series:

Mr Etherege's Answer to a Letter from Lord Buckhurst

So soft and amorously you write
Of cunt and prick, the cunt's delight,
That were I still in lantern sweating,
Swallowing of bolus or a-spitting,[1]
I should forgive each injury
The pocky whores have offered me,
And only of my fate complain
Because I must from cunt abstain.
The powerful cunt! whose very name
Kindles in me an amorous flame!
Begins to make my pintle rise,
And long again to fight Love's prize!
Forgetful of those many scars
Which he has gotten in those wars.
This shows Love's chiefest magic lies
In women's cunts, not in their eyes:
There Cupid does his revels keep,
There lovers all their sorrows steep;
For having once but tasted that,
Their mysteries are quite forgot.
This may suffice to let you know
That I to cunt am not a foe,
Though you are pleased to think me so;
'Tis strange his zeal should be in suspicion
Who dies a martyr for's religion.
    But now to give you an account
Of Cuffley, that whore paramount!

---

[1] Cures for venereal disease.

Cuffley! whose beauty warms the age.
And fills our youth with love and rage,
Who like fierce wolves pursue the game,
While secretly the lecherous dame
With some choice gallant takes her flight
And in a corner fucks all night.
Then the next morning we all hunt
To find whose fingers smell of cunt,
With jealousy and envy moved
Against the man that was beloved.
Whilst you to Echo teach her name,
Thus it becomes the voice of fame
In every corner of the Town.
We here proclaim her high renown
Whilst you within some neighbouring grove
Indite the story of your love,
And with your penknife keen and bright,
On stately trees your passion write,
So that each nymph that passes through
Must envy her and pity you.
We at the Fleece or at the Bear,
With good case knife, well whet on stair
(A gentle weapon, made to feed
Mankind and not to let him bleed)
A thousand amorous fancies scrape.
There's not a pewter dish can scape
Without her name or arms which are
The same that Love himself does bear.

Here one, to show you love's no glutton,
In the midst of supper leaves his mutton,
And on his greasy plate, with care,
Carves the bright image of the fair.

Another, though a drunken sot,
Neglects his wine and on the pot

A band of naked Cupids draws,
With pricks no bigger than wheat straws.
Then on a nasty candlestick
One figures Love's hieroglyphic,
A couchant cunt and rampant prick.
And that the sight may more inflame,
The lookers-on subscribe her name:
Cuffley! – her sex's pride and shame.
There's not a man but does discover
By some such action he's her lover.

But now 'tis time to give her over,
And let your Lordship know you are
The mistress that employs our care.
Your absence makes us melancholy,
Nor drink nor cunt can make us jolly,
Unless we've you within our arms,
In whom there dwells diviner charms.
Then quit with speed your pensive grove
And here in Town pursue your love;
Where at your coming you shall find
Your servants glad, your mistress kind,
All things devoted to your mind.

MARY DELARIVIER MANLEY

From The Royal Mischief

Homais, the central character, a wicked but sympathetically portrayed *femme fatale*, is confined in the Castle of Phasia, while her husband, the elderly, impotent Prince of Libardian, is at war. She is in love with Levan Dadian, the Prince of Colchis. In this scene, Ismael, an ambitious army officer and younger brother of the Chief Vizier, is trying to blackmail Homais, who was once his lover, back into bed with him.

ISMAEL: But must your first adorer have no favours?
  Will he not be allowed sometimes a taste,
  Some small remains of former heavenly bounty?
  Methinks you should not, sure, so far forget
  Those moments, sacred to our love and me,
  When close you grasped me – at your new found joys
  An unbeliever till you proved the wonder,
  And felt the mighty ecstasy approach –
  Then swore, whatever royal lover should
  Succeed, you never would forget the first
  Discoverer.

HOMAIS: Nor do I, Ismael, for I'll serve your fortunes,
  But for my heart, the Prince is there already,
  Now in my arms should I receive another,
  The load would be unpleasing.

ISMAEL: I'll give you leave to fancy I am him,
  For while I press you close, and feel your charms,
  No circumstance can make the joy uneasy.

HOMAIS: Oh, did you know the difference
  Between a new-born passion, and a former!
  Nothing remains but memory and wonder,
  Not the least warmth of kind desire or joy.
  Nay, scarce can we believe, or make that faith
  A miracle, how we could dote, as they reproach we did,
  How love so much, that which at present seems unlovely.

ISMAEL: When time has worn the gaudy gilding off,
   The sacred varnish that your liking gives,
   He will then seem forlorn and stale as me,
   An object less for love than wonder.

HOMAIS: Impossible! He's here for evermore,
   Fixed in my heart immovable, immortally,
   The lord of all its changes and desires.
   Nor can revolving time present my eyes
   An excellence, to tempt their faith from him,
   The greatest excellence.

ISMAEL: Madam, you speak as eager lovers use,
   Show me but one who, tho' inconstant as
   The rising winds or flowing seas, still
   Swears not fealty to the reigning object,
   Nay, fancies he shall surely keep it, too,
   Tho' he has broke ten thousand vows before,
   Took new desires, new faith for every fair,
   And loathed as much as ever he had liked.
   'Tis one great point of love, first to impose
   Upon our own belief, so self-deceived
   Are better fitted to deceive another.

IV, i

Homais's death scene

As LEVAN is embracing her, THE PRINCE OF LIBARDIAN enters with his sword drawn, runs at her, and kills her.

HOMAIS: Ah, traitor, Hellhound, thou hast done thy worst.

PRINCE OF LIBARDIAN: Thus I've discharged the debt I owed.
   Stretch Acmat's tortures to their utmost length.
   Her minion, Ismael, whom she sent to take my life
   Is by my subjects packed to Hell before her.
   Room, ye infernal powers, for three more vile
   Than ever flamed below!

HOMAIS: Thou dotard, impotent in all but mischief,
   How could'st thou hope, at such an age, to keep
   A handsome wife? Thy own, thy devil will
   Tell thee 'tis impossible.

Thus I dash thee with my gore,
And may it scatter unthought plagues around thee,
Curses more numerous than the ocean's sand,
Much more inveterate than woman's malice,
And but with never-ending time expiring.

PRINCE OF LIBARDIAN: Rail on, thou can'st deceive no more.

HOMAIS: O thou too faintly lover! can'st thou hear him?
That coward Ismael, too, who reaped my foremost joys,
What an effeminate troupe have I to deal with.
I'll meet and sink him in the hottest lake,
Nay, plunge to keep him down. Oh, I shall reign
A welcome ghost, the fiends will hug my royal mischief.
Grim Osman and his Princess grace my train,
One sent by poison, t'other by new fires.
But thou, my darling evil,
When fate had nothing else to do but join us,
When expectation beat the loudest march,
And full-blown joys within an instant of us,
'Tis more than life can bear to be defeated.
Be thou a shade and let us mingle then,
There feast at large what we but tasted here.
Thus with my utmost force I'll bear thee with me,
Thus strangle thy loved neck, thus die together,
But, oh, a curse on fate and my expiring strength.

She reaches to strangle LEVAN, *but, in the effort, dies.*

v, i

LADY CATHERINE DYER

Epitaph on the Monument of Sir William Dyer at Colmworth, 1641

My dearest dust, could not thy hasty day
Afford thy drowszy patience leave to stay
One hower longer: so that we might either
Sate up, or gone to bedd together?
But since thy finisht labor hath possest
Thy weary limbs with early rest,
Enjoy it sweetly: and thy widdowe bride
Shall soone repose her by thy slumbring side.
Whose business, now, is only to prepare
My nightly dress, and call to prayre:
Mine eyes wax heavy and ye day growes cold.
Draw, draw ye closed curtaynes: and make room:
My deare, my dearest dust; I come, I come.

MARY PIX

From The Innocent Mistress

Sir Francis Wildlove, man-about-town, is in his room dressing when his friend Beaùmont, an honest country gentleman, enters:

SIR FRANCIS: Welcome, dear friend, I pr'ythee pardon my omission, faith 'twas business that could not be left to other hands.

BEAUMONT: Women, I suppose, and that excuse I know a man of your kidney thinks almighty.

SIR FRANCIS: Even so. Well, by my life, I am heartily glad to see you. Why, thou hast been an age confined to barren fields and senseless groves, or conversation stupid and dull as they. How can'st thou waste thy youth, happy youth, the very quintessence of life, from London, this dear epitome of pleasure?

BEAUMONT: Because excess of drinking cloys my stomach, and impudence in women absolutely turns it. Then I hate the vanity of dress, and fluttering, where eternal noise and nonsense reigns. This considered, what should I do here?

SIR FRANCIS: Not much, in troth.

BEAUMONT: But you, my friend, run the career your appetite directs, taste all those pleasures I despise. You can tell me what humour's most in fashion, what ruling whim, and how the ladies are.

SIR FRANCIS: Why, faith, there's no great alteration. The money is indeed very much scarcer, yet, what perhaps you'll think a wonder, dressing and debauchery increases. As for the damosels, three sorts make a bushel, and will be uppermost. First, there's your common jilts will oblige everybody.

BEAUMONT: These are monsters, sure.

SIR FRANCIS: You may call 'em what you please, but they are very plentiful, I promise you. The next is your kept mistress, she's a degree modester, if not kind to each, appears in her dress like quality, whilst her ogling eyes, and too frequent debauches discovers her the younger sister only to the first.

BEAUMONT: This I should hate for ingratitude.

SIR FRANCIS: The third is not a whore, but a brisk, airy, noisy coquette, that lives upon treating. One spark has her to the play, another to the park, a third to Windsor, a fourth to some other place of diversion. She has not the heart to grant 'em all favours, for that's their design at the bottom of the treats, and they have not the heart to marry her, for that's her design, too, poor creature. So perhaps a year, or it may be two, the gaudy butterfly flutters round the kingdom, then if a foolish cit does not take compassion, sneaks into a corner, dies an old maid, despised and forgotten. The men that fit those ladies are your rake, your cully, and your beau.

BEAUMONT: I hope Sir Francis Wildlove has more honour than to find a mistress among such creatures.

SIR FRANCIS: Gad, honest, honourable Ned, I must own I have a fling at all. Sometimes I think it worth my while to make a keeper jealous; frequently treat the coquette, till either she grows upon me, or I grow weary of her. Then 'tis but saying a rude thing, she quarrels, I fly to the next bottle, and there forever drown her remembrance.

I, i

ROBERT GOULD

To My Lord Chamberlain at Bath

This healing stream, this Aesculapian spring,
That from all parts does such a confluence bring,
Of lame and blind, of sound and sick and sore,
Of knave and fool, and worse, of baud and whore;
Tho' wonders it is sometimes said to do,
Does yet confine those wonders to a few.
Yet vainly all expect to have a share,
The rotten wou'd be sound, the foul be fair;
The wrinkled beldam wou'd new pleasure prove,
And, like a punk of twenty, chatters love.

The stale debilitated lover here
Expects relief, and gazing on the fair,
Feels heat return; but 'tis so false a fire,
It never reaches further than desire.
How madly does that man his hours employ
That still does wish and never can enjoy?
That past the fact, is yet not past the fau't,
And damns himself by being lewd in thought?

Then for the coxcombs (not to name their cloaths,
Their dancing, raffling, drinking, noise and oaths)
Their treats and entertainments make it plain,
They come alike to be reliev'd in vain.
It never was presum'd that bathing yet
Reform'd a fool, and made him grow a wit.
Tho' thousands have been eas'd of cramps and pains,
Of palsies, itches, botches, scurfs and blains,
It fails when the distemper's in the brains.

But tho' the fops are thus deceiv'd we find
The fruitful stream to youthful ladies kind;
Who with their open breasts and swimming bowls,
(As others angle gudgeons) fish for fools;
Here still at hand, and careless of their fate,
You'll find a hundred biting at a bait:

And oft indeed, the bait is not so small,
But there's enough to satisfy 'em all.
This for the glory of the water makes,
Which hence it's kind prolifick nature takes.
Oft has the lady (her good man at home,
Invoking heav'n to unseal her steril womb)
Here first conceiv'd; then to her husband flown
With hast, to keep the theft from being known,
A fortnights time in reck'ning breaks no squares,
Or, if it shou'd, 'twere a bad day for heirs.

But now some lady, that's ador'd the most,
Is chosen out to be that morning's toast:
For her the musick plays; the health's go round
The Toast! the Toast! – and stun us with the sound:
She all the while, kind nymph, the gallery plies,
And with admiring meets admiring eyes;
Proud of the honour thus to rule the roast
She swims along the bath - the Toast, the Toast!
Pity they wou'd not one step higher go,
And drink the liquor it was soakt in too.
Who wou'd comply with such a nauseous fashion,
And rather not, with Lear, call out in passion
For civit to refresh the imagination?

But while my mind thus freely I express,
I have forgot to whom I make address.
Pardon, my Lord, that thus I entertain
Your ears with things ridiculous and vain,
And idly tread the Satyr's thorny ways,
When Dorset was so just a theme for praise.

From The Play-House, a Satyr

The Duchess of Cleveland

(of whom Rochester says 'Full forty men a day provided
for this whore,/ Yet, like a bitch, she wags her tail for
more.')

How often Cleveland, hast thou here been found
By a lascivious herd encompass'd round?
How often have you hence retir'd, and lain
A leash of stallions breathless on the plain?
Then back return'd; another leash enjoy'd,
Another after that, when those were cloy'd;
And so elsewhere, and here, has half your life
                        employ'd.

Zara, an actress

Truly said Joe, as now the matter goes,
What I shall speak must be beneath the rose.
Her mother was a common strumpet known,
Her father half the rabble of the town.
Begot by casual and promiscuous lust,
She still retains the same promiscuous gust.
For birth into a suburb celler hurl'd,
The strumpet came up stairs into the world.

At twelve she'd freely in coition join,
And far surpass'd the honours of her line.
As her conception was a complication,
So its produce, alike did serve the nation;
Till by a black, successive course of ils,
She reach'd the noble post which now she fills;
Where, Messalina-like, she treads the stage,
And all enjoys, but nothing can asswage.

From The Step-Mother, a Satyr

A young wife married to an old man

In her old dotard's feeble arms she lies,
And kindly with his impotence complies,
And when his vigor's ready to expire,
Molds his cold clay, and warms it to desire,
And blows the ember's till she finds the fire;

From To Mr Knight

London manners

In getting bastards half your town's emply'd,
And 'tis as certain that they're next destroy'd:
No privy's free; where they in ordure lie,
Yet sweeter than their mother's infamy.

From The Rival Sisters, *or* The Violence of Love

Gerardo, an old man who's in love with Catalina's woman, Ansilva, takes her to his room to give her some medicine when she pretends to feel ill. While he's searching she delivers the following monologue.

ANSILVA: I have rais'd his expectation, but on purpose indeed to deceive it, if I keep him keen, perhaps he may cut thro' his discretion to marriage. Heav'n! what monsters are we forc'd to embrace, for convenience? His closet's a perfect apothecary's shop, furnish'd with all sorts of drugs, and his conduct indeed has made it necessary – He, perhaps, gives the disease to his housekeeper; she stoops as low to the horses' heels, and transmits it to the groom; he conveys it from the stable to the landry, and from thence it goes back with the clean linnen to their master. So that the pox in his family, like the blood in his veins, is in a perpetual circulation.

IV, i

TOM D'URFEY

From the Prologue *to* The Rival Sisters

The Prologue written by D'Urfey to Robert Gould's play describes the sort of scenes and characters that are likely to endear a play to the audience of the day.

Or else how Master Justice, and his spouse,
Rated their eldest daughter, splayfoot blowse,
With mutton fist, broad face, and sorrel hair,
And chuffy cheeks, red-streak'd like Kath'rine Pear,
For letting John the Butler late prevail
O'er maiden honour for a tost and ale –
A scene like that had took, it cou'd not fail.

Or how the red-nos'd elder us'd to cackle,   [*These 3 lines in*
With holy vigour and spiritual tackle.   *a canting tone*]
Got babe of grace in porch of tabernacle.
This now had brought a harvest to us players,
Certain to please you that ne'er go to prayers.
Or did the play expose some rattling squire,
That with his fox-hounds flounders through the mire.
And, after daily teizing of his life,
At night with stubble beard halts home and scrubs his wife,
Who thus caress'd by her rough bristl'd dear,
Dreams of a hedgehog, and turns off for fear.

WILLIAM WYCHERLEY

From The Country Wife

The scene is Horner's lodgings.
Enter Horner, and Quack following him at a distance.

HORN: [*aside*] A quack is as fit for a pimp, as a midwife for a bawd; they
are still but in their way, both helpers of nature. [*Aloud.*] Well, my
dear doctor, hast thou done what I desired?

QUACK: I have undone you for ever with the women, and reported you
throughout the whole town as bad as an eunuch, with as much
trouble as if I had made you one in earnest.

HORN: But have you told all the midwives you know, the orange
wenches at the playhouses, the city husbands, and old fumbling
keepers of this end of the town? for they'll be the readiest to report it.

QUACK: I have told all the chambermaids, waiting women, tire-women,
and old women of my acquaintance; nay, and whispered it as a
secret to 'em, and to the whisperers of Whitehall; so that you need
not doubt 'twill spread, and you will be as odious to the handsome
young women as –

HORN: As the small-pox. Well –

QUACK: And to the married women of this end of the town, as –

HORN: As the great one; nay, as their own husbands.

QUACK: And to the city dames, as aniseed Robin, of filthy and contemptible memory; and they will frighten their children with your name, especially their females.

HORN: And cry, Horner's coming to carry you away. I am only afraid 'twill not be believed. You told 'em it was by an English-French disaster, and an English-French chirurgeon, who has given me at once not only a cure, but an antidote for the future against that damned malady, and that worse distemper, love, and all other women's evils?

QUACK: Your late journey into France has made it the more credible, and your being here a fortnight before you appeared in public, looks as if you apprehended the shame, which I wonder you do not. Well, I have been hired by young gallants to belie 'em t'other way; but you are the first would be thought a man unfit for women.

HORN: Dear Mr Doctor, let vain rogues be contented only to be thought abler men than they are, generally 'tis all the pleasure they have; but mine lies another way.

QUACK: You take, methinks, a very preposterous way to it, and as ridiculous as if we operators in physic should put forth bills to disparage our medicaments, with hopes to gain customers.

HORN: Doctor, there are quacks in love as well as physic, who get but the fewer and worse patients for their boasting; a good name is seldom got by giving it one's self; and women, no more than honour, are compassed by bragging. Come, come, Doctor, the wisest lawyer never discovers the merits of his cause till the trial; the wealthiest man conceals his riches, and the cunning gamester his play. Shy husbands and keepers, like old rooks, are not to be cheated but by a new unpractised trick: false friendship will pass now no more than false dice upon 'em; no, not in the city.

Enter BOY

BOY: There are two ladies and a gentleman coming up.   [*Exit*

HORN: A pox! some unbelieving sisters of my former acquaintance, who, I am afraid, expect their sense should be satisfied of the falsity of the report. No – this formal fool and women!

Enter SIR JASPER FIDGET, LADY FIDGET, *and* MRS DAINTY FIDGET

QUACK: His wife and sister.

SIR JASP: My coach breaking just now before your door, sir, I look upon as an occasional reprimand to me, sir, for not kissing your hands, sir, since your coming out of France, sir; and so my disaster, sir, has been my good fortune, sir; and this is my wife and sister, sir.

HORN: What then, sir?

SIR JASP: My lady, and sister, sir. – Wife, this is Master Horner.

LADY FID: Master Horner, husband!

SIR JASP: My lady, my Lady Fidget, sir.

HORN: So, sir.

SIR JASP: Won't you be acquainted with her, sir? [*Aside*] So, the report is true, I find, by his coldness or aversion to the sex; but I'll play the wag with him. [*Aloud*] Pray salute my wife, my lady, sir.

HORN: I will kiss no man's wife, sir, for him, sir; I have taken my eternal leave, sir, of the sex already, sir.

SIR JASP: [*aside*] Ha! ha! ha! I'll plague him yet. [*Aloud*] Not know my wife, sir?

HORN: I do know your wife, sir; she's a woman, sir, and consequently a monster, sir, a greater monster than a husband, sir.

SIR JASP: A husband! how, sir?

HORN: So, sir; but I make no more cuckolds, sir.   [*Makes horns*

SIR JASP: Ha! ha! ha! Mercury! Mercury!

LADY FID: Pray, Sir Jasper, let us be gone from this rude fellow.

MRS DAIN: Who, by his breeding, would think he had ever been in France?

LADY FID: Foh! he's but too much a French fellow, such as hate women of quality and virtue for their love to their husbands. Sir Jasper, a woman is hated by 'em as much for loving her husband as for loving their money. But pray let's be gone.

HORN: You do well, madam; for I have nothing that you came for. I have brought over not so much as a bawdy picture, no new postures, nor the second part of the *Ecole des Filles*; nor –

QUACK: Hold, for shame, sir! what d'ye mean? you'll ruin yourself for ever with the sex.   [*Apart to* HORNER

SIR JASP: Ha! ha! ha! he hates women perfectly, I find.

MRS DAIN: What pity 'tis he should!

LADY FID: Ay, he's a base fellow for't. But affectation makes not a woman more odious to them than virtue.

HORN: Because your virtue is your greatest affectation, madam.

LADY FID: How, you saucy fellow! would you wrong my honour?

HORN: If I could.

LADY FID: How d'ye mean, sir?

SIR JASP: Ha! ha! ha! no, he can't wrong your ladyship's honour, upon my honour. He, poor man – hark you in your ear – a mere eunuch.

                  [Whispers

LADY FID: O filthy French beast! foh! foh! why do we stay? let's be gone: I can't endure the sight of him.

SIR JASP: Stay but till the chairs come; they'll be here presently.

LADY FID: No.

SIR JASP: Nor can I stay longer. 'Tis, let me see, a quarter and half quarter of a minute past eleven. The council will be sat; I must away. Business must be preferred always before love and ceremony with the wise, Mr Horner.

HORN: And the impotent, Sir Jasper.

SIR JASP: Ay, ay, the impotent, Master Horner; hah! hah! hah!

LADY FID: What, leave us with a filthy man alone in his lodgings?

SIR JASP: He's an innocent man now, you know. Pray stay. I'll hasten the chairs to you. – Mr Horner, your servant; I should be glad to see you at my house. Pray come and dine with me, and play at cards with my wife after dinner; you are fit for women at that game yet, ha! ha! *[Aside]* 'Tis as much a husband's prudence to provide innocent diversion for a wife as to hinder her unlawful pleasures; and he had better employ her than let her employ herself. *[Aloud]* Farewell.

HORN: Your servant, Sir Jasper   *[Exit* SIR JASPER

LADY FID: I will not stay with him, foh!

HORN: Nay, madam, I beseech you stay, if it be but to see I can be as civil to ladies yet as they would desire.

LADY FID: No, no, foh! you cannot be civil to ladies.

MRS DAIN: You as civil as ladies would desire?

LADY FID: No, no, no, foh! foh! foh!

      [Exeunt LADY FIDGET *and* MRS DAINTY FIDGET.

QUACK: Now, I think, I, or you yourself, rather, have done your business with the women.

HORN: Thou art an ass. Don't you see already, upon the report, and my carriage, this grave man of business leaves his wife in my lodgings, invites me to his house and wife, who before would not be acquainted with me out of jealousy?

QUACK: Nay, by this means you may be the more acquainted with the husbands, but the less with the wives.

HORN: Let me alone; if I can but abuse the husbands, I'll soon disabuse the wives. Stay – I'll reckon you up the advantages I am like to have by my stratagem. First, I shall be rid of all my old acquaintances, the most insatiable sort of duns, that invade our lodgings in a morning; and next to the pleasure of making a new mistress is that of being rid of an old one, and of all old debts. Love, when it comes to be so, is paid the most unwillingly.

QUACK: Well, you may be so rid of your old acquaintances; but how will you get any new ones?

HORN: Doctor, thou wilt never make a good chemist, thou art so incredulous and impatient. Ask but all the young fellows of the town if they do not lose more time, like huntsmen, in starting the game, than in running it down. One knows not where to find 'em; who will or will not. Women of quality are so civil, you can hardly distinguish love from good breeding, and a man is often mistaken: but now I can be sure she that shows an aversion to me loves the sport, as those women that are gone, whom I warrant to be right. And then the next thing is, your women of honour, as you call 'em, are only chary of their reputations, not their persons; and 'tis scandal they would avoid, not men. Now may I have, by the reputation of an eunuch, the privileges of one, and be seen in a lady's chamber in a morning as early as her husband; kiss virgins before their parents or lovers; and may be, in short, the *passe-partout* of the town. Now doctor.

QUACK: Nay, now you shall be the doctor; and your process is so new that we do not know but it may succeed.

HORN: Not so new neither; *probatum est*, doctor.

QUACK: Well, I wish you luck, and many patients, whilst I go to mine.

[*Exit*

I, i

Later in the same scene:

Enter PINCHWIFE

HORN: Who have we here? Pinchwife?

PINCH: Gentlemen, your humble servant.

HORN: Well, Jack, by thy long absence from the town, the grumness of thy countenance, and the slovenliness of thy habit, I should give thee joy, should I not, of marriage?

PINCH: [*aside*] Death! does he know I'm married too? I thought to have concealed it from him at least. [*Aloud*] My long stay in the country will excuse my dress; and I have a suit of law that brings me up to town, that puts me out of humour. Besides, I must give Sparkish tomorrow five thousand pounds to lie with my sister.

HORN: Nay, you country gentlemen, rather than not purchase, will buy anything; and he is a cracked title, if we may quibble. Well, but am I to give thee joy? I heard thou wert married.

PINCH: What then?

HORN: Why, the next thing that is to be heard is, thou'rt a cuckold.

PINCH: Insupportable name!   [*Aside*

HORN: But I did not expect marriage from such a whoremaster as you; one that knew the town so much, and women so well.

PINCH: Why, I have married no London wife.

HORN: Pshaw! that's all one. That grave circumspection in marrying a country wife, is like refusing a deceitful pampered Smithfield jade, to go and be cheated by a friend in the country.

PINCH: [*aside*] A pox on him and his simile! [*Aloud*] At least we are a little surer of the breed there, know what her keeping has been, whether foiled or unsound.

HORN: Come, come, I have known a clap gotten in Wales; and there are cousins, justices' clerks, and chaplains in the country, I won't say coachmen. But she's handsome and young?

PINCH: [*aside*] I'll answer as I should do. [*Aloud*] No, no; she has no beauty but her youth, no attraction but her modesty: wholesome, homely, and huswifely; that's all.

DORILANT: He talks as like a grazier as he looks.

PINCH: She's too awkward, ill-favoured, and silly to bring to town.

HARCOURT: Then methinks you should bring her to be taught breeding.

PINCH: To be taught! no, sir, I thank you. Good wives and private soldiers should be ignorant – I'll keep her from your instructions, I warrant you.

HAR: The rogue is as jealous as if his wife were not ignorant. *[Aside*

HORN: Why, if she be ill-favoured, there will be less danger here for you than by leaving her in the country. We have such variety of dainties that we are seldom hungry.

DOR: But they have always coarse, constant, swingeing stomachs in the country.

HAR: Foul feeders indeed!

DOR: And your hospitality is great there.

HAR: Open house; every man's welcome.

PINCH: So, so, gentlemen.

HORN: But prithee, why shouldst thou marry her? If she be ugly, ill-bred, and silly, she must be rich then.

PINCH: As rich as if she brought me twenty thousand pound out of this town; for she'll be as sure not to spend her moderate portion, as a London baggage would be to spend hers, let it be what it would: so 'tis all one. Then, because she's ugly, she's the likelier to be my own; and being ill-bred, she'll hate conversation; and since silly and innocent, will not know the difference betwixt a man of one-and-twenty and one of forty.

HORN: Nine – to my knowledge. But if she be silly, she'll expect as much from a man of forty-nine, as from him of one-and-twenty. But methinks wit is more necessary than beauty; and I think no young woman ugly that has it, and no handsome woman agreeable without it.

PINCH: 'Tis my maxim, he's a fool that marries; but he's a greater that does not marry a fool. What is wit in a wife good for, but to make a man a cuckold?

HORN: Yes, to keep it from his knowledge.

PINCH: A fool cannot contrive to make her husband a cuckold.

HORN: No; but she'll club with a man that can: and what is worse, if she cannot make her husband a cuckold, she'll make him jealous, and pass for one: and then 'tis all one.

PINCH: Well, well, I'll take care for one. My wife shall make me no cuckold, though she had your help, Mr Horner. I understand the town, sir.

DOR: His help!

[Aside

HAR: He's come newly to town, it seems, and has not heard how things are with him.

[Aside

HORN: But tell me, has marriage cured thee of whoring, which it seldom does?

HAR: 'Tis more than age can do.

HORN: No, the word is, I'll marry and live honest: but a marriage vow is like a penitent gamester's oath, and entering into bonds and penalties to stint himself to such a particular small sum at play for the future, which makes him but the more eager; and not being able to hold out, loses his money again, and his forfeit to boot.

DOR: Ay, ay, a gamester will be a gamester whilst his money lasts, and a whoremaster whilst his vigour.

HAR: Nay, I have known 'em, when they are broke, and can lose no more, keep a fumbling with the box in their hands to fool with only, and hinder other gamesters.

DOR: That had wherewithal to make lusty stakes.

PINCH: Well, gentlemen, you may laugh at me; but you shall never lie with my wife: I know the town.

HORN: But prithee, was not the way you were in better? Is not keeping better than marriage?

PINCH: A pox on't! the jades would jilt me, I could never keep a whore to myself.

HORN: So, then you only married to keep a whore to yourself. Well, but let me tell you, women, as you say, are like soldiers, made constant and loyal by good pay, rather than by oaths and covenants. Therefore I'd advise my friends to keep rather than marry, since too I find, by your example, it does not serve one's turn; for I saw you yesterday in the eighteenpenny place with a pretty country wench.

PINCH: How the devil! did he see my wife then? I sat there that she might not be seen. But she shall never go to a play again. *[Aside*

HORN: What! dost thou blush, at nine-and-forty, for having been seen with a wench?

DOR: No, faith, I warrant 'twas his wife, which he seated there out of sight; for he's a cunning rogue, and understands the town.

HAR: He blushes. Then 'twas his wife; for men are now more ashamed to be seen with them in public than with a wench.

PINCH: Hell and damnation! I'm undone, since Horner has seen her,
and they know 'twas she.   [*Aside*

HORN: But prithee, was it thy wife? She was exceeding pretty: I was in
love with her at that distance.

PINCH: You are like never to be nearer to her. Your servant,
gentlemen.   [*Offers to go*

HORN: Nay, prithee stay.

PINCH: I cannot; I will not.

HORN: Come, you shall dine with us.

PINCH: I have dined already.

HORN: Come, I know thou hast not: I'll treat thee, dear rogue; thou
sha't spend none of thy Hampshire money today.

PINCH: Treat me! So, he uses me already like his cuckold.   [*Aside*

HORN: Nay, you shall not go.

PINCH: I must; I have business at home.   [*Exit*

HAR: To beat his wife. He's as jealous of her as a Cheapside husband
of a Covent Garden wife.

HORN: Why, 'tis as hard to find an old whoremaster without jealousy
and the gout, as a young one without fear, or the pox:

>   As gout in age from pox in youth proceeds,
>   So wenching past, then jealousy succeeds;
>   The worst disease that love and wenching breeds.

                                                            [*Exeunt*

ROBERT HERRICK

Kisses Loathsome

>   I abhor the slimie kisse,
>   (Which to me most loathsome is.)
>   Those lips please me which are plac't
>   Close, but not too strictly lac't:
>   Yeilding I wo'd have them; yet
>   Not a wimbling Tongue admit:
>   What sho'd poking-sticks make there,
>   When the ruffe is set elsewhere?

ANDREW MARVELL

To His Coy Mistress

Had we but world enough, and time,
This coyness, Lady, were no crime.
We would sit down, and think which way
To walk, and pass our long love's day.
Thou by the Indian Ganges' side
Shouldst rubies find: I by the tide
Of Humber would complain. I would
Love you ten years before the flood:
And you should, if you please, refuse
Till the conversion of the Jews.
My vegetable love should grow
Vaster than empires, and more slow.
An hundred years should go to praise
Thine eyes, and on thy forehead gaze.
Two hundred to adore each breast:
But thirty thousand to the rest.
An age at least to every part,
And the last age should show your heart:
For, Lady, you desire this state;
Nor would I love at lower rate.

But at my back I always hear
Time's wingèd chariot hurrying near:
And yonder all before us lie
Deserts of vast eternity.
Thy beauty shall no more be found;
Nor, in thy marble vault, shall sound
My echoing song: then worms shall try
That long preserved virginity:
And your quaint honour turn to dust;
And into ashes all my lust.

The grave's a fine and private place,
But none, I think, do there embrace.
   Now, therefore, while the youthful hue
Sits on thy skin like morning dew,
And while thy willing soul transpires
At every pore with instant fires,
Now let us sport us while we may;
And now, like amorous birds of prey,
Rather at once our time devour,
Than languish in his slow-chapped power.
Let us roll all our strength, and all
Our sweetness, up into one ball:
And tear our pleasures with rough strife,
Thorough the iron gates of life.
Thus, though we cannot make our sun
Stand still, yet we will make him run.

EDMUND WALLER

To one Married to an Old Man

Since thou would'st needs, bewitcht with some ill charms,
Be buried in those monumental arms:
All we can wish, is, may that earth lie light
Upon thy tender limbs, and so good night.

Of the Marriage of the Dwarfs

Design, or chance, makes others wive:
But Nature did this match contrive;
Eve might as well have Adam fled,
As she denied her little bed
To him, for whom Heaven seemed to frame,
And measure out, this only dame.

   Thrice happy is that humble pair,
Beneath the level of all care!
Over whose heads those arrows fly
Of sad distrust and jealousy;
Secured in as high extreme,
As if the world held none but them.

   To him the fairest nymphs do show
Like moving mountains, topped with snow;
And every man a Polypheme
Does to his Galatea seem;
None may presume her faith to prove;
He proffers death that proffers love.

   Ah, Chloris, that kind Nature thus
From all the world had severed us;
Creating for ourselves us two,
As love has me for only you!

JOHN DRYDEN

Prologue to An Evening's Love

When first our Poet set himself to write,
Like a young Bridegroom on his Wedding-night
He layd about him, and did so bestir him,
His Muse could never lye in quiet for him:
But now his Honey-moon is gone and past,
Yet the ungrateful drudgery must last:
And he is bound, as civil Husbands do,
To strain himself, in complaisance to you:
To write in pain, and counterfeit a bliss,
Like the faint smackings of an after kiss.
But you, like Wives ill pleas'd, supply his want;
Each writing Monsieur is a fresh Gallant:
And though, perhaps, 'twas done as well before,
Yet still there's something in a new amour.
Your several Poets work with several tools,
One gets you wits, another gets you fools:
This pleases you with some by-stroke of wit,
This finds some cranny, that was never hit.
But should these janty Lovers daily come ·
To do your work, like your good man at home,
Their fine small timber'd wits would soon decay;
These are Gallants but for a Holiday.
Others you had who oftner have appear'd,
Whom, for meer impotence you have cashier'd:
Such as at first came on with pomp and glory,
But, overstraining, soon fell flat before yee.
Their useless weight with patience long was born,
But at the last you threw 'em off with scorn.
As for the Poet of this present night,
Though now he claims in you an Husbands right,
He will not hinder you of fresh delight.

He, like a Seaman, seldom will appear;
And means to trouble home but thrice a year:
That only time from your Gallants he'll borrow;
Be kind to day, and Cuckold him to morrow.

JOHN MILTON

From Paradise Lost

Adam asks about angelic lovemaking (book VIII)

To love, thou blamest me not; for love, thou sayest,
Leads up to heaven, is both the way and guide;
Bear with me then, if lawful what I ask:
Love not the heavenly spirits, and how their love
Express they? by looks only? or do they mix
Irradiance, virtual or immediate touch?'
　　To whom the angel, with a smile that glowed
Celestial rosy red, love's proper hue,
Answered; 'Let it suffice thee that thou knowest
Us happy, and without love no happiness.
Whatever pure thou in the body enjoyest
(And pure thou wert created), we enjoy
In eminence; and obstacle find none
Of membrane, joint or limb, exclusive bars;
Easier than air with air, if spirits embrace,
Total they mix, union of pure with pure
Desiring; nor restrained conveyance need,
As flesh to mix with flesh, or soul with soul.'

Eve tempts Adam (book IX)

'On my experience, Adam, freely taste,
And fear of death deliver to the winds.'
　　So saying, she embraced him, and for joy

Tenderly wept; much won, that he his love
Had so ennobled, as of choice to incur
Divine displeasure for her sake, or death.
In recompense (for such compliance had
Such recompense best merits), from the bough
She gave him of that fair enticing fruit
With liberal hand: he scrupled not to eat,
Against his better knowledge; not deceived,
But fondly overcome with female charm.
Earth trembled from her entrails, as again
In pangs; and nature gave a second groan;
Sky loured; and, muttering thunder, some sad drops
Wept at completing of the mortal sin
Original: while Adam took no thought,
Eating his fill; nor Eve to iterate
Her former trespass feared, the more to sooth
Him with her loved society; that now,
As with new wine intoxicated both,
They swim in mirth, and fancy that they feel
Divinity within them breeding wings,
Wherewith to scorn the earth: but that false fruit
Far other operation first displayed,
Carnal desire inflaming; he on Eve
Began to cast lascivious eyes; she him
As wantonly repaid; in lust they burn:
Till Adam thus 'gan Eve to dalliance move:

　　'Eve, now I see thou art exact of taste,
And elegant, of sapience no small part;
Since to each meaning savour we apply,
And palate call judicious; I the praise
Yield thee, so well this day thou hast purveyed.
Much pleasure we have lost, while we abstained
From this delightful fruit, nor know till now
True relish, tasting; if such pleasure be
In things to us forbidden, it might be wished,

For this one tree had been forbidden ten.
But come, so well refreshed, now let us play
As meet is, after such delicious fare;
For never did thy beauty, since the day
I saw thee first and wedded thee, adorned
With all perfections, so inflame my sense
With ardour to enjoy thee, fairer now
Than ever; bounty of this virtuous tree!'
    So said he, and forebore not glance or toy
Of amorous intent; well understood
Of Eve, whose eye darted contagious fire.
Her hand he seized; and to a shady bank,
Thick over-head with verdant roof imbowered,
He led her nothing loth; flowers were the couch,
Pansies, and violets, and asphodel,
And hyacinths; earth's freshest softest lap.
There they their fill of love and love's disport
Took largely, of their mutual guilt the seal,
The solace of their sin: till dewy sleep
Oppressed them, wearied with their amorous play.

HENRY NEVILLE

The Isle of Pines

AWAY TO THE East Indies being lately discovered by sea, to the south of
Affric, by certain Portugals, far more safe and profitable than had
been heretofore; certain English merchants were encouraged by the great
advantages arising from the Eastern commodities, to settle a factory there
to the advantage of trade. And having to that purpose obtained the
Queen's Royal licence, Anno Dom. 1589, 11 or 12 Eliz. furnisht out for
those parts four ships. My master being sent as a factor to deal and nego-
ciate for them, and to settle there, took with him his whole familly, that is to
say, his wife, one son of about twelve years of age, one daughter of about
fourteen years, two maid servants, one negro female slave, and myself, who

went under him as his bookkeeper. With this company, on Monday the third of April next following, having all necessaries for housekeeping when we should come there, we embarked ourselves in the good ship called the *India Merchant*, of about four hundred and fifty tons burthen; and having a good wind, we on the fourteenth of May had sight of the Canaries, and not long after of the Isles of Cape Vert or Verd, where taking in such things as were necessary for our voyage, and some fresh provisions, we steering our course south, and a point east, about the first of August came within sight of the Island of St Hellen, where we took in fresh water. We then set our faces for the Cape of Good Hope, where by God's blessing we arrived, after some sickness, whereof some of our company died, though none of our family. Hitherto we had met with none but calm weather. Yet so it pleased God, when we were almost in sight of St Laurence, an island so called, one of the greatest in the world, as mariners say, we were overtaken and dispersed by a storm of wind, which continued with such violence many days, that losing all hopes of safety, being out of our own knowledge, and whether we should fall on flats or rocks, uncertain in the night, not having the least benefit of the light, we feared most, always wishing for day, and then for land: but it came too soon for our good. For, about the first of October, our fears having made us forget how the time passed to a certainty, we, about the break of day, discerned land, but what we knew not. The land seemed high and rocky, and the sea continued still very stormy and tempestuous. As we drew near it, perceiving no safety in the ship, which we looked would suddenly be beat in pieces, the Captain, my master, and some others got into a long boat, thinking by that means to save their lives, and presently after, all the seamen cast themselves overboard, thinking to save their lives by swimming, only myself, my master's daughter, the two maids, and the negro were left on board, for we could not swim; but those that left us, might as well have tarried with us, for we saw them, or most of them perish, ourselves now ready after to follow their fortune. But God was pleased to spare our lives, as it were by miracle, though to further sorrow. For when we came against the rocks, the ship having endured two or three blows, being now broken and quite foundred in the waters, we having with much ado gotten ourselves on the bowsprit, which being broken off, was driven by the waters into a small creek, wherein fell a little river, which being encompassed by the rocks, was sheltered from the wind, so that we had opportunity to land ourselves, though almost drown'd, in all four persons, beside the negro. When we were got upon the rocks, we could perceive the miserable wreck to our great terror. I had in my pocket a little tinder-box, and steel, and flint to strike fire upon occasion, which served now to good purpose, for its being so close, preserved the tinder dry. With this, and with the help of some old rotten wood which we got together, we kindled a fire, and dried ourselves; which done, I left my female company, and went to see, if I could find our ship's company, that were escaped, but could hear of none, though I hooted, and made all the noise I could; neither could I perceive the footsteps of any living creature, save a few birds and other fowls. At length it drawing towards evening, I went back to my company, who were very much troubled for want of me, I being now all their stay in this lost condition. We were at first afraid that the wild people of the country might find us out, although we saw no footsteps of any, no not so much as a path, the woods round about being full of briars and brambles. We also stood in fear of wild beasts. Of such also we saw none, nor sign of any. But above all, that we had greatest reason to fear, was to be starved to death for want of food. But God had otherwise provided for us, as you shall hear hereafter. This done, we spent our time in getting some broken pieces of boards, and planks, and some of the sails and rigging on shore for shelter. I set up two or three poles, and drew two or three of the cords and lines from tree to tree, over which throwing some sail-cloths, and having gotten wood by us, and three or four sea-gowns, which we had dried, we took up our lodging for that night together. The blackmore being less sensible than the rest, we made our sentry. We slept soundly that night, as having not slept in three or four nights before, our fears of what happened preventing us, neither could our hard lodging, fear, and danger, hinder us, we were so overwatcht.

On the morrow, being well refrest with sleep, the wind ceased, and the weather was very warm. We went down the rocks on the sands at low water, where we found great part of our lading, either on shore or floating near it. By the help of my company, I dragged most of it on shore; what was too heavy for us we broke, and unbound the casks and chests, and, taking out the goods, secured all; for that we wanted no clothes, nor any other provisions necessary for housekeeping, to furnish a better house than any we were like to have; but no victuals, the salt water having spoiled all, only one cask of biscuit being lighter than the rest was dry; this served for bread a while, and we found on land a sort of fowl about the bigness of a swan, very heavy and fat, and by reason of their weight could not fly, of these we found little difficulty to kill, so that they were our present food. We carried out of England certain hens and cocks to eat by the way. Some of these when the ship was broken, by some means got to land, and bred exceedingly; so that in the future they were a great help unto us. We found also, by a little river, in the flags, store of eggs, of a sort of fowl much like our ducks, which were very good meat, so that we wanted nothing to keep us alive.

The third day, as soon as it was morning, seeing nothing to disturb us, I lookt out a convenient place to dwell in, that we might build us a hut to shelter us from the weather, and from any other danger of annoyance from wild beasts, if any should find us out. So, close by a large spring which rose out of a high hill overlooking the sea, on the side of a wood (by the help of an ax and some other implements, for we had all necessaries, the working of the sea having cast up most of our goods) I cut down all the straightest poles I could find, and which were enough for my purpose, by the help of the company, necessity being our master, I digged holes in the earth, setting my poles at an equal distance, and nailing the broken boards of the casks, chests, and cabins, and such like to them, making my door to the sea-ward, and having covered the top, with sail-clothes strain'd, and nailed; I in the space of a week had made a large cabin big enough to hold all our goods and ourselves in it. I also placed our hamocks for lodging, purposing if it pleased God to send any ship that way, we might be transported home. But it never came to pass, the place, wherein we were, as I conceived, being much out of the way.

We having lived in this manner four full months, and not so much as seeing or hearing of any wild people or of any of our company, more than ourselves, they being found now by experience to be all drowned, and the place as we after found, being a large island, and disjoined and out of sight of any other land, was wholly uninhabited by any people, neither was there any hurtful beast to annoy us. But on the contrary, the country so very pleasant, being always clothed in green, and full of pleasant fruits, and variety of birds, ever warm, and never colder than in England in September; so that this place, had it the culture that skilful people might bestow on it, would prove a Paradise.

The woods afforded us a sort of nuts, as big as a large apple, whose kernel being pleasant and dry, we made use of instead of bread; the fowl before mentioned, and a sort of water-fowl like ducks, and their eggs, and a beast about the size of a goat, and almost such a like creature, which brought two young ones at a time, and that twice a year, of which the low lands and woods were very full, being a very harmless creature and tame, so that we could easily take and kill them; fish also, especially shell-fish, which we could best come by, we had great store of; so that in effect, as to food we wanted nothing. And thus, and by such like helps, we continued six months, without any disturbance or want.

Idleness and a fulness of everything begot in me a desire for enjoying the women. Beginning now to grow more familiar, I had persuaded the two maids to let me lie with them, which I did at first in private; but after, custom taking away shame, there being none but us, we did it more openly, as our lust gave us liberty. My master's daughter was also content to do as we did. The truth is, they were all handsome women, when they had clothes, and well shaped, feeding well. For we wanted no food, and living idly, and seeing us at liberty to do our wills, without hope of ever returning home. One of my consorts, with whom I first accompanied, the tallest and handsomest, proved presently with child. The second was my master's daughter. And the other also not long after fell into the same condition. None now remaining but my negro, who seeing what we did, longed also for her share. One night, I being asleep, with the consent of the others, my negro got close to me, thinking in the dark to beguile me, but I awaking and feeling her, perceiving who it was, yet willing to try the difference, satisfied myself with her, as well as with one of the rest. That night, although the first time, she proved also with child, so that in the year of our being there, all my women were with child by me; and they all coming at different seasons, were a great help to one another.

The first brought me a brave boy. My master's daughter was the youngest. She brought me a girl. So did the other maid, who, being somewhat fat, sped worse at her labour. The negro had no pain at all, and brought me a fine white girl. So I had one boy and three girls. The women were soon well again, and the two first with child again, the two last were brought to bed; my custom being not to lie with any of them after they were with child till others were so likewise; and not with the black at all after she was with child, which commonly was the first time I lay with her, which was in the night and not else; my stomach would not serve me, although she was one of the handsomest blacks I had seen, and her children as comely as any of the rest. We had no clothes for them, and therefore when they had suckt, we laid them in moss to sleep, and took no further care of them; for we knew, when they were gone more would come; the women never failing once a year at least, and none of the children, for all the hardship we put them to, were ever sick; so that wanting now nothing but clothes, nor them much neither, other than for decency, the warmth of the country and custom supplying that defect, we were now well satisfied with our condition. Our family beginning to grow large, and there being nothing to hurt us, we many times lay abroad on mossy banks, under the shelter of some trees, or such like, for having nothing else to do, I had made me several arbors to sleep in with my women in the heat of the day, in these I and my women passed the time away, they never being willing to be out of my company.

And having now no thought of ever returning home, as having resolved and sworn never to part or leave one another, or the place; having by my several wives, forty-seven children, boys and girls, but most girls, and growing up apace; we were all of us very fleshy, the country so well agreeing with us, that we never ailed anything. My negro having had twelve, was the first that left bearing, so I never meddled with her more. My master's daughter, by whom I had most children, being the youngest and the handsomest, was most fond of me, and I of her. Thus we lived for sixteen years. Till perceiving my eldest boy to mind the ordinary work of nature, by seeing what we did, I gave him a mate; and so I did to all the rest, as fast as they grew up, and were capable. My wives having left bearing, my children began to breed apace, so were like to be a multitude. My first wife brought me thirteen children, my second seven, my master's daughter fifteen, and the negro twelve, in all forty-seven.

After we had lived there twenty-two years, my negro died suddenly, but I could not perceive anything that ailed her. Most of my children being grown, as fast as we married them, I sent and placed them over the river by themselves severally, because we would not pester one another. And now, they being all grown up and gone, and married after our manner, some two or three of the youngest excepted, for, growing myself into years, I liked not the wanton annoyances of young company.

Thus having lived to the sixtieth year of my age, and the fortieth of my coming thither, at which time I sent for all of them to bring their children, and they were in number descended from me by these four women, of my children, grand-children, and great-grand-children, five hundred and forty-five of both sorts; I took off the males of one family, and married them to the females of another, not letting any to marry their sisters, as we did formerly out of necessity, so blessing God for his providence and goodness, I dismissed them. Having taught some of my children to read formerly, for I had left still the Bible, I charged it should be read once a month at a general meeting. At last one of my wives died, being sixty-eight years of age, which I buried in a place set out on purpose; and within a year after another; so I had none now left but my master's daughter, and we lived together twelve years longer. At length she died also. So I buried her also next the place where I purposed to be buried myself, and the tall maid, my first wife, next to me on the other side, the negro next without her, and the other maid next my master's daughter. I had now nothing to mind, but the place whither I was to go, being very old, almost eighty years. I gave my cabin and furniture that was left, to my eldest son, after my decease, who had married my eldest daughter by my beloved wife; whom I made king and governor of all the rest. I informed them of the manners of Europe, and charged them to remember the Christian religion, after the manner of them that spake the same language, and to admit no other, if hereafter any should come and find them out.

And now, once for all, I summoned them to come to me, that I might number them, which I did, and found the estimate to contain, in or about the eightieth year of my age, and fifty-ninth of my coming there, in all of all sorts, one thousand seven hundred and eighty-nine. Thus praying God to multiply them, and send them the true light of the gospel, I last of all dismist them; for, being now very old, and my sight decayed, I could not expect to live long. I gave this narration, written with my own hand, to my eldest son, who now lived with me, commanding him to keep it, and if strangers should come thither by chance, to let them see it, and take a copy of it if they would, that our name be not lost from off the earth. I gave this people, descended from me, the name of the English Pines, George Pine being my name, and my master's daughter's name Sarah English. My two other wives were Mary Sparkes, and Elizabeth Trevor. So their several descendants were called the English, the Trevors, and the Phils, from the Christian name of the negro, which was Philippa, she having no surname; and the general name of the whole the English Pines: whom God bless with the dew of heaven, and the fat of the earth. Amen!

THOMAS FLATMAN

An Appeal to Cats in the Business of Love

Ye cats that at midnight spit love at each other,
Who best feel the pangs of a passionate lover,
I appeal to your scratches and your tattered fur,
If the business of Love be no more than to purr.
Old Lady Grimalkin with her gooseberry eyes,
Knew something when a kitten, for why she is wise,
You find by experience, the love-fit's soon o'er,
Puss! Puss! lasts not long, but turns to *Cat-whore!*
    Men ride many miles,
    Cats tread many tiles,
  Both hazard their necks in the fray;
    Only cats, when they fall
    From a house or a wall,
Keep their feet, mount their tails, and away!

SIR JOHN SUCKLING

A Candle

There is a thing which in the light
Is seldom us'd; but in the night
It serves the maiden female crew,
The ladies, and the goodwives too.
They use to take it in their hand,
And then it will uprightly stand;
And to a hole they it apply,
Where by its goodwill it would die:
It spends, goes out, and still within
It leaves its moisture thick and thin.

The Deformed Mistress

I know there are some fools that care
Not for the body, so the face be fair;
Some others, too, that in a female creature
Respect not beauty, but a comely feature;
And others, too, that for those parts in sight
Care not so much, so that the rest be right.
Each man his humour hath, and, faith 'tis mine
To love that woman which I now define.
First I would have her wainscot foot and hand
More wrinkled far than any pleated band,
That in those furrows, if I'd take the pains,
I might both sow and reap all sorts of grains:
Her nose I'd have a foot long, not above,
With pimples embroider'd, for those I love;
And at the end a comely pearl of snot,
Considering whether it should fall or not:
Provided, next, that half her teeth be out,
Nor do I care much if her pretty snout
Meet with her furrow'd chin, and both together
Hem in her lips, as dry as good whit-leather:
One wall-eye she shall have, for that's a sign
In other beasts the best: why not in mine?
Her neck I'll have to be pure jet at least,
With yellow spots enamell'd; and her breast,
Like a grasshopper's wing, both thin and lean,
Not to be toucht for dirt, unless swept clean:
As for her belly, 'tis no matter, so
There be a belly, and –
Yet, if you will, let it be something high,
And always let there be a timpany.
But soft! where am I now? here I should stride,
Lest I fall in, the place must be so wide,

And pass unto her thighs, which shall be just
Like to an ant's that's scraping in the dust:
Into her legs I'd have love's issues fall,
And all her calf into a gouty small:
Her feet both thick and eagle-like display'd,
The symptoms of a comely, handsome maid.
As for her parts behind, I ask no more:
If they but answer those that are before,
I have my utmost wish; and, having so,
Judge whether I am happy, yea or no.

Proffered Love Rejected

It is not four years ago,
    I offered forty crowns
To lie with her a night or so;
    She answer'd me in frowns.

Not two years since, she meeting me
    Did whisper in my ear,
That she would at my service be,
    If I contented were.

I told her I was cold as snow,
    And had no great desire;
But should be well content to go
    To twenty, but no higher.

Some three months since or thereabout,
    She, that so coy had been,
Bethought herself and found me out,
    And was content to sin.

I smil'd at that, and told her I
    Did think it something late,
And that I'd not repentance buy
    At above half the rate.

This present morning early she
    Forsooth came to my bed,
And gratis there she offered me
    Her high-priz'd maidenhead.

I told her that I thought it then
    Far dearer than I did,
When I at first the forty crowns
    For one night's lodgings bid.

ANON

Stand, Stately Tavie

Stand, stately Tavie, out of the codpiece rise,
And dig a grave between thy mistress' thighs;
Swift stand, then stab 'till she replies,
Then gently weep, and after weeping, die.
Stand, Tavie, and gain thy credit lost;
Or by this hand I'll never draw thee, but against a post.

The Resolution

Nay, Silvia, now you're cruel grown;
I'll swear you most unjustly frown.
I only asked (in vain) to taste
What you denied with mighty haste;
I asked – but I'm ashamed to tell
What 'twas you took so wondrous ill –
A kiss. But with a coy disdain
You view'd my sighings and my pain:
'Twas but a civil small request,
Yet with proud looks and hand on breast,
You cried 'I'm not so eager to be kiss'd.'
Put case that I had loosed your gown,
And then by force had laid you down,
And with unruly hands had teased you, –
Too justly then I had displeased you.
Or had I (big with wanton joys)
Engaged you for a brace of boys,
Then basely left you full of nature, –
This would have been provoking matter.
But I, poor harmless civil I,
Begg'd for the meanest coolest joy,
And saw denial in your eye;
For with a squeamish glance you cried
'I hate the nauseous bliss.'
''Tis well,' said I; 'since I'm denied,
For rocks of diamonds I'll not kiss.'

In summer-time, when birds do sing,
  And country maids are making hay,
As I went forth myself alone
  To view the meadows fresh and gay,
The country maidens I espied
  With fine lawn aprons as white as snow,
And crimson ribands about their arms,
  Which made a pretty country show.
The young men fell a-prating,
  And took the maidens from hay-making
To go and tumble, tumble, tumble, tumble, tumble
  Up and down the green meadow.

The next day being holiday,
  And country maids they would be seen,
Each took his sweet-heart by the hand
  And went to dance upon the green:
The country maids incontinent
  Unto the green assembled were,
Adorned with beauty's ornament,
  Their cheeks like roses and lilies fair:

The young men fell a-skipping,
The maidens nimbly fell a-tripping,
They could not dance, but tumble, tumble, tumble
  Up and down the green meadow.

The old men that had lived long
   And viewed full many a summer's day,
Came gently walking by themselves
   To see them keep their holiday:
The married men of middle age
   Brought forth their wives to see that sport,
And they put on their best array,
   Unto the green they did resort:
There music sweetly sounding,
The maidens' hearts with joys abounding,
They could not dance, but tumble, tumble, tumble
   Up and down the green meadow.

When they with tumbling well had sweat,
   And tumbling joys had tasted well,
And Phœbus almost lost his heat,
   Each did return where they did dwell:
Their wives unto their husbands said
   The pretty sports which they had seen,
Wish'd them to teach them in their bed
   As did the lovers on the green:
The young men joyful-hearted
Each took his lass and so departed,
When they no more could tumble, tumble, tumble,
      tumble, tumble
   Up and down the green meadow.

From Wit's Cabinet

Virgins Admonished

Pretty nymph, why always blushing?
If thou lovest why art thou so coy?
In thy cheeks these roses flushing
Shew thee fearful of thy joy.
What is man that thou shouldst dread
To change with him a maidenhead?
At first all virgins fear to do it
And but trifle away their time,
And still unwilling to come to it
In foolish whining spend their time;
But when they once have found the way,
Then they are for it night and day.

From The Windsor Drollery

I'd have you, quoth he.
Would you have me? quoth she;
    O where, sir?
In my chamber, quoth he.
In your chamber? quoth she;
    Why there, sir?
To kiss you, quoth he.
To kiss me? quoth she;
    O why, sir?
'Cause I love it, quoth he.
Do you love it? quoth she;
    So do I, sir.

From The Bristol Drollery

After long service and a thousand vows,
To her glad lover she more kindness shows.
Oft had Amyntas with her tresses play'd
When the sun's vigour, drove 'em to a shade;
And many a time had given her a green gown,
And oft he kissed her when he had her down;
With sighs and motions he to her made known
What fain he would have done: then with a frown
She would forbid him, till the minute came
That she no longer could conceal her flame.
The am'rous shepherd, forward to espy
Love's yielding motions triumph in her eye,
With eager transport straight himself addrest
To taste the pleasures of so rich a feast:
When with resistance, and a seeming flight,
As 'twere t' increase her lover's appetite,
Unto a place where flowers thicker grew
Out of his arms as swift as air she flew;
Daphne ne'er run so light and fast as she
When from the god she fled and turn'd t' a tree.
The youth pursued; nor needs he run amain,
Since she intended to be overta'en.
He dropp'd no apple nor no golden ball
To stay her flight, for she herself did fall,
Where 'mongst the flowers like Flora's self she lay
To gain more breath that she might lose't in play.
She pluck'd a flower, and at Amyntas threw
When he addressed to crop a flower too.
Then a faint strife she seemed to renew;
She smiled, she frown'd, she would and would not do.
At length o'ercome she suffers with a sigh
Her ravish'd lover use his victory,

And gave him leave to punish her delay
With double vigour in the am'rous play;
But then, alas! soon ended the delight;
For too much love had hastened its flight,
And every ravish'd sense too soon awake,
Rapt up in bliss it did but now partake:
Which left the lovers in a state to prove
Long were the pains but short the joys of love.

SIR WILLIAM DAVENANT

Under the willow-shades they were
  Free from the eyesight of the sun,
For no intruding beam could there
  Peep through to spy what things were done:
    Thus sheltered they unseen did lie,
     Surfeiting on each other's eye;
Defended by the willow shades alone,
The sun's heat they defied and cool'd their own.

Whilst they did embrace unspied,
  The conscious willow seemed to smile,
That them with privacy supplied,
  Holding the door, as 'twere, the while;
    And when their dalliances were o'er,
     The willows, to oblige them more,
Bowing, did seem to say, as they withdrew,
'We can supply you with a cradle too.'

ROBERT BARON

Epithalamium

To bed ye two in one united go,
    To pleasures killing;
Embrace and struggle till your spirits flow,
    Embrace more willing
Than th' loving palms (great union's wonder),
That ne'er bore any fruit asunder.

Be young to each when winter and grey hairs
    Your head shall climb;
May your affections like the merry spheres
    Still move in time,
And may (with many a good presage)
Your marriage prove your merry age.

NICHOLAS HOOKES

To Amanda Desirous to Go to Bed

Sleepy, my dear? yes, yes, I see
Morpheus is fallen in love with thee;
Morpheus, my worst of rivals, tries
To draw the curtains of thine eyes,
And fans them with his wing asleep;
Makes drowsy love to play bopeep.
How prettily his feathers blow
Those fleshy shuttings to and fro!
O how he makes me Tantalise
With those fair apples of thine eyes!
Equivocates and cheats me still,
Opening and shutting at his will,

Now both, now one! the doting god
Plays with thine eyes at even or odd.
My stammering tongue doubts which it might
Bid thee, goodmorrow or goodnight.
So thy eyes twinkle brighter far
Than the bright trembling evening star;
So a wax taper burnt within
The socket, plays at out and in.

     Thus did Morpheus court thine eye,
Meaning there all night to lie:
Cupid and he play Whoop, All-Hid!
The eye, their bed and coverlid.

     Fairest, let me thy nightclothes air;
Come, I'll unlace thy stomacher.
Make me thy maiden chamberman,
Or let me be thy warming-pan.
O that I might but lay my head
At thy bed's feet i' th' trundle-bed.
Then i' th' morning ere I rose,
I'd kiss thy pretty pettitoes,
Those smaller feet with which i' th' day
My love so neatly trips away.

     Since you I must not wait upon,
Most modest lady, I'll be gone;
And though I cannot sleep with thee,
Oh may my dearest dream of me!
All the night long dream that we move
To the main centre of our love;
And if I chance to dream of thee,
Oh may I dream eternally!
Dream that we freely act and play
Those postures which we dream by day;
Spending our thoughts i' th' best delight
Chaste dreams allow of in the night.

MEURSIUS

From The Delights of Venus
(shortened version)

When Nature once, like Nile, the cunt o'erflows,
The clammy womb, like Aegypt fruitful grows;
Octavia now began just in her prime,
To stain her linnen with a monthly slime.
Just at sixteen her breasts began to heave
And into snow-white semi-globes to cleave.
On Venus Mount the hair a cov'ring made,
To hide love's altar with an envious shade.
Grown ripe, her itching fancy pleasure feigns,
Yet scarce knows what the titillation means.
All night she thinks on Man, both toils and sweats,
And dreaming frigs, and spends upon the sheets;
But never knew the more substantial bliss,
And scarce e'er touched a man, but by a kiss.
Her virgin cunt ne'er knew the joys of love
Beyond what dildoes or her finger gave.

Octavia goes to Tullia to find out what her bridal night was like
. . . Tullia speaks as follows:

Naked I lay, clasp'd in my Callus' arms,
Dreading, yet longing for his sweet'ning charms;
Two burning tapers spread around their light,
And chas'd away the darkness of the night,
When Callus from my panting bosom flew,
And with him from the bed, the bed cloaths drew.
I to conceal my naked body try'd,
And what he wish'd to see, I strove to hide;
But what I held, with force he pull'd away,

I blush'd, but yet my thoughts were pleas'd to find
Myself so laid, and him I loved, so kind.
Struggling I lay, exposed to his eyes;
He view'd my breast, my belly, and my thighs,
And ev'ry part that there adjacent lies.
No part, or limb, his eager eyes escap'd,
Nay my plump buttocks too he saw and clasp'd.
He dally'd thus, thus rais'd the lustful fire
'Till modesty was vanquish'd by desire.
I then look'd up, which yet I had not done,
And saw his body naked as my own;
I saw his prick with active vigour strong,
Thick as my arm, and, 'faith, almost as long,
Of cruel smart I knew I should not fail,
Because his prick so large, my cunt so small.
He soon perceiv'd my blushings and surprize.
And straight my hand unto his prick did seize;
Which bigger grew, and did more stiffly stand,
Feeling the warmth of my enliv'ning hand.
Thus far I've told of the pleasing sight;
You know that prick our darling favorite.
    It is defin'd, a hollow boneless part
Of better use, and nobler than the heart;
With mouth, but without eyes; it has a head,
Soft as the lips, and as the cherry red;
The balls hang dangling in their hairy cods
From whence proceed the spring of tickling floods,
Good pricks should be both thick as well as tall,
Your French dildoes are a size too small.
At first they're hardly in our cunts contain'd;
For maidenheads are by much labour gain'd;
But men, well furnish'd with stout pricks, are wont
To force their passage thro' a bleeding cunt.
Man's unesteem'd, a hated monster made,

When his prick's short, and can't for favour plead.
Women do not the man, but pintle wed;
For marriage joys are centred in the bed.
Now Callus strok'd and kiss'd my milk-white breast,
He fell, and saw the beauties of the rest;
Stroking my belly down, he did descend
To the lov'd place where all his joys must end.
He seiz'd my cunt, and gently pull'd the hair;
At that I trembled; there began my fear.
My soft and yielding thighs he open forc'd;
And quite into my cunt his finger thrust;
With which he grop'd, and search'd my cunt all round,
And of a maid the certain tokens found.
Then wide as could be stretch'd, my thighs he spread,
Under my buttocks too a pillow laid,
And told me then the fairest mark was made.
Then prostrate threw himself upon my breast
That groan'd with such unusual weight opprest.
My cunt's plump lips his finger drew aside,
And then to enter, but in vain, he try'd:
His body nimbly up and down he mov'd,
Against my cunt his tarse stood.
Sharp was the pain I suffer'd, yet I bor't,
Resolving not to interrupt the sport;
When suddenly I felt the tickling seed
O'erflow my cunt, my belly, and the bed.
I saw his prick, when Callus from me rose,
Limber and weak hang down his snotty nose;
For when they fuck, their stiffness then they lose,
But soon my Callus fix'd his launce upright,
Rais'd by my hand, again prepared to fight;
Tho' then within my cunt he could not spend,
Oft times he swore the error he would mend,
And the warm juice thro' every passage send.

About my cunt I felt a burning pain,
Yet long'd with more success to try again.
Callus once more new mounted to begin,
Gave me his prick, and begg'd I'd put it in.
At first against such impudence I rail'd,
But he with moving arguments prevail'd.
He kiss'd and pray'd and would not be deny'd,
And said pricks blind, and needs must have a guide.
Where there's no path, no track, he runs astray;
But in a beaten road can find his way.
I put it in, and made the passage stretch,
Whilst he push'd on, t'enlarge the narrow breach,
His prick bore forward with such strength and pow'r,
That 'twould have made a cunt had there been none before.
When half was in, and but one half remain'd,
I sigh'd aloud, and of the smart complain'd
As he push'd down, the pain I sharper found,
And drew his weapon from my bleeding wound.
Callus is vex'd to lose his half-won prize,
And spews his juicy seed upon my thighs.
My hand upon my mangled cunt I laid
To feel the monstrous wound his prick had made.

Tullia complains. Callus persuades her to another attempt. She says:

If you will try once more, I will comply,
Tho' I to fucking do a martyr die.

They go on to try another position:

Then from the window he an ointment brought,
Which his too hasty passion had forgot.
His prick smelt sweet with what he rubb'd upon't,
And seem'd as fitting for my mouth as cunt.
As soon as this was done, he made me rise,
And place myself upon my hands and thighs.

My head down stooping on the bed did lie,
But my round buttocks lifted were on high,
Just like a cannon plac'd against the sky.
My bloody smock he then turn'd up behind,
As if to bugger me he had design'd:
Then with his sweet and slipp'ry prick drew near,
And vig'rously he charg'd me in the rear.
His prick, as soon as to my cunt apply'd,
Up to the hilt into my cunt did slide.
He fucked, and ask'd me if my cunt was sore?
Or his prick hurt me as it did before:
  I answer'd, No, my dear; no, do not cease;
But oh! do thus as long as e'er you please.
This stroke did fully answer our intent
For at one moment both together spent
Just as we fuck'd, I cry'd, I faint, I die,
And fell down in a blissful extasy,
Kind Callus then drew out his prick, and said,
There, pretty fool, you've lost your maidenhead.

*   *   *

Now Callus had his rampant Fury laid,
And limber prick hung down his dangling head.
Since made a perfect woman, prick and I
Arriv'd at much familiarity.
But languishing poor prick could do no more;
Tho' not for want of will, but want of pow'r.

Callus takes aphrodisiacs and they go on with other positions. At last:

Weary with toil, and spent, while Callus slept,
I from the bed into the chamber stept,
Hoping I should not be by Callus miss'd,
I set the piss-pot to my cunt and piss'd;

But the salt water whilst 'twas trickling down,
Caus'd a sharp pain I ne'er before had known;
So whilst I sigh'd, and my poor cunt bewail'd,
And 'gainst the too large prick that made it, rail'd,
Callus awak'd; I blush'd, he laugh'd aloud,
To see upon my thighs such streams of blood.
So, to conclude, Callus no time did lose,
But fuck'd me nine times well before I rose.

Octavia is so turned on by this account that she begs Tullia to give
her a practical demonstration. She feels she can't wait for her own
wedding on the next day.

Tullia replies, my dear Octavia, you,
That I can teach, shall ev'ry secret know.
Come this way, I've a pretty engine here,
Which us'd to ease the torments of the fair;
And next those joys which charming Man can give,
This best a woman's passion can relieve.
This dildo 'tis, with which I oft was wont
T'asswage the raging of my lustful cunt.
For when cunts swell, and glow with strong desire,
'Tis only pricks can quench the lustful fire;
And when that's wanting, dildoes must supply
The place of pricks upon necessity.
Then on your back lie down upon the bed,
And lift your petticoats above your head;
I'll shew you a new piece of lechery,
For I'll the man, you shall the woman be.
Your thin transparent smock, my dear remove
That last bless'd cover to the scene of love,
What's this I see, you fill me with surprize,
Your charming beauties dazzle quite my eyes!
Gods! what a leg is here! what lovely thighs!
A belly too, as polish'd iv'ry white,
And then a cunt would charm an anchorite!

Oh! now I wish I were a man indeed,
That I might gain thy pretty maidenhead,
But since, my dear, I can't my wish obtain,
Let's now proceed t'instruct you in the game;
That game that brings the most substantial bliss;
For swiving of all games the sweetest is.
Ope wide your legs, and throw them round my back,
And clasp your snowy arms about my neck.
Your buttocks then move nimbly up and down,
Whilst with my hand I thrust the dildo home.
You'll feel the titulation by and by;
Have you no pleasure yet, no tickling joy?
Oh! yes, yes, now I faint, I die.

The poem finishes with a discussion of the joys of sex.

But now let us, with needful sleep, awhile
Refresh your limbs, tir'd with the pleasing toil.
In graceful slumbers pass the night away,
In expectation of the coming day;
Which in thy richest pride and glory dress'd
Shall give thee to the youth to be possess'd,
And reap those joys which cannot be express'd.

GIAMBATTISTA BASILE

From Il Pentamerone

The large crab-louse, the mouse, and the cricket

ONCE UPON A time there dwelt at Vommaro a very rich farmer, Miccone hight, and he had a son named Nardiello, who was the most wretched good-for-nothing to be met with amongst all the good for naught. The life of the unhappy father was embittered and darkened through his son's folly, and he knew not what to do, nor how to set him straight, nor how to make him do things as they ought to be and in good order. If he went to the tavern to eat his surfeit, he was sure to choose the most treacherous companions to quarrel with; if he had anything to do with fast women, he was sure to take hold of the worst flesh and pay for the best; if he went to a gambling-place, they would trick him, and putting him between them, they would pluck him well from right to left, so that in this way he had cast away half of his father's goods, for which reason Miccone was always up in arms, swearing, scolding, threatening, and saying, 'What dost thou think of doing, thou spendthrift? dost thou not perceive that my goods are going from high to low tide? Leave these accursed taverns, which begin with the name of foes and end with an evil signification: leave them, for they are a migraine of the brains, dropsy of the throat, and dysentery of the purse! Leave this accursed play, where thou endangerest thy life, and thy goods are eaten up, and thy monies are lost, and thy happiness is gone, and the stones bring thee to naught, and the words bring thee down to a pill. Leave the bad whoredom and that evil race, the daughters of sin, where thou spillest and spendest, and for a common fish consumest thy substance, and for some rotten flesh thou sickenest, reducing thyself over the bone that thou art gnawing: not a prostitute, but the Thracian sea, where thou art taken by the Turks; fly from the occasion, and thou shalt lose the vice; remove the cause, 'tis said, and the effect is removed. Therefore take these hundred ducats, and go to the fair at Salerno, and buy some calves, and in three or four years they will become oxen; and we will sow a field of wheat, and when the wheat becomes ripe, we will gather it, and turn corn-merchants, and if a scarcity should come, then we will measure the crowns with the corn measure; and when there is naught more to do, I will buy thee a title with the fief of some land of a friend of ours, and thou also shalt be titled like so many others; therefore listen thou to me, O my son, as every head lifteth thee higher, and whoso beginneth not cannot go forward.' Answered Nardiello, 'Leave it to me, now I shall keep proper accounts, and I have done with all other matters.' Replied the father, 'And thus I like it to be,' and handing him the money, Nardiello farewelled him, and fared to the fair.

Now he had hardly reached the waters of Sarno, that lovely river, from which the ancient family of Sarnelli taketh its name, when in an avenue of elm-trees, at the foot of a large stone which was watered continually by the fresh water, and had covered itself with a covering of creeping ivy, he beheld a fairy, who was amusing herself with a crab-louse, which played a small guitar, so that had a Spaniard heard it, he would have said that it was a most surprising and wonderful thing. Nardiello, sighting this sight, stood still, like one in a spell, to listen, saying that he would have given anything to be the owner of such a clever beast, and the fairy answered that if he would pay for it an hundred crowns, she would give it to him. Answered Nardiello, 'Never was there a better time than this, as I have them ready for thee,' and thus saying he threw down the one hundred crowns, and taking the crab-louse, which was laid inside a small box, ran to his father in great glee, happy even unto the marrow of his bones; saying, 'Now shalt thou see, O my lord, if I am a man of genius, and if I know how to do mine affair, because without even tiring myself till the evening I have found midway my fortune, and for a hundred crowns I have had such a gem.' The sire, viewing the small case, held for certain that he had bought a rough diamond, but opening the box, and beholding the crab-louse, his contempt, and anger, and vexation for the loss were as bellows puffing him with wrath, and making him swell like the toad.

Nardiello desired to relate the truth about the crab-louse and its ability, but it was impossible for him to do so, for his father would not allow him to speak one word, saying continually, 'Hold thy tongue, be silent, shut thy mouth, speak not, do not even whisper, thou seed of a mule, sense of a horse, head of an ass, and at this very moment go and take back the crab-louse to whomsoever sold it to thee. Here are another hundred crowns, I give them to thee, buy calves, and return at once; and mind not to be blinded by the evil one, or else I will make thee bite thine hands.' Nardiello took the money, and fared toward the tower of Sarno, and arriving at the same spot, he met the fairy who was now amusing herself with a mouse, which was dancing the most pretty figures of dances that ever could be seen. Nardiello stood some time with mouth wide open, staring at the bows, and jumps, and turnings, and twistings of the animal, and he wondered with excessive wonder, and enquired of the fairy if she would sell it, for he would give her an hundred ducats. The fairy accepted the offer, and took the monies, and handed him the mouse within a small box, and he returned home, and shewed to the wretched Miccone the fine wares he had bought. Again the father waxed wroth with excessive wrath, and did things out of mind, stamping about like a fantastical horse; and if it had not been for a gossip who happened to be at the show, the son would have received good measure for his hump. At last Miccone, who was in great wrath, took another hundred ducats, and said to him, 'Be careful and do thy fine tricks no more, for the third will not succeed. Go to Salerno and buy the calves, for by the soul of my dead, if thou playest me another trick, wretched will be the mother that gave thee birth.' Nardiello, with his head bowed downwards, slunk toward Salerno, and arriving at the same place, he was met by the fairy who was amusing herself with a cricket, which sang so sweetly that the folk fell asleep with the sound. Nardiello, who heard this new style of nightingale, at once longed to buy it for his wares; and agreeing to pay the hundred ducats, he laid the cricket in a small cage hollowed out of a vegetable marrow and bits of wood. Thus he returned to his father, and the latter, beholding this third bad service, lost all patience, and taking up a stump, laid it about his shoulders in bad manner, like a Rodomonte.

Nardiello, when he could escape from the claws, took up the three little animals, and left the country, and fared toward Lombardy, where lived a high and mighty lord, Cenzone hight, and he was blessed with an only daughter, named Milla, who for a certain sickness from which she suffered had become melancholy, so much so that for the space of seven years no one had seen her smile. And her sire, being in despair, had attempted a thousand remedies, and spent the cooked and the raw, and at last commanded the crier to publish a ban, that whosoever would cause the lady Milla to laugh, he would give her to him in marriage. Nardiello having heard the ban, the whim seized him to tempt his fortune, and going before Cenzone, he offered to make Milla smile, to which offer answered the lord, 'Be careful, O my comrade, for if the trial be not successful, the mould of thy blood shall pay for it.' Answered Nardiello, 'Let the shape and the shoe go, I will try it, and let happen what will happen.'

The king sent for his daughter, and seating her under the daïs, and taking seat himself, Nardiello came and stood before them, and taking out of the boxes the three animals, put them before them, and they played, and danced, and sang with such grace and sprightliness, that the princess laughed heartily. But the king wept within his heart, because by virtue of the ban, he was obliged to give a jewel of a woman to the dregs of humanity to wife. Yet as he could not withdraw his promise, he said to Nardiello; 'I will give thee my daughter in marriage and my estates as a dowry, if thou wilt agree, that if thou do not consummate within three days the act of matrimony, I will send thee to be food for the lions.' 'I am not afraid,' said Nardiello, 'for in that time I am man enough to consummate the marriage of thy daughter and of all thine house. Slowly we will go on, said the flame: at the trial are proved the melons.'

The marriage feast was spread, and the guests ate and enjoyed their sufficiency, and when the evening came, when the sun, like unto a thief, is carried with the hood over against the jail of the west, the bride and bridegroom went to bed.

Now the king had maliciously given Nardiello some opium, so that all night he did naught else but snore loudly, which thing continued to the second and the third day, when the king bade that he should be cast in the lions' den, where Nardiello finding himself in such a strait, opened the boxes which contained the three animals, saying, 'As my evil fate has brought me to such a dark pass, as I have naught to leave you, O my beautiful animals, I give you your freedom, so that ye may go whither ye please.' The animals, as soon as they were free, began to antic about, and dance, and play in such manner, that the lions remained like statues watching them.

Meanwhile the mouse spake to Nardiello, whose spirit was ready to take flight, saying, 'Hearten thine heart, O our master, that although thou hast given us our liberty, we will be thy slaves, more than ever, because thou hast fed us with so much love, and preserved us with great affection; and at the last thou hast shown unto us signs of such passionate love as to give us our freedom; but doubt not that who doeth good good expecteth. Do a good action and forget it. And thou must know that we are charmed; and to let thee see if we can and will help thee, follow us, and we will save thee from this danger.' And Nardiello followed them, and the mouse at once bored a hole the size of a man, cut stair-wise, by which they went upstairs quite safely, and they led him to an hayloft, and they said to him that he should command whatever he should desire, since they would not leave a thing undone to please him. Said Nardiello, 'The thing that would please me most, is that if the king hath given another husband to Milla, ye would oblige me, if ye were not to allow him to consummate this marriage, because it would be a consummation of this wretched life.' Answered the animals, 'That which thou requirest and naught is all one, hearten thine heart, and await for us in this hayloft, and now we will go to chase away all rottenness.' And they fared toward the court, where they found that the king had wed his daughter to an English lord, and that very night the cask would be open. When they heard this, the animals entered dexterously into the newly wedded couple's chamber, awaiting for the evening, and as soon as the banquet was ended, when the moon cometh forth to feed the chickens with the dew, the pair retired to rest. The bridegroom had loaded his gun, and bent the bow, and taken too much paper, so that as soon as he lay within the sheets, he fell asleep, as one dead. The crab-louse, hearing the snoring of the bridegroom, gently and slowly crept up the bedpost, and slid under the blanket, and quickly crawled to the bridegroom's arse, serving him as a support in such guise, that he opened the body in such wise that he could have said with Petrarch,

'From love it extracted thence a subtle liquid.'

The bride hearing the grumbling of the bowels, and the running dysentery, the zephyr, the odour, the comfort, and the shade, awakened her husband, who, beholding with what a perfume he had incensed his idol, was ready to die with shame and to burst with wrath. Rising from bed, and washing all his body, he sent for the doctors, and they said that the cause of this mishap was due to the disorder of the past banquet.

When the following evening came, again taking counsel with the valets, they one and all advised him to cover himself well, to remedy some other inconvenience; which thing being done, he went to bed, but again falling asleep, the crab-louse returned to its duties, but found the way stopped. For which reason it returned unsatisfied to its companions, saying how the bridegroom had put on repairs of bindings, a bank of ribbons, and a trench of rags. The mouse hearing this, said: 'Come with me, and thou shalt see if a good sapper can cut the way,' and reaching the place, he began to gnaw at the rags and clothes, and to make a hole in level with that other hole. Again the crab-louse entered, and gave him another medicinal dose, in such a guise that a topaz sea came forth, and the Arabian perfumes infected the whole palace. The bride being tainted with such odour awoke, and sighting the orange deluge which had coloured the white Holland sheets to Venetian tabby, holding her nose, flew to the chamber of her handmaidens. The wretched bridegroom, calling the valets, loudly and at length lamented his misfortune, that through a lax foundation the greatness of his house would be closed. His followers and servants comforted him, and advised him to be careful the third night, and related to him the story of the farting sick man, and of the mordacious doctors, the former allowing a fart to escape him, the doctors speaking to him in a learned language, said, 'Sanitatibus,' and the other letting out another, replied, 'Ventositatibus,' but a third following, he opened his mouth widely, and said, 'Asinitatibus.' 'Therefore,' continued they, 'if thy first mosaic work made in the nuptial bed was blamed upon the disorders of the banquet, the second upon the bad condition of the stomach, and this had caused the motion, the third will be imputed to natural looseness and thou wilt be expelled, in a disgraceful and shameful manner.' Said the bridegroom, 'Doubt not, as tonight, were I even to burst, I will keep watch, not allowing sleep to overcome me; and besides this, we will think of what remedy we can use to stop the master conduct, so that no one should say,

'Three times he fell, and at the third lay still.'

Having agreed thus, when the following night came, he changed room and bed, and calling his comrades, he sought their advice so as to stop up the third relaxation of the body, so that he should not be tricked for the third time. As for his remaining awake, not all the poppies in the world would make him fall asleep. Amongst his servants there was a youth whose craft was to make bombards; and as every one speaketh of his craft, he advised the bridegroom to have a wooden stopper made, as it is done for the mortars, which thing was at once done, and put in place as it should be, and he went to bed, not touching the bride, being afraid of doing some mischief and of disarranging the new invention; closing not his eyes, so as to be ready, at every move of the body, to jump out of bed. The crab-louse, who saw that the bridegroom fell not asleep, said to its companions, 'Alas, this time we will fail, and our ability will be for naught; as the bridegroom sleepeth not, and giveth me no time to follow my enterprise.' Said the cricket, 'Wait a moment, and I will serve thee,' and he began to sing sweetly, and after a little while the bridegroom fell asleep; and the crab-louse perceiving it, crept at once to its duty as a syringe. But finding the door bolted, and the way stopped, it returned in despair, and confusion to his companions, relating what had happened.

The mouse, which had no other end in view but to serve Nardiello and please him, at once fared to the pantry, and sniffing about from place to place, it came at last to a pot of mustard, wherein dipping its tail, it returned to the bridegroom's bed, and anointed the nostrils of the unhappy Englishman, and he began to sneeze so loudly and strongly, that the stopper came forth in a fury, and as he lay with his back turned to the bride, it struck her mid-breast with such a blow that it nearly slew her. And she screamed and screeched, and at her screams the king ran in, and enquired of her what ailed her. She told him that a petard had been shot at her breast. And the king marvelled with excessive marvel at such a folly, and wondered how with a petard on her chest she could speak; and lifting the bedclothes, he found the bran mine, and the petard's stopper which had hit the bride, and made a good mark in her breast; although I know not which caused her more disgust, the stink of the powder, or the blow from the ball. The king, beholding such a dirty sight, and hearing that it was the third liquidation of this instrument which he had done, expelled the bridegroom from his estates; and considering that all this evil had happened to him through the cruel treatment used to Nardiello, he struck his breast with repentance; and whilst he lamented what he had done, the crab-louse appeared before him, saying, 'Despair not, as Nardiello liveth, and for his good qualities deserveth to be the son-in-law of thy magnificence; and if thou art pleased that he should come, we will send for him at once.' Answered the king, 'O thou most welcome with the happy tidings, O my beautiful animal. Thou hast saved us from a sea of trouble, as I felt a pricking at mine heart, because of the wrong I had done to that unhappy youth. Therefore bid him come, for I long to embrace him as my son and give him my daughter in marriage.' The cricket hearing this, jumping and dancing, went to the hayloft where was Nardiello, and relating to him what had happened, led him to the royal palace, where he was met and embraced by the king, and the king led Milla to him, and the beasts gave him a spell, and by its power he became a handsome youth, and they sent for his father from Vommaro, and they all lived happily together, proving after a thousand troubles and heartaches that

'More will happen in an hour than in an hundred years.'

Transl. Sir Richard F. Burton

ANON.

From Panegyrick upon Cundums

Cundum I sing, by cundum now secure,
Boldly the willing maid by fear awhile
Kept virtuous, owns thy pow'r, and tastes thy joys
Tumultuous; joys untasted but for them.
Unknown big belly, and the squalling brat,
Best guard of modesty! she riots now
Thy vot'ry, in the fullness of thy bliss.
'Happy the man, who in his pocket keeps,
Whether with green or scarlet ribband bound,
A well-made cundum – he, nor dreads the ills
Of shankers, or cordee, or buboes dire!'[1]

* * *

[1] These four lines in quotes are probably a quotation from an older and better poem on the subject. Shankers are chancres, and cordee is the other spelling of chordee, a painful, downward curving inflammation of the penis – a possible complication of gonorrhoea.

While the hot daring youth, whose giddy lust
Or taste too exquisite, in danger's spite
Resolves upon fruition, unimpair'd
By intervening armour, cundum hight!
Scarce three days past, bewails the dear-bought bliss.
For now, tormented sore with scalding heat
Of urine, dread forerunner of a clap!
With eye repentant, he surveys his shirt,
Diversify'd with spots of yellow hue.
Sad symptom of ten thousand woes to come!
Now no relief but from the surgeon's hand,
Or pill-prescribing leach, tremendous sight
To youth diseas'd in garret high he moans
His wretched fate, where vex'd with nauseous draught
And more afflicting bolus, he in pangs
Unfelt before, curses the dire result
Of lawless revelling; from morn to eve
By never-ceasing keen emetics urg'd;
Nor slights he now his grannam's sage advice:
Nor feels he only but in megrim'd head,
Head fraught with horror – child of sallow spleen,
Millions of idle whims and fancies dance
Alternate, and perplex his lab'ring mind.
What erst he has been told of sad mischance
Either in pox or clap, of falling nose,
Scrap'd shins, and buboes, pains of ill effect!
All feels the youth, or fancies that he feels,
Nay be it but a gleet, or gentlest clap,
His ill foreboding fears deny him rest,
And fancied poxes vex his tortur'd bones;
Too late convinc'd of cundum's sov'reign use.

SIR CHARLES SEDLEY

The Fall

As Chloe o'er the meadow past
    I viewed the lovely maid:
She turned and blushed, renewed her haste,
And feared by me to be embraced:
    My eyes my wish betrayed.

I trembling felt the rising flame,
    The charming nymph pursued;
Daphne was not so bright a game,
Tho' great Apollo's darling dame,
    Nor with such charms endued.

I followed close, the fair still flew
    Along the grassy plain;
The grass at length my rival grew
And catched my Chloe by the shoe;
    Her speed was then in vain.

But, oh! as tottering down she fell,
    What did the fall reveal?
Such limbs description cannot tell;
Such charms were never in the Mall,
    Nor smock did e'er conceal.

She shrieked; I turned my ravished eyes
    And, burning with desire,
I helped the Queen of Love to rise:
She checked her anger and surprise,
    And said, 'Rash youth, retire;

'Begone, and boast what you have seen;
    It shan't avail you much:
I know you like my form and mien,
Yet since so insolent you've been,
    The Parts disclosed you ne'er shall touch.'

JOHN OLDHAM

Upon a Lady, who by overturning of a Coach, had her Coats behind flung up, and what was under shewn to the View of the Company

Phillis, 'tis own'd, I am your Slave,
This happy moment dates your Reign;
No force of Human Pow'r can save
My captive Heart, that wears your chain:
But when my Conquest you design'd;
Pardon, bright Nymph, if I declare,
It was unjust, and too severe,
Thus to attack me from behind.

Against the Charms, your Eyes impart,
With care I had secur'd my Heart;
On all the wonders of your Face
Could safely and unwounded gaze:
But now entirely to enthral
My Breast, you have expos'd to view
Another more resistless Foe,
From which I had no guard at all.

At first assault constrain'd to yield,
My vanquish'd Heart resign'd the Field,
My Freedom to the Conqueror
Became a prey that very hour:
The subtle Traitor, who unspied
Had lurk'd till now in close disguise,
Lay all his life in ambush hid
At last to kill me by surprize.

A sudden Heat by Breast inspir'd,
The piercing Flame, like Light'ning, sent
From that new dawning Firmament
Thro every Vein my Spirits Fir'd;
My Heart, before averse to Love,
No longer could a Rebel prove;
When on the Grass you did display
Your radiant BUM to my survey,
And sham'd the Lustre of the Day.

The Sun in Heav'n, abash'd to see
A thing more gay, more bright than He,
Struck with disgrace, as well he might,
Thought to drive back the Steeds of Light:
His Beams he now thought useless grown,
That better were by yours supplied,
But having once seen your Back-side,
For shame he durst not shew his own.

Forsaking every Wood and Grove,
The *Sylvane* ravish'd at the sight,
In pressing Crowds about you strove,
Gazing, and lost in wonder quite:
Fond *Zephyr* seeing your rich store
Of Beauty, undescried before,
Enamor'd of each lovely Grace,
Before his own dear *Flora*'s face,
Could not forbear to kiss the place.

The beauteous Queen of Flow'rs, the Rose,
In blushes did her shame disclose:
Pale Lillies droop'd, and hung their heads,
And shrunk for fear into their Beds:
The amorous *Narcissus* too,
Reclaim'd of fond self-love by you,
His former vain desire cashier'd,
And your fair Breech alone admir'd.

When this bright Object greets our sight,
All others lose their Lustre quite:
Your Eyes that shoot such pointed Rays,
And all the Beauties of your Face,
Like dwindling Stars, that fly away
At the approach of brighter Day,
No more regard, or value bear,
But when its Glories disappear.

Of some ill Qualities they tell,
Which justly give me cause to fear;
But that, which most begets despair,
It has no sense of Love at all:
More hard than Adamant it is,
They say, that no Impression takes,
It has no Ears, nor any Eyes,
And rarely, very rarely speaks.

Yet I must love't, and own my Flame,
Which to the world I thus rehearse,
Throughout the spacious coasts of Fame
To stand recorded in my Verse:
No other subject, or design
Henceforth shall be my Muses Theme,
But with just Praises to proclaim
The fairest ARSE, that e're was seen.

In pity gentle Phillis hide
The dazling Beams of your Back-side;
For should they shine unclouded long,
All human kind would be undone.
Not the bright Goddesses on high,
That reign above the starry Sky,
Should they turn up to open view
All their immortal Tails, can shew
An *Arse-hole* so divine as you.

From Sardanapalus

Happy, Great-Prince! and so much happier thou
In that thou thine own Happiness did'st know!
Happy, who wast content with what thy wish Enjoy'd,
Nor valued't this – what the whole World cou'd boast beside.
Restless Ambition ne'r Usurpt thy Mind,
To vex thy Pleasures, and disturb Mankind:
With gallant height of Soul, thou didst contemn
That Bauble Honor, and that Geugaw Fame,
And all the Undershrievalties of Life not worth a name!
With wiser choice, thy Judgment plac'd aright
In Cunt its noble Innocent delight:
Cunt was the Star that rul'd thy Fate,
Cunt thy sole Bus'ness, and Affair of State,
And Cunt the only Field to make thee Great:
Cunt thy whole life's fair Center was, whither did bend
All thy Designs, and all thy Lines of Empire tend:
And Cunt the sure unerring Card,
Which, plac'd at Helm, the mighty Vessel and its motion steer'd

Som Saucy Pedants, and Historians, idly Rail,
And thee Effeminate unjustly call:
How ill to him do they that Title give,
Who burnt himself, rather than be debar'd to swive?
Much of thy Ancestors they fondly prate,
By boasted Conquests, and rude War made Great:
Of *Nimrod*, *Ninus*, and *Semiramis* they tell;
Mean Heroes, who cou'd only Fight, and Vanquish well:
How to gain Empire did their Thoughts and Swords employ,
Which 'twas thy nobler Talent to Enjoy.
They now are Dust, as well as Thou,
Of Life, and all its Joys, bereft,
And nothing but their empty Mem'ries left,
An happiness which thou enjoyest too;

For thine as lasting in the Register of Fame shall be:
    And where in Fame does the vast diff'rence lye,
T'have Fought, or Fuck'd for Universal Monarchy?

Upon the Author of the Play call'd Sodom

Tell me, abandon'd Miscreant, prethee tell,
What damned Pow'er, invok'd and sent from Hell
(If Hell were bad enough) did thee Inspire
To write what Fiends asham'd would blushing hear?
Hast thou of late embrac'd some Succubus,
And us'd the lewd Familiar for a Muse?
Or didst thy Soul by Inch oth' Candle sell,
To gain the glorious Name of Pimp to Hell?
If so: go, and its vow'd Allegiance swear,
Without Press-money, be its Voluntier:
May he who envies thee deserve thy Fate,
Deserve both Heav'ns and Mankinds scorn and hate.
Disgrace to Libels! Foil to very Shame!
Whom 'tis a scandal to vouchsafe to damn!
What foul Description's foul enough for thee,
Sunk quite below the reach of Infamy?
Thou covet'st to be lewd, but want'st the Might
And art all over Devil, but in Wit.
Weak feeble strainer at meer Ribaldry,
Whose Muse is impotent to that degree,
'T had need, like Age, be whipt to Lechery.
    Vile Sot! who clapt with Poetry art sick,
And voidst Corruption like a Shanker'd Prick,
Like Ulcers, thy Imposthum'd addle Brains
Drop out in Matter, which thy Paper stains:
Whence nauseous Rhymes by filthy Births proceed,
As Maggots in some Turd ingendring breed.

Thy Muse has got the Flowers, and they ascend
As in some greensick Girl, at upper End.
Sure Nature made, or meant at least 't have don't,
Thy Tongue a Clitoris, thy Mouth a Cunt.
How well a Dildoe would that place become,
To gag it up, and make 't for ever dumb!
At least it should be syring'd –
Or wear some stinking Merkin for a Beard,
That all from its base converse might be scar'd:
As they a Door shut up, and mark't beware,
That tells Infection, and the Plague is there.

     Thou Moorfields Author! fit for Bawds to quote
(If Bawds themselves with Honour safe may do't)
When Suburb-Prentice comes to hire Delight,
And wants Incentives to dull Appetite,
There Punk, perhaps, may thy brave works rehearse,
Frigging the senseless thing with Hand and Verse;
Which after shall (prefer'd to Dressing-Box)
Hold Turpentine, and Med'cines for the Pox:
Or (if I may ordain a Fate more fit
For such foul, nasty excrements of Wit)
May they, condemn'd, to th' publick Jakes be lent,
(For me, I'd fear the Piles in Vengeance sent
Should I with them profane my Fundament)
There bugger wiping Porters when they shite,
And so thy Book itself turn Sodomite.

JOHN WILMOT, EARL OF ROCHESTER

The Earl of Rochester denied authorship of the play *Sodom* in its day, although modern critics generally ascribe it to him. An unknown, Fishbourne, was at one time credited with it.

The play contains non-stop action from such characters as Buggeranthus, Fuckadilla, Clitoris and Virtuoso, the 'Merkin and Dildoe Maker to the Royal Family'. (Merkins were pubic wigs, after which I have named a slightly shabby tortoiseshell cat who visits me.) The plot is minimal, but there are interesting discussions of the relative merits of buggery versus fucking, etc. It's a spoof on the pompous heroic genre of drama. Probably a great deal of it was satire on the court of the day. Parts of it are certainly witty enough to suggest it could have been written by Rochester. My favourite couplet is spoken by Bolloxinion, the King of Sodom:

> My prick no more, shall to bald cunts resort,
> Merkins rub off, and sometimes spoil the sport.

It would be interesting to know if this play was ever performed. The scene directions are extraordinary. One requires a fountain of a woman standing on her head 'and pissing bolt upright'. Even more unusual is the setting for Act V, scene ii:

A grove of Cyprus trees and others cut in shapes of pricks, several arbours, figures and pleasant ornaments in a banqueting house; men are discovered playing tabours and dulcimores with their pricks, and women with jews harps in their cunts.

From Sodom

BOLLOXINION: Faces may change, but cunt is but cunt still;
   And he that fucks is slave to woman's will.
   One dish to feast the palate of a king
   And strive with various sauces to invite
   The grandeur of his critic appetite?
   Yet still the meal's the same; the change doth lie
   But in the sauce's great variety.
   'Tis so with cunts' repeated dull delights;
   Sometimes you've flowers for sauce, and sometimes whites[1]
   And crablice which, like buttered shrimps appear
   And may be served for garnish all the year.

                                                            IV, ii

In the same scene, Buggeranthos, the General of the Army, tells a
sad story:

   Dildoes and dogs with women do prevail,
   I caught one frigging with a cur's bob-tail:
   My lord, said she, I do it with remorse,
   For I once had a passion for a horse
   Who in a moment griev'd and pleas'd my heart.
   I saw him standing pensive in a cart,
   With padded eyes and back with sores oppres't
   And heavy halter hanging on his chest.
   I griev'd for the poor beast, and scratched his mane,
   Pity'd his daily labour and his pain;
   When on a sudden from his scabbard flew
   The stateliest tarse that ever mortal drew,
   Which clinging to his belly, stiff did stand.
   I took and grasped it with my loving hand,
   And in a passion moved it to my cunt,
   But he, being to womankind not wont,

---

[1] Flowers are periods, the whites, leucorrhoea.

Drew back his engine, though my cunt could spare
Perhaps as much room as his lady mare.
At length I found his constancy was such,
That he would none but his dear mistress touch:
Urg'd by his scorn, I did his sight depart,
And so despair surrounded up my heart.
Now wand'ring o'er this vile cunt-starving land
I am content with what comes next to hand.

A Satyr on Charles II

I' th' isle of Britain, long since famous grown
For breeding the best cunts in Christendom,
There reigns, and oh! long may he reign and thrive,
The easiest King and best-bred man alive.
Him no ambition moves to get renown
Like the French fool, that wanders up and down
Starving his people, hazarding his crown.
Peace is his aim, his gentleness is such,
And love he loves, for he loves fucking much.

Nor are his high desires above his strength:
His sceptre and his prick are of a length;
And she may sway the one who plays with th' other,
And make him little wiser than his brother.
Poor prince! thy prick, like thy buffoons at Court,
Will govern thee because it makes thee sport.
'Tis sure the sauciest prick that e'er did swive,
The proudest, peremptoriest prick alive.
Though safety, law, religion, life lay on 't,
'Twould break through all to make its way to cunt.
Restless he rolls about from whore to whore,
A merry monarch, scandalous and poor.

To Carwell,[1] the most dear of all his dears,
The best relief of his declining years,
Oft he bewails his fortune, and her fate:
To love so well, and be beloved so late.
For though in her he settles well his tarse,
Yet his dull, graceless ballocks hang an arse.
This you'd believe, had I but time to tell ye
The pains it costs to poor, laborious Nelly,[2]
Whilst she employs hands, fingers, mouth, and thighs,
Ere she can raise the member she enjoys.
    All monarchs I hate, and the thrones they sit on,
    From the hector of France to the cully of Britain.

[1] Carwell – Louise de Keroualle, Duchess of Portsmouth, one of the King's mistresses.
[2] Nelly – Nell Gwyn.

Song

Fair Chloris in a pigsty lay;
    Her tender herd lay by her.
She slept; in murmuring gruntlings they,
Complaining of the scorching day,
    Her slumbers thus inspire.

She dreamt whilst she with careful pains
    Her snowy arms employed
In ivory pails to fill out grains,
One of her love-convicted swains
    Thus hasting to her cried:

'Fly, nymph! Oh, fly ere 'tis too late
    A dear, loved life to save;
Rescue your bosom pig from fate
Who now expires, hung in the gate
    That leads to Flora's cave.

'Myself had tried to set him free
   Rather than brought the news,
But I am so abhorred by thee
That ev'n thy darling's life from me
   I know thou wouldst refuse.'

Struck with the news, as quick she flies
   As blushes to her face;
Not the bright lightning from the skies,
Nor love, shot from her brighter eyes,
   Move half so swift a pace.

This plot, it seems, the lustful slave
   Had laid against her honor,
Which not one god took care to save,
For he pursues her to the cave
   And throws himself upon her.

Now piercèd is her virgin zone;
   She feels the foe within it.
She hears a broken amorous groan,
The panting lover's fainting moan,
   Just in the happy minute.

Frighted she wakes, and waking frigs.
   Nature thus kindly eased
In dreams raised by her murmuring pigs
And her own thumb between her legs,
   She's innocent and pleased.

The Debauchee

I rise at eleven, I dine about two,
I get drunk before sev'n; and the next thing I do,
I send for my whore, when for fear of a clap,
I spend in her hand, and I spew in her lap;
Then we quarrel and scold, 'till I fall fast asleep,
When the bitch, growing bold, to my pocket does creep;
Then slily she leaves me, and, to revenge the affront,
At once she bereaves me of money and cunt.
If by chance then I wake, hot-headed and drunk,
What a coil do I make for the loss of my punk?
I storm and I roar, and I fall in a rage,
And missing my whore, I bugger my page.
Then, crop-sick all morning, I rail at my men,
And in bed I lie yawning 'till eleven again.

To the Postboy

ROCHESTER: Son of a whore, God damn you! can you tell
    A peerless peer the readiest way to Hell?
    I've outswilled Bacchus, sworn of my own make
    Oaths would fright Furies, and make Pluto quake;
    I've swived more whores more ways than Sodom's walls
    E'er knew, or the College of Rome's Cardinals.
    Witness heroic scars – Look here, ne'er go!
    Cerecloths[1] and ulcers from the top to toe!
    Frighted at my own mischiefs, I have fled
    And bravely left my life's defender dead;[2]
    Broke houses to break chastity, and dyed
    That floor with murder which my lust denied.

[1] Cerecloths were cloths impregnated with wax, used as plasters by surgeons.
[2] 'My life's defender'. Captain Downs died of his wounds ten days after defending Rochester in a brawl at Epsom. Rochester, Etherege and others had beaten the constable there, then fled leaving Downs behind.

Pox on 't, why do I speak of these poor things?
I have blasphemed my God, and libeled Kings!
The readiest way to Hell – Come, quick!
BOY: Ne'er stir
The readiest way, my Lord, 's by Rochester.

SAMUEL BUTLER

The following poem by the author of *Hudibras* was occasioned by the public burning of a hogshead of dildoes at Stocksmarket in 1672.

Dildoides

Such a sad tale prepare to hear,
As claims from either sex a tear.
Twelve dildoes meant for the support
Of aged lechers of the Court
Were lately burnt by impious hand
Of trading rascals of the land,
Who envying their curious frame,
Expos'd those Priaps to the flame.
Oh! barbarous times! when deities
Are made themselves a sacrifice!
Some were composed of shining horns,
More precious than the unicorn's.
Some were of wax, where ev'ry vein,
And smallest fibre were made plain.
Some were for tender virgins fit,
Some for the large falacious slit
Of a rank lady, tho' so torn,
She hardly feels when child is born.

    Dildo has nose, but cannot smell,
No stink can his great courage quell;
Nor faintly ask you what you ail;

E're pintle, damn'd rogue, will do his duty,
And then sometimes he will not stand too,
Whate'er his gallant or mistress can do.
         But I too long have left my heroes,
Who fell into worse hands than Nero's,
Twelve of them shut up in a box,
Martyrs as true as are in Fox
Were seiz'd upon as goods forbidden,
Deep, under unlawful traffick hidden;
When Council grave, of deepest beard,
Were call'd for, out of city-herd.
But see the fate of cruel treachery,
Those goats in head, but not in lechery,
Forgetting each his wife and daughter,
Condemn'd these dildoes to the slaughter;
Cuckolds with rage were blinded so,
They did not their preservers know.
One less fanatic than the rest,
Stood up, and thus himself address'd:
         These dildoes may do harm, I know;
But pray what is it may not so;
Plenty has often made men proud,
And above Law advanc'd the crowd:
Religion's self has ruin'd nations,
And caused vast depopulations;
Yet no wise people e'er refus'd it,
'Cause knaves and fools sometimes abus'd it.
Are you afraid, lest merry griggs[1]
Will wear false pricks like periwigs;
And being but to small ones born,
Will great ones have of wax and horn;
Since even that promotes our gain,
Methinks unjustly we complain,

---

[1] grigg is literally a grasshopper.

If ladies rather chuse to handle
Our wax in dildo than in candle,
Much good may't do 'em, so they pay for it,
And that the merchants never stay for't.
For, neighbours, is't not all one, whether
In dildoes or shoes they wear our leather?
Whether of horn they make a comb,
Or instrument to chafe the womb,
Like you, I Monsieur Dildo hate;
But the invention let's translate.
You treat 'em may like Turks or Jews,
But I'll have two for my own use,
Priapus was a Roman deity,
And much has been the world's variety,
I am resolv'd I'll none provoke,
From the humble garlic to the oak.
He paus'd, another straight steps in,
With limber prick and grisly chin,
And thus did his harangue begin:

    For soldiers, maim'd by chance of war,
We artificial limbs prepare;
Why then should we bear so much spite
To lechers maim'd in am'rous fight?
That what the French send for relief,
We thus condemn as witch or thief?
By dildoe, Monsieur there intends
For his French pox to make amends;
Dildoe, without the least disgrace,
May well supply the lover's place,
And make our elder girls ne'er care for't,
Though 'twere their fortune to dance bare-foot.
Lechers, whom clap or drink disable,
Might here have dildoes to the navel.
Did not a lady of great honour
Marry a footman waiting on her?

When one of these, timely apply'd,
Had eas'd her lust, and sav'd her pride,
Safely her ladyship might have spent,
While such gallants in pocket went.
Honour itself might use the trade,
While dildo goes in masquerade.
Which of us able to prevent is
His girl from lying with his 'prentice,
Unless we other means provide
For nature to be satisfy'd?
And what more proper than his engine,
Which would outdo 'em, should three men join.
I therefore hold it very foolish,
Things so convenient to abolish;
Which should we burn men justly may
To that one act the ruin lay,
Of all that thrown themselves away.

    At this, all parents' hearts began
To melt apace, and not a man
In all the assembly, but found
These reasons solid were and sound.
Poor widows then with voices shrill,
And shouts of joy the hall did fill;
For wicked pricks have no mind to her,
Who has no money, nor no jointure.

    Then one in haste broke thro' the throng,
And cry'd aloud, are we among
Heathens or devils, to let 'scape us
The image of the God Priapus?
Green-sickness girls will strait adore him,
And wickedly fall down before him.
From him each superstitious hussy
Will temples make of tussy mussy[2].

---

[2] Tussy mussy, or tuzzy-muzzy, means a nosegay or bouquet garni. It is also used for old man's beard (i.e. clematis) and by association, a cunt. C.f. E. Ward: 'And salt as Lot's wife's tuzzy-muzzy'.

Idolatry will fill the land,
And all true pricks forget to stand.
Curst be the wretch, who found these arts
Of losing us to women's hearts;
For will they not henceforth refuse one
When they have all that they had use on?
Or how shall I make one to pity me,
Who enjoys Man in his epitome?
Besides, what greater deviation
From sacred rights of propagation,
Than turning th'action of the pool
Whence we all come to ridicule?
The man that would have thunder made,
With brazen road, for courser made,
In my mind did not half so ill do.
As he that found this wicked dildo.
Then let's with common indignation,
Now cause a sudden conflagration
Of all these instruments of lewdness;
And, ladies, take it not for rudeness;
For never was so base a treachery
Contriv'd by mortals against lechery,
Men would kind husbands seem, and able,
With feign'd lust, and borrow'd bawble.
Lovers themselves would dress their passion
In this fantastic new French fashion;
And with false heart and member too,
Rich widows for convenience woo.
But the wise City will take care,
That men shall vend no such false ware.
See now th'unstable vulgar mind
Shook like a leaf with ev'ry wind;
No sooner has he spoke, but all
With a great rage for faggots call:
The reasons which before seem'd good,

Were now no longer understood.
This last speech had the fatal power
To bring the dildoes' latest hour.
   Priapus thus, in box opprest,
   Burnt like a phoenix in her nest;
   But with this fatal diff'rence dies,
   No dildoes from the ashes rise.

ANON

The Tenement

If any man do want a house,
Be he prince, baronet or squire,
Or peasant, hardly worth a louse,
             I can fit his desire.

I have a tenement the which
I'm sure can fit them all;
'Tis seated near a stinking ditch,
             Some call it Cunny Hall.

It stands close by Cunny Alley
At foot of Belly Hill.
This house is freely to be let
             To whom soever will.

For term of life or years or days
I'll let this pleasant bower,
Nay, rather than a tenant want,
             I'll let it for an hour.

About it grows a lofty wood
Will save you from the sun;
Well watered 'tis, for throughout
        A pleasant stream doth run.

If hot, you there may cool yourself,
If cool, you'll there find heat;
For greatest 'tis not too little
        For least 'tis not too great.

I must confess my house is dark,
Be it by night or day,
But when you're once but got therein
        You'll never lose your way.

And when you're in go boldly on
As far as e'er you can,
For if you go to the end thereof
        You go where ne'er did man.

But though my house be deep and dark,
'T has many a man made merry,
And in't much liquor has been spent
        More precious than the sherry.

Thus if you like my Cunny Hall
Your house-room shall be good,
For such a temper as you find
        Burns neither cole nor wood,

For if it rain or freeze or snow –
To speak I dare be bold –
If you keep your nose within the door
        You ne'er shall feel the cold.

But I must covenant with him
That takes this house of mine,
Whether it be for term of life
          Or else for shorter time.

See that you dress it twice a day
And rub it round about,
And if you do dislike of this
          I'll seek a new tenant out.

LAURENCE STERNE

From The Life and Opinions of Tristram Shandy

Tom woos the Jew's widow

As Tom, an' please your honour, had no business at that time with the Moorish girl, he passed on into the room beyond, to talk to the Jew's widow about love – and this pound of sausages; and being, as I have told your honour, an open cheary-hearted lad, with his character wrote in his looks and carriage, he took a chair, and without much apology, but with great civility at the same time, placed it close to her at the table, and sat down.

There is nothing so awkward, as courting a woman, an' please your honour, whilst she is making sausages – So Tom began a discourse upon them; first, gravely, – 'as how they were made – with what meats, herbs, and spices' – Then a little gayly, – as, 'With what skins – and if they never burst – Whether the largest were not the best?' – and so on – taking care only as he went along, to season what he had to say upon sausages, rather under than over; – that he might have room to act in –

It was owing to the neglect of that very precaution, said my uncle Toby, laying his hand upon Trim's shoulder, that Count De la Motte lost the battle of Wynendale: he pressed too speedily into the wood; which if he had not done, Lisle had not fallen into our hands, nor Ghent and Bruges, which both followed her example; it was so late in the year, continued my uncle Toby, and so terrible a season came on, that if things had not fallen out as they did, our troops must have perish'd in the open field. –

– Why, therefore, may not battles, an' please your honour, as well as marriages, be made in heaven? – My uncle Toby mused –

Religion inclined him to say one thing, and his high idea of military skill tempted him to say another; so not being able to frame a reply exactly to his mind – my uncle Toby said nothing at all; and the corporal finished his story.

As Tom perceived, an' please your honour, that he gained ground, and that all he had said upon the subject of sausages was kindly taken, he went on to help her a little in making them. – First, by taking hold of the ring of the sausage whilst she stroked the forced meat down with her hand – then by cutting the strings into proper lengths, and holding them in his hand, whilst she took them out one by one – then, by putting them across her mouth, that she might take them out as she wanted them – and so on from little to more, till at last he adventured to tie the sausage himself, whilst she held the snout. –

– Now a widow, an' please your honour, always chuses a second husband as unlike the first as she can: so the affair was more than half settled in her mind before Tom mentioned it.

She made a feint however of defending herself, by snatching up a sausage: – Tom instantly laid hold of another –

But seeing Tom's had more gristle in it –

She signed the capitulation – and Tom sealed it; and there was an end of the matter.

Vol. IX, ch. VII

BENJAMIN FRANKLIN

Advice on the Choice of a Mistress

Philadelphia, June 25, 1745

My dear Friend:

I know of no medicine fit to diminish the violent natural inclinations you mention, and if I did, I think I should not communicate it to you. Marriage is the proper remedy. It is the most natural state of man, and therefore the state in which you are most likely to find solid happiness. Your reasons against entering into it at present appear to me not well founded. The circumstantial advantages you have in view by postponing it are not only uncertain, but they are small in comparison with that of the thing itself, the being married and settled. It is the man and woman united that make the complete human being. Separate, she wants his force of body and strength of reason; he, her softness, sensibility, and acute discernment. Together they are more likely to succeed in the world. A single man has not nearly the value he would have in the state of union. He is an incomplete animal. He resembles the odd half of a pair of scissors. If you get a prudent, healthy wife, your industry in your profession, with her good economy, will be a fortune sufficient.

But if you will *not* take this counsel and persist in thinking a commerce with the sex inevitable, then I repeat my former advice, that in all your amours you should prefer old women to young ones.

You call this a paradox and demand my reasons. They are these:

1 Because they have more knowledge of the world and their minds are better stored with observations, their conversation is more improving and more lastingly agreeable.

2 Because when women cease to be handsome they study to be good. To maintain their influence over men, they supply the diminution of beauty by an augmentation of utility. They learn to do a thousand services small and great, and are the most tender and useful of friends when you are sick. Thus they continue amiable. And hence there is hardly such a thing to be found as an old woman who is not a good woman.

3 Because there is no hazard of children, which irregularly produced may be attended with much inconvenience.

4 Because through more experience they are more prudent and discreet in conducting an intrigue to prevent suspicion. The commerce with them is therefore safer with regard to your reputation. And with regard to theirs, if the affair should happen to be known, considerate people might be rather inclined to excuse an old woman, who would kindly take care of a young man, form his manners by her good counsels, and prevent his ruining his health and fortune among mercenary prostitutes.

5 Because in every animal that walks upright the deficiency of the fluids that fill the muscles appears first in the highest part. The face first grows lank and wrinkled; then the neck; then the breast and arms; the lower parts continuing to the last as plump as ever: so that covering all above with a basket, and regarding only what is below the girdle, it is impossible of two women to tell an old one from a young one. And as in the dark all cats are gray, the pleasure of corporal enjoyment with an old

woman is at least equal, and frequently superior; every knack being, by practice, capable of improvement.

6 Because the sin is less. The debauching a virgin may be her ruin, and make her for life unhappy.

7 Because the compunction is less. The having made a young girl miserable may give you frequent bitter reflection; none of which can attend the making an old woman happy.

8th and lastly: They are so grateful!

Thus much for my paradox. But still I advise you to marry directly; being sincerely

Your affectionate friend,

Benjamin Franklin

JEAN-JACQUES ROUSSEAU

From the Confessions

Rousseau receives some unwelcome advances

THERE IS NO soul so vile, no heart so barbarous, that it is not susceptible of some kind of attachment. One of the two vagabonds who called themselves Moors conceived an affection for me. He was fond of accosting me, talked to me in his jargon, rendered me slight services, sometimes gave me part of his food, and frequently kissed me with an ardour which was very annoying to me. In spite of the natural alarm which I felt at his gingerbread face decorated with a long scar, and his inflamed countenance which appeared more furious than tender, I endured his kisses, saying to myself: 'The poor fellow has conceived a lively friendship for me. I should be wrong to repulse him.' He gradually began to take greater liberties, and sometimes made such curious proposals to me, that I thought he was mad. One night, he wanted to sleep with me. I refused, saying that my bed was too small. He pressed me to go to his, but I again refused, for the wretch was so dirty and stunk so strongly of chewed tobacco, that he made me quite sick.

Early on the following morning, we were both alone in the assembly-room. He recommenced his caresses, but with such violent movements, that it became quite alarming. At last, he wanted to take the most disgusting liberties with me, and, taking hold of my hand, tried to make me take the same with him. I uttered a loud cry, and, jumping back, freed myself from him; and, without exhibiting anger or indignation, for I had not the least idea what it was all about, I expressed my surprise and disgust so energetically, that he left me where I was; but, while he was finishing his efforts, I saw something white, like glue, shoot towards the fireplace and fall upon the ground, which turned my stomach. I rushed upon the balcony, more moved, more troubled, more frightened than I had ever been in my life, and prepared to find myself ill.

I could not understand what had been the matter with the wretch. I believed that he was attacked by epilepsy, or some other madness even more terrible; and in truth, I know nothing more hideous for any cool-blooded person to see than such filthy and dirty behaviour, and a frightful countenance inflamed by brutal lust. I have never seen another man in a similar condition; but if we are like it when we are with women, their looks must certainly be bewitched, for them not to feel disgusted at us.

Rousseau goes flashing

HAVING LEFT MADAME de Vercellis's house in almost the same state as I had entered it, I went back to my old landlady, with whom I remained for five or six weeks, during which health, youth, and idleness again rendered my temperament troublesome. I was restless, absent-minded, a dreamer. I wept, I sighed, I longed for a happiness of which I had no idea, and of which I nevertheless felt the want. This state cannot be described; only few men can even imagine it, because most of them have anticipated this fulness of life, at once so tormenting and so delicious, which, in the intoxication of desire, gives a foretaste of enjoyment. My heated blood incessantly filled my brain with girls and women; but, ignorant of the relations of sex, I made use of them in my imagination in accordance with my distorted notions, without knowing what else to do with them; and these notions kept my feelings in a state of most uncomfortable activity, from which, fortunately, they did not teach me how to deliver myself. I would have given my life to have found another Mademoiselle Goton for a quarter of an hour. But it was no longer the time when childish amusements took this direction as if naturally. Shame, the companion of a bad conscience, had made its appearance with advancing years; it had increased my natural shyness to such an extent that it made it unconquerable; and never, neither then nor later, have I been able to bring myself to make an indecent proposal, unless she, to whom I made it, in some measure forced me to it by her advances, even though I knew that she was by no means scrupulous, and felt almost certain of being taken at my word.

My agitation became so strong that, being unable to satisfy my desires, I excited them by the most extravagant behaviour. I haunted dark alleys and hidden retreats, where I might be able to expose myself to women in the condition in which I should have liked to have been in their company. What they saw was not an obscene object, I never even thought of such a thing; it was a ridiculous object. The foolish pleasure I took in displaying it before their eyes cannot be described. There was only one step further necessary for me to take, in order to gain actual experience of the treatment I desired, and I have no doubt that some one would have been bold enough to afford me the amusement, while passing by, if I had had the boldness to wait. This folly of mine led to a disaster almost as comical, but less agreeable for myself.

One day, I took up my position at the bottom of a court where there was a well, from which the girls of the house were in the habit of fetching water. At this spot there was a slight descent which led to some cellars by several entrances. In the dark I examined these underground passages, and finding them long and dark, I concluded that there was no outlet, and that, if I happened to be seen and surprised, I should find a safe hiding-place in them. Thus emboldened, I exhibited to the girls who came to the well a sight more laughable than seductive. The more modest pretended to see nothing; others began to laugh; others felt insulted and made a noise. I ran into my retreat; someone followed me. I heard a man's voice, which I had not expected, and which alarmed me. I plunged underground at the risk of losing myself; the noise, the voices, the man's voice, still followed me. I had always reckoned upon the darkness; I saw a light. I shuddered, and plunged further into the darkness. A wall stopped me, and, being unable to go any further, I was obliged to await my fate. In a moment I was seized by a tall man with a big moustache, a big hat, and a big sword, who was escorted by four or five old women, each armed with a broom-handle, amongst whom I perceived the little wretch who had discovered me, and who, no doubt, wanted to see me face to face.

Nineteenth-century translation

JONATHAN SWIFT

A Beautiful Young Nymph Going to Bed

Written for the honour of the fair sex

Corinna, pride of Drury Lane,
For whom no shepherd sighs in vain;
Never did Covent Garden boast
So bright a batter'd strolling toast!
No drunken rake to pick her up;
No cellar where on tick to sup;
Returning at the midnight hour,
Four stories climbing to her bower;
Then, seated on a three-legg'd chair,
Takes off her artificial hair;
Now picking out a crystal eye,
She wipes it clean and lays it by.
Her eyebrows from a mouse's hide
Stuck on with art on either side,
Pulls off with care, and first displays 'em,
Then in a play-book smoothly lays 'em.
Now dextrously her plumpers draws,
That serve to fill her hollow jaws,
Untwists a wire, and from her gums
A set of teeth completely comes;
Pulls out the rags contrived to prop
Her flabby dugs, and down they drop.
Proceeding on, the lovely goddess
Unlaces next her steel-ribb'd bodice,
Which, by the operator's skill,
Press down the lumps, the hollows fill.
Up goes her hand, and off she slips
The bolsters that supply her hips;

With gentlest touch she next explores
Her shankers, issues, running sores;
Effects of many a sad disaster,
And then to each applies a plaster;
But must, before she goes to bed,
Rub off the daubs of white and red,
And smooth the furrows in her front
With greasy paper stuck upon't.
She takes a bolus ere she sleeps;
And then between two blankets creeps.
With pains of love tormented lies;
Or, if she chance to close her eyes,
Of Bridewell and the Compter dreams,
And feels the lash, and faintly screams;
Or, by a faithless bully drawn,
At some hedge-tavern lies in pawn;
Or to Jamaica seems transported
Alone, and by no planter courted;
Or, near Fleet Ditch's oozy brinks,
Surrounded with a hundred stinks,
Belated, seems on watch to lie,
And snap some cully passing by;
Or, struck with fear, her fancy runs
On watchmen, constables, and duns,
From whom she meets with frequent rubs;
But never from religious clubs,
Whose favour she is sure to find,
Because she pays them all in kind.

    Corinna wakes. A dreadful sight!
Behold the ruins of the night!
A wicked rat her plaster stole,
Half eat, and dragg'd it to his hole.
The crystal eye, alas! was miss'd;
And puss had on her plumpers piss'd.

A pigeon pick'd her issue-peas;
And Shock her tresses fill'd with fleas.

   The nymph, though in this mangled plight,
Must every morn her limbs unite.
But how shall I describe her arts
To re-collect the scatter'd parts?
Or show the anguish, toil, and pain,
Of gathering up herself again?
The bashful Muse will never bear
In such a scene to interfere.
Corinna, in the morning dizen'd,
Who sees, will spew; who smells, be poison'd.

The Lady's Dressing-Room

Five hours (and who can do it less in?)
By haughty Celia spent in dressing;
The goddess from her chamber issues,
Array'd in lace, brocades, and tissues.

   Strephon, who found the room was void,
And Betty otherwise employ'd,
Stole in, and took a strict survey
Of all the litter as it lay:
Whereof, to make the matter clear,
An inventory follows here.

   And, first, a dirty smock appear'd,
Beneath the armpits well besmear'd:
Strephon, the rogue, display'd it wide,
And turn'd it round on every side:
On such a point, few words are best,
And Strephon bids us guess the rest;
But swears, how damnably the men lie
In calling Celia sweet and cleanly.

Now listen, while he next produces
The various combs for various uses;
Fill'd up with dirt, so closely fixt,
No brush could force a way betwixt;
A paste of composition rare,
Sweat, dandriff, powder, lead, and hair;
A forehead cloth with oil upon't,
To smooth the wrinkles on her front:
Here alum-flower, to stop the steams
Exhaled from sour unsavoury streams;
There night-gloves made of Tripsey's hide,
Bequeath'd by Tripsey when she died;
With puppy-water, beauty's help,
Distill'd from Tripsey's darling whelp.
Here gallipots[1] and vials placed,
Some fill'd with washes, some with paste;
Some with pomatums, paints, and slops,
And ointments good for scabby chops.
Hard by a filthy basin stands,
Foul'd with the scouring of her hands:
The basin takes whatever comes,
The scrapings from her teeth and gums,
A nasty compound of all hues,
For here she spits, and here she spews.

But, oh! it turn'd poor Strephon's bowels,
When he beheld and smelt the towels,
Begumm'd, bematter'd, and beslimed,
With dirt, and sweat, and ear-wax grimed;
No object Strephon's eye escapes;
Her petticoats in frowzy heaps;
Nor be the handkerchiefs forgot,
All varnish'd o'er with snuff and snot.

---

[1] Earthen pots used by apothecaries.

The stockings why should I expose,
Stain'd with the moisture of her toes,
Or greasy coifs, or pinners reeking,
Which Celia slept at least a week in?
A pair of tweezers next he found,
To pluck her brows in arches round;
Or hairs that sink the forehead low,
Or on her chin like bristles grow.

The virtues we must not let pass
Of Celia's magnifying-glass;
When frighted Strephon cast his eye on't,
It show'd the visage of a giant;
A glass that can to sight disclose
The smallest worm in Celia's nose,
And faithfully direct her nail
To squeeze it out from head to tail;
For, catch it nicely by the head,
It must come out, alive or dead.

Why, Strephon, will you tell the rest?
And must you needs describe the chest?
That careless wench; no creature warn her
To move it out from yonder corner!
But leave it standing full in sight,
For you to exercise your spite?
In vain the workman show'd his wit,
With rings and hinges counterfeit,
To make it seem in this disguise
A cabinet to vulgar eyes:
Which Strephon ventured to look in,
Resolved to go through thick and thin,
He lifts the lid; there needs no more,
He smelt it all the time before.

As, from within Pandora's box
When Epimetheus oped the locks,

A sudden universal crew
Of human evils upward flew,
He still was comforted to find
That hope at last remain'd behind:
So Strephon, lifting up the lid,
To view what in the chest was hid,
The vapours flew from out the vent:
But Strephon, cautious, never meant
The bottom of the pan to grope,
And foul his hands in search of hope.

  O! ne'er may such a vile machine
Be once in Celia's chamber seen!
O! may she better learn to keep
Those 'secrets of the hoary deep.'

  As mutton-cutlets, prime of meat,
Which, though with art, you salt and beat,
As laws of cookery require,
And roast them at the clearest fire;
If from adown the hopeful chops
The fat upon the cinder drops,
To stinking smoke it turns the flame,
Poisoning the flesh from whence it came,
And up exhales a greasy stench,
For which you curse the careless wench:
So things which must not be exprest,
When plump'd into the reeking chest
Send up an excremental smell
To taint the parts from whence they fell;
The petticoats and gown perfume,
And waft a stink round every room.

  Thus finishing his grand survey,
Disgusted Strephon stole away;
But Vengeance, goddess never sleeping,
Soon punish'd Strephon for his peeping:

His foul imagination links
Each dame he sees with all her stinks;
And, if unsavoury odours fly,
Conceives a lady standing by.
All women his description fits,
And both ideas jump like wits;
By vicious fancy coupled fast,
And still appearing in contrast.

I pity wretched Strephon, blind
To all the charms of womankind.
Should I, the Queen of Love refuse,
Because she rose from stinking ooze?
To him that looks behind the scene,
Statira's but some pocky quean.

When Celia all her glory shows,
If Strephon would but stop his nose,
(Who now so impiously blasphemes
Her ointments, daubs, and paints, and
creams
Her washes, slops, and every clout,
With which he makes so foul a rout;)
He soon will learn to think like me,
And bless his ravish'd eyes to see
Such order from confusion sprung,
Such gaudy tulips raised from dung.

MISS W.

The Gentleman's Study, In Answer to [Swift's] *The Lady's Dressing-Room*

Some write of angels, some of goddess,
But I of dirty human bodies,
And lowly I employ my pen,
To write of naught but odious men;
And man I think, without a jest,
More nasty than the nastiest beast.

In house of office, when they're bare,
And have not paper then to spare,
Their hands they'll take, half clean their bottom,
And daub the wall, O —— rot 'em;
And in a minute, with a turd,
They'll draw them out a beast or bird,
And write there without ink or pen:
When finger's dry, there's arse again.
But now high time to tell my story;
But 'tis not much to all men's glory.

A milliner, one Mrs South,
I had the words from her own mouth,
That had a bill, which was long owing
By Strephon, for cloth, lace and sewing;
And on a day to's lodging goes,
In hopes of payment for the clothes,
And meeting there, and 'twas by chance,
His valet Tom, her old acquaintance,
Who, with an odd but friendly grin,
Told her his master's not within,
But bid her if she pleased to stay,
He'd treat her with a pot of tea;
So brought her to the study, while
He'd go and make the kettle boil.

She sat her down upon the chair,
For that was all that then was there,
And turned her eyes on every side,
Where strange confusion she espied.

There on a block a wig was set,
Whose inside did so stink with sweat;
The outside oiled with jessamine,
T' disguise the stench that was within.

And next a shirt, with gussets red,
Which Strephon slept in, when in bed;
But modesty forbids the rest,
It shan't be spoke, but may be guessed;
A napkin worn [up]on a head,
Enough, infection to have bred.

For there some stocks lay on the ground,
One side was yellow, t' other brown;
And velvet breeches (on her word),
The inside all bedaubed with turd,
And just before, I'll not desist
To let you know they were be-pissed:
Four different stinks lay there together,
Which were sweat, turd, and piss, and leather.

There in a heap lay nasty socks,
Here tangled stockings with silver clocks,
And towels stiff with soap and hair,
Of stinking shoes there lay a pair;
A nightgown, with gold rich-brocaded,
About the neck was sadly faded.

A close-stool helped to make the fume;
Tobacco-spits about the room,
With phlegm and vomit on the walls;
Here powder, dirt, combs and wash-balls;
Oil-bottles, paper, pens, and wax,
Dice, pamphlets, and of cards some packs;
Pig-tail and snuff, and dirty gloves,
Some plain, some fringed, which most he loves;
A curling-iron stands upright,
False locks and oil lay down close by't;
A drabbled cloak hung on a pin,
And basin furred with piss within;
Of pipes a heap, some whole, some broke,
Some cut-and-dry for him to smoke;
And papers that his arse has cleaned,
And handkerchiefs with snuff all stained:
The sight and smells did make her sick,
She did not come to herself for a week.

A coat that lay upon the table,
To reach so far she scarce was able,
But drew it to her, resolved to try
What's in the pockets, by and by.

The first things that present her view
Were dunning-letters, not a few;
And then the next did make her wonder,
To see of tavern-bills such a number;
And a fine snuff-box there lay hid,
With bawdy picture in the lid,
And as she touched it, by the mass,
It turned, and showed a looking-glass.

The rest she found, since I'm a-telling,
Advertisements of land he's selling,
A syringe, and some dirty papers,
A bawdy-house screw,[1] with box of wafers.

Then all the shelves she searched around,
Where not one book was to be found;
But gallipots all in a row,
And glistening vials, a fine show!

[1] A bill.

What one pot held she thinks was this:
Diaclom magnum cum gummis,
And spread there was with art, *secundum*
Unguentum neopolitanum;[2]
Pots of pomatum, panacea,
Injections for a gonorrhea;
Of empty ones there were a score,
Of newly filled as many more.
In plenty too stood box of pills,
Nor did there lack for chirurgeon's bills,
Nor nasty rags all stiff with matter,
Nor bottle of mercurial water,
The use of which he does determine
To cure his itch, and kill his vermin:
'Oh heaven!' says she, 'what creature's man?
All stink without, and worse within!'

With that she rose and went away,
For there she could no longer stay;
And scarce she got in the bedchamber,
And thought herself there out of danger,
But quick she heard with both her ears
Strephon come swearing up the stairs;
She swiftly crept behind the screen,
In order not for to be seen.

---

[2] These lines refer to venereal cures.

Then in came Strephon, lovely sight!
Who had not slept a wink all night;
He staggers in, he swears, he blows,
With eyes like fire, and snotty nose;
A mixture glazed his cheeks and chin
Of claret, snuff, and odious phlegm;
And servant with him, to undress him,
And loving Strephon so caressed him:
'Come hither, Tom, and kiss your master;
Oons, to my groin come put a plaster.'

Tom dexterously his part he played,
To touch his bubo's not afraid;
Nor need he then to hesitate,
But strewed on the precipitate;
Then, in a moment, all the room
Did with the smell of ulcer fume,
And would have lasted very long,
Had not sour belches smelled as strong,
Which from her nose did soon depart,
When overcome with stink of fart,
And after, then came thick upon it
The odious, nauseous one of vomit,
That pourèd out from mouth and nose
Both on his bed, and floor, and clothes;
Nor was it lessened e'er a bit,
Nor overcome, by stink of shit,
Which, in the pot and round about
The brim and sides, he squirted out;
But when poor Tom pulled off his shoes,
There was a greater stink of toes,
And sure, a nasty, loathsome smell
Must come from feet as black as hell.

Then tossed in bed Tom left his Honour,
And went to call up Peggy Connor
To empty th' pot, and mop the room,
To bring up ashes and a broom,
And after that, mostly pleasantly
To keep his master company.
The prisoner now being suffocated,
And saw the door was wide dilated,
She thought high time to post away,
For it was ten o'clock i' th' day;
And, ere that she got out of doors,
He turns, farts, hiccups, groans and snores.

Ladies, you'll think 'tis admirable
That this to all men's applicable;
And though they dress in silk and gold,
Could you their insides but behold,
There you fraud, lies, deceit would see,
And pride, and base impiety.
So let them dress the best they can,
They still are fulsome, wretched Man.

ALAIN-RENE LE SAGE

From Le Diable Boiteux

Asmodeus is showing Cleofas various lovers

The knight

HE LIES MOTIONLESS, as you see, that a plate of lead on his forehead may have its due effect in preserving its smoothness. His hands are tied up that they may be white in the morning, and his waist braced up with an iron bodice to preserve his shape. In this extraordinary posture he is calling upon cruel Belinda; and, amidst a thousand cutting reflections on the ill success of his passion, it is no small mortification to him that, by the itching on the left side of his nose, he feels that he shall have a pimple there before morning.

From a nineteenth-century translation under the title of *The Devil on Two Sticks*

TOBIAS SMOLLETT

From Humphrey Clinker

Part of a letter from J. Melford to Sir Watkin Phillips

THEN ADDRESSING HIMSELF to my uncle, 'Sir, (said he), you seem to be of a dropsical habit, and probably will soon have a confirmed *ascites*: if I should be present when you are tapped, I will give you a convincing proof of what I assert, by drinking without hesitation the water that comes out of your abdomen.' – The ladies made wry faces at this declaration, and my uncle, changing colour, told him he did not desire any such proof of his philosophy: 'But I should be glad to know (said he) what makes you think I am of a dropsical habit?' 'Sir, I beg pardon (replied the doctor), I perceive your ancles are swelled, and you seem to have the *facies leucophlegmatica*. Perhaps, indeed, your disorder may be *oedematous*, or gouty, or it may be the *lues venerea*: If you have any reason to flatter yourself it is this last, sir, I will undertake to cure you with three small pills, even if the disease should have attained its utmost inveteracy. Sir, it is an arcanum which I have discovered, and prepared with infinite labour. – Sir, I have lately cured a woman in Bristol – a common prostitute, sir, who had got all the worst symptoms of the disorder; such as *nodi*, *tophi*, and *gummata*, *verrucæ*, *cristæ Galli*, and a *serpiginous* eruption, or rather a pocky itch all over her body. – By the time she had taken the second pill, sir, by Heaven! she was as smooth as my hand, and the third made her as sound and as fresh as a new born infant.' 'Sir (cried my uncle peevishly), I have no reason to flatter myself that my disorder comes within the efficacy of your nostrum. But, this patient you talk of, may not be so sound at bottom as you imagine.' 'I can't possibly be mistaken (rejoined the philosopher): for I have had communication with her three times – I always ascertain my cures in that manner.' At this remark, all the ladies retired to another corner of the room, and some of them began to spit. – As to my uncle, though he was ruffled at first by the doctor's saying he was dropsical, he could not help smiling at this ridiculous confession, and, I suppose, with a view to punish this original, told him there was a wart upon his nose, that looked a little suspicious. 'I don't pretend to be a judge of those matters (said he); but I understand that warts are often produced by the distemper; and that one upon your nose seems to have taken possession of the very keystone of the bridge, which I hope is in no danger of falling.' L—n seemed a little confounded at this remark, and assured him it was nothing but a common excrescence of the cuticula, but that the bones were all sound below; for the truth of this assertion he appealed to the touch, desiring he would feel the part. My uncle said it was a matter of such delicacy to meddle with a gentleman's nose, that he declined the office – upon which, the Doctor turning to me, intreated me to do him that favour. I complied with his request, and handled it so roughly, that he sneezed, and the tears ran down his cheeks, to the no small entertainment of the company, and particularly of my uncle, who burst out a-laughing for the first time since I have been with him; and took notice, that the part seemed to be very tender. 'Sir (cried the Doctor), it is naturally a tender part; but to remove all possibility of doubt, I will take off the wart this very night.'

So saying, he bowed with great solemnity all round, and retired to his own lodgings, where he applied a caustic to the wart; but it spread in such a manner as to produce a considerable inflammation, attended with an enormous swelling; so that when he next appeared, his whole face was overshadowed by this tremendous nozzle; and the rueful eagerness with which he explained this unlucky accident, was ludicrous beyond all description. – I was much pleased with meeting the original of a character, which you and I have often laughed at in description; and what surprizes me very much, I find the features in the picture, which has been drawn for him, rather softened than over-charged. –

As I have something else to say; and this letter has run to an unconscionable length, I shall now give you a little respite, and trouble you again by the very first post. I wish you would take it in your head to retaliate these double strokes upon

Yours always,
J. Melford.

NICOLAS RESTIF DE LA BRETONNE

From Monsieur Nicolas

The doctor's wife

A WEEK LATER, I was walking along the Rue Mazarine, after leaving the Comédie Française. I turned round at the sound of a light step. It was Camargo who, having seen me in front of her, had quickened her step. I greeted her as respectfully as possible and walked along beside her. 'What were you doing at our theatre today? Mademoiselle Guéant was not acting.' I told her that I had come for the tragedy, for the little play, for the ballet. I went up to her apartment without her raising any objections. She told me to knock, and a maidservant came with a lamp. She dismissed her as soon as we had entered. We chatted like old acquaintances. She put on her garters. I am sure that the first Camargo, that famous dancer at the Opera, might have had more talent, but that she did not have such voluptuously shaped legs as the second Camargo. I kissed her warmly. 'Oh!' she exclaimed. 'I am neither Guéant nor Junie!' 'But now that you have pronounced those sacred names, you will take the plunge.' And I pushed her on to her back. 'Have a care!' she cried. 'Taking the plunge is dangerous, and love is sometimes drowned.' 'I am going to drown mine!' I exclaimed. At this, Camargo burst into such immoderate laughter that I thought it was an effect of her art. In between her bursts of laughter, she cried out: 'It is . . . it is sinking . . . sinking . . . sinking!' 'I have picked the rose!' I exclaimed at last. 'And I felt the thorn,' said Camargo, pulling a face. Then she spoke to me most disobligingly, telling me that I was one of those little womanizers who were the scourge of her sex, but that all those she met she punished.

I went home reflecting on this strange adventure, and, in my turgid drunkenness, I blessed chance, swearing that henceforth I would trust it alone. Eight or ten days went by: in the meantime the prick of the thorn of Camargo's rose started festering: inflammation appeared; a burning fire, as in Phaethon's day, flowed from my veins, and water, impregnated with fire, burnt the channel which until then it had lubrefied; dull pains, like those which had made David cry out: *'Lumbi mei impleti sunt illusionibus!'* ['My loins are filled with a loathsome disease!'] almost prevented me from standing up straight. I had to confide in Loiseau. We had recourse to a medical man called Lacan. Here I must say that it is not to the surgeons that a man should turn for a cure for syphilis; they are only clumsy charlatans in this matter, while the charlatans, such as Nicole, Algeroni, etc. are the real doctors. My friend Dr Gilbert de Préval has explained to me that the reason is that the surgeons know only the old, inadequate mercury treatment, and that this method called for infinite precautions which the surgeons overlooked; whereas the *ad hoc* doctors employed a treatment which was undemanding and therefore neverfailing. Lacan began by bleeding me, and this useless treatment sent me into a swoon lasting three quarters of an hour. The treatment was lengthy, as a result of my inexperience and my physician's negligence. I was almost cured, and yet I still went to collect my pills. A young man, a handsome lad, my masseur, used to hand them over to me. One day he was absent; but I insisted on having them. A maidservant referred me to Madame Lacan, a charming young woman whom I had only glimpsed before. She asked me in. 'Are you not Monsieur Nicolas, whom Labadie has mentioned to me so often?' (Labadie was the boy.) 'Yes, Madame.' 'But you must be cured by now! You are ruining your stomach with your pills. Let us see.' (She took me into a consulting-room.) 'Undo that. A little redness but no more discharge.' (Her soft hand squeezed everything.) 'Can you feel anything?' 'Considerable pleasure,' I replied. 'That is not what I was asking you,' she went on severely; 'I am taking an interest in your health because Monsieur Loiseau has spoken highly to me of you, because Monsieur Lacan is neglecting you, and because Labadie, I do not know why, seems to want to spin out your treatment.' She had gone on examining me while she was speaking. I could not hold out any longer, and . . . *eruperunt fontes vitae* [the springs of life burst forth]. Madame Lacan coldly inspected the result and told me: 'You are cured.' She gave me a little bottle of lead salts and a little syringe, and told me how to use it. 'See no more of Camargo or her like; those women have never had either real beauty or real kindness or real health.' She dismissed me. You cannot imagine how wonder-struck I was at the stoicism, the cool self-possession of that pretty young woman – a cool self-possession far removed from the blasé passivity of Camargo who shouted odd remarks at times when she should have been crying out with pleasure.

From the autobiography of Restif de la Bretonne,
translated by Robert Baldick

FRANÇOIS-MARIE AROUET (VOLTAIRE)

From Candide

Candide in Paraguay

THE SUN WAS now on the point of setting when the ears of our two wanderers were assailed with cries which seemed to be uttered by a female voice. They could not tell whether these were cries of grief or joy; however, they instantly started up, full of that inquietude and apprehension which a strange place naturally inspires. The cries proceeded from two young women who were tripping stark naked along the mead, while two monkeys followed close at their heels, biting their backs. Candide was touched with compassion; he had learned to shoot while he was among the Bulgarians, and he could hit a filbert in a hedge without touching a leaf. Accordingly he takes up his double-barrel Spanish fusil, pulls the trigger, and lays the two monkeys lifeless on the ground. 'God be praised, my dear Cacambo, I have rescued two poor girls from a most perilous situation. If I have committed a sin in killing an Inquisitor and a Jesuit, I made ample amends by saving the lives of these two distressed damsels. Who knows but they may be young ladies of a good family, and that this assistance I have been so happy to give them may procure us great advantage in this country.'

He was about to continue when he felt himself struck speechless at seeing the two girls embracing the dead bodies of the monkeys in the tenderest manner, bathing their wounds with their tears, and rending the air with the most doleful lamentations. 'Really,' said he to Cacambo, I should not have expected to see such a prodigious share of good-nature.' 'Master,' replied the knowing valet, 'you have made a precious piece of work of it: do you know that you have killed the lovers of these two ladies.' 'Their lovers, Cacambo! You are jesting; it cannot be; I can never believe it.' 'Dear sir,' replied Cacambo, 'you are surprised at everything; why should you think it so strange that there should be a country where monkeys insinuate themselves into the good graces of the ladies? They are the fourth part of a man, as I am the fourth part of a Spaniard.' 'Alas!' replied Candide, 'I remember to have heard my master Pangloss say that such accidents as these frequently came to pass in former times; and that these commixtures are productive of centaurs, fauns, and satyrs; and that many of the ancients had seen such monsters; but I looked upon the whole as fabulous.' 'Now you are convinced,' said Cacambo, 'that it is very true; and you see what use is made of those creatures by persons who have not had a proper education.'

From a nineteenth-century translation

JOHN CLELAND

From Fanny Hill, or the Memoirs of a Woman of Pleasure

Fanny Hill observes Mrs Brown and her lover

ONE DAY, ABOUT twelve at noon, being thoroughly recover'd of my fever, I happen'd to be in Mrs Brown's dark closet, where I had not been half an hour, resting upon the maid's settee-bed, before I heard a rustling in the bedchamber, separated from the closet only by two sashdoors, before the glasses of which were drawn two yellow damask curtains, but not so close as to exclude the full view of the room from any person in the closet.

I instantly crept softly, and posted myself so, that seeing everything minutely, I could not myself be seen; and who should come in but the venerable mother Abbess herself! handed in by a tall, brawny young Horse-grenadier, moulded in the Hercules style: in fine, the choice of the most experienced dame, in those affairs, in all London.

Oh! how still and hush did I keep at my stand, lest any noise should baulk my curiosity, or bring Madam into the closet!

But I had not much reason to fear either, for she was so entirely taken up with her present great concern, that she had no sense of attention to spare to anything else.

Droll was it to see that clumsy fat figure of hers flop down on the foot of the bed, opposite to the closet-door, so that I had a full front-view of all her charms.

Her paramour sat down by her: he seemed to be a man of very few words, and a great stomach; for proceeding instantly to essentials, he gave her some hearty smacks, and thrusting his hands into her breasts, disengag'd them from her stays, in scorn of whose confinement they broke loose, and swaggered down, navel-low at least. A more enormous pair did my eyes never behold, nor of a worse colour, flagging-soft, and most lovingly contiguous: yet such as they were, this neck-beef eater seem'd to paw them with a most uninvitable lust, seeking in vain to confine or cover one of them with a hand scarce less than a shoulder of mutton. After toying with them thus some time, as if they had been worth it, he laid her down pretty briskly, and canting up her petticoats, made barely a mask of them to her broad red face, that blush'd with nothing but brandy.

His back being now towards me, I could only take his being ingulph'd for granted, by the directions he mov'd in; and now the bed shook, the curtains rattled so, that I could scarce hear the sighs and murmurs, the heaves and pantings that accompanied the action, from the beginning to the end; the sound and sight of which thrill'd to the very soul of me, and made every vein of my body circulate liquid fires: the emotion grew so violent that it almost intercepted my respiration.

Prepared then, and disposed as I was by the discourse of my companions, and Phœbe's minute detail of everything, no wonder that such a sight gave the last dying blow to my native innocence.

This over, they both went out lovingly together, the old lady having first made him a present, as near as I could observe, of three or four pieces; he being not only her particular favourite on account of his performances, but a retainer to the house; from whose sight she had taken great care hitherto to secrete me, lest he might not have had patience to wait for my lord's arrival, but have insisted on being his taster, which the old lady was under too much subjection to him to dare dispute with him; for every girl of the house fell to him in course, and the old lady now and then got her turn, in consideration of the maintenance he had, and which he could scarce be accused of not earning from her.

'A WHORE OF QUALITY'

From The Whore

Whore is my theme, ye sisters all attend,
Give your applause, and be a sister's friend;
If this ye do, and cast a fav'ring eye,
Those sons of whores, the Critics, I defy.

Of all the crimes condemn'd in women-kind,
Whore, in the catalogue, the first you'll find;
This vulgar term is in the mouth of all
An epithet, on every female's fall.
And what's a Whore? Go ask the nations round;
Is it an empty name, and nought but sound?
Is it, above all other sins, the worst?
By man despised, and by God accurs'd?
If that's the case, and scripture we believe,
What was the crime alledg'd to grandam Eve?
What was the fruit the Tree of Knowledge shew'd,
And made her break her promise to her God?
What in the serpent could o'er her prevail;
Was the great evil in his head or tail?
The Devil himself must clear up the dispute,
Who knew the virtue of the fatal fruit.

But what's a whore in life? – pray let us find,
If possible we can, among mankind.
A woman, who the worst of thoughts debase,
All void of shame, of decency, and grace;
One who for hire her person will dispose,
And take, for need, each passer-by that goes.

Is, then, necessity the only plea?
Ye sisters in high life, come tell to me;
High fed, high bred, high marry'd too, indeed,
Do you not sometimes whore to mend the breed?
Necessity, with you, can have no claim;
Wants you have none – unless you know that same;
Your spouse; perhaps, lies snoring all the night,
While you are wishing for the soft delight.
Is impotence the case? – he old, you young,
Weak in his back, while you are stout and strong;
If he can't eat, pray why should you be starv'd?
The craving Womb of Nature must be serv'd.

                    *   *   *

Will, from the pulpit, cast a side-long glance,
To damn the tenets which he dares advance;
And e'er, perhaps, he goes to evening pray'r,
Will take a bottle with some willing fair;
Will to her breasts his saint-like hands apply,
And gaze upon her with lascivious eye.
In pleasure's pulpit then will mount, and preach
A forceful doctrine, which he dares not teach;
Then, sanctify'd, will to his flock amain,
Hem, stroke his band – and rail at whores again.

ANON

The Sound Country Lass

These London wenches are so stout
   They care not what they do;
They will not let you have a bout
   Without a crown or two.

They double their chops, and curl their locks,
   Their breaths perfume they do;
Their tails are peppered with the pox,
   And that you're welcome to.

But give me the buxom country lass,
   Hot piping from the cow,
That will take a touch upon the grass,
   Ay, marry, and thank you too!

Her colour's fresh as a rose in June,
   Her temper as kind as a dove;
She'll please the swain with a wholesome tune,
   And freely give her love.

The Maid's Conjuring Book

A young man lately in our town
    He went to bed one night;
He had no sooner laid him down
    But was troubled with a sprite.
So vigorously the spirit stood
    Let him do what he can,
Sure then he said it must be laid
    By woman, not by man.

A handsome maid did undertake,
    And into bed she lept,
And to allay the spirit's power
    Full close to him she crept.
She having such a guardian care
    Her office to discharge,
She opened wide her conjuring book
    And laid the leaves at large.

Her office she did well perform
    Within a little space;
Then up she rose, and down he lay,
    And durst not show his face.
She took her leave and away she went
    When she had done the deed,
Saying 'If't chance to come again,
    Then send for me with speed.'

SUSANNAH CENTLIVRE

From The Wonder

She, who for years protracts her lover's pain,
And makes him wish, and wait, and sigh in vain,
To be his wife, when late she give consent,
Finds half his passion was in courtship spent;
Whilst they who boldly all delays remove,
Find every hour a fresh supply of love.

HENRY FIELDING

From Joseph Andrews

Betty and Joseph

ADAMS WAS GOING to answer, when a most hideous uproar began in the inn! Mrs Tow-wouse, Mr Tow-wouse, and Betty, all lifting up their voices together; but Mrs Tow-wouse's voice, like a bass viol in a concert, was clearly and distinctly distinguished among the rest, and was heard to articulate the following sounds.

'O you d—ned villain! is this the return to all the care I have taken of your family? This the reward of my virtue? Is this the manner in which you behave to one who brought you a fortune, and preferred you to so many matches, all your betters? To abuse my bed, my own bed, with my own servant! but I'll maul the slut; I'll tear her nasty eyes out. Was ever such a pitiful dog, to take up with such a mean trollop? If she had been a gentlewoman, like myself, it had been some excuse; but a beggarly, saucy, dirty servant-maid! Get out of my house, you w—!' to which she added another name, which we do not care to stain our paper with: it was a monosyllable beginning with a b—, and indeed was the same, as if she had pronounced the words she-dog; which term we shall, to avoid offence, use on this occasion, though, indeed, both the mistress and maid uttered the above-mentioned b—, a word extremely disgustful to females of the lower sort.

Betty had borne all hitherto, with patience, and had uttered only lamentations; but the last appellation stung her to the quick. 'I am a woman as well as yourself,' she roared out, 'and no she-dog; and if I have been a little naughty, I am not the first; if I have been no better than I should be,' cries she, sobbing, 'that's no reason you should call me out of my name: my be-betters are wo-orse than me.'

'Hussy, hussy,' says Mrs Tow-wouse, 'have you the impudence to answer me? Did I not catch you, you saucy—,' and then again repeated the terrible word so odious to female ears.

'I can't bear that name,' answered Betty: 'if I have been wicked, I am to answer for it myself in the other world; but I have done nothing that's unnatural; and I will go out of your house this moment; for I will never be called she-dog by any mistress in England.'

Mrs Tow-wouse then armed herself with the spit, but was prevented from executing any dreadful purpose by Mr Adams, who confined her arms with the strength of a wrist which Hercules would not have been ashamed of. Mr Tow-wouse being caught, as our lawyers express it, with the maner, and having no defence to make, very prudently withdrew himself: and Betty committed herself to the protection of the ostler, who, though she could not conceive him pleased with what had happened, was, in her opinion, rather a gentler beast than her mistress.

Mrs Tow-wouse, at the intercession of Mr Adams, and finding the enemy vanished, began to compose herself, and at length recovered the usual serenity of her temper, in which we will leave her, to open to the reader the steps which led to a catastrophe, common enough, and comical enough too, perhaps, in modern history, yet often fatal to the repose and well-being of families, and the subject of many tragedies, both in life and on the stage.

Betty, who was the occasion of all this hurry, had some good qualities: she had good-nature, generosity, and compassion; but unfortunately her constitution was composed of those warm ingredients which, though the purity of courts or nunneries might have happily controlled them, were by no means enabled to endure the ticklish situation of a chambermaid at an inn; who is daily liable to the solicitations of lovers of all complexions; to the dangerous addresses of fine gentlemen of the army, who sometimes are obliged to reside with them a whole year together; and, above all, are exposed to the caresses of footmen, stage-coachmen, and drawers: all of whom employ the whole artillery of kissing, flattering, bribing, and every other weapon which is to be found in the whole armoury of love, against them.

Betty, who was but one-and-twenty, had now lived three years in this dangerous situation, during which she had escaped pretty well. An ensign of foot was the first person who made an impression on her heart: he did, indeed, raise a flame in her, which required the care of a surgeon to cool.

While she burned for him, several others burned for her. Officers of the army, young gentlemen travelling the western circuit, inoffensive squires, and some of graver character, were set a-fire by her charms.

At length, having perfectly recovered the effects of her first unhappy passion, she seemed to have vowed a state of perpetual chastity. She was long deaf to all the sufferings of her lovers, till one day, at a neighbouring fair, the rhetoric of John the ostler, with a new straw hat and a pint of wine, made a second conquest over her.

She did not, however, feel any of those flames on this occasion which had been the consequence of her former amour; nor, indeed, those other ill effects which prudent young women very justly apprehend from too absolute an indulgence to the pressing endearments of their lovers. This latter, perhaps, was a little owing to her not being entirely constant to John, with whom she permitted Tom Whipwell, the stage-coachman, and now and then a handsome young traveller, to share her favours.

Mr Tow-wouse had for some time cast the languishing eyes of affection on this young maiden: he had laid hold on every opportunity of saying tender things to her, squeezing her by the hand, and sometimes kissing her lips; for as the violence of his passion had considerably abated to Mrs Tow-wouse, so, like water which is stopped from its usual current in one place, it naturally sought a vent in another. Mrs Tow-wouse is thought to have perceived this abatement, and probably it added very little to the natural sweetness of her temper; for though she was as true to her husband as the dial to the sun, she was rather more desirous of being shone on, as being more capable of feeling his warmth.

Ever since Joseph's arrival, Betty had conceived an extraordinary liking to him, which discovered itself more and more, as he grew better and better, till that fatal evening when, as she was warming his bed, her passion grew to such a height, and so perfectly mastered both her modesty and her reason, that, after many fruitless hints and sly insinuations, she at last threw down the warming-pan, and, embracing him with great eagerness, swore he was the handsomest creature she had ever seen.

Joseph, in great confusion, leaped from her, and told her he was sorry to see a young woman cast off all regard to modesty; but she had gone too far to recede, and grew so very indecent, that Joseph was obliged, contrary to his inclination, to use some violence to her; and, taking her in his arms, he shut her out of the room, and locked the door.

How ought man to rejoice that his chastity is always in his own power; that if he has sufficient strength of mind, he has always a competent strength of body to defend himself: and cannot, like a poor weak woman, be ravished against his will!

Betty was in the most violent agitation at this disappointment. Rage and lust pulled her heart, as with two strings, two different ways. One moment she thought of stabbing Joseph; the next, of taking him in her arms, and devouring him with kisses; but the latter passion was far more prevalent. Then she thought of revenging his refusal on herself; but whilst she was engaged in this meditation, happily death presented himself to her in so many shapes of drowning, hanging, poisoning, &c., that her distracted mind could resolve on none.

In this perturbation of spirit, it accidentally occurred to her memory that her master's bed was not made: she therefore went directly to his room, where he happened at that time to be engaged at his bureau. As soon as she saw him, she attempted to retire; but he called her back, and taking her by the hand, squeezed her so tenderly, at the same time whispering so many soft things into her ears, and then pressed her so closely with his kisses, that the vanquished fair one, whose passions were already raised, and which were not so whimsically capricious that one man only could lay them – though perhaps she would have rather preferred that one – the vanquished fair one quietly submitted, I say, to her master's will, who had just attained the accomplishment of his bliss, when Mrs Tow-wouse unexpectedly entered the room, and caused all that confusion which we have before seen, and which it is not necessary at present to take any farther notice of, since, without the assistance of a single hint from us, every reader of any speculation or experience, though not married himself, may easily conjecture that it concluded with the discharge of Betty, the submission of Mr Tow-wouse, with some things to be performed on his side by way of gratitude for his wife's goodness in being reconciled to him, with many hearty promises never to offend any more in the like manner, and, lastly, his quietly and contentedly bearing to be reminded of his transgressions, as a kind of penance, once or twice a day, during the residue of his life.

SAMUEL RICHARDSON

From Pamela, or Virtue Rewarded

Pamela writes to her parents (letter XXV)

MY DEAR PARENTS, Oh let me take up my complaint, and say, Never was poor creature so unhappy, and so barbarously used, as poor Pamela! Indeed, my dear father and mother, my heart's just broke! I can neither write as I should do, nor let it alone, for to whom but you can I vent my griefs, and keep my poor heart from bursting! Wicked, wicked man! I have no patience when I think of him! But yet, don't be frightened, for I hope – I hope, I am honest! – But if my head and my hand will let me, you shall hear all. – Is there no constable nor headborough, though, to take me out of his house? for I am sure I can safely swear the peace against him: But, alas! he is greater than any constable: he is a justice himself: Such a justice deliver me from! – But God Almighty, I hope, in time, will right me – For He knows the innocence of my heart!

John went your way in the morning; but I have been too much distracted to send by him; and have seen nobody but Mrs Jervis or Rachel, and one I hate to see or be seen by: and indeed I hate now to see anybody. Strange things I have to tell you, that happened since last night, that good Mr Jonathan's letter, and my master's harshness, put me into such a fluster; but I will not keep you in suspense.

I went to Mrs Jervis's chamber; and, oh dreadful! my wicked master had hid himself, base gentleman as he is! in her closet, where she has a few books, and chest of drawers, and such like. I little suspected it; though I used, till this sad night, always to look into that closet and another in the room, and under the bed, ever since the summer-house trick; but never found anything; and so I did not do it then, being fully resolved to be angry with Mrs Jervis for what had happened in the day, and so thought of nothing else.

I sat myself down on one side of the bed, and she on the other, and we began to undress ourselves; but she on that side next the wicked closet, that held the worst heart in the world. So, said Mrs Jervis, you won't speak to me, Pamela! I find you are angry with me. Why, Mrs Jervis, said I, so I am, a little; 'tis a folly to deny it. You see what I have suffered by your forcing me in to my master: and a gentlewoman of your years and experience must needs know, that it was not fit for me to pretend to be anybody else for my own sake, nor with regard to my master.

But, said she, who would have thought it would have turned out so? Ay, said I, little thinking who heard me, Lucifer always is ready to promote his own work and workmen. You see presently what use he made of it, pretending not to know me, on purpose to be free with me. And when he took upon himself to know me, to quarrel with me, and use me hardly: And you too, said I, to cry, Fie, fie, Pamela! cut me to the heart: for that encouraged him.

Do you think, my dear, said she, that I would encourage him? – I never said so to you before; but, since you have forced it from me, I must tell you, that, ever since you consulted me, I have used my utmost endeavours to divert him from his wicked purposes: and he has promised fair; but, to say all in a word, he doats upon you; and I begin to see it is not in his power to help it.

I luckily said nothing of the note from Mr Jonathan; for I began to suspect all the world almost: but I said, to try Mrs Jervis, Well then, what would you have me do? You see he is for having me wait on Lady Davers now.

Why, I'll tell you freely, my dear Pamela, said she, and I trust to your discretion to conceal what I say: my master has been often desiring me to put you upon asking him to let you stay –

Yes, said I, Mrs Jervis, let me interrupt you: I will tell you why I could not think of that: It was not the pride of my *heart*, but the pride of my *honesty*: For what must have been the case? Here my master has been very rude to me, once and twice; and you say he cannot help it, though he pretends to be sorry for it: Well, he has given me warning to leave my place, and uses me very harshly; perhaps to frighten me to his purposes, as he supposes I would be fond of staying (as indeed I should, if I could be safe; for I love you and all the house, and value him, if he would act as my master). Well then, as I know his designs, and that he owns he cannot help it; must I have asked to stay, knowing he would attempt me again? for all you could assure me of, was, he would do nothing by *force*; so I, a poor weak girl, was to be left to my own strength! And was not this to *allow* him to tempt me, as one may say? and to encourage him to go on in his wicked devices? – How then, Mrs Jervis, could I ask or wish to stay?

You say well, my dear child, says she; and you have a justness of thought above your years; and for all these considerations, and for what I have heard this day, after you ran away (and I am glad you went as you did), I cannot persuade you to stay; and I shall be glad (which is what I never thought I could have said), that you were well at your father's; for if Lady

Davers will entertain you, she may as well have you from thence as here. There's my good Mrs Jervis! said I; God will bless you for your good counsel to a poor maiden, that is hard beset. But pray what did he say when I was gone? Why, says she, he was very angry with you. But he would hear it! said I: I think it was a little bold; but then he provoked me to it. And had not my honesty been in the case, I would not by any means have been so saucy. Besides, Mrs Jervis, consider it was the truth; if he does not love to hear of the *summer-house*, and the *dressing-room*, why should he not be ashamed to continue in the same mind? But, said she, when you had muttered this to yourself, you might have told him anything else. Well, said I, I cannot tell a wilful lie, and so there's an end of it. But I find you now give him up, and think there's danger in staying. – Lord bless me! I wish I was well out of the house; so it was at the bottom of a wet ditch, on the wildest common in England.

Why, said she, it signifies nothing to tell you all he said; but it was enough to make me fear you would not be so safe as I could wish; and, upon my word, Pamela, I don't wonder he loves you; for, without flattery, you are a charming girl! and I never saw you look more lovely in my life than in that same new dress of yours. And then it was such a surprise upon us all! – I believe truly, you owe some of your danger to the lovely *appearance* you made. Then, said I, I wish the clothes in the fire: I expected *no* effect from them; but, if *any*, a quite contrary one.

Hush! said I, Mrs Jervis, did you not hear something stir in the closet? No, silly girl, said she, your fears are always awake. – But indeed, said I, I think I heard something rustle. – May be, says she, the cat may be got there: but I hear nothing.

I was hush; but she said, Pr'ythee, my good girl, make haste to bed. See if the door be fast. So I did, and was thinking to look into the closet; but, hearing no more noise, thought it needless, and so went again and sat myself down on the bed-side, and went on undressing myself. And Mrs Jervis, being by this time undressed, stepped into bed, and bid me hasten, for she was sleepy.

I don't know what was the matter, but my heart sadly misgave me: Indeed, Mr Jonathan's note was enough to make it do so, with what Mrs Jervis had said. I pulled off my stays, and my stockings, and all my clothes to an under-petticoat; and then hearing a rustling again in the closet, I said, Heaven protect us! but before I say my prayers, I must look into this closet. And so was going to it slip-shod, when, oh dreadful! out rushed my master in a rich silk and silver morning gown.

I screamed, and ran to the bed, and Mrs Jervis screamed too; and he said, I'll do you no harm, if you forbear this noise; but otherwise take what follows.

Instantly he came to the bed (for I had crept into it, to Mrs Jervis, with my coat on, and my shoes); and taking me in his arms, said, Mrs Jervis, rise, and just step up stairs, to keep the maids from coming down at this noise: I'll do no harm to this rebel.

Oh, for Heaven's sake! for pity's sake! Mrs Jervis, said I, if I am not betrayed, don't leave me; and, I beseech you, raise all the house. No, said Mrs Jervis, I will not stir, my dear lamb; I will not leave you. I wonder at you, sir, said she; and kindly threw herself upon my coat, clasping me round the waist: You shall not hurt this innocent, said she: for I will lose my life in her defence. Are there not, said she, enough wicked ones in the world, for your base purpose, but you must attempt such a lamb as this?

He was desperate angry, and threatened to throw her out of the window; and to turn her out of the house the next morning. You need not, sir, said she; for I will not stay in it. God defend my poor Pamela till tomorrow, and we will both go together. – Says he, let me but expostulate a word or two with you, Pamela. Pray, Pamela, said Mrs Jervis, don't hear a word, except he leaves the bed, and goes to the other end of the room. Ay, out of the room, said I; expostulate tomorrow, if you must expostulate!

I found his hand in my bosom; and when my fright let me know it, I was ready to die; and I sighed and screamed, and fainted away. And still he had his arms about my neck; and Mrs Jervis was about my feet, and upon my coat. And all in a cold dewy sweat was I. Pamela! Pamela! said Mrs Jervis, as she tells me since, O–h, and gave another shriek, my poor Pamela is dead for certain! And so, to be sure, I was for a time; for I knew nothing more of the matter, one fit following another, till about three hours after, as it proved to be, I found myself in bed, and Mrs Jervis sitting upon one side, with her wrapper about her, and Rachel on the other; and no master, for the wicked wretch was gone. But I was so overjoyed, that I hardly could believe myself; and I said, which were my first words, Mrs Jervis, Mrs Rachel, can I be *sure* it is you? Tell me! can I? – Where have I been? Hush, my dear, said Mrs Jervis; you have been in fit after fit. I never saw anybody so frightful in my life!

By this I judged Rachel knew nothing of the matter; and it seems my wicked master had, upon Mrs Jervis's second noise on my fainting away, slipt out, and, as if he had come from his own chamber, disturbed by the screaming, went up to the maids' room (who, hearing the noise, lay trembling, and afraid to stir), and bid them go down, and see what was the matter with Mrs Jervis and me. And he charged Mrs Jervis, and promised to forgive her for what she had said and done, if she would conceal the matter. So the maids came down, and all went up again, when I came to myself a little, except Rachel, who stayed to sit up with me, and bear Mrs Jervis company. I believe they all guess the matter to be bad enough; though they dare not say anything.

When I think of my danger, and the freedoms he actually took, though I believe Mrs Jervis saved me from worse, and she said she did (though what can I think, who was in a fit, and knew nothing of the matter?) I am almost distracted.

At first I was afraid of Mrs Jervis; but I am fully satisfied she is very good, and I should have been lost but for her; and she takes on grievously about it. What would have become of me, had she gone out of the room, to still the maids, as he bid her! He'd certainly have shut her out, and then, mercy on me! what would have become of your poor Pamela?

I must leave off a little; for my eyes and my head are sadly bad. – This was a dreadful trial! This was the worst of all! Oh, that I was out of the power of this dreadfully wicked man! Pray for

Your distressed DAUGHTER.

DONATIEN ALPHONSE FRANÇOIS, MARQUIS DE SADE

From Les Infortunes de La Vertu (*The Misfortunes of Virtue*)

'COME ON,' SAID Raphael, as his prodigious desires seemed to have reached the point of no return, 'it's time to sacrifice the victim; each of us must prepare to submit her to his favourite enjoyments.' And the vile man, having put me on the sofa, in the most opportune position for his deplorable pleasures, had me held by Antonin and Clément. . . . Raphael – Italian, a monk and depraved – satisfied himself insultingly, without my ceasing to be a virgin. Oh, worst of excesses! It seemed that each of these debauched men seemed to glory in leaving nature outside his choice of shocking pleasures. . . . Clément came forward, inflamed by the sight of his Superior's infamy, and even more by what he'd done while watching. He told me that he'd do me no more harm than his guardian and that the spot he'd choose for his offering would leave my virtue in no danger. He got me down on my knees, and getting tight up against me in this position, practised his false passions in a place which stopped me complaining of its irregularity while the sacrifice was going on. Jérôme followed. His temple was the same as that of Raphael, but he didn't get to the inner sanctuary and was content to stay at the vestibule; turned on by various primitive episodes of which the obscenity can't be depicted, he was unable to arrive at the accomplishment of his desires without the barbaric means which you've seen already when I was almost a victim in the house of Dubourg and of which I was completely so in the hands of de Bressac. 'What a good start!' Antonin said as he grabbed me. 'Come here, my chicken, come and let me revenge the irregularities of my brothers and pluck the first fruits that their excesses have left me. . . .' But what details . . . Great God! It's impossible for me to paint the scene for you. One might say that this wretch was the greatest libertine of the four. Although he seemed less removed from the ways of Nature, he only seemed willing to approach her with a little less nonconformity in his creed, and made up for this semblance of lesser depravity by being able to outrage me for longer. . . . Alas, if sometimes my mind had strayed on such pleasures, I had believed them pure as the God that inspired them, a gift of nature to be a consolation to mankind, born of love and tenderness. I was far from believing that man, following the example of wild beasts, wouldn't be able to enjoy himself without making his partners tremble with fear. I experienced this – the normal pain of losing a virginity was the least thing I had to bear in this dangerous attack. But it was at the moment of orgasm that Antonin finished with such ferocious cries, with such deadly excursions over the whole of my body, so like the bloody caresses of a tiger, that I believed for that moment that I was the prey of a savage animal who could only be satisfied by devouring me. When these horrors were completed, I fell back on the altar of my sacrifice, not knowing where I was and almost unconscious.

Transl. F.P.

JOHANN GEORG, RITTER VON ZIMMERMANN

From Solitude, or the Effect of Occasional Retirement

John George Zimmermann was Counsellor of State and Physician to his Britannic Majesty at Hanover.

THE FEMALE MIND is still more subject to these delusions of disordered fancy; for, as their feelings are more exquisite, their passions warmer, and their imaginations more active than those of the other sex, Solitude, when carried to excess, affects them in a much greater degree. Their bosoms are much more susceptible of the injurious influence of seclusion, to the contagion of example, and to the dangers of illusion. This may, perhaps, in some degree, account for the similarity of disposition which prevails in cloisters, and other institutions, which confine women entirely to the company of each other. The force of example and habit is, indeed, in such retreats, surprisingly powerful. A French medical writer, of great merit, and undoubted veracity, relates that in a convent of nuns, where the sisterhood was unusually numerous, one of these secluded fair ones was seized with a strange impulse to mew like a cat; that several others of the nuns in a short time followed her example; and that at length this unaccountable propensity became general throughout the convent; the whole sisterhood joined, at stated periods, in the practice of mewing, and continued it for several hours. But of all the extraordinary fancies recorded of the sex, none can exceed that which Cardan relates to have happened in one of the convents of Germany, during the fifteenth century. One of the nuns, who had long been secluded from the sight of man, was seized with the strange propensity to bite all her companions; and, extraordinary as it may seem, this disposition spread until the whole house was infected with the same fury. The account, indeed, states that this mania extended even beyond the walls of the convent, and that the disease was conveyed to such a degree from cloister to cloister, throughout Germany, Holland, and Italy, that the practice at length prevailed in every female convent in Europe.

FRANCES SEYMOUR, COUNTESS OF HERTFORD

The Story of Inkle and Yarico:
A Most Moving Tale from the Spectator [No. 11]

A youth there was possessed of every charm,
Which might the coldest heart with passion warm;
His blooming cheeks with ruddy beauty glowed,
His hair in waving ringlets graceful flowed;
Through all his person an attractive mien,
Just symmetry, and elegance were seen:
But niggard Fortune had her aid withheld,
And poverty th' unhappy boy compelled
To distant climes to sail in search of gain,
Which might in ease his latter days maintain.
By chance, or rather the decree of Heaven,
The vessel on a barbarous coast was driven;
He, with a few unhappy striplings more,
Ventured too far upon the fatal shore:
The cruel natives thirsted for their blood,
And issued furious from a neighbouring wood.
His friends all fell by brutal rage o'erpowered,
Their flesh the horrid cannibals devoured;
Whilst he alone escaped by speedy flight,
And in a thicket lay concealed from sight!

Now he reflects on his companions' fate,
His threatening danger, and abandoned state.
Whilst thus in fruitless grief he spent the day,
A negro virgin chanced to pass that way;
He viewed her naked beauties with surprise,
Her well-proportioned limbs and sprightly eyes!
With his complexion and gay dress amazed,
The artless nymph upon the stranger gazed;

Charmed with his features and alluring grace,
His flowing locks and his enlivened face.
His safety now became her tend'rest care,
A vaulted rock she knew and hid him there;
The choicest fruits the isle produced she sought,
And kindly to allay his hunger brought;
And when his thirst required, in search of drink,
She led him to a chrystal fountain's brink.

   Mutually charmed, by various arts they strove
To inform each other of their mutual love;
A language soon they formed, which might express
Their pleasing care and growing tenderness.
With tigers' speckled skins she decked his bed,
O'er which the gayest plumes of birds were spread;
And every morning, with the nicest care,
Adorned her well-turned neck and shining hair,
With all the glittering shells and painted flowers
That serve to deck the Indian virgins' bowers.
And when the sun descended in the sky,
And lengthening shades foretold the evening nigh,
Beneath some spreading palm's delightful shade,
Together sat the youth and lovely maid;
Or where some bubbling river gently crept,
She in her arms secured him while he slept.
When the bright moon in midnight pomp was seen,
And starlight glittered o'er the dewy green,
In some close arbour, or some fragrant grove,
He whispered vows of everlasting love.
Then, as upon the verdant turf he lay,
He oft would to th' attentive virgin say:
'Oh, could I but, my Yarico, with thee
Once more my dear, my native country see!
In softest silks thy limbs should be arrayed,
Like that of which the clothes I wear are made;

What different ways my grateful soul would find
To indulge thy person and divert thy mind!';
While she on the enticing accents hung
That smoothly fell from his persuasive tongue.
   One evening, from a rock's impending side,
An European vessel she descried,
And made them signs to touch upon the shore,
Then to her lover the glad tidings bore;
Who with his mistress to the ship descends,
And found the crew were countrymen and friends.
Reflecting now upon the time he passed,
Deep melancholy all his thoughts o'ercast:
'Was it for this,' said he, 'I crossed the main,
Only a doting virgin's heart to gain?
I needed not for such a prize to roam,
There are a thousand doting maids at home.'
While thus his disappointed mind was tossed,
The ship arrived on the Barbadian coast;
Immediately the planters from the town,
Who trade for goods and negro slaves, came down;
And now his mind, by sordid interest swayed,
Resolved to sell his faithful Indian maid.
Soon at his feet for mercy she implored,
And thus in moving strains her fate deplored:
   'O whither can I turn to seek redress,
When thou'rt the cruel cause of my distress?
If the remembrance of our former love,
And all thy plighted vows, want force to move;
Yet, for the helpless infant's sake I bear,
Listen with pity to my just despair.
Oh let me not in slavery remain,
Doomed all my life to drag a servile chain!
It cannot surely be! thy generous breast
An act so vile, so sordid must detest:

But, if thou hate me, rather let me meet
A gentler fate, and stab me at thy feet;
Then will I bless thee with my dying breath,
And sink contented in the shades of death.'
   Not all she said could his compassion move,
Forgetful of his vows and promised love;
The weeping damsel from his knees he spurned,
And with her price pleased to the ship returned.

JACQUES CASANOVA DE SEINGALT (CASANOVA)

From Mémoires de Casanova de Seingalt

Always anxious to oblige women, Casanova has rented a window
for three louis looking on to the square where Damiens is to be
executed. His party includes Count Tiretta, Lambertini (an
adventuress posing as a pope's niece), a fat aunt and her niece.
Damiens, who had attempted to assassinate Louis XV, was
tortured horrifically for four hours.

The martyrdom of Damiens

DURING THE TORTURE of this victim of the Jesuits, I was forced to turn
away and stop my ears when I heard his heart-rending screams, and
less than half his body was left intact; but Lambertini and the fat aunt
didn't make the slightest movement. Was it a result of their hearts'
cruelty? I had to make a pretence of believing them when they said that the
horror which inspired them at this monster's attempt stopped them from
feeling the natural pity that the sight of such unheard-of torments would
have aroused. The fact is that Tiretta kept the pious aunt occupied in a
singular fashion, throughout the execution; and perhaps that was the
reason the virtuous woman didn't dare move, or even turn her head.

   Finding himself placed close behind her, Tiretta had taken the precaution of raising her dress so that he wouldn't step on it; that was in order, no
doubt, but soon, making an accidental movement in their direction, I
noticed that Tiretta had taken too much of a precaution, and not wishing
to disturb a friend, or annoy the lady, I turned away and placed myself,

without affectation, in such a place that my beautiful friend would see nothing; this put the good woman at her ease. I heard rustlings for the next two hours, and finding the thing very amusing, I had the constancy not to move an inch throughout that time. I admired Tiretta's stamina and boldness; but, even more did I admire the beautiful resignation of the pious aunt.

Transl. F.P.

From The Life of Joseph Balsamo, commonly called Count Cagliostro

BY THE LAWS of England, if a man surprises his wife in adultery, he can commence a lawsuit against the seducer, and oblige him to pay a large sum of money.

Balsamo and his wife, during their residence in that capital, got acquainted with several Quakers; and also with a Sicilian, whom they called the Marquis de Vivona. One of the Quakers was captivated with the charms of the lady; and, in his attempts to seduce her virtue, entirely forgot the austerity of his sect. Without yielding to his wishes, Lorenza informed her husband of his passion; and he contrived, in concert with Vivona, that she should promise him a private interview; that two witnesses should watch in an adjoining chamber; and that, at the moment when the Quaker should think himself on the brink of happiness, upon a certain signal being given, Balsamo, Vivona, and the servants should rush into the apartment; and by means of threats, insults, and menaces, oblige him to pay dearly for his untasted pleasures.

Every thing succeeded according to their wishes. The Quaker, faithful to his appointment, repaired at the hour agreed upon, and began to compliment the lady in the manner made use of in Pennsylvania. Lorenza affected to be surprised at his gallantry; and asked how it was possible for one of the 'Friends' to be so polite to the ladies?

The dialogue on this became exceedingly lively and interesting: and at length the Quaker, as if preparing to *swim in bliss*, throws off his hat, his wig, and his coat. But the concerted signal being given at this instant, Balsamo, Vivona, and the rest burst into the chamber, and surprised him in this ridiculous situation. Thus *caught in the fact*, as it were, it was in vain for him to dissemble; he fumed, fretted, cursed, and swore; and at length was permitted to escape, on condition of presenting the *enraged* husband with one hundred pounds sterling, which was instantly complied with. On his departure the sharpers divided the money between them.

Transl. from the original proceedings published at Rome by Order of the Apostolic Chamber

PRISCILLA POINTON

Address to a Bachelor on a Delicate Occasion

You bid me write, Sir, I comply,
Since I my grave airs can't deny.
But say, how can my Muse declare
The situation of the fair,
That full six hours had sat, or more,
And never once been out of door?
Tea, wine, and punch, Sir, to be free,
Excellent diuretics be:
I made it so appear, it's true,
When at your house, last night, with you:
Blushing, I own, to you I said,
'I should be glad you'd call a maid.'
'The girls,' you answered, 'are from home,
Nor can I guess when they'll return.'
Then in contempt you came to me,
And sneering cried, 'Dear Miss, make free;
Let me conduct you – don't be nice –
Of if a basin is your choice,
To fetch you one I'll instant fly.'
I blushed, but could not make reply;
Confused to find myself the joke,
I silent sat till Trueworth spoke:
'To go with me, Miss, don't refuse,
Your loss[1] the freedom will excuse.'

[1] Loss – Priscilla Pointon was blind.

To him my hand reluctant gave,
And out he led me very grave;
Whilst you and Chatfree laughed aloud,
As if to dash a maid seemed proud.
But I the silly jest despise,
Since well I know each man that's wise
All affectation does disdain,
Since it in prudes and coxcombs reign:
So I repent not what I've done:
Adieu – enjoy your empty fun.

GEORGE CRABBE

From The Parish Register, Part II

Peter Pratt, the gardener

Not Darwin's self had more delight to sing
Of floral courtship, in th' awaken'd spring,
Than Peter Pratt, who simpering loves to tell
How rise the stamens, as the pistils swell;
How bend and curl the moist-top to the spouse,
And give and take the vegetable vows;
How those esteem'd of old but tips and chives,
Are tender husbands and obedient wives;
Who live and love within the sacred bower, –
That bridal bed, the vulgar term a flower.

Hear Peter proudly, to some humble friend,
A wondrous secret, in his science, lend: –
'Would you advance the nuptial hour and bring
The fruit of autumn with the flowers of spring;
View that light frame where Cucumis lies spread,
And trace the husbands in their golden bed,

Three powder'd anthers; then no more delay,
But to the stigma's tip their dust convey;
Then by thyself, from prying glance secure,
Twirl the full tip and make your purpose sure;
A long-abiding race the deed shall pay,
Nor one unblest abortion pine away.'

GEORGE SINCLAIR

From Satan's Invisible World Discovered

Jean Weir's[1] *confession*

S HE ENTREATED THAT minister to assist her, and attend her to her
death, which, at her violent importunity, he yielded unto, though it
was not his course to wait upon condemned persons. What she said in
private to himself, he says, must die with him. She avouched, that from
her being sixteen years of age, to her fiftieth, her brother had the
incestuous use of her, and then loathed her for her age. She was pretty old
at this time, and he, when he died, was about seventy. He asked her, if ever
she was with child to him? She declared with great confidence, he hindred
that by means abominable, which she beginning to relate, the preacher
stopped her. Some bystanders were desirous to hear the rest; but says he,
'Gentlemen, the speculation of this iniquity is in itself to be punished.'

[1] Jean Weir was the sister of the Scots wizard, Major Weir. They were executed separately. She
insisted on tearing off all her clothes at her execution. The ground where they had committed incest
remained barren.

An apparition of a deceased wife to her husband, at Edinburgh

S IR, THAT WHICH I narrated to you the other day, I have now sent it
under my hand, as a thing very certain and sure. I knew a servant-
maid that served a gentlewoman in the old Provost's Close, as they call it,
who was married to a butcher called John Ritchey, about twelve years ago.
She lived about five years with him, and had four children to him, and
then died. Within a few days after her burial, he went in suit of a young
woman, courting her for marriage. He had a comrade of the same trade, to

whom he revealed his intention, and desired him to meet him at such a house, near to the court of guard, down some close or other, that he might see his new mistress. The appointment was keeped. The two lovers sat down together on a bed-side, and the comrade sat opposite to them, there being a table between them, and a window or shot at the head of the room, that gave them light, the close or wynd was narrow to which they had a sight. And while the two are dallying together in the bed, the other smiling at them, behold, while this man is casting his eye about the room, he perceived distinctly the body and face of the dead wife, in her clothes; looking towards them from an opposite window; at which this man, his comrade, rose up affrighted, saying to the other, 'John, what's that?' Whereupon all stood up looking, and saw perfectly the buried woman lifting up her hands (as appeared) to take the dead-dress from her head, but could not reach it. The man threw the woman out of his arms, with a purpose to be gone quickly; but his comrade vowed he would not stir till he got something to comfort his heart; they got a little brandy, and then went away, not without wondering and fear. Upon this the man took sickness for three or four days, and his comrade coming to give him a visit, counselled him to delay, or wholly to desist from that purpose of marriage; but affection would not suffer him to forbear, and, though not fully recovered of his frenzy, he made a new address to his mistress: But, while he is putting on his shoes, his dead wife appears again in her ordinary habit; and, crossing the room in his sight, says, 'John, will you not come to me?' and with that evanished. Upon this he took sickness again, and called for his comrade, and told him of this second apparition, who most freely entreated him to desist, or at least to delay. His sickness increasing, he died. About which time, he spoke of a third visit his wife gave him, blaming him as if he had too soon forgotten her, but did not tell it distinctly; and therefore his comrade could not be positive in it. He was buried within a month of his wife's decease.

One of the ministers of Edinburgh, who had been acquaint in the house where she served, hearing some whisper of the apparition, sent a servant secretly to call for the man's comrade, who gave him a just and true narration of all that I have written. Adding, that he having seen the vision first, some told him he would quickly die, but he is yet living in the town, a flesher; the minister having married him to two wives since. The deceased wife's name was Helen Brown.

ROBERT BURNS

Air

(*Tune* – 'Sodger Laddie')

I once was a maid, tho' I cannot tell when,
And still my delight is in proper young men:
Some one of a troop of dragoons was my daddie,
No wonder I'm fond of a sodger laddie,
       Sing, lal de dal, etc.

The first of my loves was a swaggering blade,
To rattle the thundering drum was his trade;
His leg was so tight, and his cheek was so ruddy,
Transported I was with my sodger laddie.

But the godly old chaplain left him in the lurch;
The sword I forsook for the sake of the church:
He ventur'd the soul, and I risket the body,
'Twas then I prov'd false to my sodger laddie.

Full soon I grew sick of my sanctified sot,
The regiment at large for a husband I got;
From the gilded spontoon to the fife I was ready,
I askèd no more but a sodger laddie.

But the peace it reduc'd me to beg in despair,
Till I met my old boy in a Cunningham fair;
His rags regimental, they flutter'd so gaudy,
My heart it rejoic'd at a sodger laddie.

And now I have liv'd – I know not how long,
And still I can join in a cup and a song;
But whilst with both hands I can hold the glass steady,
Here's to thee, my hero, my sodger laddie.

Epitaph for Hugh Logan, Esq., of Laight

Here lyes Squire Hugh – ye harlot crew,
  Come mak' your water on him.
I'm sure that he weel pleas'd would be
  To think ye pish'd upon him.

Had I the Wyte?

Had I the wyte, had I the wyte,
  Had I the wyte? she bade me.
She watch'd me by the hie-gate side,
  And up the loan she shaw'd me.

And when I wadna venture in,
  A coward loon she ca'd me:
Had Kirk an' State been in the gate,
  I'd lighted when she bade me.

Sae craftilie she took me ben,
  And bade me mak nae clatter;
'For our ramgunshoch, glum gudeman,
  Is o'er ayont the water.'
Whae'er shall say I wanted grace
  When I did kiss and dawte her,
Let him be planted in my place,
  Syne say I was the fautor.

Wyte – blame.
Loon – lad.
Ramgunshoch – ill-tempered.
Fautor – offender.

Loan – lane.
Ayont – beyond.
Dawte – pet.

Could I for shame, could I for shame,
    Could I for shame refus'd her?
And wadna manhood been to blame,
    Had I unkindly used her?
He claw'd her wi' the ripplin-kame,
    And blae and bluidy bruis'd her;
When sic a husband was frae hame,
    What wife but wad excus'd her!

I dighted aye her e'en sae blue,
    An' bann'd the cruel randy,
And weel I wat, her willin' mou'
    Was sweet as sugar-candie.
At gloamin'-shot, it was, I wot,
    I lighted – on the Monday;
But I cam thro' the Tyseday's dew,
    To wanton Willie's brandy.

Ripplin' kame – a threshing flail.
Dighted – wiped.
Randy – Beggar.

E'en – eyes.
Gloamin' – twilight.

THE MERRY MUSES OF CALEDONIA

Our Gudewife's Sae Modest

(*Tune:* 'John Anderson, my Jo')

Our gudewife's sae modest,
    When she is set at meat,
A laverock's leg, or a tittling's wing,
    Is mair than she can eat;
But, when she's in her bed at e'en,
    Between me and the wa';
She is a glutton devil,
    She swallows cods an a'.

Laverock – lark.
Tittling – sparrow.

Duncan Davidson

There was a lass, they ca'd her Meg,
    An' she gaed o'er the muir to spin;
She fee'd a lad to lift her leg,
    They ca'd him Duncan Davidson.
                Fal, lal, &c.

Meg had a muff and it was rough,
    Twas black without and red within,
An' Duncan, case he got the cauld,
    He stole his highland pintle in.
                Fal, lal, &c.

Meg had a muff, and it was rough,
   And Duncan strak tway handfu' in;
She clasp'd her heels about his waist,
   'I thank you Duncan! Yerk it in!!!'
                    Fal, lal, &c.

Duncan made her hurdies dreep
   In Highland wrath, then Meg did say;
O gang he east, or gang he west,
   His ba's will no be dry today.

From *The Merry Muses of Caldeonia*, songs collected by Robert Burns

Hurdies – buttocks.

MATTHEW PRYOR

An Imitation of Chaucer

Fair Susan did her Wif-hede well menteine,
Algates assaulted sore by Letchours tweine:
Now, and I read aright that Auncient Song,
Olde were the Paramours, the Dame full yong.

Had thilke same Tale in other Guise been tolde;
Had They been Yong (pardie) and She been Olde;
That, by St Kit, had wrought much sorer Tryal;
Full merveillous, I wote, were swilk Denyal.

A True Maid

No, no; for my Virginity,
   When I lose that, says Rose, I'll dye:
Behind the Elmes, last Night, cry'd Dick,
   Rose, were You not extreamly Sick?

Epigram

Poor Hall caught his Death standing under a Spout
Expecting till Midnight when Nan wou'd come out
But fatal his Patience as cruel the Dame,
And curst was the Rain that extinguisht this flame.
'Who e'er thou art that reads these Moral Lines
Make Love at Home, and go to Bed betimes.'

THE
NINETEENTH
CENTURY

SPENCER ASHBEE

From Index Librorum Prohibitorum

Birching establishments

AT THE EARLY part of this century very sumptuously fitted up establishments, exclusively devoted to the administration of the birch, were not uncommon in London; and women of the town served, as it were, an apprenticeship in order to acquire the art of gracefully and effectively administering the rod. It would be easy to form a very lengthy list of these female flagellants, but I shall restrict myself to the mention of a few only. Mrs Collett was a noted whipper, and George IV is known to have visited her; she had an establishment in Tavistock Court, Covent Garden, whence she removed to the neighbourhood of Portland Place, and afterwards to Bedford Street, Russell Square, where she died. She brought up her niece in the same line, who, as Mrs Mitchell, carried on a successful business in various places, among others at No. 22 (afterwards 44) Waterloo Road, and finally at St Mary's Square, Kennington, where she died. Then came Mrs James, who had been maid in the family of Lord Clanricarde; she had a house at No. 7 Carlisle Street, Soho; she retired from business with a good fortune, and dwelt at Notting Hill in luxury, her house being decorated with pictures, and her person covered with jewels. There were, further: Mrs Emma Lee, real name Richardson, of No. 50 Margaret Street, Regent Street; Mrs Phillips, of No. 11 Upper Belgrave Place, Pimlico; Mrs Shepherd, of No. 25 Gilbert Street; Mrs Sarah Potter, alias Stewart, of various addresses, who died in 1873; and, were it not indiscreet, I might add the names of one or two other ladies who still carry on their calling. But the queen of her profession was undoubtedly Mrs Theresa Berkley, of No. 28 Charlotte Street, Portland Place; she was a perfect mistress of her art, understood how to satisfy her clients, and was, moreover, a thorough woman of business, for she amassed during her career a considerable sum of money. 'She possessed the first grand requisite of a courtizan, viz., lewdness; for without a woman is positively lecherous she cannot long keep up the affectation of it, and it will soon be perceived that she only moves her hands or her buttocks to the tune of pounds, shillings, and pence. She could assume great urbanity and good humour; she would study every lech, whim, caprice, and desire of her customer, and had the disposition to gratify them, if her avarice was rewarded in return. Her instruments of torture were more numerous than those of any other governess. Her supply of birch was extensive, and kept in water, so that it was always green and pliant: she had shafts with a dozen whip thongs on each of them; a dozen different sizes of cat-o'-nine-tails, some with needle points worked into them; various kinds of thin bending canes; leather straps like coach traces; battledoors, made of thick sole-leather, with inch nails run through to docket, and currycomb tough hides rendered callous by many years' flagellation. Holly brushes, furze brushes; a prickly evergreen, called butcher's bush; and during the summer, glass and China vases, filled with a constant supply of green nettles, with which she often restored the dead to life. Thus, at her shop, whoever went with plenty of money, could be birched, whipped, fusti-gated, scourged, needle-pricked, half-hung, holly-brushed, furze-brushed, butcher-brushed, stinging-nettled, curry-combed, phle-botomized, and tortured till he had a belly full.

'For those whose *lech* it was to flog a woman, she would herself submit to a certain extent; but if they were gluttons at it, she had women in attendance who would take any number of lashes the flogger pleased, provided he forked out an *advalorem* duty. Among these were Miss Ring, Hannah Jones, Sally Taylor, One-eyed Peg, Bauld-cunted Poll, and a black girl, called Ebony Bet.'

From the introduction to the *Index Librorum Prohibitorum*, compiled by Spencer Ashbee

GEORGE H. STOCK

The Romance of Chastisement

Dora Doveton experiences her first flogging. Martinet, the head governess, gives the order:

'FETCH TWO OF the No. 6 rods, and unlace her if necessary.' Renardeau (the French instructress) darted her hand beneath my clothes and reported that I wore no stays. Nor do I now; my waist is naturally small, and a little stiffening in the body of the dress suffices to keep my breasts in order. Steinkopf (German teacher), who had resumed her place, and Armstrong, then laid hold of me, and despite my prayers and tears, while one held my hands above my head, the other opened my dress behind and stripped off skirt, petticoats, and drawers; then with one shameless drag she furled up my shift in front and rear, and pinned it over my shoulders.

The next moment I was forced upon my knees on the block, with four hands grasping my arms and pressing my neck down. The breeze from the sky-light fanned my back, and I felt that the eyes of all present were riveted on my naked person. Could it be I that was subjected to such indignity? Though my arms were squeezed I felt it not, all my sensation seemed to have retreated to another quarter. My skin is so tender that even when bathing I tremble to expose it, and here was I fixed as in a vice, with nothing intervening between that thin skin and the murderous implements behind me.

A pause, it seemed to me an hour long, ensued, till my spine grew cold as ice twixt fear and waiting. Something had rattled on the floor, but the sound had died away, and still the expected blow came not. I looked round with half a hope. Martinet was leisurely re-adjusting a bracelet on her rod arm, her eyes the while devouring my form with a wild impassioned gaze like a lover's. Can she be relenting? Alas! the brows contract – the grasps of the holders tighten on my arms – Whir-r-r Whisp! 'Yah! Yeou! Yeoiks!' Oh! the unspeakable agony of that first murderous lash! Legions of scorpions fastened on my flesh and dug their fangs into my vitals. Vainly I hung back and screwed my front against the block, the rear would not recede; I could only diminish its width by muscular contraction. Whir-r Whisp! Whir-r Whisp! Whir-r Whisp! Nature cannot endure the pain; I struggle to my feet, receiving a fifth rasper in the act, and my shrieks rival the loudest howls of Patty (who had just before been chastised). This was the 'whipping proper', a few strokes more of which would probably have killed or maddened.

The two strong women soon resumed their clutch and dragged me to my bearings on the whipping stool – less reluctantly – for already the charm had worked; the mere act of rising seemed to have brought relief, and a change next to miraculous took place in all my thoughts and feelings. I noted the impressions shortly after they occurred, and shall endeavour to describe them.

Fear and shame were both gone: it was as though I was surrendering my person to the embraces of a man whom I so loved I would anticipate his wildest desires. But no man was in my thoughts; Martinet was the object of my adoration, and I felt *through the rod* that I shared her passions. The rapport, as the magnetisers have it, was so strong that I could divine her thoughts; had she wished me to turn my person full front to her stripes, I should have fought and struggled to obey her. Then, too, there was a thrill in a certain part, I knew magnetically, of both our persons, which every fresh lash kept on increasing. The added pang unlocked new floods of bliss, till it was impossible to tell in my case whether the ecstasy was most of pain or pleasure. When the rods were changed, I continued to jump and shout, for she liked that, but – believe me or not – I saw my nakedness with her eyes, and exulted in the lascivious joy that whipping me afforded her. This state would have continued as long as my strength, for I had no power to quit the spot till *my other self* willed it.

'ETONENSIS'

From The Mysteries of Verbena House

A protest against riding trousers for women

THE GREATEST ENEMY to a woman's chastity is contact. Let her wear her things loose, and she may keep her blood cool. Nuns – continental ones at least – don't wear drawers. Peasant women, who are chaste enough as times go, don't wear drawers; and when they stoop you may see the bare flesh of their thighs above their ungartered stockings. But the bigger the whore – professional or otherwise – the nicer will be the drawers she wears, while the prude, or the cantankerous old maid will either wear the most hideous breeches imaginable, or none at all. I positively knew a lady once who not only repudiated drawers herself, but would not allow her daughters to wear them.

'They were immodest,' she said. And so they are. They bring into immediate contact with a woman something belonging to the opposite sex.

When drawers are made of linen, and are bifurcated at the bottom and belly, they are feminised to an extent which may neutralise the elements I have spoken of; although, as far as I am concerned, it tickles me somewhat when I look from the windows of a railway carriage into suburban back gardens to see the white drawers of women hung to dry on clothes lines, and fluttering in the breeze. My imagination fills the empty galligaskins with cosy bottoms and hirsute quims. Were those drawers loquacious, like Tennyson's 'Talking Oak', what mysteries might they not reveal.

A lady, putting on her riding trousers becomes, consciously or unconsciously, akin to a hoyden assuming man's clothes, or nearer still, to a ballet girl drawing on her tights. She is subject to contact of the most perilous kind. The warm close substance that passes close to her flesh, that clasps her loins, and embraces her bum, and insinuates itself, between her thighs, has, all senseless leather, cloth, or silk, as the case may be, something of the nature of a man's hand in it.

Let the graces be stark naked, or vest them only with flowing drapery, and they may be as chaste as Susannah. Put them in drawers or tights and they become prostitutes.

If Diana had gone a hunting in trousers of 'chamois leather with black feet', she would not have behaved, I take it, quite so savagely to poor Actæon.

The Mysteries of Verbena House, or, Miss Bellasis Birched for Thieving
by 'Etonensis' was in fact started by George Augustus Sala
and finished by James Campbell Reddie

'WALTER'

From My Secret Life

Walter investigates park whores

'I SHOULD LIKE to see them doing it closer,' said I. 'Come up to the tree then: they won't mind. Stand back a minute; directly he's got his pego up her he won't notice anything, and we'll go close.'

We walked rapidly to the rear, then up to the back of the tree, and saw more and more clearly how the woman was moving up and down, as if pumping. As we got close she ceased, and the man went off, almost at a run. 'They've been quick,' said my woman. 'Has he stroked you?' I said to the other one who had just finished with the man. 'Rather!' the woman replied.

Bawdy wishes, all in conflict, all in tumult, rushed through me. I scarcely knew what I wanted or did. . . . 'He's a Scotchman,' said she. 'They always spend a lot, and quick. They doesn't do it to a gal till they can't keep it in their bollocks no longer.' 'And then they wants it for nothin',' said the other. 'Yes, they always wants it for nothin',' echoed my woman; 'cheap suits 'em, but they ain't long about it. . . .'

I groped and groped the woman who had been with the Scotchman, till she said: 'Damned if you arn't made me hot messing me about. Do me then!' 'No – no, I can't,' said I, and suddenly reflecting, withdrew my hand, wiped it on her chemise, gave both of the girls silver, and moved off rapidly, surprised and disgusted with myself, spitting on my hand, and rubbing it hard with my handkerchief. I even rubbed it on the grass where no one would see me, and at length pissed over my hand to purify it.

ANON

From Satan's Harvest Home

or the Present State of Whorecraft, Adultery, Fornication, Procuring, Pimping, Sodomy, And the Game at Flatts, (Illustrated by an Authentick and Entertaining Story) And other Satanic Works, daily propagated in this good Protestant Kingdom

*M*Y DEAR, WILL *you give me a Glass of Wine; take me under your Cloak, my Soul, and how does your precious — do?* You hear at the Corner of every Court, Lane and Avenue, the Quarrels and Outcries of Harlots recriminating upon one another, Soldiers and Bullies intermixing, the most execrable Oaths are heard, such as are seldom exceeded, but at a *Stop* of *Carts* and *Coaches* in a Winter's Evening. By and by a Brandy-Shop is going to be demolish'd, because the Master refuses to bail some Whore that's just arrested, and a Coach waiting at the Door of her Lodgings to carry her to the Officer's House, unless he does the kind Office. A Riot breaks out in another Place, a Bawd's Goods are seized on for Rent; a new Tumult ensues, a Whore's Maid in crossing the Croud, has a Misfortune to break a Bottle of red Port, with a Couple of Pipes, that she is carrying to her Mistress's Chamber, the Mob give a Shout, the Girl is beat out of Doors with her Head bloody, all the Chandler-Women and Gin People are assembled, with an *Irish* Sollicitor at their Head about the Door, with an Outcry for *Justice*; poor *Peggy's* Rashness is blamed by some, and justified by others; in an Instant half a dozen Suits of Head Cloths are torn in Pieces, and several black Eyes and bloody Noses exhibited: *Warrants, binding over,* and *Actions,* are the Subjects of all Conversation in *Coulson's-Court, Bridges-Street,* &c. A Cry of Murder is heard about twenty Yards farther, a *Mother* or *Father* being under the bastinading of a dutiful *Son* or *Daughter.* *Pimps* and *Pensioners* to the *Hundred,* you seek skulking from Bawdy-House to Bawdy-House incessantly. In short, I cannot but fancy them a Colony of *Hell-Cats* planted here by the Devil, as a Mischief to Mankind; they admit of no Comparison on this side Hell's Dominions, all this Part, quite up to *N–wtn–rs Lane Park–er's Lane*, St *Th–mas's-street*, (some few honest Shopkeepers excepted) is a Corporation of *Whores, Coiners, Highwaymen, Gamesters, Pick-pockets,* and *House-breakers,* who like *Bats* and *Owls* skulk in obscure *Holes* and *Geneva shops* by Day-Light, but wander in the Night in search of Opportunities wherein to exercise their Villany.

* * *

The greatest Evil that attends this Vice, or could befal Mankind, is the Propagation of that infectious Disease call'd the *French Pox*, which in two Centuries has made such incredible Havock all over *Europe*. In these Kingdoms, it so seldom fails to attend Whoring, now-a-days mistaken for Gallantry and Politeness, that a hale robust Constitution is esteem'd a Mark of Ungentility and Illbreeding, and a healthy young Fellow is look'd upon with the same View, as if he had spent his life in a Cottage. . . . And our Gentry in general, seem to distinguish themselves by an ill state of Health; in all Probability, the Effect of this pernicious Distemper. Nothing being more common, than to hear People of Quality complain of *rude vulgar Health*, and curse their *Porterly Constitutions*. Men give it to their Wives, Women to their Husbands, or perhaps their Children; they to their Nurses, and the Nurses again to other Children; so that no Age, Sex or Condition, can be entirely free from the Infection.

W. DUGDALE

Publisher's blurb for La Rose d'Amour

Or, the Adventures of a Gentleman in Search of Pleasure. Translated from the French.

O NE OF THE most remarkable works of the present day. Possessed of unbounded wealth, and of frame and of stamina of body apparently inexhaustible, he pursues pleasure with an appetite that grows by what it feeds on, and is never tired or wearied in the pursuit; this hero ravishes, seduces, and ruins all the females that come within his reach – rich and poor, gentle and simple, rough and refined, all fall down before his sceptre of flesh, his noble truncheon, his weapon of war. His great passion is for maidenheads, for young and unfledged virgins, for those in whom the secret instinct of propagation has hardly had time to develop itself. He travels the seas for new victims of his raging lust; he buys maidenheads by the score, he initiates them in all the mysteries of Venus, and, finally, retires to his chateau with a seraglio of beauties, such as Solomon might envy, and David long for in vain. Every page is a picture of sensual delight, and the book is illustrated with Sixteen Coloured Designs equal to the text. It is in two vols, and the price is Three guineas.

FROM *THE PEARL*

STRICTLY PRIVATE, EXCEPT TO BROTHERS,
BY ORDER

The Lady Freemason

As a brother of old, from his lodge was returning,
He called on his sweetheart, with love he was burning,
He wanted some *favours*, says she, 'Not so free,
Unless you reveal your *famed secrets* to me.'

'Agreed – 'tis a bargain – you must be prepared,
Your legs well exposed, your bosom all bared.'
Then hoodwinked and silent, says she, 'I'll be mum,
In despite of the poker you'll clap on my bum.'

To a chamber convenient his fair charge he bore,
Placed her in *due form*, having *closed tight* the door,
Then presented the point of his sharp *Instrumentis*,
And the Lady was soon made an 'entered apprentice'.

His working tools next to her gaze he presented,
To improve by them seriously she then consented,
And *handled* his *jewels* his *gavel* and *shaft*,
That she in a jiffey was passed 'fellow craft'.

She next wanted *raising*, says he, 'There's no urgency,'
She pleaded that this was a case of emergency,
His *column* looked to her in no particular way,
But she very soon made it assume perpendicular.

He used all his efforts to raise the young elf,
But found he required much raising himself;
The task was beyond him. Oh! shame and disaster,
He broke down in his *charge*, and she became *master*.

Exhausted and faint, still no rest could betide him.
For she like a glutton soon mounted astride him,
'From *refreshment* to *labour*,' says she, 'let us march.'
Says he, 'You're exalted – you are now *royal arch*.'

In her zeal for true knowledge, no labour, no shirking,
His *jewels* and *furniture* constantly working,
By night and by day, in the light or the dark,
With pleasure her lover she guides to the *mark*.

Missy's Thoughts

(At a boys' school)

I'll tell my mammy when I go home,
The boys won't let my twat alone;
They pull my frock, and beg to see.
What can they want to do with me?

My sister Mary's twice as wild,
For she's fourteen, and I'm a child;
And if they tried to plague her so,
I think what bouncing Moll would do.

But why do the boys all tease me so,
And ask if I have a mouse to show?
They say there's a mouse in Bruce's clothes,
And when he was cuddling me, it rose!

When yesterday, I climbed for pears,
The boys all came to get their shares;
They giggled, and pointed into my slit,
I didn't know they were laughing at it.

The usher pretends to be my friend,
But I don't know where his love will end;
For while he keeps his sober talk,
I catch his fingers under my frock.

They often make me lie down to show
The very inside of my belly below,
I do as they please, because they pay
A shilling among them for the play.

They're not content, though I open wide,
They grope for something or other inside;
You'd think them fools, to see how they kiss,
The smarting hole, by which I piss!

And then they show me all their shames,
And teach me all the nasty names;
I'll tell my mammy when I go home;
The boys won't leave my Cunt alone!

GEORGE GORDON, LORD BYRON

From Don Leon

Byron's married life

That time it was, as we in parlance wiled
Away the hours, my wife was big with child.
Her waist, which looked so taper when a maid
Like some swol'n butt its bellying orb displayed,
And Love, chagrined, beheld his favourite cell
From mounds opposing scarce accessible.
'Look, Bell,' I cried; 'yon moon, which just now rose
Will be the ninth; and your parturient throes
May soon Lucina's[1] dainty hand require
To make a nurse of thee, of me a sire.
I burn to press thee, but I fear to try,
Lest like an incubus my weight should lie;
Lest, from the close encounter we should doom
Thy quickening fœtus to an early tomb.
Thy size repels me, whilst thy charms invite;
Then, say, how celebrate the marriage rite?
Learn'd Galen, Celsus, and Hippocrates,
Have held it good, in knotty points like these,
Lest mischief from too rude assaults should come,
To copulate ex more pecudum.[2]
What sayst thou, dearest? Do not cry me nay;
We cannot err where science shows the way.'
She answered not; but silence gave consent,
And by that threshold boldly in I went.

[1] Lucina – goddess of childbirth.
[2] In the manner of beasts, i.e. doggy fashion.

So clever statesmen, who concoct by stealth
Some weighty measures for the commonwealth,
All comers by the usual door refuse,
And let the favoured few the back stairs use.

* * *

Who that has seen a woman wavering lie
Betwixt her shame and curiosity,
Knowing her sex's failing, will not deem,
That in the balance shame would kick the beam?
Ah, fatal hour, that saw my prayer succeed,
And my fond bride enact the Ganymede.
Quick from my mouth some bland saliva spread
The ingress smoothed to her new maidenhead,
The Thespian God his rosy pinions beat,
And laughed to see his victory complete.
'Tis true, that from her lips some murmurs fell –
In joy or anger, 'tis too late to tell;
But this I swear, that not a single sign
Proved that her pleasure did not equal mine.
Ah, fatal hour! for thence my sorrows date:
Thence sprung the source of her undying hate.
Fiends from her breast the sacred secret wrung,
Then called me monster; and, with evil tongue,
Mysterious tales of false Satanic art
Devised, and forced us evermore to part.

Don Lean was published as 'A Poem by the late LORD BYRON,
Author of *Childe Harold, Don Juan*, &c., &c. And forming
Part of the Private Journal of his Lordship, supposed to have been
entirely destroyed by Thos. Moore.' In fact, it was
almost certainly *not* by Byron.

GEORGE GORDON, LORD BYRON

From Don Juan

The love of women

CXCIX

Alas! the love of women! it is known
  To be a lovely and a fearful thing;
For all of theirs upon that die is thrown,
  And, if 't is lost, life hath no more to bring
To them but mockeries of the past alone,
  And their revenge is as the tiger's spring,
Deadly, and quick, and crushing: yet, as real
Torture is theirs, what they inflict they feel.

CC

They are right; for man, to man so oft unjust
  Is always so to women; one sole bond
Awaits them, treachery is all their trust;
  Taught to conceal, their bursting hearts despond
Over their idol, till some wealthier lust
  Buys them in marriage – and what rests beyond?
A thankless husband, next a faithless lover,
Then dressing, nursing, praying, and all's over.

CCI

Some take a lover, some take drams or prayers,
  Some mind their household, others dissipation,
Some run away, and but exchange their cares,
  Losing the advantage of a virtuous station;
Few changes e'er can better their affairs,
  Theirs being an unnatural situation,
From the dull palace to the dirty hovel:
Some play the devil, and then write a novel.

THOMAS ROWLANDSON

From Pretty Little Games

The following poems appeared below prints by Rowlandson and were probably also written by him.

The country squire new mounted

The Country squire to London came,
And left behind his dogs and game;
Yet finer sport he has in view,
And hunts the hare and cony too.
The lovely lass her charms displays,
She tips the hint and he obeys,
Within a tavern view the fair,
Each leg supported on a chair,
Her buttocks on the table seated
By which the squires joys compleated.

The hairy prospect or the Devil in a fright

Once on a time the Sire of evil,
In plainer English call'd the devil,
Some new experiment to try
At Chloe cast a roguish eye;
But she who all his arts defied,
Pull'd up and shew'd her sexes pride:
A thing all shagg'd about with hair,
So much it made old Satan stare,
Who frightened at the grim display,
Takes to his heels and runs away.

The larking cull

While on the bed the nymph's reclined,
Damons resolv'd to please his mind.
His generation tube he shews.
Between her swelling breasts it goes.
His fingers to her touch hole sent,
Alas to give her small content.
A larger thing would give more pleasure,
She always loves to have full measure.
And who for greater joys do hunt
Than rising bubbies and a Cunt.

New feats of horsemanship

Well mounted on a mettled steed,
Famed for his strength as well as speed,
Corrinna and her favorite buck
Are pleas'd to have a flying fuck.
While o'er the downs the courser strains,
With fiery eye and loosened reins,
Around his neck her arms she flings,
Behind her buttocks move like springs.
While Jack keeps time to every motion,
And pours in loves delicious potion.

Rural felicity or love in a chaise

The Winds were hush'd, the evening clear,
The Prospect fair, no creature near,
When the fond couple in the chaise
Resolved each mutual wish to please.
The kneeling youth his vigour tries,
While o'er his back she lifts her thighs.
The trotting horse the bliss increases,
And all is shoving love and kisses.
What couple would not take the air
To taste such joys beyond compare.

Published as *Pretty Little Games for Young Ladies & Gentlemen.
With Pictures of Good Old English Sports and Pastimes.*

ANON

From The Mysteries of the Court of London

The following passage comes from an extraordinary and little-known 'penny dreadful' written in the 1840s. It is a fairly early example of serial writing, bound together from weekly parts of the *Penny Magazine*. I was lucky enough to acquire this worm-eaten volume at a jumble sale for the princely sum of one penny. The style is a bit like Harrison Ainsworth and Eugène Sue trying to write porn. Although the work is over-long and over-packed with incident, in its attempts to vilify the royal family, especially the Prince Regent, it has some merit. Interestingly, *The Mysteries of the Court of London* contains one of the earliest attempts to describe a psychopath – a character who may well have been the forerunner of Stevenson's Jekyll and Hyde. The depiction of London poverty and child thieves is likely also to have influenced Dickens's *Oliver Twist.*

The Prince Regent

'IT IS IMPOSSIBLE to resist you,' said the Amazon; – and rising from her seat on the bed, she proceeded to divest herself of the apparel which became her symmetrical form so admirably.

Then, as the Prince beheld the superb bosom released from its prisonage in the closely fitting frock-coat, and appearing dazzlingly white in the lustre which filled the room, – and as his looks gloated upon the plump and sloping shoulders on which the ebon hair fell in massive tresses, – while the robust but snowy arms, now naked to about midway above the elbow, were curved gracefully behind her back as the taper fingers unloosened the fastening of the corset, – his Royal Highness regretted not that the beauteous wanton had intruded at this unseemly hour into the privacy of his chamber.

But ere she completely finished the task of undressing herself, the Amazon – as if inspired with a certain instinctive feeling of modesty, despite the position in which she was now placed – drew the rich curtain of the bed to conceal her form from the Prince: but this she did in such a manner that the night-table, whereon the soda-water and spirits stood, was left *outside* the drapery, and also hidden therefore from the view of the heir-apparent. Then, having accomplished this little manœuvre, the Amazon took a small phial from the pocket of her breeches and poured a few drops of its dark-coloured contents into the tumbler whence the Prince had already drunk the brandy, as just now stated.

In another minute the Amazon entered the royal couch and was clasped in the impassioned embrace of the fervid voluptuary.

An hour afterwards Lady Letitia Lade rose gently from the magnificent bed, and began to resume her apparel with all possible despatch.

Glancing towards the Prince, who was sleeping a profound lethargic slumber, she murmured to herself, 'The cold-blooded villain! Oh! that I was compelled to endure his detested embraces – But he imbibed the narcotic in the large dram of brandy which I gave him – and he will not awake for hours to come!'

Then a smile of triumph played on the moist coral lips of the Amazon: and, having finished dressing herself, she drew from beneath the Prince's pillow the golden chain to which was suspended the key of curious workmanship. Therewith opening the desk of his Royal Highness, she proceeded to ransack its contents; and in the course of a few minutes she found the papers for which she was searching.

''Tis as I thought!' she said to herself, again speaking low and murmuringly with her liquid, musical voice. 'The traitor – the false friend! But you shall be avenged, Mengles – you shall be avenged – even if I do not succeed in procuring your restoration to this country!'

Then, locking the desk and replacing the chain with the key underneath the pillow of the Prince, Lady Lade secured the papers about her person and took her departure by the secret staircase.

J. G. LOCKHART

From The Life of Mr Adam Blair

De Sade, perhaps, first pioneered the use of the dot-dot-dot technique in sexual scenarios; books like *The Mysteries of the Court of London* followed suit liberally. But Lockhart's novel surely contains the longest, most meaningful series of dots in publishing history.

In the following extract, Adam Blair, minister and widower, has galloped through the storm to visit the beautiful and unhappily married Mrs Campbell.

HE ROSE AND threw open the window of the apartment, and leaned over it to inhale the freshening breeze. She followed him, and resting her head upon his shoulder, gazed out along with him upon the wide silver lake, stretched out far below, and the glorious moon, which had now risen high in the heavens, and was beaming resplendent amidst all her attendant millions of twinkling stars. While they gazed, a white radiant cloud floated nearer and nearer, and at last gathering over the face of the beautiful planet, blotted her light from heaven; assuming, at the same time, a dark and frowning hue, as if mourning over the obscurity of the very luminary its own veil was concealing. The sky was darkened, and the sympathetic lake seemed to lie like a sea of ink spread out wide and far, with scarcely one solitary star here and there reflected on its surface. The winds too seemed all to have subsided; and, for a moment, earth, sky, and sea, were alike black and alike silent.

Mrs Campbell took Blair's hand and withdrew him from the window. She reseated him by the table, poured another glass of wine, and again forcing him to swallow it, began to tell him, in broken syllables, the story of her insults.

Had she never told that story, perhaps Adam Blair had never been a fallen man – nor

> 'The moon hid her light
> From *his* heaven that night.'

CHAPTER XIV

```
*   *   *   *   *   *   *
*   *   *   *   *   *   *
*   *   *   *   *   *   *
*   *   *   *   *   *   *
```

*   * The wind rose higher and higher, and the roaring waves lashed
far up against the black rocks of Uigness, and the wild voice of the tempest
howled deeper and deeper along the forest ridges, and over the waste
moors. They heard not the uproar of the elements, or if they did, it
accorded but too well with the tumults of sense and passion throughout
that long dark night, – the morning of which dawned upon slumbers, hot,
feverish, but deep, nevertheless, and lasting. An old Highland crone, the
only other inhabitant of the tower, after waiting many hours beyond the
time when she expected to be summoned, entered the chamber, and
having been in bed long before Mr Blair's arrival the night before, it may
be more easily imagined than described with what surprise she beheld her
mistress asleep in the arms of a man – and a stranger.

ANON

From Cupid's Album

The gallant monk of Mount Celenberg

DR MOORE, IN his 'View of Society,' has related an interesting incident
which fell under his own observation.

During his stay at Vienna, he and his fellow travellers had an invitation
from M. de Breteuil, to dine on the top of Mount Celenberg, in the
vicinity of that city. The steep is so rugged, that common carriages cannot
be dragged up it; they were, therefore, conveyed in one of a particular
construction, and calculated for such expeditions. Having reached the
summit, where there is a convent of monks, their eyes were directed to
two landscapes, of a very opposite character: the one consists of a range of
wild mountains; the other presents the imperial city of Vienna, with the

various branches of the river Danube, flowing through a rich champaign of boundless extent.

The dining table was covered with every delicacy of the season. Madame de Matignon, a very beautiful and sprightly lady, daughter to the host, did the honours. Some of the finest women of Vienna were of the company; and the whole of the entertainment was conducted with equal taste and gaiety.

At the dessert, some of the fathers of the convent came, and presented the company with baskets of fruit, and sallad from their garden. They were invited to sit down, and the ladies pledged them in tokay.

The ladies were afterwards admitted to the convent, and in spite of the gravity and mortified looks of the fathers, they could not but be pleased with the appearance of such a lovely assemblage, to whose society they had not been accustomed.

One lady, of a lively disposition, laid her hand on a scourge, which hung at one of the fathers' belts, and asked it of him as a present; for, having, she said, been a great sinner, she was willing to use it, when she returned home.

The father gallantly begged the lady to spare her fair skin; and to prove his sincerity, immediately fell on his knees, and began to whip his shoulders severely; declaring that when the ladies had retired he would exert more rigorous discipline; for he was determined she should be as exempt from sin as on the day of her birth.

This earnest regard melted the heart of the lady, who assured the sacred father her faults were very venial, and that she was conscious that what his tender solicitude had already prompted him to undergo, would clear her effectually.

Dr Moore put the scourge in his pocket, 'and thus the amorous contest ended'.

JOHN DAVENPORT

From Aphrodisiacs and Anti-Aphrodisiacs

The Saviour's foreskins

THE FORESKINS, STILL extant, of the Saviour, are reckoned to be twelve in number. One was in the possession of the Monks of Loulombs; another at the Abbey of Charroux; a third at Hildesheim, in Germany; a fourth at Rome, in the Church of St Jean-de-Latran; a fifth at Antwerp; a sixth at Puy-en-Velay, in the Church of Notre Dame, etc.

From Essay I, *Ancient Phallic Worship*.

Letter of Sir W. Hamilton prefixed to Payne Knight's Worship of Priapus

SIR W. HAMILTON'S account of the worship paid to St Cosmo and St Damianus is very curious. On the 27th September, at Isernia, one of the most ancient cities of the kingdom of Naples, situated in the province called the Contado di Molise, and adjoining the Aruzzo, an annual fair is held which lasts three days. On one of the days of the fair the relics of Sts Cosmo and Damianus are exposed. In the city and at the fair, ex-votos of wax representing the male parts of generation, of various dimensions, sometimes even the length of a palm, are publicly exposed for sale. There are also waxen vows that represent other parts of the body mixed with them, but of these there are few in comparison of the number of Priapi.

The distributors of these vows carry a basket full of them in one hand, and hold a plate in the other to receive the money, crying out 'Saints Cosmo and Damianus!' If you ask the price of one, the answer is, 'Più ci metti, più ci meriti!' – the more you give, the more the merit. The vows are chiefly presented by the female sex, and they are seldom such as represent legs, arms, etc., but most commonly the male parts of generation. The person who was at the fête, in the year 1780, and who gave me this account (the authenticity of which has since been confirmed to me by the Governor of Isernia) told me also that he heard a woman say, at the time she presented a vow, 'Santo Cosmo, benedetto, così lo voglio.' – Blessed St Cosmo, let it be like this! The vow is never presented without being accompanied by a piece of money, and is always kissed by the devotee at the moment of presentation.

Quoted in *Aphrodisiacs and Anti-Aphrodisiacs*

AMERICAN FOLKLORE

The Creation of a Pussy

Seven wise men with knowledge so fine,
  Created a pussy to their design.
First was a butcher, smart with wit,
  Using a knife, he gave it a slit.
Second was a carpenter, strong and bold,
  With a hammer and chisel, he gave it a hole.
Third was a tailor, tall and thin,
  By using red velvet, he lined it within.
Fourth was a hunter, short and stout,
  With a piece of fox fur, he lined it without.
Fifth was a fisherman, nasty as hell,
  Threw in a fish and gave it a smell.
Sixth was a preacher whose name was McGee,
  Touched it and blessed it and said it could pee.
Last came a sailor, a dirty little runt,
  He sucked it and fucked it and called it a cunt.

SIR RICHARD F. BURTON

Racialist Note to his Full Translation of The Arabian Nights

DEBAUCHED WOMEN PREFER negroes on account of the size of their parts. I measured one man in Somali-land who, when quiescent, numbered nearly six inches. This is a characteristic of the negro race and of African animals; e.g. the horse; whereas the pure Arab, man and beast, is below the average of Europe; one of the best proofs by the by, that the Egyptian is not an Asiatic, but a negro partially whitewashed. Moreover, these imposing parts do not increase proportionally during erection; consequently, the 'deed of kind' takes a much longer time and adds greatly to the woman's enjoyment. In my time no honest Hindi Moslem would take his womenfolk to Zanzibar on account of the huge attractions and enormous temptations there and thereby offered to them.

FROM *KRYPTADIA*

The Magic Ring

This is one of many similar tales to be found in *Kryptadia*, a nineteenth-century collection of folk tales.

ONCE UPON A time there was a tailor, who owned a magic ring. Whenever he put it on his finger, his prick shot up. One day, when he was working at a woman's place, he was so merry that when he went to bed he left his prick uncovered. The woman noticed and saw what a big prick it was. She had a great longing to try it and sent for the tailor. 'Listen,' she said to him, 'you must agree to sin with me, just once.' 'Why not, dear lady. But there's one condition – that you don't fart. If you fart, you must give me three hundred roubles.'

'Fine,' said the woman. They went to bed. The woman tried as hard as she was able not to fart under the tailor: she had ordered her young chambermaid to prepare a large onion to stop up her arse and to hold it in place with two hands and all her strength. She forced the onion into the woman's arse and it held well, but when the tailor got on top, he pressed down so hard that the onion flew out and hit the chambermaid and nearly killed her. The woman lost her three hundred roubles. The tailor took his money and went. He walked and walked for miles and miles and lay down in a field to sleep, putting the ring on his finger. His prick shot up a *verst*[1] long. He lay back and rested and then he slept. Seven wolves came up, from no one knows where, and gnawed at his prick till they were glutted. The tailor woke up thinking flies had stung it. He slipped the ring off his hand, hid it in his pocket and went on his way. He walked and he walked until he came to stay with a *moujik*.[2] The *moujik* had a young wife who really loved big pricks. The tailor slept in the courtyard and left his prick uncovered. The *moujik*'s wife saw it. How should she go about taking it? She crept up, lifted her skirt and put the prick in her cunt. The tailor realised what she was up to. Everything went well. He quietly put the ring on his finger and his prick got larger and larger until it was a *verst* high. The woman had never thought of more than a fuck. She seized the prick with both hands. The good people – her neighbours and acquaintances – all saw that the woman was planted on top of a prick. They put up a prayer that both of them would remain whole and safe. The tailor softly slipped his ring off his finger. His prick went down and the woman with it.

Transl. F.P. from *L'Anneau Enchanté*.

[1] Moujik – a type of peasant.
[2] Verst – about two-thirds of a mile.

CHARLES GODFREY LELAND

From Etruscan Roman Remains
collected by C. G. Leland.

Il moro – The moor

THERE WAS IN the Romagne a rich lady who was unkindly treated by her husband because she had no children. And he often said to her that unless she gave birth to a son or daughter, and that soon, he would leave her and take another. So the poor signora went every day to the church to pray to God that He would be so gracious as to give her a child; but it was not granted to her, therefore after a time she went no more to church and ceased to give alms.

One day she stood quite disconsolate at the window, because she loved her husband and met with no return, when, from a window opposite, a dark signore (*Signore Moro* – a Moor or Negro, as in German) called to her, and she, raising her head, asked him what he would have?

The Moor, who was a wizard, or magician (*uno streghone, o sia uno magliatore, o maliardo*), replied, 'Look me steadily in the eyes, and then all will go well with thee. And this night when thy husband shall embrace thee think steadily of me, and thus thou wilt be *incinta*, or with child.'

This came to pass, and the poor lady was very happy to regain the love of her husband, and at the same time become a mother. But joy flies like the clouds, and so did hers, for when her child was born it was dark as the Moor, yes, and looked altogether like the Moor himself. Then the husband abandoned both wife and child, saying that the infant was none of his. And the lady reproved the Moor, saying that he had betrayed her.

But the Moor replied, 'Grieve not, O good lady, for I can still make peace between thee and thy husband. Tomorrow a charity sermon will be preached, and when the friar shall give thee benediction, put the child on the ground and let it go whither it will.' So the lady did. Now her husband never went to any church, but, hearing that there was to be a famous preacher this day, he was present. And when the lady put the little babe on the ground, what was her utter amazement to see it rise and run on its little feet, and go to its father, and embrace him with its little hands, and say, in distinct words: *'Babbo, perdona mamma, è innocente'* – 'Papa, pardon mamma, she is innocent; and thou seest it is a miracle of God that I have come to thee.' And from that time the babe never uttered a word till he had come to the age when children usually talk.

Then the father, being moved by the miracle, was reconciled with his wife, and they returned home together and lived happily.

La vendetta di Pippo – Pippo's revenge

THERE WAS A man called Pippo, and he had not been long married to a young and beautiful wife when he was obliged to go on a long journey. And it so chanced that this journey was by accident prolonged, nor did his letters reach home, so that his wife, who was young and very simple, believing all the gossip and mischievous hints of everybody, soon thought that her husband had run away. Now there was a priest in the village who was *bastanza furbo* – not a little of a knave – and to him she bitterly complained that her husband had abandoned her, leaving her *incinta*, or with child.

At this the priest looked very grave, and said that it was very wicked in her husband to act as he had done; yes, that it was a mortal sin for which both she and Pippo would be damned, even to the lowest depth of hell, because she would give birth to a child which had only been begun, and not finished, for that it would probably be born without a head or limbs, and she would be very lucky if only a hand and foot, or the eyes were wanting. And that all women who bear such monsters would be certainly condemned to the worst.

Now the wife, being only a simple *contadina*, was very devout, and went frequently to confession, and, believing every word which the priest said, was terribly frightened, and asked him what could be done in this case? Then he replied that there was a way to remedy it, which he should most unwillingly employ, yet still to save her soul, and for the child's sake, he would try it. And this was that she should pass the night with him, when by his miraculous power as a priest, and by his prayers, he would so effect it that the infant would be perfected – and so she could be freed from sin. But he made her swear an oath not to tell a word of all this to any human being, and especially not to Pippo, else all would fail. So she assented, and the priest had his will.

Now no one knew it, but Pippo was a *streghone*, or wizard, and casting his mind forth to know how all was going on at home, learned all this fine affair which had passed. Then returning, instead of going to his house, he put on the form of a beautiful nun, and went to the priest's. The priest had two young sisters, famous for their extraordinary beauty, and Pippo was very kindly received by them as well as by the brother. And when he begged for a night's lodging, the two young girls bade him sleep with them, which he did, of course seducing them thoroughly.

The next morning, being alone with the priest, he first ogled him, and as the other caught eagerly at the chance of sinning with a nun, he plainly asked him if they should not go into the cellar, *per fare l'amore*[1]. At which the priest was enraptured; but when they were alone together Pippo assumed his natural form, which was a terrible one, and said: 'I am Pippo, whose wife thou didst wrong with thy lies. Evil hast thou done to me, but I have done worse to thy sisters, and worst of all to thee, for now thou art accursed before God, thou false priest!' And the *prete* could do nothing and say nothing. And there came before him all the time many spirits who mocked him, and he had to leave holy orders. And this was the revenge of Pippo.

[1] To make love.

The walnut boy

THE COUNTRY OF Benevento is in the Romagna, and that is the real *posto delle streghe*, or witch meeting-place. One evening a gentleman went to walk with his daughter whom he adored. And as they passed under a walnut-tree, and there were so many fine nuts, she desired to eat of them. But hardly had she eaten one when she felt herself ill, *allo stomaco*, and went at once home, and to bed. And all her family were in despair, because they loved her tenderly.

Nor was it long before they saw her body increasing in size, and thought she was *incinta*, or with child, and began to treat her harshly, till at the end of nine months she gave birth to a little lamb; it was very beautiful, and her parents knew not what to think of this phenomenon. And they questioned her closely as to whether she had ever had a lover, but she swore this had never been the case, and knew nothing beyond this – that she felt ill after having eaten the walnut.

Then the father took his daughter to the tree, and she ate another nut; when all at once the tree vanished, and there appeared an old witch, who touched the lamb, when it became a handsome young man, and the witch said, 'This is the lover whom you would not permit your daughter to marry. I by my sorcery made him enter and leave her (*sortire dalle sue viscere*), and so shall she be compelled to wed him.'

From The Unpublished Legends of Virgil, *collected by C. G. Leland*

Virgil and the Goddess Vesta

MANY CENTURIES HAVE passed since there was (worshipped) in Florence a goddess who was the great spirit of virtue and chastity, (yet) when a maid had gone astray she always devoted herself to worship the beautiful Avesta, as this deity was called, and the latter never failed in such case to get her devotee out of the difficulty. Her temple was that building which is now called the Baptistery of Saint John, and she was the goddess of light, as of candles, torches, and all that illuminates. And Avesta was, as I have said, known as the deity of virtue, albeit many of the people shrugged their shoulders when they heard this, being evidently strongly inclined to doubt, but they said nothing for fear of punishment.

For it was rumoured that Avesta had many lovers, and that in the rites of her religion there were secrets too dark to discover, and that as everything in her worship was involved in mystery and carried on occultly, it followed, of course, that it involved something wrong. And it was observed that once a month many women who worshipped her met in her temple by night, and that they were accompanied by their lovers, who with them adored the goddess in the form of a large lighted lamp. But that when this rite was at an end and the multitude had departed, there remained unnoted a number, by whom the doors were closed and the light extinguished, when a general orgy ensued, no one knowing who the others might be. And it was from this came the saying which is always heard when two lovers are seated together by a light and it goes out, that Avesta did it.

There was in Florence a young lord who loved a lady of great beauty. But she had a bitter rival, who to cross their love had recourse to sorcery or witchcraft, and so 'bound' or cast on him a spell which weakened his very life, and made him impotent and wretched, that his very heart seemed to be turned to water.

And this spell the witch worked by taking a padlock and locking it, saying:

'Now here I close the lock,
Yet 'tis not a lock which I close;
I shut the body and soul
Of this ungrateful lord,
Who would not meet my love,
But loves another instead,
Another whom I hate,
Whom I here lock and chain
With devil's power again.
I hold this man fast bound
That none shall set him free
Until I so command,
And bound he shall remain
Till he will marry me.'

One day Virgil was passing the Piazza del Duomo, when he met with the young man who had thus been bound or bewitched, and the victim was so pale and evidently in terrible suffering, that the great poet and magician, who was ever pitying and kind, was moved to the heart, and said:

'Fair youth, what trouble have you, that you seem to be in such suffering?'

The young man replied that he, being in love unto life and death, had been bewitched by some malignant sorcery.

'That I can well see,' replied the sage, 'and I am glad that it will be an easy thing for me to cure you. Go thou into a field which is just beyond Fiesole, in a place among the rocks. There thou wilt find a flat stone bearing a mark. Lift it, and beneath thou wilt find a padlock and chain. Take this golden key: it is enchanted, for with it thou canst open any lock in the world of door or chain. Keep the lock, open it, and then go to the Temple of Vesta and return thanks with prayer, and wait for what will come.'

So the young man did as Virgil had told him, and among the rocks found the stone and the padlock, and went to the Temple of Avesta, where he opened the lock and made the prayer to the goddess, which having done, he fell asleep, and no one beheld him.

And while he was there the young lady entered the Baptistery to worship Avesta, to offer her devotions, which being ended, she sat down and also fell into a deep sleep, and no one observed her.

But later in the night, when the doors were closed and the light extinguished, and the worshippers who remained were calling 'Avesta!' the two sleepers who were side by side were awakened by a rustling of silk, and this was caused by the dress of the goddess, who roused them. And the young man found himself restored to vigorous health and unwonted passion, and quickly noting that a lady was by him, and carried away by feelings beyond his control, embraced and kissed her – nor did she indeed resist, for the will of Avesta was on them both. But noting that the lady had a silk handkerchief partly out of her pocket, he adroitly stole it, putting in its place his own, and so with a kiss he left her, neither knowing who the other was. But on awaking, as if it were from a dream or a delirium, the lady was overcome with shame and grief, and could only think that madness or magic had overcome her reason, to cause her to yield as she had done. For this morning she felt more passionately in love with her betrothed than she had ever done before, and this was because the spell which had bound her was broken with the opening of the padlock.

But what was the astonishment of the lover, who was also restored to all his health and strength, when in the morning he looked at the handkerchief which he had carried away and found embroidered on it the arms and name of his love! So he went to visit her, and his greeting was:

'Signorina, have you lost a handkerchief?'

'Not that I know of,' replied the lady, amazed.

'Look at the one in your pocket, and then at *this*,' was his laughing reply.

She did so, and understanding all in an instant, cried out in shame and horror, while she became at first like blood and then milk. Then the gentleman said:

'It seems to me, Signorina, that we must by mistake have exchanged handkerchiefs last night in the dark, and no wonder, considering the fervency of our devotions. And since we have begun to worship and pray so devoutly, and have entered on such a good path, it were a pity for us to turn back, and therefore it were well for us to continue to travel on it hand in hand together. But I propose that instead of changing pocket-handkerchiefs, we exchange rings before the altar and get married.'

The lady laughed and replied:

'I accept with great pleasure, Signore, the handkerchief; just as the women in Turkey do when it is thrown to them. And you know the proverb:

'She who will take will give herself away,
And she who gives will sell herself, they say.'

'Even so will I sell mine for thine; but you must take the bargain on the nail, and the ball on the bound in the game of love.'

'Yes,' replied the young man; 'I do so with all my heart. But as for our handkerchiefs, I now see that it is true that the peasant does not always know what it is that he carries home in his bag from the mill. Thanks be to Avesta that we found such good flour in our sacks!'

'To Vesta and to Virgil be all praise!' replied the lady. 'But I think that while we continue our daily worship in the temple, we will go there no longer by night. *Vi sono troppo donne devote nel buio*' – There are too many lady devotees there in the darkness.

HONORÉ DE BALZAC

Two tales from Contes Drolatiques *(Droll Stories)*

From: The old gad-about

IN HIS EIGHTY-SECOND year Old Gad-About had been compelled to live chastely for about seven months, during which time he did not meet a single willing woman, and he declared it was the greatest astonishment of his life.

In this grievous state he saw in the fields in the merry month of May a girl, who by chance was a maid tending the cows. The day was so hot that the young girl was lying down in the shade of a beech tree, her face on the grass, after the fashion of people who work in the fields, who generally sleep whilst their cattle are feeding. She was awakened by the old man trying to rob her of that which a poor girl can only lose once. Finding herself outraged without receiving any pleasure she screamed so loudly that the men at work in the fields hurried to her assistance, just at the moment when she discovered the damage usually wrought on a nuptial night. She wept, she complained, declaring that the old ape should go and violate his own mother instead of her, who had not even spoken to him. The old man made answer to the girl's friends, who were threatening to murder him with their hay-forks, that he had felt compelled to do what he had done. These good people objected that he should enjoy himself without forcing a young girl to help him, lest the provost should send him straightway to the gallows, and they then took him with great clamour to the gaol at Rouen.

The girl, questioned by the provost, declared that she was asleep, and that she was dreaming of her lover, with whom she had quarrelled, because he wanted to try his strength before he married her; and in the dream she allowed him to see if everything was all right, so that there should be no disappointment either on one side or the other. He went farther than she had given him permission, and finding more pain than pleasure, she woke up and found herself in the arms of Old Gad-About, who had thrown himself upon her like a friar upon a gammon of bacon.

This affair made such a noise in the town of Rouen that the provost was commanded to attend the duke, who had a strong desire to learn whether the rumour was true. On the provost making his statement the duke sent for Old Gad-About so that he might hear what defence the man had to the charge. The poor fellow appeared before the duke and bewailed the misfortune which had befallen him through force and impulse of nature, saying that he was a true man stirred by the imperative desires of his nature; that up to this year he had had women all to himself, but that he had fasted for eight months; that he was too poor to reward girls; the honest women who had awarded charity to him were disgusted with his hair, which was getting grey, notwithstanding the vitality of his youth; and that he had been compelled to snatch at the pleasure which he saw in that horrid girl, who, in stretching herself under the beech tree had exposed her beautiful understudy and a pair of hemispheres as white as snow, that the sight of which had completely upset his reason; that the fault was with the girl and not with him, for girls ought to be forbidden to show passers-by what was known as Venus Callipge; finally, the prince ought to know what trouble it was for a man to hold his dog in during the heat of the day, for that was the time when King David was smitten by Uriah's wife; that where a God-fearing Hebrew king had failed, surely a poor destitute beggar could not be held in fault. The duke enjoyed the reasons put forward by Old Gad-About, and declared he was a man of good c—. Then he gave him back his liberty on condition that if he had such a great desire for these things he would give him an opportunity of showing it on the scaffold, to which the provost had condemned him; if, with the cord round his neck, between the priest and the hangman, he could show his desire, he should have pardon.

This affair known, a great crowd came to see the poor fellow led to the scaffold; the people lined the route as though there were about to be a ducal entry, and there were certainly more bonnets than hats. Old Gad-About was saved by a lady curious to see the finish of the old violator, and who said to the duke that religion commanded that the poor fellow should have fair play, and then assumed a posture as though she was about to dance; she showed intentionally a pair of sconces so white that the finest linen of the gorget paled before them; in fact, these beautiful fruits of love displayed themselves without a wrinkle from without her corset, like two great apples, and made the mouth water, so delightful were they. This noble lady, who was one of those who always makes a man feel strong directly he sees them, smiled at the poor man. Old Gad-About, clothed in a coat of coarse cloth, more sure of being in a position to violate after the hanging than before, came between the officers of justice, throwing his glances now here, now there, but he saw nothing but heads. 'I would give a thousand crowns,' murmured he, 'to see a girl like that one with her clothes tucked up who was looking after the cows,' for he called to mind the beautiful white columns of Venus which had brought him into this trouble and might yet save him. But as he was old the remembrance only was not powerful enough. When at the foot of the ladder he saw the two pretty possessions of the lady mentioned, also the little delta formed by their confluent contures, his master, John Chouart, was in such a rage that the old coat spoke very plainly by evincing a great uprising.

'There,' said he, to the officers of justice, 'look at once, I have gained my pardon, for I do not answer for the rascal.'

The lady was very proud of this homage to her charms.

The sergeants who had charge, on putting his coat on one side declared that the old fellow must be the very devil, for they had never seen an Ego so straight, as they found under the good man's coat. Then he was led triumphantly through the city to the duke's palace, and the sergeants and others testified to his highness what they had seen. In those ignorant times this wonderful affair was considered such an honour to the town that the people voted that a monument should be erected in the palace where the man had gained his pardon, and he was portrayed in stone as he was seen by that honest and virtuous lady. The statue could still be seen when the city was taken by the English, and contemporary historians place this narrative among the most credible and noteworthy events of this time. It was afterwards resolved that the town should furnish the good fellow with girls, to while away the rest of his days, and the good duke sent him a thousand crowns. The old man here lost the name of Old Gad-About, as the duke named him Lord de Bonne-C—. He married and his wife was put to bed nine months after with a boy, perfectly made, full of life, and which was born with two teeth. From this marriage came the house of Bonne-C—, which from very shame asked our good King Louis XI for letters patent to change the name to Bonne-Chose. The good king

remonstrated with the Lord de Bonne-C—, for there was in the State of
Venice a family named Coglioni who bore three C—t in their natural
position on their coat-of-arms. But the lords of Bonne-C— objected that
their wives were ashamed of being thus addressed in company. The king
responded that they would lose a great deal there, because with the name
the things themselves disappeared. Nevertheless, he granted the letters.
Since that time these people have been known by that name, and have
migrated into several provinces. The first lord of Bonne-C— lived
twenty-seven years longer and had another son and two daughters. But he
grieved over his riches, and that he could no longer wander at will along
the highways.

From this narrative you can learn one of the most beautiful lessons of all
the tales that you can read in your life. Those rich people who go down to
their grave with teeth still chewing, who drink wine continually in order to
prepare themselves for pleasure; these pot-bellied people repose on beds
of down whilst the Lord de Bonne-Chose slept on the hardest of beds.

This ought to make most of those who read this tale to change their life,
and to imitate Old Gad-About in his old age.

From: *The merry jests of King Louis the Eleventh*

I WILL NOT leave the heels of that great king without committing in
writing the capital trick which he played on La Godegrand, who was
an old maid, and very soured at not having found a cover for her saucepan
during the forty years of her life, and who was fretting in her yellow skin at
being as much a virgin as any mule. She lived on the other side of the
house which belonged to La Beaupertuys, so that by stooping over the
balcony close to the wall it was quite easy to see what she said and did in
the lower room where she lived, and the king often amused himself by
looking at the old maid, who did not know that she was under his eye.

Now, it happened on a market day, that the king had a young fellow of
Tours hanged for having violated a noble lady of mature age, mistaking
her for a young girl. There was no harm in that, for there would have been
no harm, but rather it would have been very meritorious for the said lady
to be taken for a virgin; but when he found out his mistake, he had
overwhelmed her with abuse, and, thinking that she had made use of a
trick, he robbed her of an enamelled silver cup, as a return for the loan
which he had just made her. This young man had long hair, and was so
handsome that the whole city wished to see him hanged, from mingled
feelings of regret and curiosity, and you may be sure that there were more

women than men present. The young fellow swung very well, and, according to the custom of the time, died gallantly, and with lance well in rest, a fact which gave rise to much talk in the town. Many ladies said with regard to this matter that it was nothing short of murder not to have preserved such a fair fellow alive.

'What do you say to putting the handsome criminal into La Gode-grand's bed?' the Beaupertuys asked the king.

'We should frighten her,' Louis the Eleventh replied.

'Not at all, Sire. You may be sure that she will gladly welcome a dead man, as she is fond of a living one. Yesterday I saw her making a fool of herself with the cap of a young man, which she had put on the top of a chair, and you would have laughed heartily at her words and antics.'

So, whilst the virgin of forty was at vespers, the king sent and had the young fellow, who had just finished the final scene of his tragic farce, cut down, and having dressed him in a clean white shirt, two grooms climbed over the wall of Mmlle Godegrand's garden, and put the man who had been hanged into the bed on the side next to the wall. As soon as they had done this, they went off, and the king remained on the balcony with the Beaupertuys waiting till it was time for the old maid to go to bed. The virgin Godegrand soon came back, 'ta! ta! fair! fair!' as the people of Touraine say, from Saint Martin's Church, to which she was quite near as the cloister wells adjoined the Rue de Jerusalem. She went home, laid aside her bag, shaplet, rosary, and other little articles which old maids burden themselves with, and then uncovered the fire, fanned it, warmed herself, sat down comfortably in her chair, and caressed her cat, for want of anything else. Next, she went to the larder, and supped whilst she sighed, and sighed whilst she supped, swallowed her food by herself, whilst she looked at her embroidery, and after drinking, emitted a loud noise, which the king heard.

'I say! Just suppose that the poor wretch hanging there were to say to her: God bless you!'

At this idea of La Beaupertuy's, they both broke out in a fit of silent laughter, but the very Christian king watched most attentively whilst the old maid undressed, admiring herself as she did it, pulling out a hair, or picking off a pimple which had been unkind enough to appear on her nose. Then she cleaned her teeth and did a number of other things which, alas! all ladies, whether they be virgins or not, do; which vexes them very much, although without these slight natural defects they would be too haughty, and we should never be able to enjoy their society. Having finished her aquatic and musical discourse, the old maid got between the sheets, and uttered a fine, loud, ample, and curious cry, when she saw and perceived the coldness of the man who had been hanged, and the pleasant fresh odour of his youth, though she jumped quite away from him out of coquetry. But as she did not know that he was really dead, she returned, thinking that he was making fun of her, and only feigning death.

'Go away, you silly joker!' she said, but you may be sure that she said these words in a very humble and gracious voice; but when she saw that he did not move, she examined him more closely, and was much astonished at this beautiful example of nature's workmanship, when she recognised the upstanding citizen, and thereupon the fancy took her to make purely scientific experiments on him, in the interests of those who might be hanged in future.

'Whatever is she doing?' La Beaupertuys said to the king.

'She is trying to resuscitate him; it is a work of Christian charity.'

For the old maid was rubbing and warming the fine young man, praying to St Mary of Egypt to aid her in restoring to life this husband who had come to her from the skies as a ready-made lover, when, suddenly, whilst she was looking at the dead man she was charitably trying to warm, she fancied that she saw a slight motion of his eyes. She, therefore, put her hand on his heart and felt it beating feebly, until at last, what with the warmth of the bed, the affection and the temperature which belongs to old maids, which is more burning than all the blasts from the deserts of Africa, she had the delight of restoring this valiant and handsome fellow, who, luckily, had been very badly hanged, to life.

'There, that is how my hangmen serve me,' said Louis the Eleventh, with a smile.

'Oh!' said La Beaupertuys, 'you will not have him hanged over again; he is far too good-looking!'

'The sentence does not say that he is to be hanged twice, but he shall marry the old maid.'

In good sooth, the kind lady went as fast as she could to fetch a barber-surgeon, who lived close to the Abbey and brought him back immediately. He at once took out his lancet, bled the young man, and as the blood would not flow, he said: 'Ah! It is too late; the blood has got into his lungs.'

But suddenly his youthful blood began to flow in drops, and then came abundantly, and the threatened apoplexy, which had only just begun, was arrested in its course. The young man moved and began to show signs of returning animation; then, in the course of nature he grew very weak and helpless, whilst his flesh grew altogether flabby. Just then, the old maid, who had been all eyes and who had followed the great and notable changes which had taken place in the person of the man who had been so badly hanged, took the barber by the sleeve, and pointing out the culprit's piteous case, said, with a curious leer: 'Will he always be like that for the future?'

'Well, yes! very often,' replied the most truthful surgeon.

'Oh! well, he was far nicer when he was hanged!'

On hearing these words, the king burst out laughing. When the old maid and the surgeon saw him through the window they were terribly frightened, as that laugh seemed to them to be a second death sentence for the unhappy man, who had already been hanged once, but the king kept his word and married him. Then, justice having been done, he gave the husband the name of Lord Mortsauf (Saved-death), in the place of that which he had lost on the scaffold. As La Godegrande had a big basketful of crowns, they founded a good family in Touraine, which exists still in all honour, as Monsieur de Mortsauf served Louis the Eleventh very faithfully on various occasions. Only for the future he had a great objection to gallows and old women, and would never make a love-assignation at night.

This teaches us to verify and recognise women thoroughly, and not make any mistake in the local difference which exists between them when they are young and old, because if we are hanged for our errors in love, there is always the danger of incurring greater risks.

Transl. R. Whittling

EDMOND DE GONCOURT

From La Faustin

Madam desires . . .

IN THIS HALL, where a series of fights had taken place, where muscular activity had been expended in a kind of fury, where drops of blood had moistened the floor; in this hall, impregnated with the secretions of strength, the still smoking pads and sandals from the skin covered with sweat gave out the wild and exciting smell of a man, tickling the feminine senses in their troubled and lascivious hours.

La Faustin got up, went to the door, then, just as she was going out, made two or three uncertain turns, and finally sat down again in the place she had just left.

The master-at-arms continued to try each weapon and take it to a dark cupboard at the end of the room.

The master-at-arms was reddish-brown, with short, curly hair, had a little coarse moustache, and the fearless expression of a bravo of the Court of the Valois, with a neck like a bullock, though very white, with the suppleness and feline elasticity and rapidity of movement which spread around him the bitter perfume of youth.

La Faustin looked at him, and while she did so her eyes became hot, and she felt the beating of the arteries of her temples.

'Monsieur Blancheron did not say when he would be back?' remarked La Faustin to break the silence.

'No,' said the young man, still engaged upon his duties, and failing to notice the woman's attention.

La Faustin remained nailed to the bench by magnetic power.

Little by little, she could only see the things around her in a vague, trembling, dazzling way; obtuse images crossed the void of her brain among the buffets of heat; a strong circulation carried through her veins warm weighty blood. She felt all the intellectual warmth of her depart and fly to other parts of her body; she had no longer a will, and there was in her ardent, moist being only sensual desire, the unbridled and frenzied appetite of a young animal, and that in a dull transport, a torpid contraction, a collective immobility, and a nervous crossing of the legs, resembling a defence against herself.

Then at that moment the woman's look, that look charged with wine and sleep, the look of intoxication beneath heavy eyelids, became obstinately fixed upon the young master-at-arms.

'You – ' she began, a quickly interrupted phase.

'Yes, madam?'

'Nothing!' she said savagely.

But their eyes met, conversed in a flash; the man indicated with a look the dark room. The woman got up from the bench with the resigned shrug of the shoulders of a vanquished creature, and joined the man.

Immediately the door was violently reopened, and La Faustin was pursued and captured in the large room by the man with eyes aflame, who tried to force her to return to the dark place. They struggled, body to body, and she dealt him with furious energy the blows in the face by which a woman defends herself from a rape by a person who is a horror to her. At last, by a supreme effort, she snatched herself from his arms, and with her dress torn, disappeared into the little garden, hearing from the outside the young master-at-arms cry out upon the threshold of the fencing-school, in anger and astonishment, 'What a strange lady! Madam desires, and then, and then madam does not!' . . .

Transl. G. F. Monkshood and Ernest Tristan

ERNEST DOWSON

Non Sum Qualis Eram Bonae Sub Regno Cynarae

Last night, ah, yesternight, betwixt her lips and mine
There fell thy shadow, Cynara! thy breath was shed
Upon my soul between the kisses and the wine;
And I was desolate and sick of an old passion,
    Yea, I was desolate and bowed my head:
I have been faithful to thee, Cynara! in my fashion.

All night upon mine heart I felt her warm heart beat,
Night-long within mine arms in love and sleep she lay;
Surely the kisses of her bought red mouth were sweet;
But I was desolate and sick of an old passion,
    When I awoke and found the dawn was grey:
I have been faithful to thee, Cynara! in my fashion.

I have forgot much, Cynara! gone with the wind,
Flung roses, roses riotously with the throng,
Dancing, to put thy pale, lost lilies out of mind;
But I was desolate and sick of an old passion,
    Yea, all the time, because the dance was long:
I have been faithful to thee, Cynara! in my fashion.

I cried for madder music and for stronger wine,
But when the feast is finished and the lamps expire,
Then falls thy shadow, Cynara! the night is thine;
And I am desolate and sick of an old passion,
    Yea, hungry for the lips of my desire:
I have been faithful to thee, Cynara! in my fashion.

EMILE ZOLA

From Nana

Nana and Muffat

ONCE SHE HAD got him in the bedroom with the doors closed, she'd entertain herself with the man's humiliation. At first, they'd have fun, she'd give him a few light slaps and force him to comply with funny wishes, making him lisp like a child and repeat little phrases.

'Say like me: "Shit! Coco doesn't care a toss!"' He was pliable to the point of imitating her accent. 'Shit! Coco doesn't care a toss!'

Or, she'd play at being a bear on all fours, on her fur rug, in her chemise, turning round growling as if she'd devour him; and she even bit his calves, for a joke. Then, getting up, she'd say: 'It's your turn now. I bet you don't make as good a bear as me.'

It was charming. She amused him as a bear, with her white skin and her mane of red hair. He would laugh and get down on all fours as well, growling and biting her calves as she got away, acting as if she was thoroughly frightened.

'Aren't we fools?' she'd say in the end. 'You have no idea how ugly you are, my pet! Ah, what if they were to see you at the Tuileries?'

But these little games soon went downhill. It wasn't cruelty in her, for she was a kind enough girl; it was as if a blast of insanity had swept its way in behind those closed doors. Their luxuriousness threw them off course and into delirious fantasies of the flesh. The old pious fears of a sleepless night turned into a bestial thirst, a mania for going down on all fours, growling and biting. Then, one day, while he was playing bear, she pushed him roughly and he fell against a piece of furniture, she burst out laughing – she couldn't help herself – seeing a bruise on his forehead. From then on, having got a taste for it with her try on La Faloise, she treated him like an animal, whipped him and followed him round with kicks.

'Gee up! Gee up! You're the horse . . . Giddy up. Filthy nag! Won't you go?'

At other times he was a dog. She'd throw her perfumed handkerchief into the corner of the room and he'd have to go over on his hands and knees to pick it up with his teeth.

'Fetch, Caesar! . . . I'll give it to you if you dawdle. Good, Caesar! Obedient dog! Nice! Do it gently!'

He revelled in his abasement, feeling the joy of being a brute. He longed to sink further and would shout:

'Hit me harder! . . . Go on, go on, I'm all worked up! Hit me for that!'

She had a sudden fancy – she ordered him to turn up one evening in his full chamberlain's uniform. What a laugh, what fun she had mocking him when he was in his full regalia with his sword, hat, white breeches and a red dress-coat emblazoned with gold embroidery and carrying the symbolic key on the right tail. This key, above all, diverted her, launching her off into a mad fantasy of dirty explanations. Laughing all the time, carried away by her lack of respect for grandeur and by the joy of demeaning him in all the official pomp of this costume, she shook him, she pinched him and yelled at him:

'Go on then, chamberlain!' She accompanied this with a series of kicks up the bum. She gave these with all her heart as against the Tuileries, the majesty of the imperial court enthroned on the summit of the fear and subjugation of the populace. That was what she thought of society! This was her revenge, a subconscious grudge of her family, bequeathed in her blood. Then, when the chamberlain was undressed, with his uniform on the floor, she shouted at him to jump on it and he jumped, she shouted at him to spit and he spat; she shouted at him to walk on the gold braid, on the eagles, on the decorations, and he walked. Scrunch! There was nothing left, everything caved in. She smashed a chamberlain as she smashed a decanter or a comfit-dish, making a complete mess of him, a heap of filth at the street corner.

In the meantime, the goldsmiths had broken their word, the bed wasn't delivered until the middle of January. Muffat happened to be in Normandy at that time, where he had gone to sell a last piece of the wreckage. Nana at once extorted four thousand francs. He wasn't due to come back until the day after next; but, having finished his business, he brought forward his return, and, without even passing Rue Miromesnil he went to the Avenue de Villiers. Ten o'clock struck. As he had a key to the little door opening on to Rue Cardinet, he went straight up. Upstairs, in the drawing-room, Zoé, who was polishing the bronzes, was struck dumb. Not knowing how to stop him, she started to tell him, in a roundabout way, that Monsieur Venot, seeming very upset, had been looking for him from the day before, and that he'd already come twice to beg her to send Monsieur home, if he stopped off first at Nana's house. Muffat heard, but couldn't make a thing of her story; then, noticing her confusion, he was seized with a fit of jealous rage – something he no longer thought himself capable of – and threw himself against the bedroom door, where he heard laughter. The door gave, the two halves flew open, while Zoé withdrew with a shrug of her shoulders. So much the worse! As Madame was going crazy she could sort matters out herself.

At the threshold, Muffat gave a cry at what he saw in front of him.

'My God! . . . My God!'

The bedroom glittered in its new royal splendour. The tea-rose velvet hangings, sewn with twinkling stars on silver bosses, were of that rosy hue the sky takes on fine evenings, when Venus shines on the horizon against the clear background of the dwindling day. Gold cords fell in the corners, gold lace framed the panels, like light flames, like heads of loose red hair half-covering the spacious emptiness of the room, heightening its voluptuous pallor. Next, just opposite, there was the gold and silver bed which sparkled with the new brilliance of its craftsmanship – a throne just large enough for Nana to be able to spread the glory of her naked limbs, an altar of Byzantine riches, worthy of the almighty power of her sex, and where she was, at this moment, uncovered, with all the religious, shameless display of a feared idol. And, near her, beneath the snowy reflection of her breasts, in the midst of her triumph as a goddess, there wallowed a disgrace, a decrepitude, a laughable and pathetic ruin, the Marquis de Chouard in his shirt.

The count had clasped his hands. A great shudder went through him.

'My God! . . . My God!'

It was for the Marquis de Chouard that the gold roses bloomed on the prow-like head of the bed, the little clusters of gold roses opening amongst the gold foliage; it was for him that the Cupids hung over, the circle of them somersaulting over a trellis of silver, laughing in amorous playfulness; and it was for him that the faun at their feet uncovered the sleeping nymph, worn out with voluptuousness, that figure of Night, modelled on the famous naked body of Nana, down to the big strong thighs by which she was known to all. Thrown there, like a human rag, marred and rotted by sixty years of debauchery, he brought a flavour of the charnel-house into the glorious display of the woman's radiant flesh. When he saw the door open, he raised himself up, seized with fear, like an ancient dotard. That night of love had turned him into a complete idiot, he'd relapsed into childhood; unable to find the right words any longer, half paralysed, stammering and shaking, he stayed in his cowering posture, his shirt rucked up on his skeletal body, one leg out of the covers, a miserable livid leg covered in grey hairs. Nana, in spite of being put out, couldn't help laughing.

'Lie down, cover yourself up in the bed,' she said, pulling him down and burying him beneath the coverlet, like a bit of filth you wouldn't want to show.

And she got up to close the door. No luck, certainly, with her little muff. He always turned up at the wrong moment. Besides, hadn't he gone to Normandy to get money? The old man had brought four thousand francs, so she'd let him have his way. She pushed back the two doors and shouted:

'So much the worse for you! It's your own fault. Is that any way to come in? I've had enough. *Bon voyage.*'

Trans. F.P.

JORIS KARL HUYSMANS

From A Rebours *(Against Nature)*

The hero, des Esseintes, is an aesthete always on the search for newer, more rarefied pleasures. One of his most satisfactory affairs is with a ventriloquist. The second passage comes from near the end of the book, where he's enjoying ill-health thanks to his erratic eating and lifestyle and starts to take an interest in enemas. The peptone enema was a standard treatment of the time, according to a turn-of-the-century French medical dictionary in my possession.

Des Esseintes and the ventriloquist

THEIR AFFAIR CONTINUED, but before long des Esseintes's sexual failures became worse. The effervescence of his mind could no longer warm the iciness of his body, his nerves were no longer obedient to his will – the lecherous follies of old men obsessed him. Feeling more and more in doubt of his powers when he was with this mistress, he had recourse to the most efficacious aphrodisiac known to aged, undependable lechers – fear.

While he was holding the woman in his arms, a drunken sot's voice would burst out from behind the door:

'Will you open up! I know very well that yo ve got a client in there with you. Just you wait, just you wait, you bitch!' Immediately, like those libertines who're turned on by the fear of being caught in the act, out in the open, on the river bank, in the Tuileries, in a urinal, or on a park bench, he recovered his powers for the moment, and would throw himself on top of the ventriloquist while the voice continued to row outside the room, and he experienced immense enjoyment in the hurry and panic of a man running a risk, interrupted and rushed in the midst of his filthiness.

The art of the enema

AT LAST HIS thoughts became more cheerful; after all his sufferings were over and the feebleness that he felt in every limb had gathered a certain sweetness and a pampered quality, at once vague and languorous. He was at once astonished and satisfied not to be encumbered with drugs and vials, and a faint smile hovered about his lips when his servant brought in an enema full of nourishing peptone and told him that he'd have to repeat this three times every twenty-four hours.

The operation was a success, and des Esseintes couldn't help silently congratulating himself on the event, which was, in a way, the pinnacle of achievement in the life he'd made for himself. His bent for the artificial had now, without any efforts on his part, attained its supreme fulfilment; no one could go further; taking nourishment in this way had to be the ultimate deviation that anyone could try.

'It would be delicious,' he told himself, 'to go on with this simple regimen when I'm well again. What a saving of time, what a radical deliverance from the aversion that meat inspires in people without appetite! What a total release from the boredom that always springs from the lack of choice involved in a limited diet! What a spirited protest against the despicable sin of gluttony! And finally, what a forceful insult to throw in the face of Nature, whose repetitive demands would be for ever silenced.'

And he went on talking to himself *sotto voce*: 'It would be easy to get up a hunger by swallowing an aperitif. Then, when you could fairly say: 'What time is it? I think it must be time to lay the table. I'm as hungry as a horse', you could set your place by putting the magic instrument on the cloth – just time to say grace and you'd have finished your meal without any of the boring, vulgar process of eating.'

A few days later, the servant brought him an enema with a different colour and smell from the peptone ones.

'But it isn't the same!' cried des Esseintes, looking anxiously at the liquid that had been poured into the apparatus. He asked for the menu, as if in a restaurant, and, unfolding the doctor's prescription, he read out:

20g Cod-liver oil
200g Beef tea
200g Burgundy
Yolk of an egg

That made him think. He had never been able to take a serious interest in cookery because of the ruinous state of his stomach, but now he surprised himself by devising recipes of a phoney epicurianism. Perhaps the doctor had realized that the recherché palate of his patient had already tired of the taste of peptone. Perhaps he'd wished, like a clever chef, to vary the flavour of his dishes, to avoid a monotony in the courses leading to a loss of appetite. Once on this line of thought, des Esseintes started to make up new recipes – meatless ones for Fridays – upping the dose of cod-liver oil and wine and dropping the beef tea because, being flesh, it was expressly forbidden by the Church.

Transl. F.P.

THE
TWENTIETH
CENTURY

FRANK HARRIS

From My Life and Loves

The Carlyles' wedding night

A T THAT DINNER Sir Richard Quain said that he had been Mrs
Carlyle's physician and that he would tell me later exactly what Mrs
Carlyle had confessed to him. Here is Quain's account as he gave it me
that night in a private room at the Garrick. He said:

'I had been a friend of the Carlyles for years: he was a hero to me, one of
the wisest and best of men: she was singularly witty and worldly-wise and
pleased me even more than the sage. One evening I found her in great
pain on the sofa: when I asked her where the pain was, she indicated her
lower belly and I guessed at once that it must be some trouble connected
with the change of life.

'I begged her to go up to her bedroom and I would come in a quarter of
an hour and examine her, assuring her the while that I was sure I could
give her almost immediate relief. She went upstairs. In about ten minutes
I asked her husband would he come with me? He replied in his broadest
Scotch accent, always a sign of emotion with him:

"I'll have naething to do with it. Ye must just arrange it yerselves."

'Thereupon I went upstairs and knocked at Mrs Carlyle's bedroom
door: no reply: I tried to enter: the door was locked and unable to get an
answer I went downstairs in a huff and flung out of the house.

'I stayed away for a fortnight but when I went back one evening I was
horrified to see how ill Mrs Carlyle looked stretched out on the sofa, and
as pale as death. "You're worse?" I asked.

"Much worse and weaker!" she replied.

"You naughty obstinate creature!" I cried. "I'm your friend and your
doctor and anything but a fool: I'm sure I can cure you in double-quick
time and you prefer to suffer. It's stupid of you and worse – Come up now
and think of me only as your doctor," and I half lifted, half helped her to
the door: I supported her up the stairs and at the door of her room, she
said:

"Give me ten minutes, Doctor, and I'll be ready. I promise you I won't lock the door again."

'With that assurance I waited and in ten minutes knocked and went in.

'Mrs Carlyle was lying on the bed with a woolly white shawl round her head and face. I thought it absurd affectation in an old married woman, so I resolved on drastic measures: I turned the light full on, then I put my hand under her dress and with one toss threw it right over her head. I pulled her legs apart, dragged her to the edge of the bed and began inserting the speculum in her vulva: I met an obstacle: I looked – and immediately sprang up: "Why, you're a virgo intacta" (an untouched virgin!) I exclaimed.

'She pulled the shawl from her head and said: "What did you expect?"

"Anything but that," I cried, "in a woman married these five-and-twenty years!"

'I soon found the cause of her trouble and cured it or rather did away with it: that night she rested well and was her old gay, mutinous self when I called next day.

'A little later she told me her story.

"After the marriage," she said, "Carlyle was strange and out of sorts, very nervous, he seemed, and irritable. When he reached the house we had supper and about eleven o'clock I said I would go to bed, being rather tired: he nodded and grunted something. I put my hands on his shoulders as I passed him and said, 'Dear, do you know that you haven't kissed me once, all day – this day of days!' and I bent down and laid my cheek against his. He kissed me; but said: 'You women are always kissing – I'll be up soon!' Forced to be content with that I went upstairs, undressed and got into bed: he hadn't even kissed me of his own accord, the whole day!

"A little later he came up, undressed and got into bed beside me. I expected him to take me in his arms and kiss and caress me.

"Nothing of the sort, he lay there, jiggling like,"' ('I guessed what she meant,' said Quain, 'the poor devil in a blue funk was frigging himself to get a cock-stand.') '"I thought for some time," Mrs Carlyle went on, "one moment I wanted to kiss and caress him; the next moment I felt indignant. Suddenly it occurred to me that in all my hopes and imaginings of a first night, I had never got near the reality: silent, the man lay there jiggling, jiggling. Suddenly I burst out laughing: it was all too wretched! too absurd!"

"At once he got out of bed with the one scornful word 'Woman!' and went into the next room: he never came back to my bed.'

Love in Athens

As I lay in bed that night about eleven o'clock I heard and saw the handle of the door move: at once I blew out the light; but the blinds were not drawn and the room was alight with moonshine. 'May I come in?' she asked. 'May you?' I was out of bed in a jiffy and had taken her adorable soft round form in my arms. 'You darling sweet,' I cried and lifted her into my bed. She had dropped her dressing-gown, had only a nightie on and in one moment my hands were all over her lovely body. The next moment I was with her in bed and on her; but she moved aside and away from me.

'No, let's talk,' she said. I began kissing her but acquiesced: 'Let's talk.' To my amazement she began: 'Have you read Zola's latest book *Nana*?' 'Yes,' I replied. 'Well,' she said, 'you know what the girl did to Nana?' 'Yes,' I replied with sinking heart. 'Well,' she went on, 'why not do that to me? I'm desperately afraid of getting a child, you would be too in my place, why not love each other without fear?' A moment's thought told me that all roads lead to Rome and so I assented and soon I slipped down between her legs. 'Tell me please how to give you most pleasure,' I said and gently, I opened the lips of her sex and put my lips on it and my tongue against her clitoris. There was nothing repulsive in it; it was another and more sensitive mouth. Hardly had I kissed it twice when she slid lower down in the bed with a sigh whispering: 'That's it; that's heavenly!'

Thus encouraged I naturally continued: soon her little lump swelled out so that I could take it in my lips and each time I sucked it, her body moved convulsively and soon she opened her legs further and drew them up to let me in, to the uttermost. Now I varied the movement by tonguing the rest of her sex and thrusting my tongue into her as far as possible; her movements quickened and her breathing grew more and more spasmodic and when I went back to the clitoris again and took it in my lips and sucked it while pushing my forefinger back and forth into her sex, her movements became wilder and she began suddenly to cry in French, 'oh, c'est fou! oh, c'est fou! oh, oh!' and suddenly she lifted me up, took my head in both her hands and crushed my mouth with hers as if she wanted to hurt me.

The next moment my head was between her legs again and the game went on. Little by little I felt that my finger rubbing the top of her sex while I tongued her clitoris gave her the most pleasure and after another ten minutes of this delightful practice she cried, 'Frank, Frank, stop! kiss me! Stop and kiss me, I can't stand any more. I am rigid with passion and want to bite or pinch you.'

Naturally I did as I was told and her body melted itself against mine while our lips met – 'You dear,' she said, 'I love you so, and oh how wonderfully you kiss.'

'You've taught me,' I said. 'I'm your pupil.'

A French mistress

i was awakened suddenly by the acutest pang of pleasure I had ever felt, and found Jeanne on top of me. How she had managed it, I don't know, but the evil was done, if evil there was, and my sensations were too intense to be abandoned. In a moment I had reversed our positions, and was seeking a renewal of the delight, and not in vain: her sex gripped and milked me, with an extraordinary strength and cleverness; such as I had never before imagined possible. Not even with Topsy had I experienced such intensity of pleasure. Taking her in my arms, I kissed her again and again in passionate surprise. 'You can kiss me now,' she said pouting: 'but you didn't believe me when I told you in the Victoria to choose me and you would profit by the exchange – my friend has only her pretty face,' she added contemptuously.

*   *   *

After a day or two I began to doubt her magic. She never tried to excite me, but whenever I sought her, I found the same diabolical power. The French have the word for her; *'Casse noisettes'* they call it, or 'nutcrackers' – a woman's sex with the contractile strength of a hand, and Jeanne knew the exact moment to use it. . . .

ANON

Eskimo Nell

When a man grows old and his balls grow cold,
And the end of his knob turns blue,
When it's bent in the middle like a one-string fiddle,
He can tell you a yarn or two:
So find me a seat and stand me a beer,
And a tale to you I'll tell,
Of Deadeye Dick and Mexico Pete,

And the harlot named Eskimo Nell.
Now when Deadeye Dick and Mexico Pete
Go forth in search of fun,
It's usually Dick who wields the prick,
And Mexico Pete the gun;
And when Deadeye Dick and Mexico Pete
Are sore, depressed and sad,
It's usually a cunt that bears the brunt,
Though the shootin' ain't too bad.
Well, Deadeye Dick and Mexico Pete
Had been hunting in Dead Man's Creek,
And they'd had no luck in the way of a fuck
For nigh on half a week;
Just a moose or two, or a caribou,
Or a reindeer or a doe,
And for Deadeye Dick with his kingly prick,
Fuckin' was mighty slow.
So do or die, he adjusted his fly,
And set out for the Rio Grande,
Deadeye Dick with his muscular prick,
And Pete with his gun in his hand.
And so they blazed a randy trail,
No man their path withstood,
And many a bride who was hubby's pride
Knew pregnant widowhood.
They made the strand of the Rio Grande
At the height of a blazing noon,
And to slake their thirst and to do their worst,
They went into Black Mike's saloon.
And as the door swung open wide,
Both prick and gun flashed free;
'According to sex, you bleeding wrecks,
You drinks or fucks with me.'
Now they'd heard of the prick called Deadeye Dick,
From the Horn to Panama,

And with nothing worse than a muttered curse
Those dagoes sought the bar;
The women too knew his playful ways,
Down on the Rio Grande,
And forty whores took down their drawers
At Deadeye Dick's command.
They saw the finger of Mexico Pete
Twitch on the trigger grip;
They dared not wait; at a fearful rate,
Those whores began to strip.
Now Deadeye Dick was breathing quick,
With lecherous snorts and grunts.
As forty arses were bared to view,
To say nothing of forty cunts.
Now forty arses and forty cunts,
You'll agree if you use your wits,
With a little bit of arithmetic,
Make exactly eighty tits;
And eighty tits make a gladsome sight
For a man with a raging stand,
It may be rare in Berkeley Square,
But not on the Rio Grande.
Our Deadeye Dick, he fucks 'em quick,
So he backed up and took his run,
And made a dart at the nearest tart,
And scores a hole in one.
He threw the whore to the sawdust floor,
And fucked her deep and fine,
And though she grinned it put the wind
Up the other thirty-nine.
Our Deadeye Dick, he fucks 'em quick,
And flinging the first aside,
He was making a pass at the second arse
When the swing doors opened wide,
And entered in, to that hall of sin

Into that harlot-hell,
All unafraid, strode a gentle maid
Whose name was Eskimo Nell.

Our Deadeye Dick, who fucks 'em quick,
Was well into number two,
When Eskimo Nell lets out a yell
And says to him, 'Hey, you!'

That hefty lout, he turned about,
Both nob and face were red,
And with a single flick of his muscular prick
The whore flew over his head.

But Eskimo Nell she took it well,
And looked him straight in the eyes,
With the utmost scorn she sneered at his horn
As it rose from his hairy thighs.

She blew a drag from her smouldering fag
Over his steaming nob,
And so utterly beat was Mexico Pete
He forgot to do his job.

It was Eskimo Nell who broke the spell
In accents calm and cool,
'You cunt-struck shrimp of a Yankee pimp,
D'you call that thing a tool?

If this here town can't wear that down,'
She sneered to the squirming whores,
'There's one little cunt that will do the stunt,
That's Eskimo Nell's, not yours.'

She shed her garments one by one,
With an air of conscious pride;
Till at last she stood in her womanhood,
And they saw the Great Divide.

She lay down there on the table bare,
Where someone had left a glass,
And with a twitch of her tits, she crushed it to bits
Between the cheeks of her arse.

She bent her knees with supple ease,
And opened her legs apart,
And with a final nod at the waiting sod,
She gave him his cue to start.

But Deadeye Dick with his kingly prick
Prepared to take his time,
For a girl like this was fucking bliss,
So he staged a pantomime.

He winked his arsehole in and out,
And made his balls inflate,
Until they rose like granite globes
On top of a garden gate.

He rubbed his foreskin up and down,
His knob increased its size;
His mighty prick grew twice as thick,
Till it almost reached his eyes;

He polished the nob with rum and gob
To make it steaming hot,
And to finish the job he sprinkled the nob
With a cayenne pepper pot.

He didn't back up to take a run,
Nor yet a flying leap,
But bent right down and came alongside
With a steady forward creep.

Then he took a sight as a gunman might
Along his mighty tool,
And shoved in his lust with a dexterous thrust,
Firm, calculating and cool.

Have you ever seen the pistons on the giant CPR?[1]
With the driving force of a thousand horse?
Then you know what pistons are;
Or you think you do, but you've yet to view
The awe-inspiring trick,

---

[1] CPR – Canadian Pacific Railway.

Of the work that's done on a non-stop run
By a man like Deadeye Dick.
But Eskimo Nell was an infidel,
She equalled a whole harem,
With the strength of ten in her abdomen,
And her rock-of-ages beam;
Amidships she could stand the rush
Like the flush of a water closet,
And she grasped his cock like a Chatswood lock
On the National Safe Deposit.
She lay for a while with a subtle smile,
While the grip of her cunt grew keener,
Then she gave a sigh and sucked him dry,
With the ease of a vacuum cleaner.
She performed this feat in a way so neat
As to set at complete defiance
The primary cause and the basic law
That govern sexual science:
She calmly rode through the phallic code,
Which for years had stood the test,
And the ancient rules of the Classic Schools
In a moment or two went west.
And now, my friend, we draw to the end
Of this copulatory epic –
The effect on Dick was sudden and quick,
Akin to an anaesthetic;
He slipped to the floor and he knew no more,
His passion extinct and dead,
Nor did he shout as his tool came out,
It was stripped right down to a thread.
Mexico Pete he sprang to his feet
To avenge his pal's affront,
With a fearful jolt, for he drew his Colt,
And rammed it up into her cunt;
He shoved it up to the trigger grip

And fired three times three,
But to his surprise she rolled her eyes
And squeaked in ecstasy.
She leaped to her feet with a smile so sweet,
'Bully,' she said, 'for you!
Though I might have guessed it's about the best
You flogged-out sods could do.
When next your friend and you intend
To sally forth for fun,
Buy Deadeye Dick a sugar-stick
And get yourself a bun.
And now I'm off to the frozen North
To the land where spunk is spunk,
Not a trickly stream of lukewarm cream,
But a solid frozen chunk.
Back to the land where they understand
What it means to copulate,
Where even the dead lie two in a bed,
And the infants masturbate.
Back to the land of the mighty stand,
Where the nights are six months long,
Where the polar bear wanks off in his lair,
That's where they'll sing this song.
They'll tell this tale on the Arctic trail,
Where the nights are sixty below,
Where it's so damn cold french letters are sold
Wrapped in a ball of snow;
In the Valley of Death with bated breath,
It's there they'll sing it too,
Where the skeletons rattle in sexual battle,
And the mouldy corpses screw!'

ALEXANDRE KUPRIN

From Yama: The Pit

The following extract comes from Kuprin's detailed exposé of
Russia's pre-Revolutionary prostitution.

'PERHAPS YOU'LL STAY with me the whole night?' she asked Gladishev,
when the others had gone away. 'Don't you be afraid, dearie; if you
won't have enough money, I'll pay the difference for you. You see how
good-looking you are, that a wench does not grudge even money for you?'
she began laughing.

Gladishev turned around to her; even his unobserving ear was struck by
Jennka's strange tone – neither sad, nor kindly, nor yet mocking.

'No, sweetie, I'd be very glad to; I'd like to remain myself, but I can't
possibly; I promised to be home toward ten o'clock.'

'That's nothing, dear, they'll wait; you're altogether a grown-up man
now. Is it possible that you have to listen to anybody? . . . But, however, as
you wish. Shall I put out the light entirely, perhaps; or is it all right the way
it is? Which do you want – the outside or near the wall?'

'It's immaterial to me,' he answered in a quavering voice; and, having
embraced with his arm the hot, dry body of Jennka, he stretched with his
lips towards her face. She slightly repulsed him.

'Wait, bear a while, sweetheart – we have time enough to kiss our fill
yet. Just lie still for one little minute. . . . So, now . . . quiet, peaceful . . .
don't stir . . .'

These words, strange and imperious, acted like hypnosis upon
Gladishev. He submitted to her and lay down on his back, putting his
hands underneath his head. She raised herself a little, leant upon her
elbow, and placing her head upon the bent arm, silently, in the faint half-
light, was looking his body over – so white, strong, muscular; with a high
and broad pectoral cavity; with well-made ribs; with a narrow pelvis; and
with mighty, bulging thighs. The dark tan of the face and the upper half of
the neck was divided by a sharp line from the whiteness of the shoulders
and breast.

Gladishev blinked for a second. It seemed to him that he was feeling
upon himself, upon his face, upon his entire body, this intensely fixed
gaze, which seemed to touch his face and tickle it, like the cobwebby
contact of a comb, which you first rub against a cloth – the sensation of a
thin, imponderous, living matter.

He opened his eyes and saw altogether near him the large, dark, uncanny eyes of the woman, who seemed to him now an entire stranger.

'What are you looking at, Jennie?' he asked quietly. 'What are you thinking of?'

'My dear little boy! . . . They call you Kolya: isn't that so?'

'Yes.'

'Don't be angry at me, Kolya – carry out a certain caprice of mine, please: shut your eyes again . . . no, even tighter, tighter. . . . I want to turn up the light and have a good look at you. There now, so. . . . If you only knew how beautiful you are now . . . right now . . . this second. Later you will become coarse, and you will begin giving off a goatish smell; but now you give off an odour of fur and milk . . . and a little of some wild flower. But shut them – shut your eyes!'

She added light, returned to her place, and sat down in her favourite pose – Turkish fashion. Both kept silent. In the distance, several rooms away, a broken-down grand piano was tinkling; somebody's vibrating laughter floated in; while from the other side – a little song, and rapid, merry talking. The words could not be heard. A cabby was rumbling by somewhere through the distant street. . . .

'And now I will infect him right away, just like all the others,' pondered Jennka, gliding with a deep gaze over his well-made legs, his handsome torso of a future athlete, and over his arms, thrown back, upon which, above the bend of the elbow, the muscles tautened – bulging, firm. 'Why, then, am I so sorry for him? Or is it because he is such a good-looking little fellow? No. I am long since a stranger to such feelings. Or is it because he is a boy? Why, only a little over a year ago I shoved apples in his pocket, when he was going away from me at night. Why have I not told him then that which I can, and dare, tell him now? Or would he not have believed me, anyway? Would have grown angry? Would have gone to another? For sooner or later this turn awaits every man. . . . And that he bought me for money – can that be forgiven? Or did he act just as all of them do – blindly? . . .'

'Kolya!' she said quietly, 'open your eyes.'

He obeyed, opened his eyes, turned to her; entwined her neck with his arm, drew her a little to him, and wanted to kiss her in the opening of her chemise – on the breast. She again tenderly but commandingly repulsed him.

'No, wait a while, wait a while – hear me out. . . . One little minute more. Tell me, boy, why do you come here to us – to the women?'

Kolya quietly and hoarsely began laughing.

'How silly you are! Well, what do they all come for? Am I not also a man? For, it seems, I'm at that age when in every man ripens . . . well, a certain need . . . for woman. For I'm not going to occupy myself with all sorts of nastiness!'

'Need? Only need? That means, just as for that chamber which stands under my bed?'

'No, why so?' retorted Kolya, with a kindly laugh. 'I liked you very much. . . . From the very first time. . . . If you will, I'm even . . . a little in love with you . . . at least, I never stayed with any of the others.'

'Well, all right! But then, the first time, could it possibly have been need?'

'No, perhaps, it wasn't need even; but somehow, vaguely, I wanted woman. . . . My friends talked me into it. . . . Many had already gone here before me. . . . So then, I too . . .'

'But, now, weren't you ashamed the first time?'

Kolya became confused; all this interrogation was to him unpleasant, oppressive. He felt, that this was not the empty, idle bed talk, so well known to him out of his small experience; but something else, of more import.

'Let's say . . . not that I was ashamed . . . well, but still I felt kind of awkward. I drank that time to get up courage.'

Jennie again lay down on her side; leaned upon her elbow, and again looked at him from time to time, near at hand and intently.

'But tell me, sweetie,' she asked, in a barely audible voice, so that the cadet with difficulty made out her words, 'tell me one thing more. But the fact of your paying money, these filthy two roubles – do you understand? – paying them for love, so that I might caress, kiss you, give all my body to you – didn't you feel ashamed to pay for that? Never?'

'Oh, my God! What strange questions you put to me today! But then they all pay money! Not I, then someone else would have paid – isn't it all the same to you?'

'And have you been in love with anyone, Kolya? Confess! Well, now, if not in real earnest, then just so . . . at soul. . . . Have you done any courting? Brought little flowers of some sort. . . . Strolled arm-in-arm with her under the moon? Wasn't that so?'

'Well, yes,' said Kolya in a sedate bass. 'What follies don't happen in one's youth! It's a matter anyone can understand. . . .'

'Some sort of a little first cousin? An educated young lady? A boarding school miss? A high school girl? . . . There has been, hasn't there?'

'Well, yes, of course – everybody has them.'

'Why, you wouldn't have touched her, would you? . . . You'd have spared her? Well, if she had only said to you: "Take me, but only give me two roubles" – what would you have said to her?'

'I don't understand you, Jennka!' Gladishev suddenly grew angry. 'What are you putting on airs for? What sort of comedy are you trying to put over? Honest to God, I'll dress myself at once and go away.'

'Wait a while, wait a while, Kolya! One more, one more, the last, the very, very last question.'

'Oh, you!' growled Kolya displeased.

'And could you never imagine . . . well, imagine it right now, even for a second . . . that your family has suddenly grown poor, become ruined. You'd have to earn your bread by copying papers; or, now, let's say, through carpenter or blacksmith work; and your sister was to go wrong, like all of us . . . yes, yes, yours, your own sister . . . if some blockhead seduced her and she was to go travelling . . . from hand to hand . . . what would you say then?'

'Bosh! . . . That can't be . . .' Kolya cut her short curtly. 'But, however, that's enough – I'm going away!'

'Go away, do me that favour! I've ten roubles lying there, near the mirror, in a little box from chocolates – take them for yourself. I don't need them, anyway. Buy with them a tortoise powder box with a gold setting for your mamma; and if you have a little sister, buy her a good doll. Say: in memory from a certain wench that died. Go on, little boy!'

Kolya, with a frown, angry, with one shove of a well-knit body jumped off the bed, almost without touching it. Now he was standing on the little mat near the bed, naked, well-formed, splendid in all the magnificence of his blooming, youthful body.

'Kolya!' Jennka called him quietly, insistently and caressingly. 'Kolechka!'

He turned around to her call, and drew in the air in a short, jerky gust, as though he had gasped: he had never yet in his life met anywhere, even in pictures, such a beautiful expression of tenderness, sorrow, and womanly silent reproach, as the one he was just now beholding in the eyes of Jennka, filled with tears. He sat down on the edge of the bed, and impulsively embraced her around the bared, swarthy arms.

'Let's not quarrel, then, Jennka,' he said tenderly.

And she twined herself around him, placed her arms on his neck, while her head she pressed against his breast. They kept silent so for several seconds.

'Kolya,' Jennie suddenly asked dully, 'but were you never afraid of becoming infected?'

Kolya shivered. Some chill, loathsome horror stirred and glided through within his soul. He did not answer at once.

'Of course, that would be horrible . . . horrible . . . God save me! But then I go only to you alone, only to you! You'd surely have told me? . . .'

'Yes, I'd have told you,' she uttered meditatively. And at once rapidly, consciously, as though having weighed the significance of her words: 'Yes, of course, of course, I would have told you! But haven't you ever heard what sort of a thing is that disease called syphilis?'

'Of course, I've heard. . . . The nose falls through . . .'

'No, Kolya, not only the nose! The person becomes all diseased: his bones, sinews, brains grow diseased. . . . Some doctors say such nonsense as that it's possible to be cured of this disease. Bosh! You'll never cure yourself! A person rots ten, twenty, thirty years. Every second paralysis can strike him down, so that the right side of the face, the right arm, the right leg die – it isn't a human being that's living, but some sort of a little half. Half-man – half-corpse. The majority of them go out of their minds. And each understands . . . every person . . . each one so infected understands, that if he eats, drinks, kisses, simply even breathes – he can't be sure that he won't immediately infect some one of those around him, the very nearest – sister, wife, son. . . . to all syphilitics the children are born monsters, abortions, goitrous, consumptives, idiots. There, Kolya, is what this disease means. And now,' Jennka suddenly straightened up quickly, seized Kolya fast by his bare shoulders, turned his face to her, so that he was almost blinded by the flashing of her sorrowful, sombre, extraordinary eyes, 'and now, Kolya, I will tell you that for more than a month I am sick with this filth. And that's just why I haven't allowed you to kiss me. . . .'

'You're joking! . . . You're teasing me on purpose, Jennie!' muttered Gladishev, wrathful, frightened, and out of his wits.

'Joking? . . . Come here!'

She abruptly compelled him to get up on his feet, lit a match and said: 'Now look closely at what I'm going to show you. . . .'

She opened her mouth wide and placed the light so that it would illumine her larynx. Kolya looked and staggered back.

'Do you see these white spots? This – is syphilis, Kolya! Do you understand? – syphilis in the most fearful, the most serious stage. Now dress yourself and thank God.'

Transl. from the Russian by Bernard Guilbert Guerney

FROM AN OLD PARIS GUIDEBOOK

LISTE ROSE

Iᵉʳ ARRONDISSEMENT

Mᵐᵉˢ	Alice	9, rue J.-J.-Rousseau
	Gaby	6, rue des Moulins
	Marie-Louise	7, rue du Pélican
	Berthy	4, rue Richepanse
	De Lierre	13, rue Molière
	De Valençais	23, rue Cambon
	Jeanne	258, rue Saint-Honoré
	Jeanne	26, rue Croix-des-Petits-Champs
	Juliette	6, rue Croix-des-Petits-Champs
	Mimi	42, rue Coquillière
	Lilia	36, rue Monconseil
	Paquita	25, rue de l'Arbre-Sec

IIᵉ ARRONDISSEMENT

(House of all nations)	12, rue du Chabanais
Charles	32, rue Blondel
Georgette	43, rue de la Lune
Léone	8, rue Colbert
Jeanne	37, rue des Petits-Carreaux
Charles	25, rue Sainte-Appoline
Alice	24, rue Sainte-Foy
Alice	32, rue Poissonnière
(Bras. du Moulin)	16, rue Blondel
Chantry	17, rue du Caire
Cléo	45, rue du Cléry
Christiane	9, rue de la Lune
Delacroix	8, rue Chénier
Denise	7–9, rue du Hanovre
D'Esmur	2, rue Chénier
Dinah	13, rue St-Augustin
Gelot	8, rue Port-Mahon
Hélène	139, rue d'Aboukir
Jeanne	30, rue Beauregard
Léone	56, rue d'Argout
Lucienne	6, rue Dalayrac
Marcelle	46, rue Beauregard
Ressaud	90, rue Montorgueil
Solange	4, rue du Hanovre
Suzy	14, rue de la Michodière
Victoria	56, rue Beauregard
Yvonne	125, rue d'Aboukir
Lise	187, rue St-Denis
Simonne	6, rue de Tracy
Fine	10, rue de Tracy
Fevra	42, rue Sainte-Anne

IIIᵉ ARRONDISSEMENT

Soreau	4, rue Blondel
De Mouy	5, rue Blondel
Berton	79, Boul. Beaumarchais
Marthe	84, rue Notre-Dame-de-Nazareth
Zoé	72, rue des Tournelles
Louisette	4, rue des Vertus

JONATHAN MEADES

Fur and Skin

A NISEED IS INSEPARABLY linked in my mind to the bodies of fallen women. It is the madeleine that evokes a Magdalene. I know what you're thinking: dirty dog, flashy talk. I can get flashier still. I can do it in French. If you do it in French it's poetry, *'C'est la madeleine qui évoque une Madeleine.'* Good, eh? What about this then: *'Mon royaume pour un ours.'* Good, eh? Pat me then. Mind you, frankly I wouldn't: I mean, give away anything, let alone a kingdom (I should be so lucky), for a horse *or* a bear. Especially not a bear. Have you ever got a whiff of a bear's breath? I have. That's the sort of thing you get to smell in my line of business. Guess what I'm in then. Go on. What d'you think my line is then, squire? (I'm aping Stobey, the ape. Prod ribs.) Guess, strewth, guess! (Prod kidneys.) Don't be a wal. A long one to a primate you won't get it . . . But own up, you know me already.

Anyway, my Magdalenes – that's what they were, you could tell because they all had their jars of ointment. And, no, it wasn't feet they anointed. But otherwise they were the very picture of that whore in her pre-penitent state. Pernod, Ricard, Berger, Chinchon, all the gaudy bottles of Asturias, fennel, fenouillette, Sambuca, ouzo, raki, the umbelliferous Levantine plant, 16 March 1915, the Pharisees' tithes, check trousers, the Albigensian dwarf Lautrec – these provoke, without my bidding, a seemingly infinite parade of mental tableaux showing women of all races (the erotic imagination is a catholic and egalitarian machine) in their transports, in beds, in ones and twos and threes, in clothes that don't keep them warm, in novel congas with exotic companions . . . I have seen them too often, these scenes of complicated abandon. Very lively, of course, but they pall. I often find myself in them. There, that's my keen tongue, pink as a shepherd's delight – I'm talking about the German shepherd, you understand. And my teeth – fine and white and you have to admire the canines. And my eyes, by Dunstan! are decorative semi-spheres of liquid amber. And look at my spry pointed ears and my taut body and piston-potent haunches. Look most of all at my glorious pelt. 'You're a furrier's delight,' Eva told me once, running a blood-red nail across my tummy. Joking? I'd like to think she was, but you never can tell with these boudins from Belleville; they'll do *anything* to get their *appartements* on Wagram or Kléber. I'll tell you later about some of the things that Eva did.

There was a time when I hadn't even heard of aniseed. In those days all I knew was the beach that was white and curved like a paring from a giant's big-toe-nail. Out in the bay the sea that used to be rivers and before that rain turned into white horses – no wonder you people believe in progress. Rusty and I rushed into the waves. We rolled and squealed and tumbled. We boxed on two legs like the hares we had heard about but never seen. The moon made the sea stretch this far or *this* far and sometimes it over-stretched itself so that the sand dried quickly, as if a cloud had rushed from in front of the sun. In the half-wet sets our bodies made we'd lick the salt from each other and dream – one dream for two – of how we would emulate Romulus and Remus, be suckled by a she-human, lead a belligerent band of sheep-dogs and found a city on the site where we had been nurtured.

Alas, only one half of the first part of this attractive prospectus came to be, *viz.* I got to be suckled by a she-human, several in fact, want to know how many John and that'll be another kirsch-fantaisie. Thanks. What else was there? There were Rusty's footprints, there was his scent – no brother ever smelled sweeter, there were the cliffs (gnawed sponge-cake, green topping), there were the wind-twisted tamarisks. I can't remember a day when there wasn't at least a breeze. Sometimes the vital wind still gets my face, strikes it just as it used to all that time ago and everything comes back to me, even Stobey and Old Nunc.

It was Stobey that sold me into this life. I was outside Chatsworth early one morning and was, oh, playful as a pup when Old Nunc bellowed from within:

'Ere, Stobey, where you lurking then my son?'

Stobey was lurking on a tattered Lloydloom just a few feet from me. The chair's legs were sunk deep in the ground beneath his weight and all around us the grass rippled the way that fur does when subjected to a wind-effect machine. He was fashioning a Jack-Me-Lad from an empty Players' packet. This was a base form of origami – a tear here, a notch there, a notch thus . . . What it added up to was a device with which Stobey impressed people of his ilk in public houses. He would pull the sliding part of the packet and to his cry of 'Jack-Me-Lad' up would spring a sort of tumescent robot. (You can imagine what people of Stobey's ilk were like.)

He took no notice of Old Nunc's cry, just carried on, his tongue leeching towards his ear in artisanal absorption. Away in the middle distance, on the slab of concrete beside a communal tap. Rusty lay on his back with his feet cycling in air; he looked happier than I had ever seen him. Every now and then his legs obscured a midget's handkerchief of sail in the bay. Old Nunc called Stobey's name again, stretching the vowels into howling parade-ground diphthongs. Stobey clenched his jaw in irritation, stared at me through half-closed eyes and carried on again, this time whistling softly through the mauve chipolatas that God had given him in lieu of lips.

I suppose you might say that I brought it on myself. I was oh so rash to pay no heed to that dextrous bully's minatory squint: I knew what it meant. I knew that man had a massive capacity for spite. There was silence within. Old Nunc must have thought that Stobey was off performing one of the chores with which he filled his day when he wasn't reading *Glass's Guide* in the caballeros between Blenheim and Wentworth Woodhouse. I gave him away. I shopped him with a raucous peal, rruff, ruf rarf, rruff, ruf rarf. Old Nunc was at the door before the shadow of my last euphonic note had died away.

'You gone mutt 'ave you Stobey?'

He stood there with a pocket calculator and a cigarette in one hand and his new day's beaker of St Raphael in the other, glaring. Stobey was glaring too, at me. (Does *glare* suggest murderous intent? It's meant to, he meant it to.)

'Mhungry. I wan' breakfas'.'

'I'll go down the Bag's then,' said Stobey.

'Nah. I fancy armstrongs. Big plate o' them. An' lamb's ones. Not yer pig's. You go down Oliver's now and you tell 'im it's for me and not to give yer pig's. An' rashers, nice fat rashers. You say it's for me an' to give yer nice fat rashers.'

'Oh Christ Nunc on me muvver's spleen sfreequarters a bleedin' hour down Oliver's an' back.'

'Well you'd 'ave better get goin' then 'adn't yer. On yer bike my son.'

But Stobey didn't have a bike. He had the van but he had lost his licence and, as Old Nunc kept reminding him, he didn't know where to find it. Old Nunc peeled him a couple of corrugated banknotes.

He set off, trudging resentfully across the field in the direction of Osborne and Compton Wynyates. I trotted along beside him, pitying him for his frayed trouser cuffs. He aimed a couple of kicks at me but I was as agile then as I am, famously, now; he missed. I sprinted across the grass to Rusty and for a few moments (that become more precious and more achingly vivid as the years go by) we somersaulted through the air with the sumptuous harmony and synchronous ease that only those sprung from the same egg can achieve. (The dainty little leaps of circus poodles –

topiary on four legs – are to our soaring arcs what Miss Mamie van Doren was to Miss Marilyn Monroe. I draw my simile from the cinema because that's my world, the world I frequent.) Then Rusty wanted to play Hunt The Stash – he longed to accompany a policeman like Constable Constable on a raid on a pop star's house and be the one to find the cache of drugs in a tooled box from Tangier or to collar the roadie, a Stobey look-alike, as he tried to flush the lavatory. I didn't want to play, so Rusty searched for mines instead and I ran after Stobey, thinking as usual that the way *I* would like to serve society was as a blind dog, proud in my cream harness, leading my master with gentle dignity through teeming streets, happy to be the apex of the trinity (whose other parts are black glasses and white stick) that signifies sightlessness. Stobey made to hit me but I didn't flinch so he threw a stick for me to chase. I brought it back and as we turned out on to the road beside Harlaxton (unlet because of the traffic noise) he threw it again. High this time and looping and I was already in pursuit when it was still way up in the air. The slipstream of something vast and noxious shunted me across the verge, put my hair *en brosse*; shaken, I looked back at Stobey, who was grinning with canicidal glee, almost. The stick was now a mat of splinters in the middle of the road save for a cylinder of lichen-grey bark that bobbed about the tarmac. A belching milk tanker was racing away down the hill.

Stobey waited to be served behind a harassed slattern. Her little boy squatted on his haunches whining wretchedly about his bellyache and eating copperish rabbit droppings from a paper bag. The scattered sawdust was patterned like iron filings subjected to a magnetic field or like the stubble on the back of a madman's head. Oliver held up a red and yellow wedge that bled down his arm. A short man and a big blonde joined the queue behind me, they wore scent, they both wore jewellery. The slattern picked up her package.

'Two pounda lamb's kidneys an' halfa streaky,' said Stobey.

'C'mon Lance,' said the slattern to her son who spilled his bag of rabbit droppings. They rolled all over the floor. I don't know what came over me; I didn't then, I mean. I do now. The smell of the things! Bliss! Olfactory wipe-out! Their perfume was not luxury, it was *necessity*. This was nosejoy as few know it. It was, of course, aniseed. I rooted, I slipped on the sawdust. Then I tasted and swooned. I hardly felt Stobey's boot as it connected with my shoulder.

The big blonde was tittering. The short man said:

'Impwessive ahnd you got there. Vewy intwestin' indeed. 'E's not for sale I don't suppose?'

Stobey and the short man huddled together under a picture showing a pig before and after its fatal accident. The big blonde gave blubbing Lance a coin. The short man spat on his fingers and, impeded only by his cluster of rings, counted a sum off a roll of notes so thick that Stobey gaped open-mouthed. I looked up and found that the big blonde was running her eyes over me in a most unusual way.

We do not gnaw bones because we want to, you know. We gnaw bones because they are all that we are given. We do not determine the course of our lives. The notion of *la carte* is foreign to us. We get what's thrown to us. Choice? Ha! We live in an open prison of the will. It's not for nothing that it's called a *dog's life*. It's not for nothing that *dog* is a universal word of deprecation. It's not for nothing that *dog* is synonymous with, variously, coward, churl, traitor, braggart, bully, head-case, shirker, spoil-sport.

Sammi and Lou promoted my fondness for aniseed. They gave it me all the time, in all sorts of ways; sometimes, I suspect, they tried to disguise the fact that they were giving it to me – this would be characteristic. I had Pal enriched with marrowbone jelly and ground aniseed balls. I had quivering bricks of meat and jelly smothered in pastis. I had mounds of Chum in which Sammi's surgeon-gloved hands had buried quantities of star anise that scraped my palate. I had everything Lou left on the side of his plate – and he liked to leave a lot as a sign of his profligacy – covered in fennel seeds. Sometimes the water in my bowl was oily and viscous, which meant that a bottle of Sambuca had been tipped into it during the night by Lou as he stumbled about in his shorty towelling gown. After a few weeks during which my dreams grew increasingly lush and my waking life got ever more sybaritic – chocolate truffles, laps, pats, carpets with canapés to be found deep in the pile – Sammi and Lou returned with me to Back Up The Smoke. We sped past Harlaxton with my head out of the window over Sammi's shoulder and my ears swept back to render me the perfect paradigm of sleek streamlining. Rusty was nowhere to be seen but I hardly cared – I was intoxicated by my new life, I was in love with the future and all it held. Rusty was just part of the past, like the dank space beneath Chatsworth where we used to shelter from the stinging rain or like the mother that I had quite forgotten.

At Back Up The Smoke everything is red, dangerous, quick, loud, and the quoins, obeying a law of progressive diminution, march away to a horizon that is so close and dismal it is an obviation of all hope. There they fostered my addiction. They made me an *addict*. They made me dependent. Then they became dependent on me. They were, you see, parasites who had to create their own host – me, lucky me. I of course had no idea that I was dependent on aniseed till one evening when I realized that none of the dishes I had been served that day had contained a trace of the stuff and that I ached – sore head, intercostal neuralgia, tight hamstrings. That night I scraped the suede from the walls of Lou's pool room. The next day my food again lacked my drug. I further damaged Lou's pool room and again went unpunished. I could smell burnt flesh. Rats painted in gay Dayglo stripes sprinted along the pool table. A hairless man poked his head through the ceiling and said the Iron Duke was dead. I often shook. I lay on my flank and heard myself howl. I was locked in the room, my meagre rations were pushed round a just-opened door. One corner of the room I filled with brown coils. Then they came for me. Two men, both of them unfamiliar to me, both of them wearing thick gauntlets in case I should sink my teeth into them, led me to the top of the house.

Although it was daytime the windows of this room were covered. The brightest lights I had ever seen were aimed at static white kites. Four men with bad eyesight stared at Sammi through complicated black spectacles. Although it was daytime she lay on a bed wearing a coat which looked as if it was made from the coats of my cousins. No doubt she is ill, cold, and these men are physicians: my thoughts ran thus, and their rightness was confirmed by the way that Lou consulted with each of these specialists. He looked worried. Then he smiled at me and leaned over Sammi. I couldn't see what he was doing, but I heard a seal break and I realized that he was showing the doctors where Sammi's pain was, just near her tummy. Then he said 'Shoot' and I ducked because I hadn't forgotten what Stobey was like with a gun and these men with their severe myopia were likely to be even worse. Then I smelled aniseed. Up on the downs are two identical tumuli, rosily autumnal. It must be that season because the copse that is way this side of them is crisp and russet. And the aniseed is just south of the copse.

But I must draw a curtain over this scene. From beyond the curtain you can, however, hear me panting, you can hear water lapping, you can hear Sammi humming, you can hear one of the doctors whistling 'My Ship Is Coming In', you can hear Lou saying 'That's my boy . . . My Cwist this is goin' to be an earner . . . Jus look at 'im go.' The film was, of course, *The Alsatian and Lorraine*. If you are shy about such things you can always attribute your knowledge of it to newspaper reports of the wrongful dismissal of twenty West Midlands car workers who spent their night shifts enjoying repeated viewings of it. Both Sammi and Lou were impressed by the counsel provided for the men by their trade union. He argued that given its high price, poor finish, lack-lustre design and the difficulty encountered in selling the model on which they were 'working' it was in everybody's interest that they should continue to watch films between their teabreaks. The firm was censured and fined.

'That,' pronounced Lou, jabbing the newspaper with his jet and sapphire finger, 'is just the sort of bwief we got to 'ave on *The Twue Meaning of Cancan.*'

Lou was having a spot of bother with a Watch Committee in the sticks on account of his – our? – follow-up to *The Alsatian and Lorraine.* This film made it clear that *cancan* is derived from *concon.* (The lexicographic wimps at the OED throw in the towel with a crummy 'said to be L'.)

The pattern of my life was soon established: three weeks during which I was encouraged to indulge my habit; three unspeakable days of enforced abstinence; three or so days when I was allowed aniseed on the set but not off it. I was trapped. It was by these means that my best performances were coaxed from me. By the end of my first year I had appeared in many films, some of them 'genre classics', others . . . Well, even such dogs as Lassie and Cerberus had their off-days. As my fame grew and more films and feats came between me and my pre-stellar self so did I increasingly yearn to be reunited with Rusty. And I'd have given it all up to be a blind dog, to have really *helped.* But I was, as I say, trapped by my addiction.

I suppose things might have been worse, they were to get worse. I was, however, immune to the diseases that are attendant on my kind of stardom. They are not transmittable to dogs. The spirochaete – the slow assassin that corkscrewed through Lord Randolph Churchill, Boswell, most poets, Frederick Delius, my precursor Errol Flynn and millions more besides – might know me but could never enter me. And just as I required no prophylaxis so could my co-stars dispense with the chemical and mechanical apparatus of contraception; my seed can do nothing to you people, don't worry. I should, I must admit, have liked to have been the co-author of one of those fabulous mixes – a head, say, like Delon's and a body like mine. Of course the hapless beast might have had the body of a Hitchcock or Welles and my head. The latter would, doubtless, have had the infinite sadness of G. F. Watts's *Minotaur,* but the former . . . Oh, what a big plump Whitstable his world would have been. And I should have liked my co-author to have been Eva; faithless, flighty, fickle Eva. You *dog. Volage!*

The ozonic bite of the breeze across a plain where a million ears of corn turned to listen as we passed by was the first sign I received that I was going home: I still thought of Chatsworth as my home. All they would have heard was Eva's invariable, promiscuous cry of *'Oh, comme c'est marrant – tu trouves pas, Henri?'*; she said this of every house, field, horse, church. I sat between her and Henri in the back of Lou's big, brand-new silver car which he had bought 'dead cheap, wock bom pwice', presumably because it had no roof – the workers, in all likelihood, had been watching *The Things Girls Do With Sauerkraut* when they were meant to be putting it on. Then the crust-gold fields gave way to the downs of my puppyhood, we reached the top of a hill and a wedge of blinding, mirror-bright sea appeared. My heart thumped. The sea came into and out of sight tantalizingly. I rode the green folds like a happy boy on a roller-coaster. Then we were surging along the road towards Harlaxton; I was all a-quiver; we rounded the bend, and it had gone. It wasn't there, and Audley End wasn't there, and Speke Hall and Wollaton . . . they had disappeared. Where once there had been bright caravans and life and obeliscal chemical-toilet tents now there was nothing, nothing. A field, just a field. With cows in it. And where was Rusty? Where had my brother gone?

Eva's story was the story that I had heard from all my co-stars, with the exception of Glyn (*A Shepherd's Life*) who had never wanted to be a 'proper' actress and wasn't just filling in time before he got his break. Eva was unexceptional on that score. In every other way she was special. She was gentle, voluptuous, soft as milk; her self-interest was so patent it was touching, it informed everything she did. I thought she was lovely. I enjoyed making *Chien de Pompier* more than any other film. I enjoyed Eva more than any other co-star. She smelled so fresh and crisp and *biscuit-like* – this despite having only recently worked with a ram, a bear, a disgraced zoo-keeper, twin midgets and lots of charcuterie. Henri, I am sure, was aware of my infatuation. His small eyes, whose parchment bags advertised some hepatic cock-up, followed us as we ran together along the beach, with me vainly searching for a sign of Rusty and her pretending, I suppose, that she was playing the climactic scene of a cinematic romance and that Trintignant or Depardieu was bounding through the edge of the spray towards her.

We made a film in a former aircraft hangar that sat baldly astride an old runway, where tansy and thistles grew. The runway ran to the sky in both directions; when the doors at both ends were open the effect was disorientating, disconcerting. I spent hours between takes lying in Eva's arms, snuggling greedily against her, gazing up at the far-off reflection of us together in the vast mirror that was suspended from the building's superstructure. This mirror was the biggest that anyone had ever seen;

Lou was proud of that. It was, along with the fire-engine, the film's most important prop. I thought that we looked just right together. (I felt like a prince. The conjunction of fur and skin is a happy one.) Eva would blow into my ear and, rapturously, we would rehearse while the technicians – concave-chested men with Capstan hawks and meat-beaters' eyes – hooted and hissed and whistled and stamped. Henri would strut about threatening the sack to anyone who so much as took a swig of the many Marie Brizard anisette bottles that rested in a corner. Supine and sated, I stared at my twin on the ceiling; it was as if Rusty had found his own paramour and was forever fixed in vertiginous sprawl with her. I was happy for him.

Eva told me all about Henri, then we rehearsed again. (*Répétition*, apt word.) Henri, she said, was a jealous man. He was also a greedy man, and a cynical one. His cynicism had made him his first fortune. Did you ever meet a Frenchman who wasn't a hero of the Résistance? Who hadn't strangled a battalion of Boches with his own hands? Who didn't have an inventory of marshalling yards, bridges, barracks and canal basins that he had blown up? Who didn't have a tattered photograph that he'd pull out at every opportunity to show him wearing a beret and a bullet belt, clutching a sub-machine gun, standing with his Pétainophobic dog in a landscape of maquis and rocks? Henri took that photograph. He took thousands. He transformed men who had sold their daughters to Hansi and Karl Heinz for half a pound of butter, men who had betrayed their brothers, men who had led the soft life, into men who might walk proudly through post-war France.

I'd have drawn the line at participating in those photographs. Henri's baseness made me love Eva all the more, and when the last scene was shot and the coughing onanists began to dismantle the set that had been our home I wept. The bed, *our* bed, that blissful site was perfunctorily wheeled and carried to a van that waited down the runway – the surface was too pitted to drive it any closer. The fire-engine was parked in long grass beside the runway. The sound-recordist carried away his worn machine towards it. The vast mirror was lowered from the ceiling, five crouching men moved it slowly past me; I was thankful that its black back was towards me and that I was spared the sight of my abjectness.

Eva and Henri were embracing, his hands moved beneath her clothes making the material jut and bulge like inarticulate puppets; she giggled and sighed. My tongue was still numb with anisette, I could still taste her, my coat was smooth where she had pulled some goose-grass from it, the body that I was forced to occupy was the one that only minutes before she had toyed with languorously, dextrously, savagely. Lou sloped away with his arm round Sammi, telling her that he had heard about a book called *Kennelworth* that might make a good film. I was desolate. I walked hang-dog away past the fire-engine through canyons of tickling grass.

Then I heard it. A bark that rose and rose sweetly as if carried by cherubim. It was a bark that was an echo of mine. I turned, and there, back beyond the red and chrome appliance near where the van had been parked, was my double, my twin, my brother Rusty. As one we set off towards each other, matching each other sinew for sinew, muscle for muscle; our rhythm was as balanced and harmonious as it had been the last time we tumbled together – how long ago was that? And how long it seemed, that spring towards eternal reunion. He got bigger all the time. Now I could see his bouncing pelt and his springy tongue. Now I leapt, straight from stride into air. And he leapt as I leapt. He had been crying too – I could see his eyes. They were the last thing I saw. I went, they tell me, straight through the mirror (which disobligingly turned out to be made of tingling splinters) and discovered that on the other side of the looking-glass there is, aptly, blackness. Also there was the van and the sound-recordist with his tape of my voice; he got cut.

Some of the shards that pierced my corneas were as fine as hair and are still there. Giulia gives me pills for those times when it gets bad. I wish I could see her. I'd like to see her leading me, the blind dog, to Lou's new studio where we are making *Hot Dog, Sausage Dog*. Is she as bad and lovely as Eva? Please tell me. Her scent is that of aniseed.

J. R. ACKERLEY

From My Dog Tulip

Tulip in heat

TULIP ENTERED HER heat on the first of March, and even I never envisaged the consequences that rapidly developed. Within a few days 'Mon Repos' was in a state of siege. My cousin began by thinking this rather amusing, and sent me cheerful accounts of the 'sweet' little Scotties and Sealyhams who had come to call. She found it less amusing when they accumulated and would not go away; when the larger dogs took to scrambling over the white-washed wall in front, which, by repeated leapings against the winter jasmine that had been carefully trained to ornament it, they could just manage to do; when their smaller associates, not to be outdone and left behind, contrived to smash the flimsy latch of the gate by constant rattling at it, and all camped out all night, quarrelling and whining, among the Seven Dwarfs. Nor did she find it amusing when the other ladies of Ferring, deprived of and anxious about their pets who returned not home even for their dinners, called round to retrieve them, not once but every day and a number of times a day, in a progressively nastier frame of mind. The soft answer that turneth away wrath is no part of the diplomatic equipment women claim to possess; my cousin was not one to be spoken to sharply without giving as good as she got. Very soon to the sound of Tulip's excited voice within and the replies of her devotees without was added a recurrent chorus of equally incontinent human voices raised in revilement and recrimination. And my cousin found it less amusing still when she tried to take Tulip for walks and fell into the error I had made of attempting to beat off her escort, which resulted not only in a more formidable incursion of enraged owners complaining that she had been seen ill-treating their pets, but, more affectingly, in her clothes and flesh getting torn. Before the first week was over, Tulip was not taken out at all; but now there was no lovely lift to waft her out of sight, sound and scent of her admirers; good though she always was, no desirable and desiring bitch could be expected to behave with restraint in a small bungalow all the windows of which presented her with the spectacle of a dozen or so of her male friends awaiting her outside; she barked at them incessantly, hastening from window to window; they barked back; then, like the siren, she would break into song; the expensive net curtains were soon all in tatters, and these, in the end, I had to replace.

I could not replace 'Mon Repos' itself. By the close of the affair it is no exaggeration to say that it was practically wrecked. The walls still stood, of course; but what walls! A tepid rain had been falling for some time to add to the general melancholy of the scene, and their fresh white paint was liberally stippled with filthy paw marks where the excited creatures had tried to clamber in at the windows; the pale blue paint of the doors, at which they had constantly knocked, was scratched and scored; the Seven Dwarfs were prostrate in a morass that had once been a neat grassy border. Siege became invasion. The back of the bungalow held out a little longer than the front; its garden was protected by a fence; but as Tulip's ready time approached and the frustrated besiegers realised that this was where she now took the sea air, they set about discovering its weak spots. This did not take long. By the time I was able to come down for my second visit during this period, to stay now and supervise the marriage, they had already forced their way in at several points, and my cousin was hysterically engaged in ejecting dogs of all shapes and sizes from dining-room, sun parlour and even in the night from her bedroom.

Into the midst of this scene of chaos Mountjoy, at the appropriate moment, was introduced. Tulip had not seen much of him during her wooing week; the Tudor-Smiths had thought it undesirable that he should mix in such low company; she was pleased to see him now. As soon as he made his wishes clear she allowed him to mount her and stood quietly with her legs apart and her tail coiled away while he clasped her round the waist. But, for some reason, he failed to achieve his purpose. His stabs, it looked to me standing beside them, did not quite reach her. After a little she disengaged herself, and, assuming her play attitude, began to flirt in front of him. But he had graver ends in view. Again she stood, with lowered head and flattened ears, her gaze slanted back, apprehensively, I thought, to what he was doing behind. This time he appeared to have moved further forward, and now it did look as though he would succeed; but suddenly she gave a nervous cry and escaped from him once more. They tried again and again, the same thing always happened, whenever he seemed about to enter her she protested, as though she were still a virgin, and pulled herself free. And now it was quite upsetting to watch his continual failure to consummate his desire and the consequent frustration of these two beautiful animals who wished to copulate and could not manage to do so. Nor could I see any way to help them, except to lubricate Tulip, which I did, for they seemed to be doing themselves all that could be done, except unite. It was, indeed, very moving, it was sorrow, to watch them trying to know each other and always failing, and it was touching to see Tulip give him chance after chance. But of course she was getting tired, she was panting; compared with him she was a small, slender creature, and it could not have been anything but burdensome for her to have the weight of his massive body upon her back and the clutch of his leonine arms about her waist. Yet, at the same time, he was as gentle with her as he could be; he took hold of her in a careful kind of way, or so it looked, manoeuvring his arms tentatively upon her as though to get a purchase that did not grip her too hard; and sometimes, when she made a nervous movement or uttered an anxious cry, he would dismount and, going round to her head, put his nose to hers as if to say: 'Are you all right?' But at last, in his own weariness, his jabs got wilder and wilder, quite wide of the mark; finally she would have no more to do with him and, whenever he approached her, drove him away.

Now what to do I did not know. Who would have supposed that mating a bitch could be so baffling a problem? Perhaps, in spite of her coiling tail, she was not ready. I set them together the following day, and the day after, only to watch them go through the same agonising performance. And now it was her twelfth day. Was there truly something wrong with her, or was I muddling away her third heat like the others? I sent for the local vet. Next morning he came and stood with me while the animals repeated their futile and exhausting antics.

'It's the dog's fault,' he said. 'He can't draw.'

This term had to be explained to me. It meant that his foreskin was too tight to enable him to unsheathe, a disability that could have been corrected when he was a puppy. Besides this, the vet announced after examining him, which Mountjoy permitted with extraordinary dignity, he was a 'rig' dog, that is to say he had an undescended testicle, a not uncommon thing, said the vet, and a serious disqualification in mating, since it was heritable. It is scarcely necessary to add that neither of these terms, nor any of this information, is mentioned in the dog books, at least in none that I have ever come across. Mountjoy's owners themselves, who had never offered him a wife before, were totally ignorant of these facts, if facts they were, and therefore of the corollary that their noble and expensive beast was relatively worthless.

There was nothing now to be done but to phone Colonel Finch. In the late afternoon Tulip was hustled into a taxi and conveyed to Gunner. Of the outcome of this I never was in doubt and was not therefore disappointed. She would have nothing to do with him at all. He was willing, she was not; it was the bully's turn to be bullied, and when the Colonel decided that his positive lamb had had enough, Tulip re-entered her taxi and was driven back to 'Mon Repos'.

Dusk was now falling. I restored her to the ravaged garden, and it was while I stood with her there, gazing in despair at this exquisite creature in the midst of her desire, that the dog-next-door emerged through what remained of the fence. He had often intruded before, as often been ejected. Now he hung there in the failing light, half in, half out of the garden, his attention fixed warily upon me, a disreputable, dirty mongrel, Dusty by name, in whom Scottish sheep-dog predominated. I returned the stare of the disconcertingly dissimilar eyes, one brown, one pale blue, of this ragamuffin with whom it had always amused Tulip to play, and knew that my intervention was at an end. I smiled at him.

'Well, there you are, old girl,' I said. 'Take it or leave it. It's up to you.'

She at once went to greet him. Dusty was emboldened to come right in.

360 The Literary Companion to Sex

There was a coquettish scamper. She stood for him. He was too small to manage. She obligingly squatted, and suddenly, without a sound, they collapsed on the grass in a heap. It was charming. They lay there together, their paws all mixed up, resting upon each other's bodies. They were panting. But they looked wonderfully pretty and comfortable – until Tulip thought she would like to get up, and found she could not. She tried to rise. The weight of Dusty's body, united with her own, dragged her back. She looked round in consternation. Then she began to struggle. I called to her soothingly to lie still, but she wanted to come over to me and could not, and her dismay turned to panic. With a convulsive movement she regained her feet and began to pull Dusty, who was upside down, along the lawn, trying from time to time to rid herself of her incubus by giving it a nip. The unfortunate Dusty, now on his back, now on his side, his little legs scrabbling wildly about in their efforts to find a foothold, at length managed, by a kind of somersault, to obtain it. This advantage, however, was not won without loss, for his exertion turned him completely round, so that, still attached to Tulip, he was now bottom to bottom with her and was hauled along in this even more uncomfortable and abject posture, his hind-quarters off the ground, his head down and his tongue hanging out. Tulip gazed at me in horror and appeal. Heavens! I thought, this is love! These are the pleasures of sex! As distressed as they, I hastened over to them, persuaded Tulip to lie down again for poor Dusty's sake, and sat beside them to caress and calm them. It was a full half-hour before detumescence occurred[1] and Nature released Dusty, who instantly fled home through the gap in the fence and was seen no more. As for Tulip, her relief, her joy, her gratitude (she seemed to think it was I who had saved her), were spectacular. It was more as though she had been freed from some dire situation of peril than from the embraces of love.

[1] It could have been longer.

GUILLAUME APOLLINAIRE

From Les Onze Mille Verges

The title of Apollinaire's erotic novel, *Les Onze Mille Verges*, is an untranslatable joke. Give the last word an extra 'i' and it would become virgins – 'The Eleven Thousand Virgins' – the famous co-martyrs of St Ursula. As it is, it means 'The Eleven Thousand Rods' (or Pricks), a title far more appropriate to this non-stop romp of sex and sadism in all its forms.

The great dane

SHE MASTURBATED ME but would not let me touch her. Then she called her dog, a beautiful Great Dane, and rubbed his tool for a moment. When his pointed prick was erect, she made the dog mount her, ordering me to help the beast. His tongue was lolling out and he was panting with lust.

My suffering was so intense that I fainted as I climaxed. When I came to, Florence was calling me urgently. The dog's penis, once it had penetrated, refused to come out again. For half an hour both the woman and the beast had been making fruitless efforts to separate. A nodule on the Great Dane's prick held it firmly in my wife's clenched vagina. I threw cold water over them and this soon restored them to liberty. Since that day, my wife has shown no desire to make love with dogs. As a reward, she masturbated me, then sent me off to bed in my own room.

The song of the Preobajenski Regiment

> Alas, you poor peasants, you're off to the war,
> They'll fuck your old mothers behind and before,
> The bulls in your stables will service your wives
> And give them the time of their natural lives.
> As for you, all you'll have is Siberian flies
> To tickle your bollocks and give you a rise,
> But on Fridays don't give them a bite of your prick,
> For meat is forbidden, it might make them sick.
> And don't give them sugar or white ration bread,
> They make it by grinding the bones of the dead.
> So come on and fuck now, you young farmer-boys,
> The officer's mare, for she's full of sweet joys,
> And they say that her hole isn't nearly as wide
> As the cunt of a hefty young Tar-ar-tar bride.
> Oh, who cares if they screw all our sweethearts and wives?
> We're off to the wars and we're risking our lives!

'Masturbation is a military virtue'

A COSSACK WHOSE hands were cold was warming them in his mare's cunt. The beast was neighing softly. Suddenly, the randy Cossack leapt on to a chair behind his animal and, pulling out a prick as long as a wooden lance, slipped it joyfully into the creature's vagina, which must have dripped a very aphrodisiac hippomaniac juice, for the human brute discharged three times, his arse convulsing violently, before he finally withdrew.

An officer who had observed this act of bestiality approached the soldier with Mony. He reproached him sternly for having succumbed to his passion.

'My friend,' he said to him, 'masturbation is a military virtue. Every good soldier should know that, in wartime, onanism is the only act of love permitted. Toss yourself off, but don't touch women or animals.

'Besides, masturbation is an admirable thing, for it allows men and women to become accustomed to their imminent and prolonged separation. The habits, ideas, clothing and tastes of the two sexes are becoming more and more disparate. It is high time we took account of this fact, and it seems to me essential, if one wishes to be a master in this world, to obey this natural law which will shortly impose itself upon us.'

Transl. Nina Rootes

PHILIP ROTH

From Portnoy's Complaint

Whacking off

THEN CAME ADOLESCENCE – half my waking life spent locked behind the bathroom door, firing my wad down the toilet bowl, or into the soiled clothes in the laundry hamper, or *splat*, up against the medicine-chest mirror, before which I stood in my dropped drawers so I could see how it looked coming out. Or else I was doubled over my flying fist, eyes pressed closed but mouth wide open, to take that sticky sauce of buttermilk and Clorox on my own tongue and teeth – though not infrequently, in my blindness and ecstasy, I got it all in the pompadour, like a blast of Wildroot Cream Oil. Through a world of matted handker-chiefs and crumpled Kleenex and stained pajamas, I moved my raw and swollen penis, perpetually in dread that my loathsomeness would be discovered by someone stealing upon me just as I was in the frenzy of dropping my load. Nevertheless, I was wholly incapable of keeping my paws from my dong once it started the climb up my belly. In the middle of a class I would raise a hand to be excused, rush down the corridor to the lavatory, and with ten or fifteen savage strokes, beat off standing up into a urinal. At the Saturday afternoon movie I would leave my friends to go off to the candy machine – and wind up in a distant balcony seat, squirting my seed into the empty wrapper from a Mounds bar. On an outing of our family association, I once cored an apple, saw to my astonishment (and with the aid of my obsession) what it looked like, and ran off into the woods to fall upon the orifice of the fruit, pretending that the cool and mealy hole was actually between the legs of that mythical being who always called me Big Boy when she pleaded for what no girl in all recorded history had ever had. 'Oh shove it in me, Big Boy,' cried the cored apple that I banged silly on that picnic. 'Big Boy, Big Boy, oh give me all you've got,' begged the empty milk bottle that I kept hidden in our storage bin in the basement, to drive wild after school with my vaselined upright. 'Come, Big Boy, come,' screamed the maddened piece of liver that, in my own insanity, I bought one afternoon at a butcher shop and, believe it or not, violated behind a billboard on the way to a bar mitzvah lesson.

JOHN WHITWORTH

Youth and Andrew Marvell

I drink my presbyterian soul's
Election to unhappiness
At various local watering holes
And plot the moves of sex like chess.
Between each Laura Ashley dress
Hot dreams of boys keep cropping up:
Reflections in a poison cup

Of what you mustn't say or think on,
Showers and rugger socks and squash
And bitter beer and bars to drink on
And bare legs in a mackintosh,
Behaving prole while talking posh
Where echoing adolescence loiters
Down dateless days designed for coitus.

So young in deed, so old in sin,
I showed Jack Champion my tool
And spiked our orange juice with gin
In the churchyard after Sunday School.
The girls I love are pure and cool;
I want to spread their thighs with syrup.
Then lick it off to make them chirrup.

I do not ask or hope for pardon.
I do not wish it otherwise
But that each unassisted hard-on
Should wake me with a fresh surprise
Outside the gates of Paradise
Where two by two the blessed pass
And stretch long bodies on the grass.

Friday I put my hand upon it.
I did indeed and very nice.
Though indigence can help a sonnet,
Enough of solitary vice.
Better to carve yourself a slice
Of life, for, as the poet said,
There's fuck-all fucking when you're dead.

DAVID DABYDEEN

Nightmare

Bruk dung de door!
Waan gang sweat-stink nigga
Drag she aff she bed
Wuk pun she
Crack she head
Gi she jigga[1]
Tween she leg!

Dem chase she backdam:
Waan gang cane-stiff cack
Buss she tail[2] till she blue an black
Till she crawl tru de mud an she bawl an she beg.

[1] *Jigga* – a severe itching and peeling of the flesh as a result of contact with putrid matter.
[2] *Buss she tail* – a Guyanese expression (usually 'buss she tail wid licks', i.e. 'burst her tail with lashes') meaning to beat severely on the buttocks.

Dem haul she canal-bank like bush-haag
Cut she troat over de dark surging wata
When dem dun suck dem raise dem red mout to de moon
An mek saang,

Deep in de night when crappau[3] call an cush-cush[4]
Crawl dung hole, lay dem egg in de earth
When camoudie[5] curl rung calf dat just drap
An black bat flap-flap-flap tru de bush . . .

Wet she awake, cuss de daybreak!

[3] *Crappau* – a native frog.
[4] *Cush-cush* – type of ants.
[5] *Camoudie* – a type of snake.

WENDY PERRIAM

From The Fifty-Minute Hour

To quote Wendy Perriam: 'The pious Catholic housewife Mary makes her first attempt at masturbation, which she decides to do as a penance, making it as painful as possible, and expressing her horror at the new world of vibrators and sex-toys she has just discovered. She offers up the pain to her psychoanalyst John-Paul, but gradually pain changes to ecstasy, and she climaxes to the throbbing pumping imagery of the Steam Museum which she has recently visited with her sons.'

S HE REFILLED HER sherry – it would help her to relax – drifted back upstairs. The double bed was rumpled and dishevelled, the way she'd left it earlier. She grimaced in distaste, smoothed the sheets and blankets, still reluctant to get in. That bed had such bad memories, seemed always to accuse her, hiss 'failure' at her, 'boring'. She sometimes wished secretly that James could be neutered as Horatio had been – just a whiff of anaesthetic, a tiny snip, and total transformation. No more mounting, rutting, coupling, sniffing round the females, leaping five-foot walls to reach a bitch on heat. It had also made him much more docile – placid, almost soppy, which would be nice in James as well.

She straightened the blue counterpane, backed out of the room. Perhaps she'd use the other bed, the spare-room bed, the one she always thought of as her daughter's – that non-existent daughter she chatted to in secret, had even named, bought clothes for. The shrine was still set up, the candles and the vases, though no fresh flowers, no recent smell of wax or burning flesh. John-Paul hadn't appreciated her spiritual bouquet. She sank down on the bed, disappointment struggling with new hope. Why not make him a different one, one he'd really relish? He had encouraged her to masturbate, to give herself an orgasm, so she could experience the feel of it, help herself to pleasure – which he seemed to see as duty, despite the fact such practices were forbidden by the Church. Now she saw a way of solving the dilemma, satisfying everyone, including even herself. If she made the masturbation really painful, she'd be obeying John-Paul's mandate (at least to the letter, if not exactly the spirit), offering him a new and quite unusual spiritual bouquet, while avoiding Father Fox's wrath and her own sense of guilt in indulging in what the Church condemned as 'solitary and sinful pleasure'.

She checked her watch. Nearly ten to seven. Nobody would call now. It was the suburban dinner hour, sacred to husbands and to families, when no bells rang except the oven-timer. She crept back to her bedroom, scrabbled through the bottom drawer where she kept her sanitary towels, drew out not a small soft pad but an eight-inch hard vibrator. Well, she'd had to hide it somewhere, and James so hated periods he would no more touch her Kotex than approach a nuclear reactor with a leak.

She felt much the same about that plastic monster. Even James's was not as big or ugly, and did at least deflate at times, folded down quietly after use; wasn't labelled 'Super-Stud' around its rampant rim. 'Super-Stud' came complete with batteries, also labelled 'super'. In fact, everything was super – super-power, super-thrust, super-satisfaction. The catalogue had quite appalled her. Up till now, she had more or less ignored the existence of vibrators – known (vaguely) people used them, but only hardened people like prostitutes on clients, or perverts on themselves. She had regarded them as something rather shameful and obscene which went on far away, in another world from hers, like those brutish men who killed elephants for ivory, or turned tigers into hearth-rugs. But that catalogue had sold them like cereals or slippers – cosy everyday things which any normal woman needed. And even John-Paul seemed to champion them, saying with a little smile (which she couldn't see, but had picked up from his voice) that an artificial penis was often more obliging than the flesh-and-blood variety, since it wouldn't let you down. He'd told her a vibrator would be under her exclusive control and would go at her own pace: as long, as short, as fast, as slow, as she could cope with at each practice-session. It seemed incredible to her – to derive satisfaction, ecstasy, from something with no hands nor heart nor voice. James rarely talked himself, but he did at least make noises, or sometimes grunted 'Lovely tits' when she first removed her brassière.

She'd spent two whole mornings goggling at the pictures – yes, huge full-colour pictures with descriptions underneath, and such a wild variety – vibrators in soft latex, or gold, or rigid plastic; matt black ones, shiny silver; some with studs, or nobbles, or light-up tips, or 'thrill-frills'; or with several different screw-on heads which rotated or gyrated, or flexible extensions to reach something called a G-spot (which made them sound like carpet-cleaners); some shaped like little grinning men or even teddy bears. And those dreadful punning names: 'Wonderbar' and 'Joy Stick', 'Bully Boy', 'Banana'. If she'd been cool before, that catalogue had frozen her completely, sent her sexual temperature plunging below zero. But penance was another thing entirely. The more you hated something, then the better as a penance, like their soft-boiled eggs at school, which were actually more raw than soft, and had little bloody specks in, which her best friend said were the beginnings of new chicks. From the age of seven to the age of seventeen, she'd swallowed every nascent chick she could, marked them on her spiritual bouquet. At least she'd learnt willpower, developed a strong stomach.

She got up from her knees, concealing the vibrator beneath the jacket of her suit, still vaguely anxious that someone might be watching – if not an actual neighbour prying with a telescope from the house across the street, then the Blessed Edwin Mumford, observing her from heaven, and distinctly disapproving. She lit the candles, removed her tights and pants again (left her other clothes on, which made her feel less blatant), then lay back on the bed. She wished she had some flowers, or even music. Ritual was important – she knew that from the Church. But at least the candles cast strong shadows, gave a certain atmosphere, and she'd set up a small photograph of John-Paul, like an icon. She had snipped it from the dust-jacket of his latest publication: *Eros and Thanatos: a Re-examination*. The book was very difficult – made *Psychology Today* seem as painless as the *TV Times* – but she'd bought it for the photograph and the blurb about the author, which made him sound so busy and so brilliant she'd felt quite overcome to be allowed the privilege of paying for an hour each week of his time and genius.

She opened her legs a grudging inch, positioned the vibrator. You were meant to use a lubricant – some cherry-flavoured sticky stuff called 'Joy Jelly', which had arrived with the vibrator (and also with its 'supers' – 'super-rich, super-sexy, super-lubricating'). It would hurt more without the jelly, especially as her burns had not yet healed. Even using just one finger for five minutes, as she'd done at five o'clock, had made them twinge and shock. The vibrator had a setting like an oven – high for roasts, 'simmer' for just stewing. She turned it on to high, rammed it in, violently and suddenly. Her Pain Score soared to nine, jumped higher still as she directed it specifically against the largest of the burns. She closed her eyes to concentrate on pain, take it up to twelve, or even over.

'It's for *you*, John-Paul,' she whispered. 'All for you – the pain.' One burn had even festered, was throbbing, really griping, as she stabbed it with the rigid plastic shaft. Pleasure he had called it, but what were words so long as she obeyed him? 'As fast, as slow, as long, as short, as you can cope with at each practice-session.' She took it slower, turned the pressure down, let it almost idle – in and out, in and out, like a finger in a . . . . It felt different from a finger, seemed to go in further, hurting still – oh, certainly – but a restrained and rhythmic pain now, which was soothing, almost kindly. The noise had changed, as well – no longer a harsh skirl, but a gentle droning purr, which seemed to calm her, reassure her. She had never known that pain could be relaxing; that she could want it to continue, not just for John-Paul's sake, but for her own. Maybe that was wrong, though, and she was being far too lax. Angrily, abruptly, she turned the power to highest, reeled back to her Pain Score, tried to tot it up again, as her burns cried out for pity. Thirteen, was it, fourteen? Still not high enough. She could hear the vibrator screaming now, as she reached twenty, twenty-one.

Perspiration was sliding down her breasts, sticking to her slip. She'd have to take it off, remove her skirt and jacket too, so she was less hampered, less restricted, could concentrate on pain. She put the vibrator down a moment, as she struggled with her clothes, tried to force the zip. The silence seemed unkind, and there was a strange ache between her legs – an ache for that lost rhythm, which had become part of her, had sprung from her, and which she felt she'd known from way back, known in dreams, or even in past lives. She drained her sherry first, dark sweet sherry, like John-Paul's rich brown voice. He was talking to her now, his voice very close and intimate from his seat behind the couch; his words warm amoroso dribbling down her body. 'You're doing very well, Mary. Just relax a little more – that's it. Now turn it on again and let it throb between your fingers, to try to get the feel of it, establish the best rhythm.

That's good, that's very good. Now stroke it down your body – yes, slowly, very s-l-o-w-l-y, right across your breasts and down your belly and your thighs, until you reach your . . .'

'Genitals,' she said out loud. She had to practise all those words: forbidden words, exquisite words, words which made her hot and so ashamed. Her legs were opening wider, opening for John-Paul. Yes, of course she longed to open them – open them and please him, split apart and bleed for him. 'Vulva,' she said lingerly. 'Clitoris.' 'Vagina.' Nobody could hear her. The vibrator was too loud. The noise was whirring out again, gasping, almost panicky, laboured like her breathing. Why should she be panting when she was just relaxing on a bed? Why drenched with sweat, why feverish? Had John-Paul switched her on, pulled some giant lever like the one in the Steam Museum where they'd taken all three boys this last July – a lever which set flywheels into motion, started rods and pistons, mobilised huge pumping-engines, which had all begun to thwack and thrust, drowning conversation, dwarfing even James?

She'd felt threatened at the time, alarmed not just for the boys who might get trapped in all that dangerous machinery, but frightened on her own account. It was so masculine, so violent, that powerhouse of trapped steam, those bursting throbbing boilers and swollen cylinders; that overwhelming beam-engine rearing to the roof, its gigantic metal beam weighing fifteen tons at least, heaving up and down as it drove its frantic flywheel (which the man had told her would plunge straight through the solid wall if it ever broke off from its bearings). She had watched the pressure-gauges slowly rising, rising; the shiny oil-slicked piston-rods thrusting in and out; had felt some strange excitement suddenly curdling with the terror, longed to be connected to those wildly pulsing engines, part of that machinery – a feed-pipe or a blow-valve which could share its pounding rhythm. 'DANGER!' said the notice in huge red capitals. She'd deliberately ignored it, stepped closer to the piston-rods, even slipped inside the barrier.

She shut her eyes. She could feel the heat again, that stifling claustrophobic heat which reeked of oil and steam; could hear the steady rhythmic slam of the engines pumping, pumping; see the scalding water-drops swelling on the glistening pipes, bursting, running down; could almost taste the clogging grease on the inflamed and sweating metal. Her own body was inflamed, running with hot oil, spurts of steam condensing into droplets, leaking down the insides of her thighs. She had forgotten pain completely. Did wheels feel pain? Or piston-rods? She just had to keep on thrusting, driven on, driven on – yes, right to danger-point.

She had reached that point – and passed it – could feel her axle cracking up, wrenching from its bearings, her rev-counter so fast now it was spinning out of control. She was breaking off, flying free, plunging through a three-foot solid wall. She felt the crash, the impact, yet experienced no pain – only elation and amazement as she blasted into heat and light, heard John-Paul's shout behind her, a shout of triumph, sheer relief. He seemed to have arranged some celebration in her honour. She was aware of voices, noises, reverberating bangs; glimpsed a sudden hail of rockets snipering the sky, exploding in a shower of coloured sparks – laser-blue, throbbing-pink, strobing knife-blade silver.

She could hear another noise, coming from much nearer – footsteps on the stairs, an angry voice she knew too well.

'Are you deaf or something, Mary? I've been shouting for five minutes and you haven't heard a word. The dog's gone mad as well. It's those damn-fool bloody fireworks they're letting off next door.' The footsteps tramping closer, right up to the door; the handle slowly turning. 'Mary!' the voice lower now, and scandalised, almost disbelieving. 'What in God's name are you *doing*?'

© Wendy Perriam 1990.

ERICA JONG

From Fear of Flying

Bennett Wing

BENNET WING APPEARED as in a dream. On the wing, you might say. Tall, good-looking, inscrutably Oriental. Long thin fingers, hairless balls, a lovely swivel to his hips when he screwed – at which he seemed to be absolutely indefatigable. But he was also mute and at that point his silence was music to my ears. How did I know that a few years later, I'd feel like I was fucking Helen Keller?

Wing. I loved Bennett's name. And he was mercurial, too. Not wings on his heels but wings on his prick. He soared and glided when he screwed. He made marvelous dipping and corkscrewing motions. He stayed hard forever, and he was the only man I'd ever met who was never impotent – not even when he was depressed or angry. But why didn't he ever kiss? And why didn't he speak? I would come and come and come and each orgasm seemed to be made of ice.

The eternal limp prick

Besides, the older you got, the clearer it became that men were basically
terrified of women. Some secretly, some openly. What could be more
poignant than a liberated woman eye to eye with a limp prick? All history's
greatest issues paled by comparison with these two quintessential objects:
the eternal woman and the eternal limp prick.

'Do I scare you?' I asked Adrian.

'*You?*'

'Well some men claim to be afraid of me.'

Adrian laughed. 'You're a sweetheart,' he said, 'a pussycat – as you
Americans say. But that's *not* the point.'

'Do you usually have this problem?'

'*Nein*, Frau Doktor, and I bloody well don't want to be interrogated
further. This is ab*surd*. I do *not* have a potency problem – it's just that I am
awed by your stupendous ass and I don't *feel* like fucking.'

The ultimate sexist put-down: the prick which lies down on the job.
The ultimate weapon in the war between the sexes: the limp prick. The
banner of the enemy's encampment: the prick at half-mast. The symbol
of the apocalypse: the atomic warhead prick which self-destructs. *That*
was the basic inequity which could never be righted: not that the male had
a wonderful added attraction called a penis, but that the female had a
wonderful all-weather cunt. Neither storm nor sleet nor dark of night
could faze it. It was always there, always ready. Quite terrifying, when you
think about it. No wonder men hated women. No wonder they invented
the myth of female inadequacy.

Refusals

I thought back to my days of having fantasies of men on trains. It's true
that I never did anything about these fantasies and wouldn't have dared to.
I wasn't even brave enough to *write* about them until much later. But
suppose I *had* approached one of these men, and suppose he had rejected
me, looked away, shown disgust or revulsion. What then? I would have
immediately taken the rejection to heart, believed myself in the wrong,
blamed myself for being an evil woman, a whore, a slut, a disturber of the
peace. . . . More to the point, I would have immediately blamed my own
unattractiveness, not the man's reluctance, and I would have been
destroyed for days by his rejection of me. Yet a man assumes that a
woman's refusal is just part of a game. Or, at any rate, a lot of men assume

that. When a man says no, it's no. When a woman says no, it's yes, or at least maybe. There is even a joke to that effect. And little by little, women begin to believe in this view of themselves. Finally, after centuries of living under the shadow of such assumptions, they no longer know what they want and can never make up their minds about anything. And men, of course, compound the problem by mocking them for their indecisiveness and blaming it on biology, hormones, premenstrual tension.

ANAÏS NIN

From Little Birds

Fay's lover

FAY HAD BEEN born in New Orleans. When she was sixteen she was courted by a man of forty whom she had always liked for his aristocracy and distinction. Fay was poor. Albert's visits were events to her family. For him their poverty was hastily disguised. He came very much like the liberator, talking about a life Fay had never known, at the other end of the city.

When they were married, Fay was installed like a princess in his house, which was hidden in an immense park. Handsome coloured women waited on her. Albert treated her with extreme delicacy.

The first night he did not take her. He maintained that this was proof of love, not to force oneself upon one's wife, but to woo her slowly and lingeringly, until she was prepared and in the mood to be possessed.

He came to her room and merely caressed her. They lay enveloped in the white mosquito netting as within a bridal veil, lay back in the hot night fondling and kissing. Fay felt languid and drugged. He was giving birth to a new woman with every kiss, exposing a new sensibility. Afterwards, when he left her, she lay tossing and unable to sleep. It was as if he had started tiny fires under her skin, tiny currents which kept her awake.

She was exquisitely tormented in this manner for several nights. Being inexperienced, she did not try to bring about a complete embrace. She yielded to this profusion of kisses in her hair, on her neck, shoulders, arms, back, legs. . . . Albert took delight in kissing her until she moaned, as if he were now sure of having awakened a particular part of her flesh, and then his mouth moved on.

He discovered the trembling sensibility under the arm, at the nascence of the breasts, the vibrations that ran between the nipples and the sex, and between the sex mouth and the lips, all the mysterious links that roused and stirred places other than the one being kissed, currents running from the roots of the hair to the roots of the spine. Each place he kissed he worshipped with adoring words, observing the dimples at the end of her back, the firmness of her buttocks, the extreme arch of her back, which threw her buttocks outwards – 'like a coloured woman's', he said.

He encircled her ankles with his fingers, lingered over her feet, which were perfect like her hands, stroked over and over again the smooth statuesque lines of her neck, lost himself in her long heavy hair.

Her eyes were long and narrow like those of a Japanese woman, her mouth full, always half-open. Her breasts heaved as he kissed her and marked her shoulder's sloping line with his teeth. And then as she moaned, he left her, closing the white netting around her carefully, encasing her like a treasure, leaving her with the moisture welling up between her legs.

One night, as usual, she could not sleep. She sat up in her clouded bed, naked. As she rose to look for her kimono and slippers a tiny drop of honey fell from her sex, rolled down her leg, stained the white rug. Fay was baffled at Albert's control, his reserve. How could he subdue his desire and sleep after these kisses and caresses? He had not even completely undressed. She had not seen his body.

She decided to leave her room and walk until she could become calm again. Her entire body was throbbing. She walked slowly down the wide staircase and out into the garden. The perfume of the flowers almost stunned her. The branches fell languidly over her and the mossy paths made her footsteps absolutely silent. She had the feeling that she was dreaming. She walked aimlessly for a long while. And then a sound startled her. It was a moan, a rhythmic moan like a woman's complaining. The light from the moon fell there between the branches and exposed a coloured woman lying naked on the moss and Albert over her. Her moans were moans of pleasure. Albert was crouching like a wild animal and pounding against her. He, too, was uttering confused cries; and Fay saw them convulsed under her very eyes by the violent joys.

Neither one saw Fay. She did not cry out. The pain at first paralysed her. Then she ran back to the house, filled with all the humility of her youth, of her inexperience; she was tortured with doubts of herself. Was it her fault? What had she lacked, what had she failed to do to please Albert? Why had he had to leave her and go to the coloured woman? The savage scene haunted her. She blamed herself for falling under the enchantment of his caresses and perhaps not acting as he wanted her to. She felt condemned by her own femininity.

Albert could have taught her. He had said he was wooing her . . . waiting. He had only to whisper a few words. She was ready to obey. She knew he was older and she innocent. She had expected to be taught.

That night Fay became a woman, making a secret of her pain, intent on saving her happiness with Albert, on showing wisdom and subtlety. When he lay at her side she whispered to him, 'I wish you would take your clothes off.'

He seemed startled, but he consented. Then she saw his youthful, slim body at her side, with his very white hair gleaming, a curious mingling of youth and age. He began to kiss her. As he did so her hand timidly moved towards his body. At first she was frightened. She touched his chest. Then his hips. He continued to kiss her. Her hand reached for his penis, slowly. He made a movement away from it. It was soft. He moved away and began to kiss her between the legs. He was whispering over and over again the same phrase, 'You have the body of an angel. It is impossible that such a body should have a sex. You have the body of an angel.'

Then anger swept over Fay like a fever, an anger at his moving his penis away from her hand. She sat up, her hair wild about her shoulders, and said, 'I am not an angel, Albert. I am a woman. I want you to love me as a woman.'

Then came the saddest night Fay had ever known, because Albert tried to possess her and he couldn't. He led her hands to caress him. His penis would harden, he would begin to place it between her legs, and then it would wilt in her hands.

JEREMY REED

Playing with Fire

You going down, contortionist
to give me head with pink lipstick,
a black girl with red hair,
your face a locket. A green curtain drawn
on the afternoon rain.

Your vibrations drew the volcanic core
to a white tributary of fire
eased out as pearls.
Your drop-earrings shook
diamanté flashes, two waterfalls
responsive to your rhythmic tongue,
you lying in a black g-string,
conical breasts with nipples
like purple anemones.

I came, imagining seraglios
and all the positions that we'd achieved,
the best one, your legs right over your head
in a three quarter somersault,
I straddling as though suspended
in taking off into a gymnast's vault.

Shoe Fetishist

His intimacy with hotels
clarifies the anatomy
of his circuit from the inside,
hall-porters, how to slip a key

from a receptionist, coerce
by adopting a strategy
of hinting at discrepancies
inherent in their policy

of desk-bribes, turning a blind eye
to the hooker using a suite
that's officially occupied.
His preoccupation's with feet,

the small, tapered, red toe-nailed foot
that silks into a stiletto,
wine-glass stemmed heels, the metal cap
exciting when he traces slow

abrasions with it on his skin.
Snakeskin, patent, black satin bows,
he adds them to his collection,
imagining silk-stockinged toes

forming a sensuous glove-fit
in the hard elongated point.
Smell, colour and tactility,
shape in his mind a sculpted joint

between the arched sole and his sex,
an erotic intersection,
cupped in his hand intangibly
with variants of position.

His wardrobes are stashed with leather
exhibits; they're his solitary
communion with occupants
he's come to love vicariously;

and recalls the fired stimulus
of his great cache, his standing back
before thigh-high and knee-high boots,
almost uncrinkled in their black

austerity, the hotel dead,
mid-afternoon and how the air
was scented with them as he'd knelt
like one dropped to his knees in prayer.

Purple Banana

Her finger trick creates a banana:
it is ophidian how he erects
and telescopes into her lipsticked pout
and undulates a slow motion
in and out, not a sixty-nine,
she crouched down on her haunches, bottom up
in air-sheer white panties.

She imagines a tongue teasing her crack
and he additional fingers on his balls,
they need inventives to participate
in sensory extravagance;
the weird conjunction of geometries,
two side by side, one flipped over,
the other on his back.

He eases his purple banana free
before it shoots its seeding galaxy.
Fellatio as an aperitif
stimulates the volcanic impetus
to other pleasures.

                    She ascends a scale
of excruciating laughter;
it's guess work what he does to her
and where he is and over and over
their tensions twist around a molten core.

SUJATA BHATT

Shérdi[1]

The way I learned
to eat sugar cane in Sanosra:
I use my teeth
to tear the outer hard *chaal*
then, bite off strips
of the white fibrous heart –
suck hard with my teeth, press down
and the juice spills out.

January mornings
the farmer cuts tender green sugar-cane
and brings it to our door.
Afternoons, when the elders are asleep
we sneak outside carrying the long smooth stalks.
The sun warms us, the dogs yawn,
our teeth grow strong
our jaws are numb;
for hours we suck out the *russ*, the juice
                        sticky all over our hand.

So tonight
when you tell me to use my teeth,
to suck hard, harder,
then, I smell sugar cane grass
                in your hair
and imagine you'd like to be
shérdi   shérdi   out in the fields
          the stalks sway
               opening a path before us.

[1] Sugar cane in Gujerati, the poet's first language.

JOE ORTON

From The Orton Diaries

March 1967

THE PUBLICITY HAS been good for the play. Mark tells me that the matinée was up and the evening performance was sold out except for a few seats. When I left, I took the Piccadilly line to Holloway Road and popped into a little pissoir – just four pissers. It was dark because somebody had taken the bulb away. There were three figures pissing. I had a piss and, as my eyes became used to the gloom, I saw that only one of the figures was worth having – a labouring type, big, with cropped hair, and, as far as I could see, wearing jeans and a dark short coat. Another man entered and the man next to the labourer moved away, not out of the place altogether, but back against the wall. The new man had a pee and left the place, and, before the man against the wall could return to his place, I nipped in there sharpish and stood next to the labourer. I put my hand down and felt his cock, he immediately started to play with mine. The youngish man with fair hair, standing back against the wall, went into the vacant place. I unbuttoned the top of my jeans and unloosened my belt in order to allow the labourer free rein with my balls. The man next to me began to feel my bum. At this point a fifth man entered. Nobody moved. It was dark. Just a little light spilled into the place from the street, not enough to see immediately. The man next to me moved back to allow the fifth man to piss. But the fifth man very quickly flashed his cock and the man next to me returned to my side, lifting up my coat and shoving his hand down the back of my trousers. The fifth man kept puffing on a cigarette and, by the glowing end, watching. A sixth man came into the pissoir. As it was so dark nobody bothered to move. After an interval (during which the fifth man watched me feel the labourer, the labourer stroked my cock, and the man beside me pulled my jeans down even further) I noticed that the sixth man was kneeling down beside the youngish man with fair hair and sucking his cock. A seventh man came in, but by now nobody cared. The number of people in the place was so large that detection was quite impossible. And anyway, as soon became apparent when the seventh man stuck his head down on a level with my fly, he wanted a cock in his mouth too. For some moments nothing happened. Then an eighth man, bearded and stocky, came in. He pushed the sixth man roughly away from the fair-haired man and quickly sucked the fair-haired man off. The man beside me had pulled my jeans down over my buttocks and was trying to push his prick between my legs. The fair-haired man, having been sucked off, hastily left the place. The bearded man came over and nudged away the seventh man from me and, opening wide my fly, began sucking me like a maniac. The labourer, getting very excited by my feeling his cock with both hands, suddenly glued his mouth to mine. The little pissoir under the bridge had become the scene of a frenzied homosexual saturnalia. No more than two feet away the citizens of Holloway moved about their ordinary business. I came, squirting come into the bearded man's mouth, and quickly pulled up my jeans. As I was about to leave, I heard the bearded man hissing quietly, 'I suck people off! Who wants his cock sucked?' When I left, the labourer was just shoving his cock into the man's mouth to keep him quiet. I caught the bus home.

May 1967

We went to the Alhambra for dinner. I had a glass of wine because it works well with hash. Kenneth already with hash and valium inside him decided *not* to risk vino as well. We went for a stroll. Sat on the boulevard at the Café de Paris and, at ten, rose to go, only to meet Nigel, Frank and Kevin who persuaded us to stay a little longer. In the re-allotment of places, I sat next to a rather stuffy American tourist and his disapproving wife. They listened to our conversation and I, realising this, began to exaggerate the content. 'He took me right up the arse,' I said, 'and afterwards he thanked me for giving him such a good fucking. They're most polite people.' The American and his wife hardly moved a muscle. 'We've got a leopard-skin rug in the flat and he wanted me to fuck him on that,' I said in an undertone which was perfectly audible to the next table. 'Only I'm afraid of the spunk you see, it might adversely affect the spots of the leopard.' Nigel said quietly, 'Those tourists can hear what you're saying.' He looked alarmed. 'I mean them to hear,' I said. 'They have no right to be occupying chairs reserved for decent sex perverts.' And then with excitement I said, 'He might bite a hole in the rug. It's the writhing he does, you see, when my prick is up him that might grievously damage the rug, and I can't ask him to control his excitement. It wouldn't be natural when you're six inches up the bum, would it?'

The American couple frigidly paid for their coffee and moved away. 'You shouldn't drive people like that away,' Nigel said. 'The town needs tourists.' 'Not that kind, it doesn't,' I said. 'This is *our* country, *our* town, *our* civilisation. I want nothing to do with the civilisation they made. Fuck them! They'll sit and listen to buggers' talk from me and drink their coffee and piss off.' 'It seems rather a strange joke,' Frank said with an old school-teacher's smile. 'It isn't a joke,' I said, 'there's no such thing as a joke.'

Nigel, who was drinking some strange brandy, got very excited by a girl who passed. She looked like a boy. She was German. We discussed women for a bit and I wrote them off as a mistake. 'Who wants a girl to look like a boy?' I said. 'Or a boy to look like a girl? It's not natural.' 'I really think, Joe,' Nigel said, 'that you shouldn't bring nature into your conversation quite so often, you who have done more than anyone I know to outrage her.' 'I've never outraged nature,' I said. 'I've always listened to her advice and followed it to wherever it went.'

July 1967

Later on I walked him to King's Cross where he caught a bus home. On the way we talked about sex. 'You must do whatever you like,' I said, 'as long as you enjoy it and don't hurt anyone else, that's all that matters.' 'I'm basically guilty about being a homosexual you see,' he said. 'Then you shouldn't be,' I said. 'Get yourself fucked if you want to. Get yourself anything you like. Reject all the values of society. And enjoy sex. When you're dead you'll regret not having fun with your genital organs.' He told me how he'd visited an East End pub. 'And all these young chaps were crowding round. One of them said to me, "Kaw! Ken, it's legal now, you know." And he started to pull his trousers down. And the landlady said, "Ernie! Now then! We'll have none of that." "But he's a celebrity, we've got to put on a show," Ernie said. "Not that kind of a show," the landlady said. She was the disapproving type,' Kenneth said. 'And what happened?' I said. 'Oh, nothing. We went back about a week later and the pub was empty.' 'You should've seized your chance,' I said. 'I know,' Kenneth said, 'I just feel so guilty about it all.' 'Fucking Judeo-Christian civilisation!' I said, in a furious voice, startling a passing pedestrian. We parted and I hope I'd done him a bit of good. At least I'd told him not to feel guilty. It isn't as simple as that, but at least I've tried to help him.

Orton's last sexual experience

In the evening, braving the rain in a mac borrowed from Oscar, we all went into Brighton. Our intention was to see the new James Bond film –

You Only Live Twice. We couldn't get in. The others, including Kenneth, decided to see *In Like Flint.* I couldn't face the idea. I said I'd go for a walk and then go home. Eileen gave me the keys of the house. I was surprised that they only seemed to possess one set. I left them going into the box office and trudged through the drizzle about the town. After walking for a long while I found a gent's lavatory on a patch of grass near a church. I went in. It was v. dark. There was a man in there. Tall, grand and smiling. In the gloom he looked aristocratic. When the lights were turned on (after about five minutes) I could see that he was stupid, smiling and bank-clerkish. He showed his cock. I let him feel mine. 'Oo!' he gasped, not noticing the sinister sore that he had developed on the end over the last week or so. 'Oo!' I asked if he had anywhere to go back to. 'No,' he said, 'I don't have the choice of my neighbours, you see. They're down on me and I couldn't take the risk.' He nodded to a dwarf skulking in the corner of the lavatory. 'He'll suck you off, though. I've seen him do it.' He made a motion to the dwarfish creature, rather as someone would call a taxi. The dwarf sucked me off while the other man smiled benevolently and then, I suppose, went back to his neighbours refreshed.

SIDONIE-GABRIELLE COLETTE

From La Vagabonde

Colette writes of a man's misunderstanding of lesbians:

Two women enlaced will never be for him anything but a depraved couple, he will never see in them the melancholy and touching image of two weak creatures who have perhaps sought shelter in each other's arms, there to sleep and weep, safe from man who is so often cruel, and there to taste, better than any pleasure, the bitter happiness of feeling themselves akin, frail, and forgotten. What would be the good of writing, and pleading, and discussing? My voluptuous friend can only understand love.

Transl. Enid McLeod
© Colette and Enid Bagnold, from *The Collected Stories of Colette.*
Reprinted by kind permission of Martin Secker and Warburg Ltd.

MICHÈLE ROBERTS

Magnificat

(for Sian, after thirteen years)

oh this man
what a meal he made of me
how he chewed and gobbled and sucked

in the end he spat me all out

you arrived on the dot, in the nick
of time, with your red curls flying
I was about to slip down the sink like grease
I nearly collapsed, I almost
wiped myself out like a stain
I called for you, and you came, you voyaged
fierce as a small archangel with swords and breasts
you declared the birth of a new life
in my kitchen there was an annunciation
and I was still, awed by your hair's glory

you commanded me to sing of my redemption

oh my friend, how
you were mother for me, and how
I could let myself lean on you
comfortable as an old cloth, familiar as enamel saucepans
I was a child again, pyjamaed
in winceyette, my hair plaited, and you
listened, you soothed me like cakes and milk
you listened to me for three days, and I poured
it out, I flowed all over you

like wine, like oil, you touched the place where it hurt
at night we slept together in my big bed
your shoulder eased me towards dreams

when we met, I tell you
it was a birthday party, a funeral
it was a holy communion
between women, a Visitation

it was two old she-goats butting
and nuzzling each other in the smelly fold

VIOLETTE LEDUC

From La Bâtarde

Hermine and Violette

'DOES YOUR WIFE play the piano?' Hermine asked.
    I stamped on her foot.
'My wife is an invalid. No, she doesn't play,' he answered.
The conversation languished.
Help me, since I already know you a little, begged the man's faded eyes.
I didn't dare.
'We could meet another time somewhere more private,' he said.
He turned toward me.
'Would the Rue Godot-de-Mauroy suit you?' came his urgent whisper.
Hermine hung on my lips, begging me to refuse. Rue Godot-de-Mauroy. . . .
'Does that suit you?' she asked.
'Why not?' I answered, lighting a *Camel*.
He paid the waiter.
'Have you read *Sanctuary*?' I asked suddenly, hoping to give us an air of consequence.
He was already shaking our hands.
'We'll talk about that next time, on the Rue Godot-de-Mauroy.'
We arranged to meet again the following week.

Couples and men on their own were coming into the bar; Hermine watched him walk away.

Suddenly Hermine felt intimidated by the bar.

'Say we won't go, tell me you were lying to him,' she cried.

She pulled her satin jacket back on to her shoulders.

'We shall have plenty of time to talk about it later,' I replied.

She admitted how terrified she felt the following week, as we walked along the Boulevard Malesherbes. She stuttered like an old idiot woman. We caught sight of him suddenly, on the Rue Godot-de-Mauroy. He looked rather decrepit and sad. Hermine regained her calm.

'After all, he may be very nice really,' she said.

'I didn't think you'd come,' he said, as though we'd just brought him back to life.

'Is your wife any better?' Hermine asked with a lovely open smile.

He turned away his head.

'I'll go in first. You can follow me.'

The affair was already settled. His manner was different from the week before at the Ritz. He was forcing his pace.

Hermine watched him as he walked away. 'Let's go, squirrel, let's go while there's still time.'

I got annoyed: 'He's going in, we must follow him.'

'Why do you want to do it? Why?' Hermine begged.

I pushed her after him.

'Let's go right up,' the man said, quivering now.

I was already buried with my fears in the thick pile of the carpets.

A young housemaid showed us into a little drawing room with a mirrored ceiling and a triple mirror on one wall. There were naked women floating on clouds, and a large pouffe welcoming us.

'What are we doing here?' Hermine asked. 'It isn't a bar.'

'You're not a child, mademoiselle. Sit down. They are bringing you champagne on ice.'

The maid came in. She set down the tray and vanished again.

Hermine questioned me. She pretended she was unaware of the man's presence. Was it a hotel or a private apartment?

'Both,' he answered. 'People make love here. Don't you think it's a charming love nest?' he asked me.

Hermine poured the champagne. It was a respite for her. He didn't smoke: he lit our cigarettes for us.

'Let's go now,' Hermine said. 'I'll pay for the champagne, then we need never think about it again. . . . The whole thing can be settled, Violette.

We'll pay for the champagne and leave.' Hermine opened her purse.

'Rotten spoilsport,' I hissed. 'What can you possibly have against this gentleman? You're always afraid of everything.'

'I can see you're broad-minded,' the man said to me.

'Squirrel, is it you talking like this? Do you like being here? The champagne is too sweet.'

'The champagne is dry, Hermine!'

'It's too warm.'

'The champagne is on ice, Hermine.'

'I like seeing you both draw yourselves up like that,' the man said. 'Now we're getting somewhere, yes . . .'

He crossed his legs. For him, the performance was beginning at last.

Hermine took off her hat. 'Very well. I'll stay here, since you don't want to leave.'

She refilled our glasses.

'Come and see your room,' he said eagerly.

'Our room? You've been deceiving me,' Hermine said.

He opened the door. Hermine went in first, plunging into the abyss so as to face the worst as quickly as possible. She hid her face in her hands and moaned: 'Mirrors, mirrors . . .'

She moved into my arms. She was sobbing.

'Let's leave, my baby, let's go away from here. You shall have whatever you want.'

The man was circling around the bed, his image reflected in all the mirrors.

'I'm terribly sorry. Do leave if she really wants to.'

He sat down on the satin bedcover. I stood rooted to the spot as I wiped away Hermine's tears. I was supporting the weight of her head on my shoulder.

He left the room but returned with another bottle of champagne.

The alcohol had turned me into a faun that day. I was promising Hermine the most extravagant sensations. Broken in my arms, she listened and watched me in the mirror.

'Yes, if you like, but he must go away,' she moaned.

He left the room again.

We clinked our glasses together and drank.

'He's bored out there, Hermine, he's all alone.'

'Yes. It's just that I'm never bored, I'm never alone. I try to understand. But I don't.'

'He may be unhappy.'

'Yes, he may be unhappy. Let's drink to us, my little darling.'

'To us. I don't think he can be dangerous.'

'Yes, he may not be dangerous. It's true, he's alone and there are two of us,' Hermine went on, as though she were referring to some mystery.

It was then that I suggested we undress. She wept for her wretchedness and her docility as I helped divest her of her principles.

He came in on tiptoe. It would be impossible to imagine a man more correctly dressed, more proper, more strictly made to measure. I undressed without taking my eyes off myself in the mirror.

And it was to the mirror that he ventured coldly: 'You look like a Saint Sebastian.'

A compliment is a springboard.

Lying on her belly, Hermine was waiting for me. I threw off the bedclothes, I forgot the man in the mirror, and I forgot Hermine, the better to worship the victim I had sacrificed.

'Make love to her. That is all I ask,' I heard before I plunged into the abyss.

Close your eyes, don't look at them and they won't see you, I said to Hermine when her eyes encountered the mirrors with the man's face working on the ceiling.

The fleshless fingers handed me a glass of champagne as I lay there streaming.

Leaving the hotel was not easy. The man disappeared before we were ready, leaving us some money. We walked along the street without exchanging a word, deprived of the breeze or the wind that would have refreshed us. I asked Hermine why she'd decided to go through with it. She answered that she wanted to show she was brave. Should we laugh or cry? She said I could buy the lacquer table next day.

Transl. Derek Coltman

KINGSLEY AMIS

Nothing to Fear

All fixed: early arrival at the flat
Lent by a friend, whose note says *Lucky sod*;
Drinks on the tray; the cover-story pat
And quite uncheckable; her husband off
Somewhere with all the kids till six o'clock
(Which ought to be quite long enough):
And all worth while: face really beautiful,
Good legs and hips, and as for breasts – my God.
What about guilt, compunction and such stuff?
I've had my fill of all that cock;
It'll wear off, as usual.

Yes, all fixed. Then why this slight trembling,
Dry mouth, quick pulse-rate, sweaty hands,
As though she were the first? No, not impatience,
Nor fear of failure, thank you, Jack.
Beauty, they tell me, is a dangerous thing,
Whose touch will burn, but I'm asbestos, see?
All worth while – it's a dead coincidence
That sitting here, a bag of glands
Tuned up to concert pitch, I seem to sense
A different style of caller at my back,
As cold as ice, but just as set on me.

SEBASTIAN BARKER

I meditate on Sex because of Yeats on the flight of a
    swallow.
Fucking hell! I am not describing that. The purpose of
    sex,
In my opinion, is not the received joy nor the mellow
Ecstasy. Who isn't bored with these. It's the pretext
Of life. The sum, goal, aim, target, direction,
The be-all and end-all, the common spiritual omphalos
(Which we may here compare to the belly-button):
It's the reason we go to work, wash, or buy new shoes.
It is, in fact, the thing to aim for, not a pleasure
Picked up *en route*. It is the heart of life, the heart
Of life. It would be wrong to think I'm a sexual huckster.
I am religious, and sex to me is the start
Of the pilgrimage. But what is sex? The adolescent kiss
Matured through orange-juice, brandy, LSD, war,
    marriage, or this.

JOHN UPDIKE

From A Month of Sundays

The narrator of *A Month of Sundays* is a minister who has lost his
faith. He takes to having a series of affairs with his women
parishioners. He is always impotent with Frankie.

'I CAN ONLY think,' I said, 'it has something to do with your being such a
staunch churchwoman.'
   'But – ' She delicately halted.
   'The others are too? Jane and Alicia? Jane doesn't believe in God, she
believes in the Right Thing. Alicia even less. She likes music and men and
that's all she has the spiritual budget for.'

'And am I,' Frankie asked, shedding shyness, 'the only other – ?'

'Not exactly.' The melancholy and muffled one-shots behind the choir robes I did not want to betray, even to her. Right of therapeutic privacy. 'But even if the woman *is* a church member, she doesn't embody faith like you do. You seem really hipped on it. The way you used to look up at me through your veil.'

'I'm not veiled now,' she precisely said, and bit a Butter Nutter cookie with her smile. 'And *am* I' – speaking crumbs, one hand cupped beneath her chin to catch them, lest they make the sheets hurt – 'so hipped on it?'

'I think so. Do you believe in God the Father Almighty, maker of Heaven and Earth?'

She blushed and, her voice as modest as possible, answered, 'Yes.' A fury gathered within me, an amateur plumber's frustrated rage at being unable to dissolve my lump and unclog my ability, my after all hideously common and as they say God-given ability, to deliver myself into this loved woman's loins.

'Say you don't,' I commanded.

Frankie didn't understand.

'Say you don't believe in God. Say you think God is an old Israeli fart. Say it.'

She wanted to, she even took breath into her lungs to utter something, but couldn't.

Easy stages, I thought. 'Say "fart."' She did. I gave her more words to say. She passed them through her lips obediently, untastingly, like a child in catechetical class. The corners of her lips curved, pronouncing; she was amused. Our litany excited me; she noticed this, and moved to capitalise; at a new angle I admired the sequence of her vertebrae and the symmetrical flats of her winglike scapulae; I pushed her off, and brought her face up to the level of mine, and held it so hard her cheekbones whitened and her eyes went round. '*How* can you believe, Frankie? How can any sane person?'

'Many do,' she told me. Then amended, 'Some do.'

'It's *so* ridiculous,' I said. 'It's always been ridiculous. There was this dreadful tribal chauvinism of the Jews. Then some young megalomaniac came along and said, Look at Me. And about a dozen people did. And then. . . . We don't know what happened, nobody knows, all we know is that as the Roman Empire went rotten one mystery cult prevailed over the many others. People were as messy then as they are now – it could have been any cult. And the damn thing's still among us. It's an establishment, Frankie love. A racket. Believe me. The words are empty. The bread is just bread. The biggest sales force in the world selling empty calories – Jesus Christ. What is it, Frankie? A detergent? A deodorant? What does it do, Frankie? This invisible odorless thing.'

'It lets people live?' The feel of her fragile small jaw struggling to move under my fingers was exciting. My grip had tightened the fine wrinkles from her face.

'It lets them die,' I corrected. 'It likes them to die. This summer among many delightful distractions I watched a fifteen-year-old boy die of leukemia. He was an ordinary boy, a little duller than most; he couldn't understand why him, and I couldn't either. But he was old enough and bright enough to know what a meaningless foul trick it was; why don't you? Suppose it had been Julie? She's fifteen now, isn't she? Suppose she's struck by a car, while we lie here? How would you feel?'

'Terrible. Sinful.' Her eyes, though watering with pain, still searched my face for what I wanted, so she could give it.

I dropped my hands to her throat. A fasces of veins, pumping. I asked her, 'If a demon were to enter me and make me strangle you, do you think God would stop it?'

'No.' She was frightened, yet tittered; my sudden touch had tickled.

I hit her. First a tap with a cupped hand, then really a hit, with open palm and stiff wrist so our chamber split at the noise, and all the gossamer threads her love had spun were swept away. 'You dumb cunt,' I said, 'how can you be so dumb as to believe in God the Father, God the Son, and God the Holy Ghost? Tell me you really don't. Tell me, so I can fuck you. Tell me, you know down deep there's nothing. The dead stink, Frankie; for a while they stink and then they're just bones and then there's not even that. Forever and ever. Isn't that so? Say it.'

'I can't.'

'Why not, sweet? Why not? Please.' I got to my knees and crouched above her, I wanted to lift her away, to safety, away from myself. Paradoxically, I suppose.

'I can't,' she cried under me, lightly twisting.

I brushed away the hair agitation had tossed into her eyes. 'Why can't you? You know there's nothing. Tell me there's nothing. Tell me it's a fraud, I'm a fraud, it's all right, there's just us and we'll die, there's just your dear cunt, just your dear ass, your tits, your dear mouth, your dear, dear eyes.' I touched her eyelids and thought of pressing down.

She bit her lower lip rather than speak.

I crouched lower, urging, clowning. 'There is Noboboddy, Frankie, with his faithful dog Nada. There must be nothing. You can't think there's a God. You know you can't. What's your reason? Give me one reason, Frankie.'

'You,' she said, in a voice half-hostile, and this hostility brought her soul so close I moaned and bowed my head to take my gaze from hers; I saw my own phallus erect up to my navel. She spread her legs quickly, but not quickly enough, for though I entered her, repentant tenderness overtook me; her pelvic bone gnashed against mine as I melted inside her; she came, wide to whatever was, while I couldn't, and it became my time to weep again. She pulled my face down to hers, so roughly I resisted; she thirstily kissed my tears.

'Forgive me,' I of course said, 'I don't know what happens to me. But at least it was something for you, this time, wasn't it?'

She nodded tremulously, still lapping my tears; her tongue felt so large and strong and single I remembered the kiss when her mouth had seemed to have many petals. She formed words. 'You must think of this,' she told me, 'as holy too.'

I rolled from her, her fair body sunk in a trough of sweat. The fresh air on my skin reconstituted the world. 'OK,' I said. 'That's good practical theology. I'll try. I think I'll get there next time.'

And events did not prove me a false prophet. There was no next time. Distilling my ministry, I find this single flaw: Frankie Harlow never did get to feel my seed inside her, sparkling and burning like a pinch of salt.

ROGER WODDIS

Look the Other Way

(After T. S. Eliot's 'Whispers of Immortality')

When Shri Pranukh Swami, leader of a celibate sect, arrived in Britain he had not seen a woman for forty years.

The Swami is much possessed by sex
And sees the distaff side as sin;
Their double features, soft and round,
Induce a crawling of his skin.

Temple bells instead of balls
Stare from the sockets of his eyes;
He does not share the thoughts of those
Who long for elongated thighs.

His eyes are down, lest golden girls
Should drain and draw him into vice;
The rigour of his code precludes
Sugar and spice and all things nice.

The female of the human kind
Must never come within his view;
Nothing so corrupts the soul
As women in a shopping-queue.

There vibrates in his memory
No mother's mammary embrace;
And curtained from his inward eye
Is more than half the human race.

D. H. LAWRENCE

From The First Lady Chatterley

The style of the first version of *Lady Chatterley's Lover* is much clearer and simpler than most of Lawrence's writing. There is also more of a marked class difference in the speech of the gamekeeper, Parkin (Mellors in later versions).

HIS EYES WERE flashing and changing, and he was rather pale. She sat down on the sofa in the small, cosy room. He sat down in his Windsor arm-chair, and began to unfasten his leather gaiters and take off his heavy boots. The dog in the scullery was rather noisily lapping something.

She looked round. The varnished dresser stood on glass supports and had on it various cottage ornaments. Over it hung an enlarged photograph of a young, fairish man with a rather thin, sticking-out moustache and square shoulders, and a woman, dark and with frizzed hair, wearing a black satin blouse and a big lace collarette. She looked common.

'Do you ever see your wife?' she asked.

'Eh?'

He had placed his boots and leggings at the side of the white hearth, and was in grey worsted stockings. He glanced up quickly, and followed her glance to the enlarged photograph.

'My wife! No! She's livin' wi' somebody else.'

'Don't you want to see her?'

'No.'

'Why not?'

He glanced at her quickly. Their eyes met, and from his a spark flew.

'I dunna want to. – Should we go up then? Shanna ter take thy things off?'

'Yes. Upstairs!' she said.

He lit a candle, blew out the lamp, and she followed him to the stairs.

'Shut stairfoot door,' he said, 'for t' dog.'

Balanced on one stair, she carefully closed the stairfoot door behind her. The steep stairs creaked as he went up in stocking feet, and she followed. Probably the other woman had followed him like this.

On the tiny landing were two doors, one open. She followed him into the crowded small bedroom. The big iron bedstead was pushed against the wall, the bed covered with a white quilt. A yellow chest of drawers was against the opposite wall, and by the window, under the slope of the roof, a dressing table with a swivel mirror stood penned down. The room was colourless and ordinary.

'Do you always sleep here?' she asked.

'Me? Ay! I sleep in this bed.'

She took off her hat and mackintosh and hung them on the nail behind the door. Then she sat down on the edge of the bed and slowly pulled off her shoes.

'Did you never like your wife?' she asked him.

He had been standing motionless by the door. He gave a writhing movement of repudiation.

'Dunna talk about her. It's not what ter's come for, is it?'

He looked at her strangely, anxiously.

'No!' she said. 'Only I had to think about her.'

'Eh!' he said. 'Er's not a nice woman, an' 'er niver was.'

'But you liked her once?'

'Eh! I liked what I had of her – for a bit. An' then I didn't like 'er – an' don't. It's enough.'

She slowly pulled off her stockings and garters, while he still stood there against the door, motionless and inscrutable. Then she slipped her dress over her head, and stood in her thin, delicate white nightgown. She laid her dress and stockings over the bed-rail. And he still had not moved.

'Shall yer sleep agen t'wa?'

She got quietly into bed.

And then, only then, he sat down heavily on the edge of the bed and untied his tape garters and pulled off his stockings. He stood up to push off his cord breeches, and she saw his feet white and clean but gnarled out of shape by clumsy heavy boots.

He stood in his shirt – she had known he wouldn't change it – and looked at her.

'I canna believe as yer really want me,' he said, looking down at her with dark, glowing eyes. He was a mature man, not a boy.

She smiled at him faintly. And the last thing she saw was his face as he bent near the candle and blew out the light with a quick breath. His face, lit up intensely like that, had something – it seemed so ridiculous – of the pure masculine angel about it. She smiled again, in the dark room, as he touched her. She realised how he had recoiled from all women after that common wife of his: and how his desire fought against his recoil and mistrust; his old dislike of the hard, unloving woman he had known in his mother also fighting furiously against his intense desire of a mature, lonely man for a woman to believe in with his body. A woman with a gentle, warm soul and a warm, soft desirous body! that was the burning flicker of his hope. But the ache of experience drew back and resisted, told him not to want her.

She had understood a good deal, looking at the 'enlargement' of a bold woman in a black satin blouse, and that young man with the square shoulders and defiant eyes.

'There then!' she thought, as she softly stroked his male, live body. 'I won't deceive you in my heart, at least.'

Because, when he did break away from his cramping mistrust, his was such a clean passion.

He slept with her right breast cupped in his left hand, for she had her back to him. And she knew that at first he must have slept with his wife like that, because his hand came like a child's, and gathered her breast and held it as in a cup. If she moved his hand it came back while he slept, by instinct, and found her breast and held it softly enclosed. And it was as if he balanced the whole of her gently in the hollow of his hand, as if she were no more than a dove nestling, all nestled in the strong palm of his hand.

She lay perfectly still, yet not asleep. All her body was asleep under the heavy arm laid across her. Only her mind, like a small star of consciousness, shone faintly and wondered. His arm lay across her, her breast was balanced in his hand, she was encircled and enclosed by him even while he slept.

So this was what it was to be a wife! How implicitly he made a wife of her even if he had got her only for this one night! The curious united circle of the man and the woman! It was a kind of prison too.

MOLLY PARKIN

Mother's Pride

The kid crept in again last night
to sleep between me and his dad.
I know it's not normal,
not now he's sixteen.
But he wakes with these nightmares, this terrible dream,
I swear half the time he doesn't know where he's been.
He was always a sensitive lad.

Perhaps the fact of his father –
you know, being so old,
affected his blood. Oh, does he feel the cold!
Why, at night would you credit
he shivers so much! Yet his hands
are quite clammy, I can tell by their touch
even under my nightie (brushed nylon from Marks,
not see-through of course. None of those silly larks).

He still wets the bed. Well, I say 'wet', I mean
that when I turn down the sheets I can see where he's been.
But boys do, don't they really, I'd say as a rule.
And he clings to my bosom! Yes, he did as a child
but just lately it's different –
they're driving him wild.

'Silly boy,' I say sometimes
and give him a kiss.
But he offers his mouth, making sure I won't miss.
And the feeling disturbs me. I don't know why,
but in the dark and the quiet I feel I could cry . . .
So I cuddle him close
and I stroke his soft hair.
It gives such a feeling of comfort, him there.
And old dad, he sleeps on.
When he's gone, yes, he's gone!
Oh no – nothing will wake him,
not even the shaking. Our boy gets so worked up,
like a frisky young pup.
All the jiggling and joggling
and the giggling and gobbling –
dear, oh dear, what a noise!
Oh well – boys will be boys. . . .

© Molly Parkin.
from *Purple Passages*.

LIZ LOCHHEAD

Morning After

Sad how
Sunday morning finds us
separate after All,
side by side with nothing between us
but the Sunday papers.
Held like screens before us.
    Me, the Mirror
reflecting only on your closed profile.
    You, the Observer
encompassing larger, Other issues.

Without looking up
you ask me please to pass the colour section.
I shiver
while you flick too quickly
　　　too casually through the pages, with
　　　too passing
　　　an interest.

Inventory

you left me
　　　nothing but nail
　　　parings orange peel
　　　empty nutshells half filled
　　　ashtrays dirty
　　　cups with dregs of
　　　nightcaps an odd hair
　　　or two of yours on my
　　　comb gap toothed
　　　bookshelves and a
　　　you shaped
　　　depression in my pillow.

© Liz Lochhead – *Dreaming of Frankenstein* and *Collected Poems*
(Polygon 1984).

LISA ALTHER

From Original Sins

Sally, an ex-cheerleader, bored to death by having to stay at home
all day, is trying desperately to be a good wife to Jed.

SALLY WAS SITTING in the living room clipping a recipe for Cherry
Cheese Delight out of *Modern Wife* when Jed walked in.

'Hey,' he said, kissing her.

'What's wrong, honey?'

'What makes you think something's wrong? Can't a man be in a bad
mood without always having to explain himself?'

'Sure, honey. Here, have a seat.' She went into the kitchen.

She called 'It's Coach Clancy, isn't it?'

No answer.

'You must be real sad.'

'Stop telling me what I feel.'

'OK, honey.' She was seized with anxiety. What if it wasn't Coach
Clancy? What if it was something she'd done? Was it that she'd asked him
to put his clothes in the hamper? Did he have himself another woman who
wouldn't ask him to do this? She went into the bathroom and looked in the
mirror, tracing the faint wrinkles at the corners of her eyes with her
fingertips. She fluffed up her hair, molded her breasts with her hands and
lifted them. Not all that much sag yet. She smiled her pep squad smile.

For breakfast Sally cooked Jed's favorite – fried eggs, grits, fried
potatoes, sausage, toast and coffee. He declined to speak while eating.
Sally only wished she'd been struck dumb before asking him to put his
clothes in the hamper. He'd been doing it ever since – and speaking and
making love very little. She thought about strewing dirty clothes around
the bedroom, so he'd get the idea it really was OK. If he resumed
dropping his clothes on the floor, maybe he'd resume speaking and
making love.

During the afternoon Sally was in the kitchen making corn bread for
supper, using Mother Tatro's ghastly sugarless recipe. The kids had just
gone down for naps. She heard Jed calling from the garage.

He was lying on his back under the Chevy with just his legs, in green
work trousers, sticking out. She stooped and called, 'What, honey?'

He pulled himself out from under the car. His face and hands were black with grease. 'I'm having me a crisis here. I wonder could you run down to Ben's Body Shop and ask him for an oil pan for a '58 Chevy Impala?'

'Will you listen for the kids?'

'Yeah, sure. Take some money out of my wallet on the dresser.'

She drove out to the highway, thrilled to have him let her do something for him. Maybe he was going to forgive her. She got the oil pan and crept through heavy traffic back to the mill village.

As she walked over to the Chevy, she had an inspiration. The kids were asleep. The house blocked the garage from the street. Jed wanted her to surprise him. . . . She crept up to the car, squatted, put down the oil pan. Then she quickly unzipped his green trousers, and began stroking his penis, fighting repulsion at the pale squishy little thing.

A voice croaked, 'What the . . .' He tried to double up. There was a dull thud, and he lay still.

She laughed. 'Just relax and enjoy it, darling.'

He wasn't getting hard.

'Bad idea, huh?' she called anxiously.

No answer.

'You don't like this, Jed?' What a horrible mistake. He wouldn't even speak to her now.

'Here's the oil thing anyway.' She shoved it under the car, feeling frantic. She put his penis back in his trousers and zipped them up. What could she do to win his love again? Who was this other woman she was competing with anyway? Was it someone she saw every week at church, passed every day on the sidewalk, shopped with side by side in Kroger's? Did everyone in town know about it except herself? Were they pitying her behind her back? How could Jed make it so humiliating for her? What had she ever done except love him and try to make his life easier and more pleasant? She walked in the kitchen door, tears streaming from her eyes. Jed walked out of the bathroom. She stared at him.

'Any luck with the oil pan?' he asked pleasantly.

'It's under the car,' she whispered.

He started for the back door.

'Jed?'

'Huh?'

'Who's under the car?'

'Oh, Hank come over to help me out.'

'I thought it was you.

'Huh-un.'

He pushed open the screen door.

'Jed?'

He turned. She blurted out what she'd done. He laughed. Relieved, she joined him through her tears. They could laugh together. He'd forgiven her for whatever it was she'd done. They went out to the garage.

'Hank?' he yelled. 'How's that for hospitality, buddy?'

No answer.

'Hank?'

He grabbed Hank's ankles and dragged him out. He was motionless, a gash across his forehead. 'Christ, you've killed him!'

She stood with her hands to her mouth, her eyes wide.

'Well, call the Lifesaving Squad or something! But shit, how do I explain this?'

'Just tell what happened.'

'What, that my wife was playing with my best friend's dick?'

'But I thought it was you, Jed.'

'That my wife can't tell my dick from my best friend's? Shit, Sally, what the hell did you think you was doing?'

'I was just trying to be how you wanted me to be – surprising you and all.'

'I never asked for no hand jobs under the Chevy.'

Her chin began quivering.

'Well, shit, Sally, don't start crying again. Go call the Lifesaving Squad, and then stay in the house and let me handle it.'

She sat in the living room reading in *Modern Wife* 'Can This Marriage Be Saved?' It sounded unlikely. The ambulance arrived and departed, Jed with it. Laura began whimpering, and Sally got both kids up and gave them juice and cookies.

Jed walked in. She was scared to look at him. 'How is he?'

'He'll be all right. Some stitches in his head and a broken arm.'

'Broken arm? I didn't touch his arm.'

'Well, at first I wasn't going to tell them lifesavers nothing. But when we got to the hospital, I realized when Hank came to, he might think it was me feeling him up or something.'

'You? Why would you do something like that?'

'Well, I wouldn't.'

'Why would Hank think you might?'

'Well, he wouldn't.'

'So why were you worried?'

'Ah shit, I don't know! I had to tell them something, didn't I?'

'I guess.'

'So I told them the truth. They got to laughing so hard, they dropped him and broke his arm in two places.'

'Oh poor Hank. I feel awful.'

'Some of them lifesavers is on over at the mill. It's probably all over town by now.'

Sally began putting sweaters on the kids. 'Well, I'm sorry.'

'I don't know, Sally. It just ain't right. The mother of my kids and all, acting like some kind of . . . whore or something. And now it's all over town.'

Sally clenched her teeth. 'I can't figure out what you want, Jed. If I could, I'd do it. But I just can't.'

E. E. CUMMINGS

From the Collected Poems

she being Brand

-new;and you
know consequently a
little stiff i was
careful of her and(having

thoroughly oiled the universal
joint tested my gas felt of
her radiator made sure her springs were O.

K.)i went right to it flooded-the-carburetor cranked her

up,slipped the
clutch(and then somehow got into reverse she
kicked what
the hell)next
minute i was back in neutral tried and

again slo-wly;bare,ly nudg. ing(my

lev-er Right-
oh and her gears being in
A l shape passed
from low through
second-in-to-high like
greasedlightning)just as we turned the corner of Divinity

avenue i touched the accelerator and give

her the juice,good
                    (it

was the first ride and believe i we was
happy to see how nice she acted right up to
the last minute coming back down by the Public
Gardens i slammed on

the
internalexpanding
&
externalcontracting
brakes Bothatonce and

brought allofher tremB
-ling
to a:dead.

stand-
;Still).

————————————

                    may i feel said he
                    (i'll squeal said she
                    just once said he)
                    it's fun said she

(may i touch said he
how much said she
a lot said he)
why not said she

(let's go said he
not too far said she
what's too far said he
where you are said she)

may i stay said he
(which way said she
like this said he
if you kiss said she

may i move said he
is it love said she)
if you're willing said he
(but you're killing said she

but it's life said he
but your wife said she
now said he)
ow said she

(tiptop said he
don't stop said she
oh no said he)
go slow said she

(cccome?said he
ummm said she)
you're divine!said he
(you are Mine said she)

HENRY MILLER

From Tropic of Cancer

Germaine

GERMAINE WAS DIFFERENT. There was nothing to tell me so from her appearance. Nothing to distinguish her from the other trollops who met each afternoon and evening at the Café de l'Eléphant. As I say, it was a spring day and the few francs my wife had scraped up to cable me were jingling in my pocket. I had a sort of vague premonition that I would not reach the Bastille without being taken in tow by one of these buzzards. Sauntering along the boulevard I had noticed her verging toward me with that curious trot-about air of a whore and the run-down heels and cheap jewelry and the pasty look of their kind which the rouge only accentuates. It was not difficult to come to terms with her. We sat in the back of the little *tabac* called L'Eléphant and talked it over quickly. In a few minutes we were in a five franc room on the Rue Amelot, the curtains drawn and the covers thrown back. She didn't rush things, Germaine. She sat on the *bidet* soaping herself and talked to me pleasantly about this and that; she liked the knickerbockers I was wearing. *Très chic!* she thought. They were once, but I had worn the seat out of them; fortunately the jacket covered my ass. As she stood up to dry herself, still talking to me pleasantly, suddenly she dropped the towel and, advancing toward me leisurely, she commenced rubbing her pussy affectionately, stroking it with her two hands, caressing it, patting it, patting it. There was something about her eloquence at that moment and the way she thrust that rosebush under my nose which remains unforgettable; she spoke of it as if it were some extraneous object which she had acquired at great cost, an object whose value had increased with time and which now she prized above everything in the world. Her words imbued it with a peculiar fragrance; it was no longer just her private organ, but a treasure, a magic, potent treasure, a God-given thing – and none the less so because she traded it day in and day out for a few pieces of silver. As she flung herself on the bed, with legs spread wide apart, she cupped it with her hands and stroked it some more, murmuring all the while in that hoarse, cracked voice of hers that it was good, beautiful, a treasure, a little treasure. And it *was* good, that little pussy of hers! That Sunday afternoon, with its poisonous breath of spring in the air, everything clicked again. As we stepped out of the hotel I looked her over again in the harsh light of day and I saw clearly what a whore she was – the gold teeth, the geranium in her hat, the run-down heels, etc., etc. Even the fact that she had wormed a dinner out of me and cigarettes and taxi hadn't the least disturbing effect upon me. I encouraged it, in fact. I liked her so well that after dinner we went back to the hotel again and took another shot at it. 'For love,' this time. And again that big, bushy thing of hers worked its bloom and magic. It began to have an independent existence – for me too. There was Germaine and there was that rosebush of hers. I liked them separately and I liked them together.

CHARLES THOMSON

From The Penis Poem

I am a penis,
the masculine totem.
My base is a bag
that is known as the scrotum.
I'm not muscle or bone
and don't call me vein –
though I can in most men
take the place of a brain –
and I can't say my character's
lacking a stain.

I am a penis:
I'm hairy and squat,
but sex appeal's something
I've definitely got
(this last observation
is mainly intended
for the ears of the person
to whom I'm appended –
who otherwise seems
to get rather offended).

I am a penis,
a bit of a card,
mostly quite soft
but at times rather hard.
Without warning I'm pulled out
and fondled and flattered
then rubbed up the wrong way
and pummelled and battered
until I collapse
feeling totally shattered.

When I'm no longer seen
as a source of abuse
it's good to get back
to my natural use:
pissed out of my head,
I can really let rip
and then I'm hung over
till I feel just a drip –
but not half what I feel
if I'm trapped in the zip.

The pain, yes, the pain
if I ever get caught.
No wonder the life
of a penis is fraught.
It's a job that provides
rather limited views,
so most of the time
I curl up for a snooze –
especially after
he's been on the booze.

At such times (though it's not,
I am grateful, the norm)
I can be required
to stand up and perform;
and I must say that's something
that just isn't right.
For I always feel tired
at the times he gets tight:
though he shakes me, he often
can't rouse me all night.

Of course, there's a function
I've so far been ducking.
The job that I'm known
most of all for is farming.
They say you can judge
a man best by his deed:
I don't make manure,
or harvest, or weed –
I'm merely a tool
for the spreading of seed.

Without me humanity
wouldn't exist
(and I don't need the wisecrack
'it wouldn't be missed').
I think this is quite
a large service to render.
When I suffer from fever
and feel rather tender
I'm due for what's known
as the opposite gender.

The actual process
I find rather scary.
I'm pushed through an entrance
that's slimy and hairy
to a tunnel that's dark,
cramped, pulsating and smelly,
then pumped up and down
inside somebody's belly –
I wish there'd been football
results on the telly.

I feel a bit
like a motorcar piston,
or a boxing glove
on Sonny Liston.
It's the task in life
for which I'm fated:
it's known in the trade
as getting mated
(I think it's rather
over-rated).

This carries on
at quite a length
until I've used up
all my strength,
when I lose control
in a great convulsion
which always involves
a violent expulsion
resembling a knocked-over
can of emulsion.

*   *   *

There is of course
a complication
which fills me with
exasperation:
I'm on the job
when, without exception,
it's all tools down
for contraception –
an act that baffles
my conception.

The best for me
is called the pill
(though the thought of its hormones
makes me ill).
Then there's the coil –
not bad for a chap
and better than reeling
with slap after slap
from a piece of elastic
that's known as the cap.

Next, we come in contact
with what's called a sheath.
Though it helps repulse VD
and Aids and sharp teeth,
I will stand up to state
that this method's the worst:
I'd strangle the geezer
who thought of it first
and each time I'm in one
I pray it will burst.

I'm sentenced to a stop
in a cellophane bracket.
I squirm round like mad
in my plastic strait-jacket
attempting to put
matters into reverse,
but they pull me up quick
with a short breathless curse
and push it back harder
which makes me feel worse.

We all have our time
of endurance allotted,
but I really do wish
that the sheath would get knotted:
I get so restricted
when one is around,
I feel so uptight
and I can't hear a sound,
and then at the climax
I nearly get drowned.

© Charles Thomson.

JAMES BERRY

Moment of Love

Sweetrose Sweetrose you pretty
Lawd Lawd hol' this time
hol' it like Joshua still the sun
She lyin' here I full
I brimful with joy
   brimful with joy –
no empty pocket on me to drag me
no lockedhead of mine to fail me
no government debate to bug me
Only she lyin' here needin' not a word
An' I sing sweeter than any blackbird
Sweetrose Sweetrose you pretty
Stay good an' don' get baby
   Stay good an' don' get baby

ZYGMUNT FRANKEL

WITH ALL THE
pills
IUDs,
condoms
diaphragms,
safe periods,
coitus interuptus,
abortions,
accidents,
wars,
and emigration,

why is the bus so crowded?

INDEX

Also available from Mandarin Paperbacks

Kate Saunders & Peter Stanford

CATHOLICS & SEX

'It sounds like just a silly dirty little book to make money'
Victoria Gillick

'The main problem that the Catholic laity experiences
with sex can be summed up by one word: priests. The
main problem that priests experience with sex can be
summed up in two words: the Pope. The writers present
some fairly cogent arguments to show why priests should
be allowed to marry and why the teaching on sexual
behaviour has little to do with what Christ preached but
has everything to do with pre-Christian attitudes to
women and sex'
Harriet Waugh, LITERARY REVIEW

'*Catholics and Sex* deserves to be widely read and
discussed. I agree with [its] conclusions'
Father John Metcalf, CATHOLIC HERALD

'If this book was another attack on Catholic repression it
would surely be greeted in Ireland with a yawn. But what
makes it compelling reading is its authors' palpable belief
in their Church, and their disgust that its strong teachings
should be overshadowed by the sexual equivalent of
angels on pinheads'
IRISH TIMES

THE JOURNALS OF JAMES BOSWELL
1762–1795

Selected and introduced by John Wain

'I thought of my valuable spouse with the highest regard and warmest affection, but had a confused notion that my corporeal connection with whores did not interfere with my love for her. Yet I considered that I might injure my health, which there could be no doubt was an injury to her. This is an exact state of my mind at the time. It shocks me to review it.'

'If we only knew Boswell, as did his contemporaries, as the author of *The Life of Johnson*, we would still think of him as a genius, but to know him via his *Journals* makes us set him above all other self-confessing writers . . . John Wain arranges the immortal episodes in chronological order, and creates all around them a sense of freshness and urgency. The youthful Boswell hobnobs, travels and chases the girls. The flamboyant Boswell pursues fame. The magical Boswell records himself and his universe as no writer has done before or since. Both the fragrance and the stink of the 18th Century rise from his pages . . .'
Ronald Blythe, COUNTRY LIFE

'Boswell's journals are his *Prelude*, as they are his *Ulysses*, his *Fleurs du Mal*, his *A la Recherche du Temps Perdu*, his *Catch 22* . . . The rediscovery of Boswell has been one of the great literary detective stories of the century . . . One might hazard a guess that from now on the truly popular edition will be this new one-volume selection of John Wain's'
Fiona MacCarthy, THE TIMES

Ruth Brandon

BEING DIVINE

The most spellbinding actress of her age, Sarah Bernhardt was a goddess of her own making, a beauty, a genius, a legend – the first genuinely original world idol. In a career that spanned sixty years, her superhuman creativity compelled her to play to packed houses all over the world, and well into old age. Her beautiful voice, her extraordinary seductiveness – on stage and off – and her superhuman energy earned her the adulation of countless admirers, and the fulfilment of a completely free woman.

'A remarkable story . . . Clearly the attraction for Ruth Brandon, in this breathless book, is of a woman of extraordinary independence'
Anita Brookner, OBSERVER

'*Being Divine* celebrates the first true celebrity of stage and screen'
SHE

'Eminently readable . . . A must for anyone interested in theatre, and a treat for anyone besides'
SPECTATOR

'Brandon, who turns a wry phrase and has an excellent eye for detail, gives us a Sarah who was both magnificent and absurd, a precursor of a very modern phenomenon: the superstar'
TIMES LITERARY SUPPLEMENT

Errol Flynn

MY WICKED WICKED WAYS

'Errol Flynn's autobiography is eventful (of course), entertaining (naturally) and – surprisingly – very well written with the flair of a born raconteur disciplined by something like the skill of a born writer'
TIMES LITERARY SUPPLEMENT

'A big, brash, fundamentally sad book. It sounds very much like the man himself'
Patrick Campbell, SUNDAY TIMES

'Daring, bold, amusing and just a little sad . . . A story admirably told with vigour and style'
IRISH TIMES

'. . . eye-and-cork popping, shockingly candid autobiography that names names, calls spades spades, queens queens, and kings bums . . .'
NEW YORK HERALD TRIBUNE

'A shocker . . . Flynn uses strong language, and writes with as much colour as his life deserves . . . There is no doubt that he lived one of the fullest, most active lives of his period, and this is an extraordinarily readable, enjoyable, revealing view of it'
NEW YORK POST

Peter Ustinov

DEAR ME

Peter Ustinov had his first acting lessons from a parrot, spent much of his childhood as a motor car, and played his first stage role as a pig (when his performance was deemed 'adequate'). Since then he has become the playwright, actor, author, designer, director, film star and entertainer *par excellence* so familiar to his worldwide public. He is also Sir Peter Ustinov Kt., CBE, Chancellor of Durham University, tireless worker and propagandist for UNICEF, and thoughtful, philosophical citizen of the world.

Comic, controversial and full of anecdotes about the rich and famous, Peter Ustinov's autobiography reveals a courageous and exquisitely funny man, engaged in a lifelong search for truth.

'He writes both books and plays, he acts, he sings, he paints, he thinks, he cares. And he tells a very amusing story'
DAILY MIRROR

'Hugely enjoyable . . . written as if it were a collaboration between Jean-Jacques Rousseau and Groucho Marx'
FINANCIAL TIMES

'*Dear Me* is hilariously funny but underneath the clowning, which he admits is a method of survival, there is a shrewd and exceptional understanding'
SUNDAY TELEGRAPH